# Behold His Glory

# Behold His Glory

*Daily Meditations for Adults
on the Beauty and Meaning of Christ's Life*

WILLIAM G. JOHNSSON

REVIEW AND HERALD® PUBLISHING ASSOCIATION
WASHINGTON, DC 20039-0555
HAGERSTOWN, MD 21740

Copyright © 1989 by
Review and Herald® Publishing Association

The author assumes full responsibility for the accuracy of all facts and
quotations as cited in this book.

This book was
Edited by Richard W. Coffen and Raymond H. Woolsey
Designed by Bill Kirstein
Cover Photo by Four By Five Inc.
Type set: 10.5 pt. Garamond Book

## Acknowledgments

I am grateful to Corinne Russ for the 100-plus hours spent in typing the
manuscript, to friends and dear ones who encouraged the effort, and most
of all to the Lord who revealed Himself anew through the study.

Texts credited to NEB are from *The New English Bible*. © The Delegates of
the Oxford University Press and the Syndics of the Cambridge University
Press 1961, 1970. Reprinted by permission.

Texts credited to NIV are from the *Holy Bible, New International Version*.
Copyright © 1973, 1978, International Bible Society. Used by permission of
Zondervan Bible Publishers.

Bible texts credited to Phillips are from J. B. Phillips: *The New Testament
in Modern English*, Revised Edition. © J. B. Phillips 1958, 1960, 1972.
Used by permission of Macmillan Publishing Co., Inc.

Bible texts credited to RSV are from the Revised Standard Version of the
Bible, copyrighted 1946, 1952 © 1971, 1973.

Texts credited to RV are from the Revised Version, Oxford University Press,
1911.

PRINTED IN U.S.A.

**R&H Cataloging Service**
Johnsson, William George, 1934-
    Behold His glory.
    1. Devotional literature.    2. Jesus
Christ. I. Title.
            242.2
ISBN 0-8280-0538-9

# Dedication

For Cheryl—
the second daughter we wanted

# About the Author

William George Johnsson has lived on three continents. Born and raised in Adelaide, South Australia, he went to India as a missionary immediately after marrying Noelene Taylor, also an Australian. After serving more than 15 years in India, the Johnssons were called to the United States in 1975.

Johnsson's first degree was in chemical technology from Adelaide University, and he worked as a research chemist for three years. Leaving chemistry for the ministry, he subsequently earned degrees from Avondale College, Andrews University, the University of London, and Vanderbilt University (Ph.D. in biblical studies). His denominational service includes the following: academy dean of boys, evangelism, Bible teacher, college teacher, and seminary professor and administrator. He joined the *Adventist Review* in 1980 and since December 1982 has been editor in chief.

The Johnssons have two children—Terence Bryce and Julie Margaret, both born in India.

Johnsson has authored about 400 periodical articles. *Behold His Glory* is his tenth book.

This series of morning devotional readings springs from a statement by Ellen White: "It would be well for us to spend a thoughtful hour each day in contemplation of the life of Christ. We should take it point by point, and let the imagination grasp each scene, especially the closing ones. As we thus dwell upon His great sacrifice for us, our confidence in Him will be more constant, our love will be quickened, and we shall be more deeply imbued with His spirit. If we would be saved at last, we must learn the lesson of penitence and humiliation at the foot of the cross" (*The Desire of Ages*, p. 83).

Like many other statements from Ellen White, this counsel is easier to memorize than to practice. This year, however, we shall attempt to follow it out. We shall see Christ in all the Scriptures as we trace the marvel of His incarnation for us. Predicted long before, born, growing up as a boy in Nazareth, baptized, tested, ministering, dying, rising, ascended, coming again—we shall behold His glory!

# "BEHOLD HIS GLORY"

| | |
|---|---|
| January: | His Coming Foretold |
| February: | The Incarnation (birth, youth, etc.) |
| March: | The Ministry Commences (John the Baptist, Baptism, Temptations) |
| April: | The Healer |
| May: | The Teacher |
| June: | The Liberator |
| July: | The Beauty of His Life |
| August: | Life in Christ ( =Discipleship) |
| September: | Toward Jerusalem ( =Facing the Cross) |
| October: | The Final Week |
| November: | Death and Resurrection |
| December: | High Priest and Coming Again |

# THE WORD MADE FLESH

*And the Word was made flesh, and dwelt among us,*
*(and we beheld his glory, the glory as of the only begotten*
*of the Father,) full of grace and truth. John 1:14.*

What is God like? Is He severe and demanding, hovering over us like a heavenly policeman? Is He cruel and vindictive, a cosmic tyrant who plays sport with the creatures of His hand? Or is He like a benevolent grandfather, wishing us well but unable to arrest the mad rush of evil through the universe?

Across the face of the globe, in every time and place, men and women have wondered what God is like. Because we all have within us a God-hunger, a restless longing after Him that He put there when He made our first parents in His image (Gen. 1:26, 27), we all try to imagine God. But we end up making God after *our* image, just like ourselves (Rom. 1:23).

We can never know what God is like unless He reveals Himself to us. But He has! And He does! The Bible is the record of His self-manifestation, His gracious condescension to us in our separation, loneliness, and poverty. Because God loves us He does not leave us alone, groping, bewildered, making Him after our likeness.

Great as were the portrayals of God in the Old Testament, the supreme revelation came in Jesus Christ. In Him the eternal Word, one with God (John 1:1, 2) was "made flesh." He is the special one, the one in unique relation to the Father—"the only begotten of the Father." To know Jesus is to know what God is like. "If ye had known me, ye should have known my Father also. . . . He that hath seen me hath seen the Father," He said (John 14:7-9). "All that man needs to know and can know of God has been revealed in the life and character of His Son, the Great Teacher" (*Medical Ministry*, p. 95).

Seeing Jesus, we see how false are the gods that human imagination has dreamed up. God is not severe and demanding, nor is He a cosmic tyrant. And He is not a passive or impotent heavenly being. Rather God is love—love caring, love acting, love dying to save.

What a difference this year might make if we too could behold the glory of the Word made flesh! If we could turn our eyes from ourselves, from our false gods, and just see Him, everything else would fade to nothingness.

# BEHOLD HIM

*But we all, with open face beholding as in a glass the glory of the Lord, are changed into the same image from glory to glory, even as by the Spirit of the Lord. 2 Cor. 3:18.*

Recently some interesting studies were made of hardened criminals. Someone noticed that many of the most incorrigible men and women were physically ugly. They had grown up with taunts, the butt of jokes. When they looked in the mirror they saw an unpleasant, repulsive image. So with the permission of these unfortunate people, corrective surgery was arranged. In many cases the results were dramatic. Not only was there change in physical appearance; conduct also took a quantum leap to the better. Instead of being morose and antisocial, these people began to find a useful place among their fellows. They had a new self-image, a new self-respect, and a new sense of responsibility.

Jesus Christ is the greatest agent for change in the world. If we would be like Him, we must behold Him. He is the man of matchless charms, the one altogether lovely, the fairest of ten thousand (S. of Sol. 5:10, 16).

Jesus did not come to this earth with a halo around His head. He laid aside the majesty of the heavenly courts as He emptied Himself in the Incarnation (Phil. 2:5-8). Nor did He come with a retinue of angels, or with fine clothes, or with glitter and pageantry. "He hath no form nor comeliness; and when we shall see him, there is no beauty that we should desire him," predicted Isaiah (53:2). So the "glory" of Jesus was not in outward appearance, not in grandeur and splendor. His glory was in *what He was*—in that inner being that glowed with a holy passion to do the divine will and a selfless love to save men and women. His was the glory of a life—a life of kindness, goodness, and service.

How do we behold that glory? By spending time to think about that life. By making the effort to read the Bible and other books that will uplift the story of His life—especially *The Desire of Ages*. By talking with Him. And by keeping our eyes open each day to see His continuing ministry as He moves among men and women today—and in our own experience.

When you look in the mirror, what do you see? "He shall glorify me," said Jesus of the Spirit (John 16:14). That Spirit will change us into His image today, if we will behold Him.

# CHRIST IN ALL THE SCRIPTURES

*Search the scriptures; for in them ye think ye have eternal life: and they are they which testify of me. John 5:39.*

We believe in the study of the Scriptures, but not as an end in itself. The religious leaders of Jesus' day spent their lives in the close investigation of the Old Testament, memorizing long portions, disputing over minute details of interpretation. Yet when the Son of God appeared they failed to recognize Him and set about to kill Him. Today some scholars devote their energies to the linguistic, historical, and literary analysis of the Bible, but never find a heart experience with the Man of the Bible. They are "ever learning," but "never able to come to the knowledge of the truth" (2 Tim. 3:7).

So our study of the Scriptures must have a different purpose than becoming wise in knowledge or being able to report our diligence to others at church. We should study to find Christ. It is He to whom the Scriptures—Old and New—testify. Without Him they are a jigsaw puzzle, a conglomeration of history, poetry, prophecy, advice. With Him as the key, the puzzle comes together: the Bible is a unity, with one Author and one Center. Without Christ, the Old Testament is a book of movement toward a goal—but the goal is never attained. With Him promise meets fulfillment, prediction is realized.

We commonly isolate "Messianic prophecies" of the Old Testament—and rightly so. But the whole Old Testament in fact is a Messianic prophecy. It is the record of the acts of God, who comes to His people in their lostness to bring them deliverance. More and more these saving acts of God point ahead to the great act when God Himself will intervene personally, becoming incarnate to deliver the world from the bondage of sin.

If we would understand the Bible, then, we need to read it Christologically. Not only should we ask what any passage meant in its original setting and what it means to us today; we should also ask what it tells us about Christ and His saving mission. We should ever read Scripture in the light of "the Lamb slain from the foundation of the world" (Rev. 13:8).

And the Scriptures *do* testify of Him! His promise is: "And ye shall seek me, and find me, when ye shall search for me with all your heart" (Jer. 29:13).

# ON THE EMMAUS ROAD

*And beginning at Moses and all the prophets, he ex-pounded unto them in all the scriptures the things con-cerning himself. Luke 24:27.*

I would like to have joined Cleopas and his friend that Sunday afternoon. The road to Emmaus wasn't a long one, only about seven miles. But the journey seemed endless to the two heavy-hearted disciples. Their hopes had died two days before, outside Jerusalem, as Jesus of Nazareth had breathed His last on a Roman cross.

I would like to have seen the difference Jesus made when He joined them. They should have recognized Him, but they did not. So burdened by the thought of His death were they that "their eyes were holden that they should not know him" (Luke 24:16). But nevertheless the Stranger began to transform the journey. As He expounded the Scriptures, they forgot about the road, forgot about their grief. In the light of understanding, distance and doubts rolled away. Then at last "their eyes were opened, and they knew him" (verse 31).

Sometimes we too set out to go to Emmaus. We feel desolate, grieving. Every now and then life caves in on us, and we set out for Emmaus. The Emmaus road seems long, hot, and dusty. Then a Stranger draws near and requests our company. If we let Him (He will not force Himself on us), He walks with us—and strikes up a conversation. As we begin to hear His words, we forget the way and begin to understand. We suddenly realize that God has not left us on our own, that once again He has come to us to revive our drooping spirits and show us His leading, even in the midst of heartache. The Emmaus road—the road of despair and grief—becomes a place to find our Lord anew.

Cleopas and his companion first found Christ in the Scriptures, then they were able to recognize Him in the Stranger by the way. Our experience may be similar to theirs. The Christ we find by studying the Bible will help us to know better the Christ who walks and talks with us along the road of life.

On the road to Emmaus, Jesus began at the books of Moses and expounded in all the Scriptures the things about Himself. During the rest of this month we also will turn to those same Scriptures, beginning with Genesis, as we seek to know better the Stranger by the way.

# THE TWO GARDENS

*And I will put enmity between thee and the woman, and between thy seed and her seed; it shall bruise thy head, and thou shalt bruise his heel. Gen. 3:15.*

There once was a garden. In it were heard only the sounds of laughter and holy joy. God planted that garden and put our first parents in it "to dress it and to keep it" (Gen. 2:15). But the garden of life became the garden of death. The chill wind of transgression blew across its face and blighted the innocence and holy joy. Made in the image of God, made to enjoy the fellowship of God and angels, Adam and Eve hid, afraid, from the face of God (Gen. 3:8).

But God came seeking them. "Where art thou?" He called (verse 9). This question rings through every book of the Bible. God is seeking humanity—seeking us because we are lost, because we cannot help ourselves, because we cannot find Him. So God comes to us. And when He comes, it is to bring us salvation, to offer us hope in the provision He already has made to meet the emergency of sin.

So to our first parents in their shame came a word of hope from God. God promised a "seed" of the woman who, in God's own time, would come to crush the head of the serpent. Though that child of Eve would suffer in the process—"thou shalt bruise his heel"—He would be the divine agent to assure the triumph of right in the great controversy with evil.

There was another garden. In it, on a Thursday night when the moon was at the full, a Man knelt to pray. He had often come to this place, seeking quiet communion with God; always He had left refreshed. But now His sweat was like great drops of blood. Agonizing, He cried out: "O my Father, if it be possible, let this cup pass from me: nevertheless not as I will, but as thou wilt" (Matt. 26:39). That garden, which became the garden of death for Jesus of Nazareth, is the garden of life for us. By His struggles, submitting to drain the bitter cup to its dregs, tasting death for every man and woman (Heb. 2:9), He reversed the loss of the first garden. Though His heel was wounded, dying He saved us, freeing us from our guilt and breaking the power of the enemy over us. Thank God for "the seed" of the woman!

# MY BROTHER'S KEEPER

*And the Lord said unto Cain, Where is Abel thy brother?*
*And he said, I know not: Am I my brother's keeper? Gen.*
*4:9.*

One of the most tragic signs of the times is the callous disregard for human life. Men and women are concerned only about themselves. They trample upon others, literally and figuratively, seeking to gain the ascendancy, seeking to "get ahead" no matter what the cost to others. Crimes of violence—murder, rape, assault—are proliferating. Many cities are becoming modern jungles where anarchy and brute force hold sway.

Life in the world is like a pyramid. The higher a person climbs, the fewer people there are above him. So scratch and struggle, sweat and strive, pulling yourself up on the backs and shoulders of others so that you stand higher than they.

But Jesus Christ inverts the pyramid. His value system is the complete reversal of the world's. In Jesus' kingdom we live, not to climb above our fellows, but to bear them on our shoulders. "Whosoever will be great among you, let him be your minister; and whosoever will be chief among you, let him be your servant: even as the Son of man came not to be ministered unto, but to minister, and to give his life a ransom for many" (Matt. 20:26-28). And so at the apex of this inverted pyramid we find one Man, Jesus Christ. Instead of lording His power over all, He is carrying the entire human race on His back, bearing its sins to the cross of redemption.

Am I my brother's keeper? Cain's insolent retort is answered by Jesus: Yes, Cain, you are your brother's keeper. As I have made mankind all "of one blood" (Acts 17:26) and as I have died for all as the new Adam (Rom. 5:12-21), so every man and woman is now one in Me.

What a difference such a concept could make to our society! Think of it—every person concerned, genuinely caring for his neighbor. We could do away with the police, with the courts, with lawyers. We could buy a used car without any qualms! Life would be like heaven on earth.

In your sphere, in my sphere, heaven is to begin now. *We* are to show the world that we care. Because Jesus died for every person, every Abel is our brother and we are his keeper.

# THE COVENANT OF PROMISE

*I do set my bow in the cloud, and it shall be for a token of a covenant between me and the earth. Gen. 9:13.*

This chapter introduces explicitly one of the greatest words of the Bible—"covenant." It signifies a contract into which God and humanity enter, a solemn agreement binding both parties. But the divine covenant is not like a normal human contract. We are familiar with the latter—when we buy a house, purchase a new car, get married, or enter into business partnership. In the biblical covenant, however, the parties are not equal. Nor are the terms hammered out across the table before either party signs. Rather, it is God—one wholly greater than us—who stipulates the conditions of the covenant.

So here is God entering into covenant with Noah and his sons after the Flood. Promising never again to bring the waters of destruction on the world, God makes an "everlasting covenant" (Gen. 9:16) and signifies it by the rainbow (verses 13, 14, 17). To men and women in fear of another cataclysm, He gives a sign of His promise.

Throughout Scripture we read about covenants. God makes a covenant with Abraham (Gen. 17:7-16), then with Israel at Sinai (Ex. 19:3-6), with the people under Joshua (Joshua 24:1-27), and so on. Jeremiah foretells a new covenant (Jer. 31:31-34), and in the New Testament it comes to fruition (Heb. 8:6-13).

What is the significance of this "covenant" language? It shows the gracious condescension of a God who cares enough for us that, in order to reassure us, He even enters into a way of bonding Himself to us after a human practice. The covenant is trying to tell us that God *can* be trusted, that He really does care. And that it is He alone who specifies the way of salvation—we cannot haggle with God about the terms of the salvation He offers us.

While covenants are often mentioned in the Bible, they all spring from the "everlasting covenant" (Heb. 13:20), ratified not with the blood of animals but with the blood of Christ. Every promise of the Old Testament, whether to Adam and Eve, Noah, Abraham, or Israel, looked forward to what God's Lamb would accomplish, and rested on the certainty of that accomplishment. That is why every time we see a rainbow, we should think of the rainbow about God's throne (Rev. 4:3).

# THE LAMB GOD PROVIDES

*And Abraham said, My son, God will provide himself a lamb for a burnt offering: so they went both of them together. Gen. 22:8.*

After nearly 4,000 years the story of Abraham and Isaac on Mount Moriah still wrenches our hearts. We marvel at the fortitude of the old man: how did he ever find strength to obey the divine voice? How could he be sure that it was indeed the voice of God and not the whisper of a demon? How could he ever bring himself to take up the knife to the throat of his only son, beloved with years of longing?

And we marvel at the clear-eyed courage of the boy. As he and his father had gone on the journey, curiosity had turned to anxiety and anxiety to foreboding and foreboding at last to stark truth as the boy looked death in the face. His question haunts us: "Behold the fire and the wood: but where is the lamb for a burnt offering?" (Gen. 22:7). Then at last, when the altar is built and the wood set out, without a struggle, without a protest, he is bound, awaiting death.

And we marvel at the provision of God in this heartrending test of humanity. Although Abraham had spoken of the Lord's providing a lamb, he did not realize the depth of his own words. He took the knife to slay his own son, "accounting that God was able to raise him up, even from the dead; from whence also he received him in a figure" (Heb. 11:19). But God had Himself provided a sacrifice! "And Abraham lifted up his eyes, and looked, and behold behind him a ram caught in a thicket by his horns" (Gen. 22:13). So he called the place Jehovah-jireh, "the Lord will provide" (see verse 14).

Near that place nearly 20 centuries later, God again provided a Lamb. Another Father gave His only Son; another Son went willingly to His death. "It was to impress Abraham's mind with the reality of the Gospel, as well as to test his faith, that God commanded him to slay his son. The agony which he endured during the dark days of that fearful trial was permitted that he might understand from his own experience something of the greatness of the sacrifice made by the infinite God for man's redemption" (*Patriarchs and Prophets*, p. 154).

# THE HEAVENLY WRESTLER

*And Jacob was left alone; and there wrestled a man with him until the breaking of the day. Gen. 32:24.*

Here is Jacob, attacked in the night, fighting for his life. He was at his wits' end. The well-laid plans of Jacob the deceiver had collapsed about him; all his schemes were in ruins. He had made an ungraceful exit from the home of Laban, his father-in-law, sneaking away without a word of farewell. As he neared his home he heard the bad news: his twin brother Esau, whom he had tricked years before, was coming to meet him—with 400 men! So Jacob, fearing what the new day would bring forth, had decided to spend the night alone by the brook Jabbok. And now this! An assailant confronts him in the darkness and they wrestle through the night.

God's ways of reaching us are strange and ingenious. Because He loves us, He will not let us go without a struggle. We may think the devil is working hard to win us; God is working even harder. He comes to us again and again, through a multitude and variety of ways, wrestling with us to make us His own. Who would have thought that the stranger in the night, coming out of the darkness upon the disconsolate Jacob, was God Himself? Yet He was. Jacob came to realize it at last, after hours of struggle. The next morning he said, "I have seen God face to face, and my life is preserved" (Gen. 32:30). It was Christ who fought with Jacob, striving to subdue his soul by subduing his body. He was the heavenly wrestler by the Jabbok.

Would we try to run away from God? He will not give us up without a struggle. Have we come to the end of our rope, feeling the loss of our plans and forsaken by both men and God? He will come to us, perhaps in a totally unexpected way, wrestling with us so that we may learn new dimensions of faith:

In vain Thou strugglest to get free;
I never will unloose my hold;
Art Thou the Man that died for me?
The secret of Thy love unfold;
Clinging, I will not let Thee go,
Till I Thy name, Thy nature, know.
—Charles Wesley

# SHILOH

*The sceptre shall not depart from Judah, nor a law-giver from between his feet, until Shiloh come; and unto him shall the gathering of the people be. Gen. 49:10.*

Judah was not the oldest son of Jacob; by the law of descent, the role of leadership should not have been his. Reuben, the firstborn, was entitled to that position. But God does not abide by those human rules and categories that we set up to assign some people as superior and others as inferior. God breaks through the man-made roadblocks of caste, color, sex, and status to accomplish His purposes. So He passed over the weak-kneed Reuben, "unstable as water" (Gen. 49:4), and designated Judah as the chief of the tribes of Israel.

When Israel wanted a king, Saul, a Benjamite, emerged as the nation's first monarch. Saul's reign soon fell into disobedience and failure, however, and God turned to a man after His own heart (1 Sam. 13:14). He chose a shepherd boy, fresh from the hills of Bethlehem, tanned by the wind and the sun, a poet, and filled with unpretentious courage—David, a Judahite. Like his ancestor who received the promise of our text, David was not the oldest son in the family.

This shepherd boy rose to become Israel's most famous king. Mighty in war, strong in peace, the sweet singer of his people, he was a king admired and loved by the nation, despite his personal failures. Ever after, Israel looked back on the Davidic era in their history as the zenith of their fortunes.

And they looked forward to the new Davidic King. Though the nations went into captivity, they hoped for the tree, hacked down by enemies, to sprout again; for a shoot to grow out of Jesse, a Branch out of his roots (Isa. 11:1). They lived in hope, because the ancient promise foretold of such a King. Out of Judah at last would arise the supreme ruler, Shiloh—"he . . . whose right it is" (Eze. 21:27). Not a usurper, not a political hack, not a grasping general—but Shiloh. Israel's true King would appear, "and unto him shall the gathering of the people be."

After more than 2,000 years of waiting, a voice was heard: "Lo, I come . . . to do thy will, O God" (Heb. 10:7). A new son of David, a new Judahite, had come. In a Bethlehem stable a baby's cry broke the stillness of night. Shiloh, Israel's true King and He who would gather the nations to God by Himself, had come!

# GOD OF THE BURNING BUSH

*And God said unto Moses, I AM THAT I AM: and he said, Thus shalt thou say unto the children of Israel, I AM hath sent me unto you. Ex. 3:14.*

God comes to us in unpretentious ways. What could be more common to a shepherd than a bush? That was all that Moses, now 40 years a shepherd, saw in the situation, except that the bush was on fire. He could not have dreamed that this day and this bush would launch his career as God's leader to deliver his people from bondage. He had abandoned that career four decades earlier, when his ambitious schemes had crashed in ignominious ruin.

But God was in the burning bush. The divine majesty was concealed in the flames; the place was "holy ground" (Ex. 3:5). The God of Abraham, Isaac, and Jacob had not forgotten His people, and He was about to act on their behalf: "I know their sorrows; and I have come down to deliver them," He said (verses 7, 8). Moses was to be His agent to bring them out of Egypt, but it was Yahweh's act: "I will be with thee" (verse 12).

When Moses, thinking of the plethora of deities in Egypt, asked the name of the God of the burning bush, he was told: "I AM THAT I AM . . . I AM." This was a strange name, one utterly unlike the gods of Egypt, where the sun, the Nile, the ruler of the dead, and many others were worshiped. The name of the God of the burning bush is not to be identified with the sun, or the river, or mountains, or human beings, or any creature. His name signified His eternal being: He is what He is, He will be what He will be. Eternally, He—and He alone—can say, I AM. We measure time by lifespans, cutting off our little yardstick into segments marked "past," "present," and "future." But the God of the burning bush has no beginning and no end; He always is; He is I AM.

The God of the burning bush appeared to people throughout Israel's history. At its climax He again came unpretentiously. So low-keyed was His appearing that the "experts" could not believe it was He. Like Moses, they asked Him, "Who are you?" (John 8:25). And like Moses they heard, "Before Abraham was, I AM" (verse 58). But unlike Moses, they did not heed the voice from the burning bush. The record says: "Then took they up stones to cast at him" (verse 59).

# THE BLOOD ON THE DOORPOSTS

*And the blood shall be to you for a token upon the houses where ye are: and when I see the blood, I will pass over you, and the plague shall not be upon you to destroy you, when I smite the land of Egypt. Ex. 12:13.*

There was wailing in Egypt that night. Across the land, from the palace of Pharaoh to the hut of the lowliest peasant, the firstborn of every household lay dead, smitten by the angel of death.

But in one section there was no grief—only haste, busy preparation, gathering the few belongings for a long trek. The tribes of Israel, dwellers in Egypt for hundreds of years and slaves for generations, were about to march out as free men and women. No firstborn child had died among them. When the angel of death crossed the land on his grim mission, he saw the blood on their doorposts and passed over.

Today the Jews still observe the Passover festival. They eat the roast lamb with bitter herbs and unleavened bread, according to the directions given to Moses (Ex. 12:8). They recount the story of how their ancestors were delivered from bondage.

We Christians do not observe the Passover. Or rather, we do not keep up the traditions commanded to Moses and handed down by generations of his race. We keep the Passover, not once a year, but throughout the year. Says Paul: "Christ our passover is sacrificed for us" (1 Cor. 5:7).

Jesus, on the last night of His earthly life, ate the Passover with His friends. Then He went out to His death—the Passover Lamb Himself. Like the symbolic lamb He was "without blemish" (Ex. 12:5), untainted by sin. Like that lamb His blood brings deliverance—He died to set us free.

But is the blood on the doorposts? God made *provision* to the Israelites in Egypt: if they would kill the lamb and put the blood on the doorposts, they would be spared by the angel of death. And God has made provision for the world in His Son, "the Lamb of God, which taketh away the sin of the world" (John 1:29). His blood saves us from eternal death; His blood sets us free. But this is only if the blood is on the doorposts of our heart, only if we each—personally, individually—have accepted it.

Is the blood on the doorposts?

# WATER FROM THE ROCK

***Behold, I will stand before thee there upon the rock in Horeb; and thou shalt smite the rock, and there shall come water out of it, that the people may drink. Ex. 17:6.***

Thirst makes men and women desperate. Thirsty people will fight, lie, and kill for a canteenful of water. Thirsty people lose their judgment; their whole being becomes focused on their bodies, crying out for water.

Israel was being tested by God; Israel was thirsty. They forgot the miracle of the plagues in Egypt, they forgot the miracle of the Red Sea, they forgot the miracle of the manna. All they could think of was "Give us water that we may drink" (Ex. 17:2). They were almost ready to stone Moses; their religious experience had dried up and they were tempting God Himself.

But God provided water from the rock. Moses smote the rock at His command, and water flowed out—water for the multitude. I have hiked high in the Himalayas, where the glaring sun beats down in the rare atmosphere. And then I too have found water in the rock—a spring of ice-cold water bubbling out of the burning mountainside. How cool, how refreshing, to the weary traveler. The water from the mountain springs from which I have drunk, however, is just a trickle, altogether insufficient for a crowd of Israelites.

If Israel could have looked beyond their own physical needs, they might have learned a lesson of the gospel in this Meribah experience. "They drank of that spiritual Rock that followed them: and that Rock was Christ," said Paul (1 Cor. 10:4). Christ was the smitten Rock out of whose side would flow rivers of living water to quench the thirst of a weary world (John 7:37, 38). But the Rock was smitten once, and once only. Once He died, to save the world, and no more. That is why, when at a later point in time Moses impetuously struck the rock, he was rebuked severely by God.

Jesus still gives "living water." He satisfies our longings, our deepest cravings. He is "an hiding place from the wind . . . ; as rivers of water in a dry place, as the shadow of a great rock in a weary land" (Isa. 32:2). There are many fountains in this world—fountains of learning, fountains of pleasure, fountains of beauty. But when we taste the water from the Rock, we drink and are satisfied, never to thirst again.

# THE LORD OUR BANNER

*And Moses built an altar, and called the name of it Jehovah-nissi. Ex. 17:15.*

On one of the darkest nights of the battle of Britain, in World War II, when the island nation seemed on the brink of defeat, Prime Minister Churchill came out from his underground headquarters to see a man writing on the wall, "Home rule for Wales!" That man had a cause, but it was a woefully misguided one in view of the times.

Today we see a proliferation of pressure groups. They all have their special interests, their causes that they seek to bring to the attention of political leaders and the public. Processions, pickets, demonstrations, banners—they are part of our age. Sometimes we see them, on a limited scale, even within the church.

But we have a cause. "Is there not a cause?" queried the shepherd boy David as he loaded the stones into his sling and went against Goliath (1 Sam. 17:29). The cause was the Lord's—the honor of His name in the defense of His people. And we have a cause today. We are soldiers for Jesus Christ, commissioned to tell the good news of His cross and second coming to a world in despair. We have the everlasting gospel to preach to every nation, kindred, tongue, and people (Rev. 14:6, 7).

When the armies of Israel defeated the Amalekites, Moses built a memorial altar and called it Jehovah-nissi, "The Lord is my banner" (Ex. 17:15, RSV). It was a name of ringing confidence, serving notice on the enemies of the 12 tribes that, although the children of Israel were ill-trained and broken psychologically by slavery, the Lord was at their head. In His name they had defeated Amalek; in His name they would be victorious over every foe ahead.

Now is the time for us to raise our standard to the world: "The Lord Our Banner." When the world tells us that our task of preaching the everlasting gospel to the last corner of earth is impossible, let us raise that banner. When the world would come in like a flood to turn us away from God's ideal for us, let us raise it. When we would fall into diversions, internal strife, and suspicion, let us raise it. It is the bloodstained banner of Prince Emmanuel. He is our leader. By His cross He has won the right to this world, and in His name we shall overcome at last.

# THE TENT GOD PITCHES

*And let them make me a sanctuary; that I may dwell among them. Ex. 25:8.*

Why did the Lord command the people of Israel to make Him a tent? Later, at the dedication of the Temple—a structure vastly superior to the tabernacle—Solomon declared, "But will God indeed dwell on the earth? behold, the heaven and heaven of heavens cannot contain thee; how much less this house that I have builded?" (1 Kings 8:27). If the glorious Temple of Solomon was too small for God, why should He tell them to make a tent, "that I may dwell among them"?

While God fills the universe, He delights to dwell with people. Despite all the misconceptions of God that have flourished in the past and that still abound, the Bible teaches us that God does care. He *is* interested in us; He *is* love (1 John 4:16). He is on our side. He is trying to get us into heaven, not trying to make the entry requirements so exacting as to keep us out. In fact, that any soul is lost is a matter of grief to God. He weeps over each person as He wept over His people of old: "How shall I give thee up, Ephraim? how shall I deliver thee, Israel?" (Hosea. 11:8). That is why He commanded Israel to pitch a tent for Him. He wanted to give them something concrete to grasp, something visible upon which to focus their faith.

The entire sanctuary system was for this same purpose. It educated Israel, teaching them lessons about the seriousness of sin and the way God had provided to deal with it. It was God who laid down the whole set of laws about sacrifices and rituals, and the man or woman who believed God took Him at His word and found forgiveness through the sanctuary and its sacrifices.

Later another tent was pitched for God. John 1:14 reads literally: "And the Word was made flesh, and pitched His tent among us." God came to live with us, sharing our lot, feeling our pain, dying our death. "He suffered the death which was ours, that we might receive the life which was His" (*The Desire of Ages*, p. 25).

One day God again will pitch His tent among us. "Behold, the tabernacle of God is with men, and he will dwell with them, and they shall be his people, and God himself shall be with them, and be their God" (Rev. 21:3).

# ATONEMENT BY BLOOD

*For the life of the flesh is in the blood: and I have given it to you upon the altar to make an atonement for your souls: for it is the blood that maketh an atonement for the soul. Lev. 17:11.*

In recent years many Christian denominations have given up talking about the blood of Jesus. They find such hymns as "O now I see the crimson wave, the fountain deep and wide . . ." repulsive. They feel that the language of blood belongs to a primitive conception of God and religion, and wish to update religious vocabulary so that modern psychological terms are used to describe the benefits of Calvary.

I question the value of this "updating." Our text today lays down a spiritual law: "It is the blood that maketh an atonement for the soul." That law is echoed by Hebrews, the book of the New Testament that especially elaborates and explains Leviticus: "Without shedding of blood is no remission" (Heb. 9:22). Scores of other passages of Scripture, from both Old and New Testaments, highlight the idea of atonement by blood as a divine axiom.

The thought of animal sacrifices is a grisly one. The ancient office of priest reminds us of a consecrated butcher. Could there not have been some other way? we cry out, as we read of massive slaughter of animals at the dedication of Solomon's Temple (2 Chron. 7:5). The picture of the sanctuary service is not a pretty one.

But neither was the cross pretty. So accustomed are we to think of the blessings of the cross that accrue to us that we forget what it meant to Jesus. Today His cross is bathed in light, a symbol of His victory. But that picture is the cross *after* Calvary. By taking it He transformed it. For Him it was a grisly instrument, an execution device, Satan's trump card. It belongs in the macabre company of the firing squad, the hangman's noose, and the electric chair.

For the mystery of sin God provided the mystery of the cross. Sin is not a light matter. Sin costs—even the death of God's own Son. There was no other way. The life of Jesus, perfect as it was, was not enough. His life had to be poured out in death—"it is the blood that maketh an atonement for the soul." Let this mystery of the cross seep through our beings until we hate the sin that led to Calvary. And let us today live in the joy and victory His blood has won!

# LOOK AND LIVE

*And the Lord said unto Moses, Make thee a fiery serpent, and set it upon a pole: and it shall come to pass, that every one that is bitten, when he looketh upon it, shall live. Num. 21:8.*

What a stupid idea! Whoever heard of treating snakebite in such a manner? What possible good could come from looking at a brass serpent attached to a pole?

What good? Much good—healing, in fact. For God had commanded, laying down this prescription for life. Israel had erred, bringing upon themselves the plague of snakes; but God immediately provided the remedy. Look and live—this was the essence of the cure He commanded. There was no other way out: no antivenom serum available, no field hospital, no magic potion to bring relief. Only by taking God at His word could dying men and women find hope and healing.

It sounds simple, doesn't it? What could be easier than just to look and live? And yet we sometimes find it hard to do. In fact, we try everything *else* but God's way. We go through our line of special anti-snakebite cures, trying one and then moving to another. We don't want to admit that we are at our wits' end. Surely *something* we can find or do will give us life!

All the while that we are trying to prove to ourselves—and to God—that we can get by on our own, He waits. He waits, presenting before us His prescription: Look and live. He says: Just believe Me, just accept that I *have* provided the cure in Jesus my Son. "As Moses lifted up the serpent in the wilderness, even so must the Son of man be lifted up: that whosoever believeth in him should not perish, but have eternal life" (John 3:14, 15).

Am I desperate enough to take God at His word? Am I ready to forsake all my efforts to cure the snakebite—am I suffering enough—to look and live? Am I ready yet to receive without deserving; to take the Man of the cross as my Saviour and Lord? Ellen White put it well: "To him who is content to receive without deserving, who feels that he can never recompense such love, who lays all doubt and unbeliefs aside, and comes as a little child to the feet of Jesus, all the treasures of eternal love are a free, everlasting gift" (letter 19e, 1892).

# THE STAR OF JACOB

*I shall see him, but not now: I shall behold him, but not nigh: there shall come a Star out of Jacob, and a Sceptre shall rise out of Israel. Num. 24:17.*

Balaam was an apostate prophet, but he spoke these words by divine revelation. His greed had led him to disobey God's instructions, and he had come with Balak, king of Moab, to curse Israel. But when he fell into prophetic trance he spoke from God. Instead of cursing, he blessed. So the fact that we may be led of God and used of God is not in itself proof that we are walking in the path of God's will. Neither should we interpret hardship and pain as a sure sign of God's displeasure with us.

Balaam's words strike our ears with unusual power in these times. Ours is the era of the "stars." I do not mean the heavenly bodies, although almost every paper and magazine includes a "Your Week by the Stars," and presumably millions of readers follow this humbug. It is not this astrological hocus-pocus but earthly "stars" that characterize our age.

We see the "stars" on the silver screen or on the playing field. They loom larger than life, every well-groomed hair in place, every wrinkle covered over. They have just the right word, delivered at the precise moment and with the correct intonation for maximum effect. They perform superhuman feats, rescuing the maiden in distress, catching the touchdown pass as time runs out, hitting the home run to win the game. How many young men and women—and older ones, too—spend hours dreaming about the "stars"? Just to get their autograph is a great achievement. To be a "star"—that would be heaven!

We have a Star. Higher than our most exalted conception is the Man, Jesus of Nazareth. In an age when the world flocks after its human idols, we will turn our eyes on Him. When we see Him, we see true and full humanity. All else and all others fade away into the wings. They cannot abide the genuine qualities He displays. He *deserves* to be a star—for what He is and for what He has done.

Balaam's graphic prophecy nevertheless strikes a sad note: "I shall behold him, but not nigh." Balaam foresaw the Star of Jacob, but not as one of His. He would be outside His kingdom. May we today not be so blinded by earthly "stars" that we share Balaam's place!

# A SAVIOUR'S COMMANDS

*I am the Lord thy God, which have brought thee out of the land of Egypt, out of the house of bondage. Ex. 20:2.*

Our attitude toward law is different when we know the lawgiver. Each of us is born with a perverse streak. The very presence of rules makes us want to break them. If you want someone to touch your newly painted fence, just hang a sign that says "Don't Touch—Wet Paint." When I was a dean of boys in academy, I noticed how the faculty would try to solve problems by inventing new rules. They thought that simply by making laws, they could remove all difficulties. But new and better laws were simply a challenge to the students to find new and better ways to get around them, or to break them without being caught.

But when we know the lawgiver, our attitude changes. When there is a personal relationship, a deep trust and respect, then we know that the rules he has laid down are not given to burden us. They don't come from a desire to fence us in, to crush our free spirits. He gives them for our best good.

It makes all the difference in our relationship to the Ten Commandments when we realize that they begin with the words of our text today. He who commanded Israel was the one who had saved them. First He saved, then He commanded. He did not say, Obey these laws, then I will save you. No; He came to the 12 tribes in their slavery, working miracles to deliver them from Egypt. Then He brought them out to Sinai and revealed the Decalogue to them.

Jesus did a similar thing in New Testament times. In the Sermon on the Mount He elaborated the law. He showed that its demands speak to our inner being, testing even our desires and motives. But before Jesus gave this stringent interpretation of the law, He "went about all Galilee, teaching in their synagogues, and preaching the gospel of the kingdom, and healing all manner of sickness and all manner of disease among the people" (Matt. 4:23). He who commanded had first delivered.

Without the Lawgiver, the Ten Commandments are a prison, every bar marked "Thou shalt not!" But when we know Jesus the Lawgiver, the Ten Commandments are a promise, every one marked "Because you are Mine, thou shalt not."

# MOSES AND THE LAMB

*The Lord thy God will raise up unto thee a Prophet from the midst of thee, of thy brethren, like unto me; unto him ye shall hearken. Deut. 18:15.*

When Jesus put His famous question to the disciples at Caesarea Philippi, "Whom do men say that I the Son of man am?" (Matt. 16:13), they gave a variety of answers. Elijah, John the Baptist, Jeremiah, or one of the prophets—these were the speculations that were circulating about Jesus. Apparently no one suggested the Old Testament figure most like Jesus—Moses. Christ is the great leader of the people of God, prominently revealed in the New Testament but in fact their captain in all ages. But Moses, the preeminent person of the Old Testament, is a striking anticipation of Him.

Each was threatened at birth by a wicked king. Both lived for a time in Egypt. Both confronted the religious and political hierarchy of their day. Both led Exodus movements—Moses took Israel through the Red Sea and the Sinai to the borders of the promised land; Christ called out a people from the shackles of sin and disease. Both were concerned with the Ten Commandments— Moses as the recipient of the tables of stone on Mount Sinai, and Christ as the lawgiver who elaborated the Decalogue by example and precept during His earthly life. Both were involved with the sanctuary and its services—Moses as the person given the instructions for the wilderness tabernacle and sacrificial rituals, and Christ as high priest and sacrifice in the "true" sanctuary, which is in heaven (Heb. 8:1, 2).

Moses was a meek man, humble "above all the men which were upon the face of the earth" (Num. 12:3). So was Jesus: He emptied Himself to live among us, bearing His head to mockery, scorn, spitting, and a crown of thorns. Moses endured a people who were stubborn, slow to learn, and often complaining. So did Jesus: He labored patiently with His "little ones" (Matt. 10:42), despite their ambitious rivalry, pettiness, and dullness of heart.

Like Christ, Moses was resurrected. He joins in the victory that His Lord has won for us all. No wonder that the redeemed will sing in heaven "the song of Moses the servant of God, and the song of the Lamb" (Rev. 15:3).

# THE CAPTAIN OF THE LORD'S HOST

*And the captain of the Lord's host said unto Joshua,*
*Loose thy shoe from off thy foot; for the place whereon thou*
*standest is holy. And Joshua did so. Joshua 5:15.*

We often forget this truth—that as members of God's church
we stand on holy ground. In many respects the church looks like
any other human institution. It has its organization, management
principles, and politics. It can be studied sociologically, analyzed,
and to a certain extent explained. But, while the church is a human
institution, it is much more. Paul said we are "stewards of the
mysteries of God" (1 Cor. 4:1), pointing to the transcendent
element, the key divine factor that lifts the church beyond merely
human considerations.

We need especially to remember that the head of the church is
Jesus Christ. He was the one who appeared to Joshua as he went
apart to pray before the battle of Jericho. "It was Christ, the
Exalted One, who stood before the leader of Israel" (*Patriarchs
and Prophets*, p. 488). He still goes before His people. John the
revelator saw Him in a striking vision: "And I saw heaven opened,
and behold a white horse; and he that sat upon him was called
Faithful and True, and in righteousness he doth judge and make
war" (Rev. 19:11). As Commander in Chief of the armies of
righteousness He leads His people on to victory in His name.

To Joshua, wondering how the Hebrew tribes would fare in
their first battle, the Captain of the Lord's host gave assurance:
"See, I have given into thine hand Jericho, and the king thereof, and
the mighty men of valour" (Joshua 6:2). To us today He says: "No
weapon that is formed against thee shall prosper" (Isa. 54:17).
Because He is at the head of the church, we shall be triumphant at
last.

Often our work is small. Are you the only Adventist in your
town? Are you the only Christian in your family? Do you meet for
worship in a little structure on a back street or in a hired hall? Do
the odds seem overwhelming against the giving of the gospel to
every person on earth? Let us find again the Captain of the Lord's
host and loose our shoes from off our feet.

# HIS NAME IS WONDERFUL

*And the angel of the Lord said to Him, "Why do you ask my name, seeing it is wonderful?" Judges 13:18, RSV.*

In this story of Manoah and his wife we meet one of the recurring characters of the Old Testament, "the angel of the Lord." He appeared to Abraham as he sat in the door of his tent in the heat of the day (Gen. 18:1, 2, 33), to Gideon as he was threshing wheat in secret (Judges 6:11, 20), to various other people of the Old Testament. In each visit the men or women involved first saw Him as no more than a human being; in this story Manoah and his wife at first call him "the man of God," or simply "the man" (Judges 13: 6, 8, 10, 11). But in each story the supernatural character of the angel is at length revealed, and Abraham, Gideon, and the others come to realize that they have been talking with God. So Manoah says: "We shall surely die, because we have seen God" (verse 22).

What is the name of the angel of the Lord? Call His name Wonderful. We know Him by His earthly name Jesus, given by the angel in a dream to Joseph before He was born of the virgin Mary. "Jesus" is the same as the Hebrew name Joshua, and means "savior" or "deliverer." "Christ" is a title; it means "Messiah," the anointed one. But His eternal name, His name before the Incarnation, we do not know. He is designated as the Word and as the Son, but both names describe His function in the plan of salvation.

Have you discovered that His name is Wonderful? Men and women, boys and girls, in first-century Palestine found that the Jesus of Nazareth who had left the carpenter's bench for a ministry of teaching, preaching, and healing had another name—a secret name. Although they first had seen Him as just a man, He revealed Himself as someone far more than a man. In Him they found peace; in Him they found forgiveness; in Him they found new life; in Him they found God! Isaiah had foretold it: "Unto us a child is born, unto us a son is given: . . . and his name shall be called Wonderful" (Isa. 9:6).

So call His name Wonderful. He is our wonderful Saviour, wonderful Counselor, wonderful Mediator, wonderful Healer, wonderful Priest, wonderful Lord, wonderful King! When we behold His glory, we fall at His feet and exclaim, "His name is Wonderful!"

# A THREEFOLD LOVE STORY

*And Ruth said, Intreat me not to leave thee, or to return from following after thee: for whither thou goest, I will go; and where thou lodgest, I will lodge: thy people shall be my people, and thy God my God. Ruth 1:16.*

Nestled between the bloody battles of Judges and the wars of 1 Samuel we find the little book of Ruth. A jewel of both literature and spiritual insight, it sets forth a threefold love story.

The famous words of our text for today tell the first love story—a woman's love for her mother-in-law. It is an extraordinary affection, one altogether without thought of gain or return. Ruth's husband was dead, Naomi had no more sons, and the two women were from different races and cultures. For centuries jokes have been made about in-laws. But Ruth was an unusual person and Naomi an even more unusual one. A pure, selfless bond of love united these two women who had so little in common.

Ruth, a young widow and a stranger "amid the alien corn," meets Boaz. So is set in motion the second love story of the book of Ruth. Boaz is famous in the town, "a mighty man of wealth" (Ruth 2:1). He owns fields and hires and fires workers. He speaks as though he is considerably older than Ruth, calling her "my daughter" (verse 8). It is an unlikely match—the rich landowner and the poor, foreign widow—but they fall in love. Ruth, the Moabitess, becomes a member of the line from which Messiah will come (Ruth 4:13-22; Matt. 1:5-16).

Is there a third love story here? Indeed there is. For Boaz, who acts so graciously toward Ruth, is also the "near kinsman," the one who has the right to redeem (Ruth 3:12; 4:4-6). The law of the kinsman, given by God to the Israelites, was a wise provision to help families in time of need. By its operation people who had fallen upon hard times could not be sold and driven from the land, their most precious possession. Instead, the closest relative would step in to "redeem" the land, ensuring that it would stay in the family. The law extended to the care of a widow who was left childless.

So Boaz and Ruth tell the third love story—it is the story of Christ's love for us. We are in poverty, alone, aliens; but He is the near kinsman. By becoming man, by becoming one with us, He won the right to redeem us.

# LIMPING BETWEEN OPINIONS

*And Elijah came unto all the people, and said, How long halt ye between two opinions? if the Lord be God, follow him: but if Baal, then follow him. 1 Kings 18:21.*

The Hebrew of this text gives an interesting insight into its meaning. "Halt" has the idea of limping along, as the RSV translates: "How long will you go limping with two different opinions?"

Limping between opinions—these words sum up much of Israel's history. Through the books of Samuel, Kings, and Chronicles the nation often is like the "doubleminded" person of James 1:8—unstable in all its ways. First, it seeks to be like its neighbors and asks to have a king. With the inception of the monarchy, the fortunes of Israel rise and fall with the quality of leadership that comes from the throne. Unfortunately, they fall more than they rise, as the record of Israel's kings relentlessly notes: "And he did evil in the sight of the Lord." Israel limps between two opinions, trying to share the worship of Yahweh with Baal, her loyalties divided. Inevitably the flower of the kingdom fades and at last Israel is taken captive, her Temple laid desolate, her capital wasted. Even after some of the exiles returned and began to restore the land, many of the people were still limping spiritually.

We need to hear Elijah's challenge in these times. We need to be torn away from our worship of modern Baals and come back to the first commandment—"Thou shalt have no other gods before me" (Ex. 20:3). For many people today, Christianity is a club, a status symbol, a comfortable feeling. There is little sense of its distinctiveness, that "there is a wall of separation which the Lord Himself has established between the things of the world and the things He has chosen out of the world and sanctified unto Himself" (*Testimonies*, vol. 1, p. 283).

In universal terms the conflict between Yahweh and Baal of Elijah's time is the controversy between Christ and Satan. If Christ be God, let us follow Him! Let us give Him our undivided loyalty.

Early in the second century, Bishop Ignatius, on his way to martyrdom at Rome, wrote to Polycarp. "The times demand you," he exhorted, "as pilots demand wind and a storm-tossed man a harbor." May we be true to our times, not limping between two opinions, but single-minded for Christ.

# MY REDEEMER LIVES

*For I know that my redeemer liveth, and that he shall stand at the latter day upon the earth. Job 19:25.*

Some of our deepest insights are forged in the crucible of suffering. Here is Job, feeling utterly forsaken, giving voice to perhaps the finest expression of faith in the entire Old Testament. The whole chapter up to this text has given no hint of the glorious sunburst that we suddenly find here.

Job has been lamenting how God has turned against him: "He hath also kindled his wrath against me, and he counteth me unto him as one of his enemies" (Job 19:11). His relatives have abandoned him (verses 13, 14); even the house servants (verses 15, 16) and young children (verse 18) disregard him. He appeals to his friends, but in vain (verses 21, 22), and even makes a fanciful entreaty that posterity will understand him (verses 23, 24). All—every human source of comfort and encouragement—has failed. He has been reduced to nothing. But out of that nothingness rises the song of faith: "I know that my Redeemer lives" (verse 25, RSV). The cup of suffering has a jewel among its dregs.

On Christmas Day, 1865, while at Rochester, New York, Ellen White saw in vision a vine entwined around a cluster of trees. Then the trees began to sway as though moved by a powerful wind, and the vine was shaken loose from its support. Finally a person came up and severed the last clinging tendrils of the vine and it collapsed to the ground. People passed by and pitied it, but no one raised a hand to lift up the vine.

But then an angel came to the vine and, placing his arms beneath it, raised it upright. The angel commanded the vine, "Stand toward heaven, and let thy tendrils entwine about God. Thou art shaken from human support. Thou canst stand, in the strength of God, and flourish without it. Lean upon God alone, and thou shalt never lean in vain, or be shaken therefrom." When Ellen White inquired as to the meaning of the vision, the angel said, "Thou art this vine" (*Testimonies*, vol. 1, pp. 583, 584).

Job earlier had cried out for a "daysman" (Job 9:33)—that is, a mediator or umpire. Now faith grasps that there is One who stands in man's behalf in the heavenly courts. It is He who "always lives to make intercession" for us (Heb. 7:25, RSV). He is the Defender par excellence!

31

# DAVID'S LORD

*The Lord said unto my Lord, Sit thou at my right hand, until I make thine enemies thy footstool. Ps. 110:1.*

Of all the Messianic prophecies of the Old Testament, this is the one most frequently referred to in the New Testament. Doubtless its popularity among the early Christians stemmed from Jesus Himself.

During the last few days of His public teaching, and as the cross loomed stark ahead, Jesus bested His adversaries by quoting this passage. They had been raising difficult questions, hoping to get Him to provide a reason to arrest Him; now they found the tables turned. "How say the scribes that Christ is the son of David"? asked Jesus. "David therefore himself calleth him Lord; and whence is he then his son?" (Mark 12:35, 37).

The religious leaders were left speechless. So-called experts in interpreting the Scripture, they had been defeated on their own grounds. Their theology was unable to cope with the concepts brought out by Psalm 110:1. They looked forward to Christ (the Messiah), the son of David—but Messiah would be another powerful king, ruling and conquering the surrounding nations as had the son of Jesse in Israel's golden age. He would be *another* David—no less, but also no more. Their expectations did not allow for Messiah to be David's *lord* as well as his son. So Matthew's account of the scene closes with: "And no man was able to answer him a word" (Matt. 22:46).

David's Lord—the concept expressed by Psalm 110:1—still boggles the mind. The multitude still can accept that He is son of David. Perhaps a great man. Perhaps the greatest figure in history. Maybe the supreme teacher of the ages. Even a good man, the noblest person to have walked this planet.

All these evaluations of Jesus will still be given by the wise men of the world. They will raise Jesus to the front place among men—provided He is nothing more.

But He *is* more. To call Him merely a great teacher is to make Him out to be a liar; to say He is only a good man makes Him a deceiver or a madman. He *cannot* be only a teacher or a good man. He is either what He claimed to be—Lord, of David and of you and me—or He is the worst of people. But those who "taste and see" *know*. They know Him, and fall at His feet.

# THE SERVANT OF THE LORD

*Behold my servant, whom I uphold; mine elect, in whom my soul delighteth; I have put my spirit upon him: he shall bring forth judgment to the Gentiles. Isa. 42:1.*

The prophecies of the Messiah, which commence with the promise of the "seed of the woman" (see Gen. 3:15) and run throughout the Old Testament like a joyous refrain, reach a crescendo in the book of Isaiah. We shall frequently turn to these pages as we study in succeeding weeks the life and death of Jesus. In particular we shall notice a series of four brilliant passages that portray Messiah as "the servant of the Lord" (Isa. 42:1-7; 49:1-9; 50:4-9; 52:13—53:12).

Our text for the day marks the commencement of these passages. It sets out a threefold description of the Servant of the Lord.

First, Messiah will be a "servant." That idea is strange to most of us: we did not grow up in a wealthy home with butlers, maids, footmen, chauffeurs, and gardeners. Even further distant is the thought of "slave," to which the original word comes close. These are the days of equal rights and democracy; we are concerned to get our fair share; we do not want to be trampled on by anyone. But, says the Scripture, Messiah will be primarily a servant! No drums and pomp for Him, no political program, no grasping for office—He came to serve. "In His life no self-assertion was to be mingled. The homage which the world gives to position, to wealth, and to talent was to be foreign to the Son of God. None of the means that men employ to win allegiance or to command homage was the Messiah to use" (*Prophets and Kings*, pp. 692, 693).

Second, although a servant, Messiah was the one in whom God delighted. He spoke the words of approval at His baptism, and sealed the divine mission with His blessing. The lowly preacher-healer from Nazareth, whom the "great" passed by, was in fact God's Man, a Servant of the will of heaven.

Third, Messiah's mission was not merely for Israel. It would be worldwide: "he shall bring forth judgment to the Gentiles." In Him the hopes and dreams of mankind find a home; in Him the whole human family finds rest.

Thank God for His Servant!

# THE LORD OUR RIGHTEOUSNESS

*In his days Judah shall be saved, and Israel shall dwell
safely: and this is his name whereby he shall be called,
THE LORD OUR RIGHTEOUSNESS. Jer. 23:6.*

Many people are ready to say "The Lord Our Deliverer." When
the ship begins to sink, even the ungodly and so-called atheists
begin to cry out to God. Other people are happy to say, "The Lord
Our Protector." They look upon God as a heavenly safety net, one
whose benevolent care will guard them from accident and sickness. Some others—certainly a group smaller in number—still say
"The Lord Our Judge." Like the philosopher Kant, who ruled his
life by the eternal verities of the paths of the stars above and the
moral law he felt within, they see that the universe must at last give
account to its Maker.

But it is a broad step to be able to say "The Lord Our
Righteousness." It means that we don't look to God merely for
those areas of life over which we have no control—when the ship
starts sinking, or we get sick, or the day of final reckoning—but
even for what we think we can control: ourselves. It means that we
forsake ourself and all our claims to righteousness, our secret
pride, our self-justifying excuses, our rationalization. After all,
when we think for a while, we can list plenty of points in which we
are a pretty fine sort of people and certainly come up with a score
that puts us ahead of a lot of others, even in the church. That is why
it is hard to say from the heart, "The Lord My Righteousness."

It is interesting to read the confession of the famous French
thinker Rousseau. He describes at length his weaknesses and
failures, not sparing himself to the world. But he also shows how
circumstances encouraged his weaknesses and how, even when he
failed, his motives were good. The upshot is that, all things
considered, even with his "warts," he is the best of men!

Two people went to pray. One said, "I thank You, God, that I'm
not like the other people." But the other said, "God, be merciful to
me a sinner!" (Luke 18:9-14). It is still hard to say: "The Lord Our
Righteousness." Only when we behold Jesus in His glory will we
*want* to say it.

# NEW HEARTS FOR OLD

*A new heart also will I give you, and a new spirit will I put within you: and I will take away the stony heart out of your flesh, and I will give you an heart of flesh. Eze. 36:26.*

The Great Physician is also the Great Surgeon. He alone, He who made the human heart, can give new hearts for old. And He has never lost a patient.

One of the most dramatic advances in modern medicine has come in the treatment of heart disease. The first successful heart transplant, performed by Dr. Christiaan Barnard of South Africa, created a wave of excitement and admiration that rippled around the world. Open-heart surgery has become common: men and women whose effectiveness had been curtailed by diseased hearts are now walking, working, and running. Even mechanical hearts have been developed.

Great as these advances are, they are strictly limited in scope. They cannot change the essential human nature, the sin-diseased heart. They cannot take men and women who are selfish and make them unselfish; men and women who are greedy and unkind, and make them generous and kind; men and women who are cruel and malicious, and make them loving and thoughtful.

How much we need new hearts for old! How much we need Someone to cut out our stony, hardened, scarred hearts and give us a "heart of flesh"—a heart that is tender and gentle, a heart that is pure, a heart that is noble, a heart like Jesus'! The symptoms of spiritual atherosclerosis are all through society. Murder, rape, robbery, cheating, waste, gluttony, fraud—sin is no respecter of education or bank account. Every 23 minutes someone is killed on U.S. highways by a drunken driver—more than 20,000 people each year. Society is diseased because we are—I am—diseased.

That is why Jesus' words to Nicodemus are as true today as they were nearly 2,000 years ago: "Ye must be born again" (John 3:7). His diagnosis, though we may find it unwelcome, is 100 percent accurate. But He, the Great Physician, is also the Great Surgeon. If we let Him, He will give us new hearts for old. And He has never lost a patient.

# MESSIAH THE PRINCE

*And after threescore and two weeks shall Messiah be cut off, but not for himself. Dan. 9:26.*

When we think of the visions of the book of Daniel we usually recall the rapacious beasts that represent the kingdoms of this world. As Adventists we often spend much time on the religio-political "little horn" power of the seventh and eighth chapters of Daniel. But the evil "little horn" is not the central character of Daniel's prophecy, nor is any earthly king or kingdom.

In fact, every line of prophecy in Daniel focuses on Christ. He is the stone cut out without hands in chapter 2. He is "one like the Son of man" who receives the kingdom after the judgment in chapter 7 (verses 13, 14). It is against Him that the desecrating little horn power rises up in chapter 8 (verses 10-14, 23-26). He "stands up" in chapter 12 on behalf of the people of God (verses 1, 2).

Above all, the prophecy of the 70 weeks (Dan. 9:24-27) sets out Messiah the Prince. In terms of both literary structure and development of thought, this striking passage is the heart of the book of Daniel. To the prophet, agonizing in prayer over the wasted city and desolated sanctuary comes God's word of hope: the city is to be rebuilt and Messiah will come. He is Israel's true prince or ruler, the one whom all the monarchs in her history had but dimly foreshadowed.

But wonder of wonders, Messiah will be "cut off." Daniel must have been astonished. First came the glad word of Messiah's soon appearing—but now this! How could it be that the Prince would be "cut off, but not for himself" (RSV: "be cut off, and shall have nothing")? How could Israel's long-awaited King be subjected to the rejection sketched by these words? Surely the nation would acclaim Him, not disown Him!

In light of the first advent of Jesus we understand the paradox of Daniel's prediction. We now know that the prophecy of the 70 weeks itself supplies the answer: by His cutting off, Messiah the Prince would "make an end of sins . . . make reconciliation for iniquity, and . . . bring in everlasting righteousness" (verse 24). By His cutting off we are grafted in; by His becoming nothing we have life more abundant.

# THE DESIRE OF ALL NATIONS

*And I will shake all nations, and the desire of all nations shall come: and I will fill this house with glory, saith the Lord of hosts. Haggai 2:7.*

Do you meet for worship each Sabbath in a little church on a back street of town? Do you ever meet in a hall hired from some other organization? Perhaps you sometimes sit in your humble church and dream of the big Adventist centers—Loma Linda, Sligo, Pioneer Memorial—or the cathedral you attended as a child.

The people of God of Haggai's day were feeling down. They had come back from Babylonian exile full of hope. They had started to rebuild the Temple, wasted by the invaders. But the work seemed pitifully humble. Some of the old people could remember the first house of the Lord—Solomon's magnificent Temple—and they wept when they saw how poor the new structure seemed by comparison. As its foundations were laid, "the people could not discern the noise of the shout of joy from the noise of the weeping of the people" (Ezra 3:13).

Even after the new Temple was begun, work on it proceeded painfully slowly. Hindered by enemies, shortage of materials, and discouragement, its construction was still unfinished some 15 years later when Haggai appeared on the scene. He was a prophet with a single message: Arise and build.

And to those who mourned over the glory of the former Temple—"Who is left among you that saw this house in her first glory? and how do ye see it now?" (Haggai 2:3)—he had a prediction of thrilling assurance. Although this new house was as nothing compared with Solomon's Temple, it would be filled with glory. Into it—yes, this structure on which they now toiled in discouragement—would step "the desire of all nations." "The Lord, whom ye seek, shall suddenly come to his temple" (Mal. 3:1).

And as we worship in our little church or hall, if *He* is present—the Desire of all nations—our humble structure is filled with glory. Without Him, the finest cathedral is empty.

So the line of predictions, stretching from Genesis through the Psalms and to Malachi, the last of the Old Testament prophets, has prepared Israel for Messiah. Her King *will* come, Messiah the Prince, the Lord's Servant, the seed of the woman. The Old Testament rests in anticipation.

# THE MYSTERY OF GODLINESS

*And without controversy great is the mystery of godliness: God was manifest in the flesh. 1 Tim. 3:16.*

How could the eternal God become man? How could the One who is without beginning or end of days, whose fingers flung the stars into space and shaped the world, condescend to become human, one with us, bone of our bone, flesh of our flesh?

One night in Bethlehem a baby's cry cut through the stillness. Mary, wife of Joseph but still a virgin, had given birth. The Word had become flesh!

See Him lying in the manger—so tiny, so helpless, so dependent, so like us! Could it be that Mary's child, conceived of the Holy Spirit but so obviously like us, is the eternal God, He whose goings forth were from eternity? How can it be, that *this* babe is both man—and God?

We can study, probe, philosophize, and argue, but we can never explain this mystery. To explain the God-man would require the ability to understand God. Why, we but poorly understand man; we know far less about God, except what He has told us about Himself.

But we don't have to be able to *explain* Jesus in order to know Him (in fact, I'm not sure I understand my wife very well, even after 30 years of happy life together!). Genuine Christianity always will retain the element of mystery about the Babe of Bethlehem. He is like us—but not exactly. He *is* human; but He is so much more!

"That God should thus be manifest in the flesh is indeed a mystery," wrote Ellen White, "and without the help of the Holy Spirit we cannot hope to comprehend this subject. The most humbling lesson that man has to learn is the nothingness of human wisdom, and the folly of trying, by his own unaided efforts, to find out God" (*Selected Messages*, book 1, p. 249).

Instead of debating, we should rather be like Moses when he came to the burning bush, and take off our shoes in awe of the presence of God. We should fall down in adoration—amazed, wonder-struck, and grateful at God's act of self-sacrifice.

Jesus, child of Mary,
So frail, so weak, so small,
At Thy crib I worship
And own Thee Lord of all.

# HYMN NO. 1

*Great indeed, we confess, is the mystery of our religion:*
*He was manifested in the flesh, vindicated in the Spirit,*
*seen by angels, preached among the nations, believed on*
*in the world, taken up in glory. 1 Tim. 3:16, RSV.*

Pliny, governor of the Roman province of Bithynia early in the
second century, had a problem. A strange new religion was
spreading among the people. These followers of the Jew Jesus,
called Christians, had no churches or public meeting places. In
fact, their religion wasn't recognized by the state, so they could
meet only privately in homes to worship or tell others about their
ridiculous Teacher, crucified 80 years earlier in Jerusalem.

And yet the new faith was spreading. Silently but powerfully,
Christianity was leavening the entire province. And that was the
problem—it was affecting the regular religion. Fewer people were
going to the temples; trade in animals for sacrifice and idols was
falling off. Something had to be done!

Pliny decided to arrest anyone who could be identified as a
Christian and examine him thoroughly. Eventually an array of
people came before him—men and women of all ages, even
children. Pliny couldn't discover any crime these people had
committed; nevertheless, they were a nuisance, a threat to the
long-established order. Pliny asked each person three times, "Are
you a Christian?" If after the third opportunity the Christian still
clung to his faith, Pliny sentenced him to death—on the grounds of
obstinacy!

We know about this early chapter in Christianity because Pliny
wrote his boss—the Roman emperor Trajan—to inquire if he were
acting aright. Pliny's letter has been preserved, and it contains one
further insight into Christian life in the early second century. Pliny
tells us that he learned that the Christians had a curious practice of
rising early and gathering together before daybreak to sing an
antiphonal (voice against voice) hymn of praise to Christ as God.

Now look at our Scripture for today. Notice, it is a hymn, and
it praises Christ as God. Observe also that each line balances the
next: "He was manifested in the *flesh*," *but* He was "vindicated in
the *Spirit*." He "was seen by angels," *but* He was "preached among
the nations"; He was "believed on in the world," *but* He was "taken
up in glory."

Paul here is quoting an early Christian hymn—a hymn of
adoration to Christ. Maybe, just maybe, this is what the Christians
of Bithynia met to sing together at daybreak.

# THE SAVIOUR

*Therefore, when Christ came into the world, he said: "Sacrifice and offering you did not desire, but a body you prepared for me. . . . Then I said, 'Here I am—it is written about me in the scroll—I have come to do your will, O God.'" Heb. 10: 5, 7, NIV.*

A few yards offshore, a woman is floundering among the ice floes of the river. A rescue helicopter lets down a life preserver. She grabs it, but it slips from her hands. The helicopter pilot tries again. She does not have the strength, maybe not even the will, to grasp it. The television cameras catch the look of helpless terror in her eyes.

A group of rescue workers and onlookers are standing along the riverbank. Suddenly a young man breaks away from them and plunges into the river. With strong strokes he swims toward the woman, who has laid her head back on the water. He reaches her, seizes her, turns for the shore. A man in a yellow slicker rushes forward to meet them with a rope, and soon the woman is eased onto the snowy slope.

Lenny Skutnik has saved the life of Priscilla Tirado.

Lenny Skutnik, 28-year-old messenger at the Congressional Budget Office, had been let off work early that snowy afternoon of January 13, 1982. Making his way home, he saw the commotion on Washington's 14th Street Bridge, the ambulances, the helicopters—and passengers bobbing in the icy water. Air Florida Flight 90 had plunged into the Potomac River.

Skutnik stopped his car and joined the curious crowd on the bank. But unlike the other bystanders, he shucked off his coat and his boots and dived in.

Skutnik became an instant hero. Asked what led him to dive into a freezing river, at dusk, in a snowstorm, he replied: "If I hadn't done it, she would have died."

But what if Lenny Skutnik had recognized the woman in the river as one who had broken his heart? Would he still have risked his life to save her? What if she had been an evil woman? or Hitler? What would he have done then?

"But God shows his love for us in that while we were yet sinners [before His grace had made us anew] Christ died for us" (Rom. 5:8, RSV). God, taking a human body, plunged into the icy waters to ferry us to eternal safety.

# THE LIBERATOR

*And she shall bring forth a son, and thou shalt call his name JESUS: for he shall save his people from their sins. Matt. 1:21.*

Call Him Liberator, this virgin's firstborn son, plucked from the womb of eternity, flung into an alien land.

The baby, Liberator of humanity, cries. He cries just as my firstborn son, plucked from the womb of life and flung into an alien land, cried.

So the author of "Away in a Manger" had it wrong when he wrote "The cattle are lowing, the baby awakes, the little Lord Jesus, no crying He makes."

He was wrong. Jesus cried at birth. Jesus cried when He awoke. For the Liberator came in no alien flesh to set us free. Bone of our bone, He would walk our trails, suffer our heartaches, bear our pain. He would know the lure of temptation, brave the laser bolts of the ancient enemy. He would drink life's cup to the dredges.

And at last—death itself. A lonely, despairing, God-forsaken death, rending heaven asunder with its awful cry, "My God, my God, why hast thou forsaken me?" (Matt. 27:46).

Where is the face of the little Boy in the manger, that face so smooth and innocent and full of mystery? Bethlehem's Babe hangs contorted in death, wracked by the woe of a world gone wrong.

And thereby—liberation! Once temptation fled in defeat; now death itself falls, slain by the Liberator's death.

Every time we look into the face of a little child we see mystery—the mystery of being, of where we came from, of what we may be. Every babe is a song of hope in a silent world.

That is because of the virgin's firstborn Son, who cried, who is the liberator. He has set humanity free, free to be fully human, free to be sons and daughters of God.

The Babe's birth also guarantees our future. The Desire of ages, He sustains our lives. The Desire of all nations, He will come again. The Liberator, victor over sin, victor over death, will come back to reign!

Look into the Babe's face—so smooth, so soft, so peaceful, so full of mystery.

And with the Wise Men, fall down and adore Him; bring your gifts, offer Him all.

# EMMANUEL

*Behold, a virgin shall be with child, and shall bring forth a son, and they shall call his name Emmanuel, which being interpreted is, God with us. Matt. 1:23.*

When life closes in and its burdens seem almost too hard to bear, I remember Emmanuel—God with us. When I must pass through deep waters, when sorrow and disappointment would overwhelm me, I think of Emmanuel—God with us.

God did not provide for our salvation by transporting us out of this sin-racked earth, by destroying the planet gone wrong and plucking His people away. No—He brought salvation by coming Himself to live among us. God took human nature! He walked in our moccasins, felt our pain, struggled with us, suffered with us, sorrowed with us.

Nor does God put His people today in a protective cocoon. True, the principles of the Christian life, faithfully practiced, do provide freedom from many of the scourges that bad living brings. Furthermore, occasionally God intervenes in a miraculous way to deliver His people from evil. But usually He does not: the Christian knows his share of suffering, sorrow, and even tragedy.

But there is a difference. In all our suffering, God is with us. In all our sorrow, Emmanuel—God with us. Even when tragedy strikes, we know the assurance of His presence. He promises: "I will never leave thee, nor forsake thee" (Heb. 13:5). And again: "When thou passest through the waters, I will be with thee; and through the rivers, they shall not overflow thee" (Isa. 43:2).

An elderly church member wrote to me over the course of several years. She had had a hard life—the loss of her husband, and then three of her children. Now she lived alone, frail and infirm, with scarcely a friend in the world. To compound her troubles, her daughter lay dying. This sister thought she could not bear such sorrow; she prayed to be laid to rest before her daughter.

It was not to be. But God did something better: He sustained her through the most severe trial of her life. When she went to the funeral home for her last vigil with her daughter, it was as though a Presence met her at the door, took her by the hand, enabled her to walk steadily to the casket, and spoke words of comfort. In the days and months that followed, although she felt the grief over her daughter's loss, not once did the Presence forsake her.

Today, dear friend, no matter what may befall you, remember Emmanuel—God is with you!

# CAN I TRUST THIS MAN?

*He saith unto them, But whom say ye that I am? Matt. 16:15.*

The Child of Mary became the most controversial person in history. Although He was called Prince of Peace, wars were fought in His name. Although He poured out His life to bring healing of body and mind to all around Him, families would be divided—children against parents and parents against children—because of Him.

Who was He? The question troubled those who heard Him and saw Him. It has troubled every generation since. It troubles us, too: since the birth of that Babe in Bethlehem, Jesus of Nazareth has been a nagging question on the conscience of humanity, refusing to let it rest.

He Himself challenged His generation with the question "Who do you say I am?" And when Peter replied spontaneously, "You are the Messiah, the Son of the Living God," Jesus acknowledged the answer with "Simon son of Jonah, you are favoured indeed! You did not learn that from mortal man; it was revealed to you by my heavenly Father" (Matt. 16:15-17, NEB).

What answer will I give today?

If I say "He was a good man," that's true, but not good enough. *He claimed to be God!* If I say "He was a great teacher and healer," that's also true—but remember what He said about Himself! Jesus either made false claims about Himself (in which case He certainly *wasn't* a good man), or He was deluded, or He was crazy, or—He was what He claimed to be.

Can I trust this Man? If He is God, He can claim my life, my soul, my all. Can I trust Him?

It isn't a matter of proof. If it were, the wisest men and women could prove His deity and would be believers. But we *can* find an answer. We can know Him, just as Peter and the other disciples knew Him nearly 2,000 years ago.

As we read the Gospels and meditate on this remarkable person, He comes to us in the stillness, just as He came to them by the lakeside. Out of the shadows, in the quiet, He will speak to us His mysteries. And we will know. We will know that in meeting Jesus of Nazareth we meet God!

We don't give ourselves to someone—we don't exchange marriage vows—unless we can trust that person. And we can't give ourselves to Jesus unless we can trust Him, unless we can be sure that He really is what He claimed to be.

But we *can* trust Him! We can put Him to the test, find that He is the most trustworthy person on earth.

He has never failed me, and He will never fail you.

# A GIFT IS FOREVER

*For unto us a child is born, unto us a son is given. Isa. 9:6.*

It was Christmas and we were far from home, missionaries in a developing country. Christmas doesn't seem the same when the vast majority of the population belong to non-Christian religions, when the streets don't hang with colored lights, and when the radio doesn't play "Jingle Bells" or "Silent Night" during December.

It was Christmas and I was feeling far from home. I thought of the red, crisp, juicy Jonathan apples that grow in the hills above Adelaide in southern Australia where I grew up. How I longed for an apple! Here the few apples available in the bazaar came from far away and were way beyond our meager budget.

"I'll get you an apple, Daddy!" Terry, our 3-year-old, had heard my expressions of longing. He ran from the room, while Noelene and I looked at each other in surprise. Within a few minutes he was back, right fist tightly clenched, eyes laughing in anticipation. "Here's your apple, Dad," he exclaimed as he opened his hand and presented me with—a bright-red marble!

Of course, we all had a good laugh. But I have often thought back on that incident, now more than 25 years ago. Terry's gift was an act of pure unselfishness, pure love, pure delight, pure joy.

God's gift of Jesus was like that. An act of grace, an act of joy.

A gift is forever. You can't take back a gift—if you do, it wasn't a gift in the first place.

God didn't lend His Son to us for 33 years—He *gave* Him to us. And a gift is forever. "To assure us of His immutable counsel of peace, God gave His only-begotten Son to become one of the human family, forever to retain His human nature" (*The Desire of Ages*, p. 25).

To live today in the sense of that Gift is the most liberating experience I know. To sense that because of that Gift I *belong* here, that the world is *for* me and not against me, that God is on my side, that my day is surrounded by His grace as truly and as fully as the air I breathe so that I cannot get away from that grace—that is living!

# JESUS' FAVORITE NAME

*For the Son of man is come to seek and to save that which was lost. Luke 19:10.*

In the New Testament we find various names and designations for Jesus—Christ (which means Messiah), Lord, Son of God, Son of man, and so on. Which of these, do you think, was *Jesus'* favorite?

Overwhelmingly, "Son of man." In fact, Jesus hardly ever referred to Himself as the Messiah. Perhaps that term had become so associated with thoughts of militaristic campaigns, grandeur, and liberation from the bondage of the hated Romans that Jesus deliberately avoided it. He *was* the Messiah—but the Messiah of God's plan, not of Israel's expectations.

So Jesus turned to another name, one rich in Old Testament associations. In the book of Ezekiel, God frequently addressed that prophet as "son of man"—apparently indicating that Ezekiel was representative of humanity, not merely of Israel. And in the book of Daniel we read about "one like the Son of man" who comes in the clouds of heaven and receives the kingdom (Dan. 7:13).

Jesus used "Son of man" in several connections. He spoke of the Son of man in terms of His mission: "For the Son of man is come to seek and to save that which was lost" (Luke 19:10). Likewise in connection with His passion and sacrificial death: "And truly the Son of man goeth, as it was determined: but woe unto that man by whom he is betrayed!" (Luke 22:22). Finally, with reference to His second coming: "When the Son of man shall come in his glory, and all the holy angels with him, then shall he sit upon the throne of his glory" (Matt. 25:31).

Here is an interesting fact: in the Gospels, no one else called Jesus by His favorite name, Son of man. They called Him "Son of David," "Lord," occasionally "Son of God" or "Messiah"—never "Son of man."

Have you ever thought how curious Jesus' use is? He doesn't say "*I* have come to seek and to save the lost," but "*The Son of man* has come to seek and to save the lost." It's like the president of the United States saying "The president will go to Dallas," or the team leader of the Washington Redskins saying "The quarterback will throw a bomb to the wide receiver." We rarely speak like this—only when we wish to draw attention to our *role* or *function*.

And that's what Jesus was doing by using His favorite name. Over and over He wanted to remind men and women that He was *truly* man, human, one with us—and also the long-promised Son of man from Daniel's prophecy.

Maybe He wants to remind us today of that truth.

*February 9*

# WHEN OUR HOUSE COMES TUMBLING

***Since the children have flesh and blood, he too shared in their humanity. Heb. 2:14, NIV.***

When our house comes tumbling down, we will put our hand into His and walk away and leave it all behind.

When people misunderstand us and spread false reports about us and twist our words, we will remember that the Saviour of the world, who took our flesh and blood, also was falsely accused.

When we face lonely days and lonely nights and wonder how we can make it through one more hour, we will find strength to carry on in the One who prayed alone in Gethsemane and died alone on Calvary.

When we weep for a dear one laid to rest, or a child gone astray, or a friend so tortured by life's pressures that he took his own life, we will think of the Man of sorrows, who bore all our griefs, who is afflicted in all our afflictions.

When our bones ache and our body cries out for cessation of pain, we will cast our sicknesses upon Him who bore all our diseases.

When we feel crushed and disappointed because we have lost our job or failed the exam, when we feel rejected and forgotten, we will remind ourselves that One in heaven has walked in our moccasins and understands.

And when our hearts feel light and our feet skip and it seems as though the night will never come, we will recall Jerusalem's most popular dinner guest, whose conversation held even Pharisees spellbound, whose warm arms and laugh held the little children, whose words turned water into wine at a wedding long ago.

But when the night comes and the long, low call sounds our name, we will go out into the dark fearing no evil, knowing that He went before us through death's door and will be with us.

When our house comes tumbling, we will put our hand into His and walk away and leave it all behind.

46

# THE POWER OF A MOTHER'S PRAYERS

*But Mary treasured up all these things and pondered them in her heart. Luke 2:19, NIV.*

I am coming to think that a mother's prayers find a special place in the heart of God. I have heard a mother supplicating the throne of God with weeping, and I have been moved. If her prayers so moved me, how much more the heart of a loving heavenly Father!

Mary pondered the ways of her firstborn. Scripture tells us twice that she treasured away words and events that pointed to the mystery of Jesus (Luke 2:19, 51). She knew that her child, flesh of her flesh, was destined for greatness in God's plan—but that the path of greatness would be crossed by tragedy. "A sword will pierce your own soul too," the aged Simeon told her when she brought the 8-day-old boy to the Temple (Luke 2:35, NIV).

She saw her son grow to manhood—and continued to wonder. She knew Him as every mother knows her child—and yet she could not understand how the predictions of greatness and of tragedy would find fulfillment.

When the wine ran out at Cana's wedding feast she came to Him, challenging Him to act: "They have no more wine."

"Dear woman, why do you involve me?" He replied in gentle rebuke. "My time has not yet come" (John 2:3, 4, NIV).

Mary saw her Son rise to greatness. She saw the crowds flock to hear Him and to touch Him. She saw Him ride in triumph into Jerusalem as Israel's Messiah.

And she saw Him nailed to the cross. She stood by while He breathed His last.

We talk of the prayer life of Jesus; what about Mary's prayers —for Him?

Friend of mine, do you weep as you pray for your son or daughter? Listen to the word of the Lord: "This is what the Lord says: 'A voice is heard in Ramah, mourning and great weeping, Rachel weeping for her children and refusing to be comforted, because her children are no more.' This is what the Lord says: 'Restrain your voice from weeping and your eyes from tears, for your work will be rewarded,' declares the Lord. 'They will return from the land of the enemy'" (Jer. 31:15, 16, NIV).

# THE PYRAMID OF LIFE

*Your attitude should be the same as that of Christ Jesus: who, being in very nature God, did not consider equality with God something to be grasped, but made himself nothing, taking the very nature of a servant, being made in human likeness. Phil. 2:5-7, NIV.*

The *Wall Street Journal* is the most influential newspaper in the world. Scores of thousands of business executives and lawyers arrive at their offices each day, shut their doors, and open the *Journal*. They do nothing until they have scanned its message for the day.

Some years ago a theology student, Carnegie Samuel Calian, set out to discover the secret of the *Journal's* hold on the American mind. He interviewed scores of businesspeople; he spent time with the editors of the paper, probing their philosophy. Out of the study emerged a book, *The Gospel According to the Wall Street Journal*.

"In the course of my interviews, one industrial executive spoke bluntly, 'Everybody is in business to make money. . . . There's no trust when things are tight. . . . When things are going well, people are generous.' He also added, 'Sure, there's a need for some measure of trust . . . but collateral is the basis for any credit. The days of gentlemen's agreements are over.'

"Another manager, on discovering that I was a theologian studying business practices, took me aside for some lessons in the hard realities of life. 'Do you know,' he said, 'that in life you must go out to win—if you want to be a loser, then be a "good guy" like teachers, ministers, and social workers.'

"He also felt that trust is a luxury in our world. Once the trust placed in someone is destroyed, you are the loser. 'When you learn how to lose,' he said, 'you learn to compensate a loss with a win. Losses are an education; winning is your diploma. As for myself, I don't believe in losses; I make winners out of everyone.'

"The manager that I was interviewing was, by the way, an active churchgoer, but he had long ago decided that Sunday and Monday were two different worlds. To try to integrate them would be an exercise in futility. 'In fact,' he said, 'if you ask me how to be a Christian in business, my answer is that you can't, or you won't survive. Any book on the topic would be the shortest on record' " (p. 52).

For many people who set the compass of their life by the *Wall Street Journal*, life is a pyramid—a pyramid in which men and women struggle and claw and trample others in order to get to the top.

But Jesus Christ upends life's pyramid. In His kingdom, success is measured in terms of giving, not getting; in helping others, not ruling over them. And He alone is at the apex of this inverted pyramid, bearing the weight of the world's burdens on His shoulders.

At the top of a pyramid, said John Wesley, you find only two creatures—lizards or eagles. Which will I be today?

*February 12*

# ROOTS

***The book of the generation of Jesus Christ, the son of David, the son of Abraham. Matt. 1:1.***

For most of us the search for our origins is simply a matter of curiosity. We'd like to know when our forebears came to the New World; we'd like to be able to trace them to some hamlet or village in England, Germany, Scandinavia, or Africa.

However, for some people the search for roots is deadly serious. The Mormons compile huge lists of genealogies because they believe they can be baptized on behalf of their dead ancestors—and so give them a place in heaven! Occasionally, for a few others, a will is contested over the questions of paternity and heirship: fortunes ride on the quest for roots.

In ancient times roots were important. When the Jews returned to Jerusalem after the Babylonian exile, some of the priests were excluded from the Temple services because they could not establish their genealogy (Ezra 2:61-63).

Matthew sets out for us Jesus' roots. He establishes that Jesus was both son of Abraham and son of David. Being son of Abraham made Jesus one of the chosen people. Jesus was a Jew. He had brown eyes, not blue; a long nose; dark hair, not blond. He was son of Abraham.

He also was son of David. This put Him in the royal line, a possible heir to the throne of Israel. When later the crowds wanted to place the crown on His head, they weren't totally off the mark—He *was* the Messiah. Where they misunderstood Him was in failing to realize that God's Messiah would conquer by love, not force. He would be crowned with thorns, not gold.

So Matthew sets it all out—the proof of Jesus' roots as son of David and son of Abraham. Since descent was traced through the male line, as it still is, he gives us the legal evidence.

But at the end of the list of names we learn that the genealogy presents no more than the *legal* situation. For when Matthew comes to Joseph, last name on the list, he breaks the pattern. Joseph was *not* the father of Jesus—he was only the *husband* of Mary (Matt. 1:16).

God, not Joseph, was the Father of Jesus!

*February 13*

# THE GREAT COMMUNICATOR

*When all things began, the Word already was. The Word dwelt with God, and what God was, the Word was. The Word, then, was with God at the beginning. John 1:1, 2, NEB.*

Have you ever wondered why it was the Son rather than the Father or the Holy Spirit who came to earth to be our Saviour?

We have but faint glimmerings of the answer to this question. The Trinity boggles our human minds: God is one, but in three persons. Our minds seek analogies drawn from our knowledge of the world, but every attempt falls short. In past centuries theologians likened the Trinity to the sun rising, the sun at noonday, or the sun setting; or to body, soul, and spirit. Given our familiarity with the committee system, we Adventists tend to imagine the Trinity as the Heavenly Committee, or its three officers!

All these efforts fail. God is unlike us and cannot be reduced to our terms. We can know of Him only what He has revealed about Himself in the Scriptures.

Those Scriptures, however, call the Son "the Word." They tell us that the Son *always* was the Word. "In the beginning," says John, "the Word was God"—in the beginning before the beginning of Genesis 1:1, before the world was, before the universe was, before the big bang or whatever act God used to speak matter into existence. Before all else, when only God was, the Word was. And the Word was God.

From eternity the Godhead communicated itself through the Son. He was God's thought made audible, Ellen White tells us, the expression of the character and purposes of God.

So when God came to man in Old Testament times—walking in the garden, dining with Abraham, speaking from Sinai, appearing to the young man Isaiah as he worshiped in the Temple—it was the Word that people saw and heard. The Son of God communicated the mind of God.

In the mysterious councils of eternity, when God foresaw the fall of the human family, He made provision to meet our desperate need. God Himself would come to earth, not simply to visit mankind, but to *become* man. He would take our nature and our lot; He would bear our burdens; He would die in our place.

And so, in the fullness of God's time, the Word became flesh. The Word, the Great Communicator, the Eternal Communicator, showed us what God is like—"full of grace and truth."

*Jesus, eternal Word made flesh, God come to us, we now come to You. Take us in your hands and whisper your will for us this day.*

# FOUR MOTHERS IN ISRAEL

**For what the law could not do, in that it was weak through the flesh, God sending his own Son in the likeness of sinful flesh, and for sin, condemned sin in the flesh: that the righteousness of the law might be fulfilled in us, who walk not after the flesh, but after the Spirit. Rom. 8:3, 4.**

Matthew's genealogy of Jesus contains three surprises. Ancient records followed only the paternal line—mothers didn't count. But Matthew broke with precedent and listed four women in the ancestry of Jesus—Tamar (Matt. 1:3), Rahab (verse 5), Ruth (verse 5), and Bathsheba (verse 6).

When we go back to the Old Testament to try to discover why he singled out these four, we get a shock. Each of these mothers in Israel represented a marital situation that fell far short of God's ideal.

Tamar, daughter-in-law of Judah, posed as a prostitute and tricked Judah into giving her a son (Gen. 38:13-30)—a marital tangle as messy as any we can find today!

Rahab was a prostitute—at least she was when the Israelite spies sneaked into Jericho (Joshua 6:22-25).

Ruth, in contrast, was a virtuous woman. But she was a Moabite, member of a nation the children of Israel had been forbidden to marry, and excluded from the tabernacle services (Deut. 23:3).

And Bathsheba became wife of King David after he committed adultery with her, got her pregnant, and arranged to have her husband, Uriah the Hittite, killed in battle.

Every one of these marriages was irregular and/or illicit. But each of these relationships produced a male that became part of the genealogy of Jesus.

We live in a world of fractured relationships. The edenic ideal of marital bliss, of faithfulness to one man or one woman for life, often is shattered. Divorce, perversion, incest, abused children, battered wives—that's our world.

But into such a world came a Saviour. He came, not to rebuke or to tell us how far from the ideal we had fallen, but to rescue us. To give us hope—to give us forgiveness. To lift us up and give us power to start over.

The four mothers in Israel represent us—in all our need, in all our pain. And they represent God's plan for every son and daughter of Adam and Eve, His universal effort to save us out of our lostness.

*February 15*

# MY FATHER'S BUSINESS

*And he said unto them, How is it that ye sought me? wist ye not that I must be about my Father's business? Luke 2:49*.

What is your earliest memory? Building sandcastles at the beach? Fireworks on the Fourth of July? A childhood hurt that your mother comforted?

Sometime between infancy and age 12, the boy Jesus began to sense that He was different from other children. He began to realize that Joseph, the husband of His mother, wasn't His father, that the sheltered circle of Joseph's home could not be His forever, that one day God's call would take Him beyond the carpenter's shop where He helped Joseph.

In the early centuries of Christianity various apocryphal Gospels were written. Some of them speculated about "the hidden years at Nazareth"—the period of Jesus' boyhood, adolescence, and growth to manhood before He commenced upon His public ministry. In one of these Gospels we find the child Jesus making pigeons from clay. He throws them into the air, and presto—they fly away! In another incident Mary supposedly is teaching Him the alphabet. But soon He begins to instruct her—He not only knows the alphabet already, but gives secret meanings to the letters!

These portrayals of the boy Jesus are not only fictional—they are false. The infant Jesus didn't have perfect knowledge of His identity or of His mission. His mind grew, His consciousness gradually expanding to differentiate Himself from others. As he was nurtured by the godly Mary, instructed by the Holy Spirit as He communed with His real Father, the awareness gradually dawned.

How early this happened, and through what means, we cannot say. But today's scripture makes clear that by age 12 Jesus had a remarkably sharp idea of who He was and the task for which He had been born.

That visit to the Temple made a profound impression. "For the first time the child Jesus looked upon the temple. He saw the white-robed priests performing their solemn ministry. He beheld the bleeding victim upon the altar of sacrifice. . . . Every act seemed to be bound up with His own life. New impulses were awakening within Him. Silent and absorbed, He seemed to be studying out a great problem. The mystery of His mission was opening to the Saviour" (*The Desire of Ages*, p. 78).

And boys and girls today also may discern clearly who they are and what God would have them be. They do not—indeed, cannot—know all that God has in store for them. Nor did Jesus at age 12. But they may know that they are sons and daughters of God, and that our Father's business is the grandest enterprise in the world.

*February 16*

# ON BEING DIFFERENT

*And the child grew, and waxed strong in spirit, filled with wisdom: and the grace of God was upon him. Luke 2:40.*

It's hard to be different.

We hate to arrive at a social gathering wearing casual clothes and find that everyone else has come in formal dress, or to be the only one in jacket and tie when the others have dressed casually. Children don't want to be different. And teenagers most of all seek to conform with their peers.

Jesus was different. He grew through the tumultuous teen years, when the currents and drives of life bring uncertainty, awkwardness, and conflict, remaining different from His peers.

He was different from His own brothers and sisters. Scripture mentions the names of His brothers—James, Joseph, Judas, and Simon (Mark 6:3). They were stepbrothers and stepsisters, probably the children of Joseph, husband of Mary, by a previous marriage. Because Joseph was the legal father of Jesus but not Jesus' natural father, Jesus had no direct blood ties with these other family members.

The differences extended much deeper, however. We read that many years later Jesus' brothers told Him how He ought to be going about His mission (John 7:3-8). The dialog reflects misunderstandings and tensions that reach back to sibling rivalry in Jesus' childhood. On another occasion His family members tried to intervene in His ministry: "When his family heard about this, they went to take charge of him, for they said, 'He is out of his mind' " (Mark 3:21, NIV).

"Jesus was misunderstood by His brothers because He was not like them," writes Ellen White. "His standard was not their standard. . . . The example of Jesus was to them a continual irritation. He hated but one thing in the world, and that was sin" (*The Desire of Ages*, p. 88).

The home, which should be a haven of acceptance and security, often is a place of meanness and cruelty. Siblings can be thoughtless or thoughtfully unkind, jealous of parental approval, inventive in inflicting hurt upon a sensitive brother or sister. Childhood injustices, real or imagined, leave lasting scars and turn the adult away from God and the church. Rivalries and wrongs fester over the years and at last boil over in anger and hatred.

The hardest place to be different is the home. But that is where religion comes closest to life—many a preacher acclaimed publicly fails there—and where Jesus grew in love, faith, and knowledge of His Father's will.

*February 17*

# THE MAN NOBODY KNOWS

### *"Isn't this the carpenter's son? Matt. 13:55, NIV.*

Nobody knows what Jesus looked like. Although we have four Gospel accounts, no writer gives us a hint anywhere as to His physical appearance. We read that people exclaimed over His teachings and were amazed at His miracles, but apparently no one ever said "See how tall He is!" or "What a handsome man He is!"

"He had no beauty or majesty to attract us to him, nothing in his appearance that we should desire him," predicted the gospel prophet (Isa. 53:2, NIV). And so He did not stand out in the crowd because of His appearance. His was the beauty of a life, not of physical features.

54

Nor do the traditional portraits of Jesus represent Him accurately. In fact, they are downright misleading. The earliest portrayals of Jesus that we have come from centuries after His time, when His appearance had long been forgotten—and when many Christians had begun to turn to the monastic ideal.

These men, who had forsaken life in the world to contemplate, fast, and pray, painted Jesus after their own likeness. Jesus appeared pale, weak, emaciated. The gaunt figure hanging on the cross had sunken cheeks and sunken chest, sad eyes, an otherworldly look.

That wasn't the Jesus of the Gospels. He was the carpenter's son. The 30 years He spent working with His hands made Him strong, muscular. His eye was trained to cut a straight line, to plane a surface smooth, to erect a beam upright.

After He left the carpenter's shop for three years of itinerant ministry, He traveled on foot. His face was bronzed from the days in the sun, His skin ruddy with the glow of life in the open. Often He slept outside: "The foxes have holes, and the birds of the air have nests; but the Son of man hath not where to lay his head," He said (Matt. 8:20). When He came to Jerusalem, He often spent the night on the Mount of Olives: "Then each went to his own home. But Jesus went to the Mount of Olives" (John 7:53—8:1, NIV).

The Man on the cross wasn't weak, pale, emaciated. He was strong, bronzed, muscular. His eyes weren't otherworldly; though etched with suffering, they were bright, intelligent, friendly.

Over the centuries the Christian church, desiring to show the divinity of Jesus Christ, has reduced His humanity to shadow, a shell. The Jesus of the Gospels, the real Jesus, the warm, flesh-and-blood Jesus, has become the man nobody knows.

*February 18*

# LOSING JESUS

*After the Feast was over, while his parents were returning home, the boy Jesus stayed behind in Jerusalem, but they were unaware of it. Luke 2:43, NIV.*

It's terrible to be lost.

When I was a boy my brother Gordon, who was then about 18, worked in a lumber camp in the Australian bush. One night the horses broke their traces and ran away. The next day Gordon set out to get them back, following their tracks through the bush. He went on for several miles but wasn't concerned—he knew he would strike a fence in due course. What he didn't realize was that a stretch of the fence was out: the horses had gone through the gap and he had followed them far beyond what he had expected when he left the camp.

The Australian bush is harsh. Hot, dry, and flat, it exacts a grim toll on the lost traveler. Gordon was lost—and without water. I first learned of his predicament when police came to our door with the news. That evening the newspapers carried a report of the search.

Happily, Gordon chanced upon a remote homestead. An old couple scratched the soil and kept a few animals. They took him in and saved his life—even though they took another day before harnessing the wagon and driving to notify the police.

It's even more terrible to lose Jesus.

We lose Jesus when we think He is safe with us. We get busy, caught up in our labors, go on our way—and don't realize He is no longer with us.

We lose Jesus in Jerusalem. We think that when we are among Christians—when we are at an Adventist college, working for the church, assembled for worship—that the very environment will keep Jesus with us. But when we look for Him we find He has gone.

Relationships take years to build, but they shatter in a moment. Trust based on a long period of shared experiences can be snapped by one foolish or unfaithful act.

And Christian experience, nurtured on study of the Bible, prayer, and witness, can leak away in front of the television set. Jesus is easily lost!

But the good news is that Jesus can be found again! When like Mary and Joseph we seek Him earnestly, seek Him with tears, seek Him regretting our foolishness and unfaithfulness, we will find Him. We will find Him where they found Him—in His Father's house, the place of God's will.

*February 19*

# THE OBEDIENCE OF JESUS

*Then he went down to Nazareth with them and was obedient to them. Luke 2:51, NIV.*

The New Testament tells of the obedience of Jesus in three different places.

The boy Jesus, Luke tells us, was obedient to Joseph and Mary. Even though Jesus knew His real Father was in heaven, He submitted to Joseph. Think of it: the Creator of the universe, who

56

upholds "all things by the word of his power" (Heb. 1:3), took instruction from His earthly parents, meekly striving to please them in all His tasks.

The man Jesus, the book of Hebrews tells us, "learned obedience from what he suffered" (Heb. 5:8, NIV). Jesus did not learn as we often do—by tasting the bitter fruit of disobedience. Rather, He learned through progressive submission to the Father's will. That will led Him through deep waters, even to the stark suffering of Gethsemane, when He cried out, "O my Father, if it be possible, let this cup pass from me: nevertheless not as I will, but as thou wilt" (Matt. 26:39).

And finally the path of obedience took Him to Calvary. "He humbled himself and became obedient to death—even death on a cross!" the apostle Paul tells us (Phil. 2:8, NIV). There, impaled between two felons, He took upon Himself the sins of the world. In the horror of separation from the Father, He cried out in despair, "My God, my God, why hast thou forsaken me?" (Matt. 27:46).

"Christ was treated as we deserve, that we might be treated as He deserves. He was condemned for our sins, in which He had no share, that we might be justified by His righteousness, in which we had no share. He suffered the death which was ours, that we might receive the life which was His. 'With his stripes we are healed' " (*The Desire of Ages*, p. 25).

Some Christians think obedience is a dirty word. They say it smacks of legalism, that it negates grace. They need to take another look at the obedience of Jesus. By His obedience we have hope of eternal life—a life of loving obedience to the divine will.

We may know the power of His love in our work and play today. As He obeyed His father and His Father, so may we, by His Spirit, walk in the path of the divine will. So, friend, put your hand into His and go out to a new day in new life!

# THE PRIEST AND THE VIRGIN

***And Mary said, Behold the handmaid of the Lord; be it unto me according to thy word. Luke 1:38.***

The angel Gabriel had more success with the young woman Mary than with the Lord's priest Zechariah. He came to each in turn, bringing tidings of a miraculous act that God was about to perform. Mary believed him, but Zechariah doubted.

Yet the prediction made to Mary was more difficult to accept than Zechariah's message. Gabriel told the priest that Elizabeth, who had passed the time of childbearing, would conceive and bear Zachariah's son. The child would be filled with the Holy Spirit and grow up to prepare a people for the Lord; he would be the fulfillment of Malachi's prophecy of the coming of Elijah (Mal. 4:6).

All this was too much for Zechariah. "Whereby shall I know this? for I am an old man, and my wife well stricken in years," he replied (Luke 1:18). Even though he was a priest, even though Gabriel came to him in the Temple as he offered sacrifice, his faith could not lay hold on God's promised word.

Contrast the virgin Mary. We do not know her age when Gabriel appeared before her with the startling pronouncement that she would conceive a child by the Holy Spirit—the long-awaited Son of David, Israel's Messiah. Most likely she was still in her teens, however.

But the girl knew her God. When Gabriel greeted her with, "Hail, thou that art highly favoured, the Lord is with thee: blessed art thou among women" (verse 28), Mary did not feel a surge of pride. Instead, she was troubled, wondering what the salutation foreshadowed. But when Gabriel laid out the plan of the Lord for her, that she would experience a conception even more miraculous than would come to Elizabeth, Mary simply said, "Behold the handmaid of the Lord; be it unto me according to thy word" (verse 38).

Youth is not necessarily the time of folly, just as old age is not necessarily the time of piety. The heart of a young man or woman may be more ready to say yes to the Lord's call for the impossible—more ready than the heart of a minister of long experience.

We who work for the church get used to ordinary measures of the Lord's power. We do our duties, blessed of the Lord, enveloped in a covering of prayer and sacrifice. But when Gabriel suddenly appears with a startling pronouncement, our faith may seek the protective cocoon of religious routine.

That's why today God needs young men and women for whom nothing is impossible, who will say, "I am the Lord's servant. . . . May it be to me as you have said" (verse 38, NIV).

*February 21*

# MARY'S SON

*And Mary said: "My soul glorifies the Lord and my spirit rejoices in God my Savior." Luke 1:46, 47, NIV.*

When our children were young we had happy times together singing around the piano for family worship. We sang our way up through "With Jesus in the Family" to "Do, Lord."

But then they entered their teen years. They seemed to be always on the run—to school functions, music lessons, games—and we were always driving them somewhere. It became more and more difficult to get together for worship. And when we did, they would sit silent, mouths closed when we suggested we sing. The music stopped. Parents with teenage children, does this sound familiar?

This bothered me. I love to sing, especially for worship.

The good news, for you who also may be bothered right now, is that the music started again—eventually. Our children passed through their teens (yes, it "came to pass"!), when they were more interested in *listening* to music than in singing—often to music that Noelene and I didn't understand—and came back to enjoying singing with us at worship. By this time we were working through the new *Seventh-day Adventist Hymnal*.

Singing Christians, I think, are growing Christians. Just as a lot of the music of our times reflects the despair and meaninglessness of those who compose and perform it, so songs of faith come from a heart that knows and trusts in God.

Mary's song, sung in the home of her cousin Elizabeth, is an outpouring of praise. It's commonly called the Magnificat, from its first words: "My soul doth magnify the Lord." The Magnificat, which runs through 10 verses of Luke's Gospel (Luke 1:46-55) overflows with a sense of what God has done for Mary. "The Mighty One has done great things for me—holy is his name," sings Mary (verse 49, NIV).

But it goes further: Mary represents the "little people" of earth, the poor and the humble, whom society doesn't notice—but whom God notices. God turns from the proud, the powerful, and the rich to lift up the humble, to fill the hungry with good things. The Magnificat doesn't *boast* over God's choosing the weak over the strong; rather, it pours out praise that God's kindness would condescend to those whom the world passes by.

In heaven, too, God's people will sing together. We will sing the song of Moses and of the Lamb (Rev. 15:2-4), ascribing glory to the Lord who has done great things for us. Today let's practice that chorus!

# DAUGHTERS ARE SPECIAL

*Now Adam knew Eve his wife, and she conceived and bore Cain, saying, "I have gotten a man with the help of the Lord." Gen. 4:1, RSV.*

In the Bible no one ever rejoices over the birth of a daughter. Many people rejoice that they have a son, however. Eve rejoices. Rebekah rejoices. Rachel rejoices. Hannah rejoices. Naomi rejoices. And wives that are childless grieve that they haven't been able to give their husband a son.

By this emphasis on sons and lack of interest in daughters, the Bible writers were merely reflecting the times in which they lived. Most ancient peoples kept women in inferiority.

Henry VIII of England divorced Catherine of Aragon because she didn't bear him a son. In our century the last king of Egypt, Faruk, set aside his wife and married another for the same reason. The king's ego was wounded when his wife could give him only daughters. He blamed her—obviously being ignorant of elementary laws of genetics that hold if anyone was to be faulted, it was he!

More tragically, in some poor societies baby daughters have been, and still are, left to die at birth. When food is scarce, spare it for the males!

But daughters are special. A daughter is every much a gift from God as a son, and every bit as precious. Some would say more precious.

The coming of the Son of Mary, who was the Son of God, made the difference. He broke with the rabbinical traditions to exalt women to a place of equality with men. Whereas the pious Jew in his morning prayer thanked God each day that "Thou hast not made me a Gentile, a slave, or a woman," Jesus accepted women as His disciples. Time and again He set aside custom and tradition, risking criticism or censure, to show that daughters are special.

Jesus' emancipation of women was recognized later in the apostle Paul's words, "For as many of you as have been baptized into Christ have put on Christ. There is neither Jew nor Greek, there is neither bond nor free, there is neither male nor female: for ye are all one in Christ Jesus" (Gal. 3:27, 28).

Those of us who have a daughter don't need to be told: daughters are special. And we want for them everything that Jesus, the Great Emancipator, wanted for them.

# WHEN TIME STANDS STILL

*And, lo, the angel of the Lord came upon them, and the glory of the Lord shone round about them: and they were sore afraid. Luke 2:9.*

Some moments seem frozen in time. We can look back on them years later and recall the exact circumstances when time stood still.

On a snowy January day I held Noelene's hand tightly as she summoned strength from deep within to give birth to our first-born—a son. I can tell you just what that cold delivery room in the mountains of India looked like, the conversation between the nurses during the hours of protracted pain and struggle.

Nearly six years later, again in India—a telegram. "Regret to inform you that Father passed away this morning. Mother." The shock, the numbness, friends moving in with comfort. Frantic attempts to call Australia: at last the operator routes the call via London, and I hear my mother's voice. But there is no conversation—I can hear her, but she cannot hear me.

I will never forget that day.

Weddings. Graduations. Coffins and cold ground. Thanksgivings and Christmases. Vacations by the seaside.

Days imprinted indelibly on the mind.

Another unforgettable day is coming. Then the heavens will burst open and the Son will come to earth with trumpets and angel choirs of jubilee.

Ages hence we will remember that moment.

But the Son's first coming was utterly unlike it. Israel slept when the Saviour was born. Priests saw nothing unusual in the child of Mary and Joseph—poor child of poor people. Pharisees and scribes debated rabbinical law, arguing over minutiae according to the school of Hillel (liberal) or the school of Shammai (conservative).

In heaven, time stood still. On earth, all things continued without missing a beat.

Not quite. Those most removed from the halls of Israel's religious elite—illiterate shepherds and foreigners—knew that something great, something unforgettable, was happening at that moment. Passing by the great, the learned, the privileged, God revealed the meaning of the heart-stopping moment to those who were open to receive it.

61

# THE MAIDEN AND THE MONSTER

*The dragon stood in front of the woman who was about to give birth, so that he might devour her child the moment it was born. Rev. 12:4, NIV.*

Israel slept while her King was born. But the dragon, "that ancient serpent, called the devil or Satan" (Rev. 12:9), was wide awake. The struggle that began in heaven long before—and that saw the dragon cast out in defeat before the armies of the Son of God—was about to enter a new and decisive phase.

As Mary looked down at the still face of her baby lying in the manger, she must have wondered what dangers and fears lay before Him. How innocent, how frail, He looked! Could she have known that the ancient enemy had long waited for this moment, that he already had formed a strategy to snuff out the child's life before He could even grow to maturity to commence His mission, she would have trembled in terror.

We look into the face of our newborn child and try to pierce the future. Will he or she become a mighty worker for God? a leader in society? a leader in the arts? In that face we see the dreams, hopes, potentiality of the human race, created in the image of God.

But we feel, too, the stab of fear. Suddenly the world seems dangerous—diseases known or scarcely named strike without warning, crippling, maiming. Infants die in their sleep—"crib death," a name that tells us that we know nothing except the vulnerability of babies and the fragility of human life. And along the road of life dangers lurk, threatening body, mind, and soul. The ancient enemy waits—waits to devour our child.

But the world is a safer place now. Yes, crime may have increased, evil men and seducers may wax worse and worse in these last days before the Second Coming (2 Tim. 3:13), but the Babe of Mary has smashed the power of the dragon.

The Son of God bested the dragon in heaven, when His angels fought with Satan and his angels. Then alone, dependent on the Father as we are dependent, He met the dragon on the dragon's enchanted ground. Alone He met him; alone He bested him. It took a cross, but that cross gave the death blow to the serpent, delivering every son and daughter of Adam and Eve, setting our hearts free as we look into the face of our newborn child.

"Then I heard a loud voice in heaven say: 'Now have come the salvation and the power and the kingdom of our God, and the authority of his Christ. For the accuser of our brothers, who accuses them before our God day and night, has been hurled down'" (Rev. 12:10, NIV).

# THE CONTRASTS OF THE CHRIST

*And she brought forth her firstborn son, and wrapped him in swaddling clothes, and laid him in a manger; because there was no room for them in the inn. Luke 2:7.*

Every baby is a bundle of contradictions. So small and helpless, it rules the household—every ear listens for its cry, every foot hastens to help. Unable to utter a word, its concerns become everyone's concerns. The weakest member of the family, it marshals all the energy of the family.

How much more the Babe born of Mary—Son of God and Son of man, King of the universe, laid in a manger because there was no room for His parents in the inn!

In Stuttgart, Germany, a baby boy was born on October 15, 1758—Johann Heinrich von Dannecker. Although his father was employed in the stables of the duke of Wurttemberg, the boy began to dream dreams of greatness. Realizing how short life is and how transient the works of our hands, he decided to become a sculptor. Then, after he was dead and gone, his deeds would live on in stone.

Von Dannecker applied himself to his vocation with fierce concentration. After studying under masters, when he was only 22 he was appointed sculptor to the ducal palace. Within three years he had left for Paris, then on to Rome. His succession of sculptures of Greek and Roman gods and goddesses made him the talk of Europe. Illustrious persons commissioned him to do their portrait busts.

Von Dannecker now had achieved fame and a lasting place in history. But he was not yet satisfied—he felt that the crowning work of his art still lay before him. He withdrew to think, to look within himself. He began to contemplate the One who is greater than any pagan god, the One who was God in the flesh. If he could capture in stone that mystery of *that* One—that would be his supreme work!

Von Dannecker set himself to the task. After months of work his effort was ready for unveiling. Instead of calling in his friends, he invited a group of children to be the first to see his new creation. When he pulled aside the covers, a boy spoke up, "He was a *great* man!"

Von Dannecker destroyed the work.

After months of renewed labor he had a new Christ ready. Once again he wanted to see how children—the most honest critics—would react. As he unveiled the statue a girl said, "He was a good man!"

Von Dannecker was more pleased, but not yet satisfied. He destroyed the work.

And so at last to the third statue, and another group of children. This time, at the unveiling, no one spoke; but a boy took off his cap and several dropped to their knees.

And Von Dannecker was satisfied.

*February 26*

# THE EMPTY BEDS IN BETHLEHEM

***Then Herod, when he saw that he was mocked of the wise men, was exceeding wroth, and sent forth, and slew all the children that were in Bethlehem, and in all the coasts thereof, from two years old and under, according to the time which he had diligently enquired of the wise men. Matt. 2:16.***

Although no document from Roman history records Herod's slaughter of the infants of Bethlehem, his diabolical deed is in full harmony with his other acts of atrocity and cruelty of which we know. By the time of the birth of Jesus this would-be murderer of the Christ child had become the embodiment of evil.

Herod was now old—in his late 60s—and approaching death. He had experienced a long reign over Palestine—more than 30 years. Adept at sensing which way the political winds were blowing, he had supported in turn Julius Caesar, Caesar's murderers, Mark Antony, and finally Antony's conqueror, Octavian, who became the emperor Augustus. With the support of Rome and a policy of ruthless suppression of opposition, Herod kept the peace in Judea.

Trust, however, wasn't his forte. In fact, being a "friend" of Herod put one on dangerous ground—his suspicions could find a ready object to light upon. Even relatives learned to walk in fear—he had three of his sons and one of his 10 wives murdered. One of his last acts, only a few days before his own demise, was to have his son Antipater put to death.

He planned to go out in style! Knowing the people of his kingdom would rejoice at his death, he ordered the imprisonment of leading Jews in the stadium in Jericho. They were to be killed as soon as Herod died—so that at least someone would be mourning at the time of his death! Fortunately his sister Salome and her husband, Alexas, who were charged with carrying out Herod's order, thwarted his plan. At his death the noblemen were released and the Jews rejoiced.

But not in Bethlehem. There some beds were empty, some cribs were silent. Mothers wept, fathers stood numb, uncomprehending at the monstrous act of their demented ruler.

"Power tends to corrupt and absolute power corrupts absolutely," said Lord Acton. Herod the Great had become great in evil. He had become the agent of the dragon, the ancient enemy of Christ and His followers. Another act in the drama of the ages had played out. The conflict that began in heaven had flared up in fury on earth.

Meanwhile, far away in Egypt, the child Jesus was safe. But strange twist: He, who had come from heaven to give His life for every boy, left behind in Bethlehem a row of infant graves.

*February 27*

# PREPARED FOR HIS COMING

*But when the fulness of the time was come, God sent forth his Son, made of a woman, made under the law. Gal. 4:4.*

Like the stars in their appointed courses, says Ellen White, God's purposes know no haste and no delay. We pick up the newspaper and read about murders and robberies, the clangor of war in far-off places. The course of human history seems chaotic, the product of random events. But could we see the curtain of the world drawn back and look upon the whole as God looks, we would see the Eternal One silently, methodically working out the purposes of His will.

Christ came in the fullness of time. God had prepared the world for His coming. He arrived through a window of opportunity—the world was more peaceful, more unified, more connected than it had been for centuries or would be again for many more centuries.

Rome ruled the world. The Pax Romana ("peace of Rome"), despite some oppression, brought stability and security to a large portion of the globe. Latin, the language of administration, and

65

Greek, the language of literature, united diverse cultures. The highways were safe for travelers, as were the seas—Rome subdued the pirates. Rome constructed a network of major roads, paved, leading like arteries to the heart of the empire on the banks of the Tiber. And Rome established a postal system: couriers sped along the highways, carrying messages to the outposts of the empire.

God had prepared the world in other ways. The system of Greek philosophy and the traditional religion based on the gods had broken down. Philosophy pointed to the good life and the good man, but could not provide the power to make them possible. People had become dissatisfied with the worship of the Greek and Roman deities—the gods seemed remote, detached from everyday life and cares. Men and women cried out for a spiritual leader.

And then He came. He came in the fullness of time.

He will come again in the fullness of God's time. Although the time seems prolonged, although His coming seems delayed, God is still in control and will send forth the Son once more when God's moment strikes.

Just as the gospel spread like wildfire in the second century, so today it is leaping from hamlet to hamlet, from mountaintop to jungle outpost. Soon it will have reached every creature under heaven, and Jesus will return (Matt. 24:14).

God has prepared the world for that Coming. Have I let Him prepare me?

*February 28*

# REJOICING TO SEE THE STAR

*When they saw the star, they rejoiced with exceeding great joy. Matt. 2:10.*

Although tradition has given to the Magi the names of Gaspar, Balthasar, and Melchior, we do not know their real names. We don't even know that they were three in number—that is another legend, based on the record in Matthew's Gospel that they brought three types of gifts—gold, myrrh, and frankincense (Matt. 2:11). Although Christmas pageants often feature "the three Wise Men," there may have been more. Interestingly, Ellen White nowhere suggests there were only three.

She does shed other light, however. Identifying the Magi as "philosophers," she includes them among the "upright men who studied the indications of Providence in nature, and who were honored for their integrity and wisdom" (*The Desire of Ages*, p. 59).

I am intrigued by these men. Where did they come from? What happened to them afterward? Did they later hear about Jesus' death on Calvary? Did they become followers in a far-off land, disciples long before the good news arrived by the hand of missionaries?

And the star—what about it? The Magi noticed it—a new, bright, heavenly body—and saw in it the fulfillment of Balaam's prophecy given 1,400 years earlier: "There shall come a Star out of Jacob, and a Sceptre shall rise out of Israel" (Num. 24:17).

But why didn't the Jews notice the star? Or if they noticed it—and remember, the star "went before" the Magi until it stood right over the house where the child Jesus lay (Matt. 2:9)—why didn't they also follow it to Bethlehem?

The answer to these questions can only be—discernment. The Magi were open to God. They were ready to see, ready to notice, ready to be led.

And so they, and not the high priest, or the theologians, or the king, were led to Bethlehem.

Perhaps the star still shines. Perhaps those whose eyes are open today will see God's sign and follow it, bringing their gifts of love to lay at the feet of the Christ child.

*O God of the star, who anciently led Wise Men to the Babe of Bethlehem, open our eyes to the path of Your will today. We bring our gifts; show us where we must follow. And like the Wise Men, may we rejoice in Thy star.*

*March 1*

# THE CALL

**Then Jesus came from Galilee to the Jordan to be baptized by John. Matt. 3:13, NIV.**

"Tidings of the wilderness prophet and his wonderful announcement spread throughout Galilee. The message reached the peasants in the remotest hill towns, and the fisher folk by the sea, and in these simple, earnest hearts found its truest response. In Nazareth it was told in the carpenter shop that had been Joseph's, and One recognized the call. His time had come. Turning from His daily toil, He bade farewell to His mother, and followed in the steps of His countrymen who were flocking to the Jordan" (*The Desire of Ages*, p. 109).

How did Jesus know it, know that His time had come?

He was now about 30 (Luke 3:23)—certainly no age for impetuous action. Nazareth may have been provincial, but it was safe. Nazareth stood for home and security.

But when Jesus closed the door on the carpenter's shop, He chose the unknown. He opted for the open road instead of security, for unpredictable happenings and misunderstandings and abuse. And at last—for a cross.

God calls. No one can explain it: how, when, or why. There are false calls—God doesn't call everyone who feels called; but God calls.

And when God calls, the heart must respond. It must weigh Nazareth against Calvary.

For three years I worked as an industrial chemist. I had earned a Bachelor of Technology degree by age 19 and went into industry, working at a lab bench in research and development.

I had friends; the salary was good; the job offered security, prospects for promotion. But one day I left it all behind. For some months I'd been wrestling with a sense of God's calling, trying to argue God and myself out of it. At last I yielded to the divine imperative. I wrote a letter of resignation and left it on the desk of the chief chemist.

He was amazed, shocked. He thought at first I had been bought out by a rival company in the same city. When I told him I was quitting chemistry—despite my love for it—for the uncertain prospect of ministry he stared at me, uncomprehending.

God calls. That was the hardest decision of my life. Harder by far than the call to go to India that came just three years later.

So Jesus shut up the shop, said goodbye to Mary, and set out for the Jordan. I'm glad He did: His sense of mission gives me my place in the world.

*March 2*

# THE MAN FROM THE DESERT

*I tell you the truth: Among those born of women there has not risen anyone greater than John the Baptist; yet he who is least in the kingdom of heaven is greater than he. Matt. 11:11, NIV.*

He stood tall, the man from the desert. His face was bronzed by the sun and scorching east winds, yet it had a freshness about it that was immediately noticed. No worry lines there; just the glow of a vigorous disposition. No doubt his years in the wilds had made him tough.

After two years he was killed, and if you were writing his biography, this is how his life might appear on balance:

Assets at death: none. He left no bonds or stocks; he didn't have a bank account; he didn't even leave money behind to pay his funeral expenses; he owned no home and no automobile.

Degrees earned: none. He didn't finish high school; he didn't even go to school. He wrote no books or articles. He was never invited to tour as a guest lecturer, never called upon to deliver a commencement address. No honorary degrees were ever conferred upon him.

Age: about 32. If length of days is a criterion for success, he was a failure.

Place in a hall of fame: doubtful. Though for a time some people thought he might be the next national leader, he himself discounted any such possibility. He attracted huge crowds for a while, but after he made a politically injudicious speech, he was arrested, and his movement collapsed. He had really attracted only a very small core of genuine followers—it was never a grass-roots surge, and none of them was significant.

But no man was greater than he.

In modern society, status is generally linked to salary, success to material possessions. By this standard, John failed totally. But so did Jesus Christ. The Saviour of the world had only one item of value at His death—His coat, for which the Roman soldiers gambled.

What about educational qualifications? John didn't have any degree or diploma, but he was an educated man. He was brilliant after a fashion.

It has been a maxim among people of all races that a long life is a blessing, an early death a tragedy. But is length of days a true criterion of success? The man from the desert died young, but so did Jesus Christ. Clearly, it is not so much how long we live as what we do with the years we have that really counts.

*March 3*

# LIGHTS THAT SHINE FOREVER

*He was a burning and a shining light: and ye were willing for a season to rejoice in his light. John 5:35.*

The intensity of a life counts far more than its length. Better a life of 30 or only 20 years packed full of energy, creative endeavors, and service to God and to our fellows than one of 100 years spent in sluggishness and small-mindedness.

I read once about a man named Gulbenkian. He was supposed to be the wealthiest person alive—although no one really knew, such a wretched recluse was he. He was so miserly that he wouldn't even treat himself to a decent meal—He subsisted on a few crusts. Despite the allure of his fabulous riches, no woman could stand to live with him.

Gulbenkian, so the report went, had but one ambition in life—to live longer than his father. And even in that he failed; although he passed 90 years, he died younger.

How much more worthwhile John's life! Although he was dead at only 31 or 32, although his public ministry lasted only a year or two, his life shone and flared with a fire that lightened his generation. Lights like that shine forever. As long as men and women tell the story of Jesus, John the Baptist's example will inspire and challenge young people to lives of Christian commitment.

Thirty years before America won independence a young man named David Brainerd burned with a godly passion like John's. Converted in his early 20s, he felt a burden to take the good news of Jesus to the Delawares, the Six Nations, the Senakes, and the Tutelas. In terms of numbers converted, he had but scant success. In terms of achievement as the world counts achievements, Brainerd was a nobody: he died at 29 from consumption.

But through his diaries Brainerd lives on. Frank, honest, they tell his hunger for God and the Holy Spirit. "I thirst, I thirst, for the rivers of living waters," he writes over and over. And thousands of young men and women have read those diaries (they have been printed) and given themselves to Christ and His mission.

The greatest Man who ever lived died at only 33—crucified between two felons. But He completed the work for which He had been born; He lit a light that will shine forever.

*March 4*

# JESUS AND JOHN

*The Son of man came eating and drinking, and they say, Behold a man gluttonous, and a winebibber, a friend of publicans and sinners. Matt. 11:19.*

Jesus was a lot like His cousin John the Baptist—but also very different. They were born only about six months apart; and both were unexpected children, born outside the course of nature. Both were commissioned by the Lord for special missions. They preached the same message: "Repent: for the kingdom of heaven is at hand" (Matt. 3:2; 4:17). And both died in their early 30s, deprived of justice and executed. But there the similarities stop.

John did no miracle (John 10:41); the greater part of Jesus' ministry was devoted to healing the sick.

John preached repentance because One greater than he was soon to appear. Jesus was that one.

John declared that the kingdom of God was soon to arrive. With Jesus the kingdom arrived.

John was an ascetic. He withdrew from the society of his fellows, living on locusts and wild honey. He and his disciples fasted often. Jesus liked company. Whenever He came to Jerusalem He received a rash of invitations to Sabbath dinner. Sometimes He invited Himself. He enjoyed a good meal with interesting conversation. He and His disciples did not fast.

John preached in the desert, where he had grown up. The people came to him, and he instructed them and baptized them. But Jesus went to the people. He was a city man as much as a country person. He grew up in a town. Wherever people were in need—the cry of pain, the pangs of hunger, the leaden weight of death—that's where Jesus went. The people came out to John, but Jesus *went* to them.

John died tragically, sacrificed to satisfy the hatred of an immoral woman and to save the face of a drunken monarch. Jesus died tragically, victim of the machinations of the religious establishment, but God's sacrifice for the sins of a lost world.

John's body was buried by his grieving disciples. Nobody knows where his remains lie. Jesus was buried in the new tomb of Joseph of Arimathea. But after three days He rose from the dead, leaving the grave empty.

*March 5*

# HUMAN ERROR

*And so John came, baptizing in the desert region and preaching a baptism of repentance for the forgiveness of sins. Mark 1:4, NIV.*

En route from southern California to Seattle for an appointment at Walla Walla College, I picked up the in-flight magazine. Just inside the cover was a full-page message from the airlines' president. He was young and good-looking, and if he authored the article that carried his byline, he also could write well.

His concern was to explain—as pleasantly as possible—why his airlines enforced stricter policies for carry-on baggage. I had checked one suitcase, which contained materials for a handout during my presentation at the college next day. Under the seat I placed a carry-on briefcase.

We landed at Seattle; I transferred to the flight to Pasco. No problem—same airline, just the next gate, lots of time.

At Pasco I went to the baggage area—no suitcase! Then to the claims desk. "Sorry, sir; we'll put out a tracer."

I gave my talk at Walla Walla—without notes! I slept that night without pajamas. Next morning I awoke composing a letter to the good-looking airlines president. I got my suitcase at last—with my notes and change of clothing—at Pasco on my way home (someone in Seattle had sent it on to Portland instead of to Pasco!).

Human error! Despite our best plans and the marvels of our modern technology, things go wrong. The best computers depend on information from fallible human beings.

We can get by without our materials for a lecture, or pajamas for a night. But when human error causes a nuclear disaster like Chernobyl, people die.

We are dreamers, we humans. We can *imagine* the perfect, the flawless, the infinite, the unconditioned. We can imagine, but never attain it.

That's why we need repentance—which means "turning." We need to turn away from our self-sufficiency, turn to God, who alone is perfect, and in whom we find healing, wholeness.

We need continually to repent, to turn. Repentance is a state of mind. "Repentance includes sorrow for sin and a turning away from it. We shall not renounce sin unless we see its sinfulness; until we turn away from it in heart, there will be no real change in the life" (*Steps to Christ*, p. 23).

*O God of our hopes and desires for wholeness, we turn again to You. Keep us this day in an attitude of repentance, stayed upon Your grace.*

*March 6*

# ELIJAH'S MANTLE

**But I tell you that Elijah has already come, and they did not know him, but did to him whatever they pleased. So also the Son of man will suffer at their hands. Matt. 17:12, RSV.**

The Jews still look for Elijah. As they observe Seder (Passover) each year, they set an extra place. The empty chair and unused table setting remind them of the promise with which the Old

Testament closes: "Behold, I will send you Elijah the prophet before the coming of the great and dreadful day of the Lord" (Mal. 4:5).

But Jesus said that Elijah had already come. That voice in the wilderness preparing the way for Jesus' ministry had been he.

John was not Elijah come back from heaven. Before John was conceived, the angel Gabriel told Zechariah, "And he shall go before him [the Messiah] in the spirit and power of Elias" (Luke 1:17). John would be like Elijah—in devotion to God and in work.

And so he was. Even his clothing—the camel's hair garment and the leather girdle—recalled the great prophet of 800 years before (cf. 2 Kings 1:8). Like Elijah, John dwelt in the desert. And like Elijah, he called Israel to repentance, to turn from all systems of false worship and to put God first.

It's interesting that when John was asked if he was Elijah, he refused the designation (see John 1:21). Apparently he didn't want to be identified with the false expectations of his fellows, who presumably thought Elijah himself would come to earth. John took up Elijah's mantle, however.

But the story doesn't end with John, for Malachi's prophecy predicts that God will send Elijah "before the great and dreadful day of the Lord." In Revelation 14 we read about the Second Coming and a warning message that immediately precedes it. That message, which is to go to all the world, challenges men and women to "fear God, and give glory to him; for the hour of his judgment is come: and worship him that made heaven, and earth, and the sea, and the fountains of waters" (verse 7). Could this be a fulfillment of Malachi 4:5, 6?

Adventists think so. We see ourselves as the last link in the chain that stretches from Elijah of the Old Testament to John the Baptist to the Second Coming. What a heritage!

*March 7*

# UNDER CHRIST'S LORDSHIP

*From that time Jesus began to preach, and to say, Repent: for the kingdom of heaven is at hand. Matt. 4:17.*

Archaeologists digging under the Palatine Palace in Rome uncovered mute evidence of what it meant to be a Christian in the first century. A crude drawing portrays a slave kneeling before a cross. On that cross the figure has the body of a man but the head of an ass. Underneath the sketch we find the mocking words: "Alexamenos adores his lord!"

Christianity spread rapidly among the slaves in the Roman Empire. Like the underprivileged classes in later times, they were more receptive to the call of Jesus. But not all slaves embraced Christ. Alexamenos witnessed to his faith amid taunts and mocking.

The lordship of Jesus—that was the decisive issue that divided men and women in the first century. Will I bow before the Man on the cross? was the question that challenged every person confronted by Christianity.

It's still the $64,000 question, even in North America and other so-called Christian lands. Being brought up in a Christian home, even going to church and saying "Jesus is Lord" in hymns and prayers, doesn't make one a Christian. The issue is: Is Jesus Lord of my life? Have I come under His rule?

The New Testament texts that speak about "the kingdom of God" or "the kingdom of heaven" highlight this challenge. The terms appear with almost equal frequency and apparently mean the same thing. And the word translated "kingdom" can just as well be rendered as "rule" or "reign."

Jesus preached the kingdom of God, He proclaimed the rule or reign of God. That probably has more impact on most of us today than talk of kingdoms. Wherever a person comes under the lordship of Jesus—under His rule or reign—the kingdom of heaven is present in that place.

Will I go out into this day under the lordship of Christ? Will the kingdom of heaven be wherever I am—at home, at work, at school?

*O Jesus, Lord of the kingdom, rule in my heart today. Be Lord of my life; be my all.*

*March 8*

# BETWEEN THE TIMES

**And from the days of John the Baptist until now the kingdom of heaven suffereth violence, and the violent take it by force. Matt. 11:12.**

This is a strange text. How could the kingdom of heaven be taken by force? Didn't Jesus tell us just the opposite in the Sermon on the Mount: "Blessed are the poor in spirit: for their's is the kingdom of heaven" (Matt. 5:3)?

Modern translations help a little, but not much: "From the days of John the Baptist until now, the kingdom of heaven has been forcefully advancing, and forceful men lay hold of it" (Matt. 11:12, NIV).

When we look at the context, however, we see a pattern. Verse 11 tells us that, great as John the Baptist was, "he that is least in the kingdom of heaven is greater than he." Verse 13 tells us that "all the prophets and the law prophesied until John."

Jesus is describing in these verses the parting of the ways, the end of an era and the dawning of a new age.

The old era was that of the law and the prophets. John was part of that age: he was the final voice—and how mighty a voice he was!—of it.

But with the coming of Jesus a new era broke in upon mankind—the kingdom of heaven. This is why John preached, "The kingdom of heaven is *at hand*," and why Jesus commenced His ministry with the same words (Matt. 3:2; 4:17).

The kingdom of heaven surpasses the previous age—the age of the law and the prophets—to the extent that reality surpasses shadows and fulfillment surpasses expectation and the light of the sun surpasses a candle. So John, great as he was, was "least in the kingdom of heaven" because he belonged to the old era that was passing away with the coming of Jesus.

The kingdom of heaven is also the era of the common man. The common people heard Jesus gladly, Mark tells us (Mark 12:37). No longer was religion the prerogative of the learned and the wealthy. Ordinary men and women pressed into the kingdom when they saw and heard Jesus' ministry.

That is our privilege still. The Sun of righteousness has risen upon us. We live in the new age—the kingdom of heaven.

*O God, may we live as children of Your kingdom throughout this day. May we press forward into the light of Your salvation and Your love.*

*March 9*

# THE PRIMARY VIRTUE

**But when he saw many of the Pharisees and Sadducees come to his baptism, he said unto them, O generation of vipers, who hath warned you to flee from the wrath to come? Matt. 3:7.**

I marvel at the boldness of John the Baptist. He minced no words when the leaders of the religious establishment came out to hear him. "And do not think you can say to yourselves, 'We have Abraham as our father,'" John said. "I tell you that out of these stones God can raise up children for Abraham" (Matt. 3:9, NIV). To the soldiers John said, "Don't extort money and don't accuse people falsely—be content with your pay" (Luke 3:14, NIV).

Courage, said Sir Winston Churchill, is the primary virtue, because without it no other quality can find expression. Churchill, that old British bulldog, knew what he was talking about—he rallied his people in their darkest hour, when Hitler's invasion seemed imminent. His speeches—"We shall fight on the beaches, we shall fight on the landing grounds, we shall fight in the fields and in the streets, we shall fight in the hills"—galvanized the island kingdom.

Whence the boldness of John the Baptist? Not from an awareness of physical strength; not from an overbrimming self-confidence; not from a chain of successes in life. John the Baptist, during his years in the desert, had found God. God was his friend, his strength, his enabling.

"He looked upon the King in His beauty, and self was forgotten. He beheld the majesty of holiness, and felt himself to be inefficient and unworthy. He was ready to go forth as Heaven's messenger, unawed by the human, because he had looked upon the Divine. He could stand erect and fearless in the presence of earthly monarchs, because he had bowed low before the King of kings" (*The Desire of Ages*, p. 103).

In the end of time, just before the second coming of Jesus, God again will have men and women, and young people, and boys and girls, who go boldly forth for Him. Against the scorn and allurements of the world, they will keep His commandments and hold the faith of Jesus (Rev. 14:12). Like the worthies of old they will "do exploits" because they "know their God" (Dan. 11:32).

When we know our God, we will not fear men.

*March 10*

# PLAYING SECOND FIDDLE

### *He must increase, but I must decrease. John 3:30.*

"We're number one! We're number one!" The chant goes up from fans of winning Super Bowl teams, or after the World Series—even after a high school sports victory. In America, winning has become not just part of the game but *the* contest. Television coverage drums home "the thrill of victory, the agony of defeat."

John the Baptist was happy to be number two. He didn't mind the shift in popularity—the crowds who previously had waited on his every word swung their attention over to Jesus. It bothered

John's disciples, but not John. He had played first violin and played the part well; now he was content to assume the role of second fiddle.

It's harder to play second fiddle. It's harder to be number two. We all like the limelight, the attention, the praise. But society and the church depend on second fiddlers. If everybody played first violin, where would the orchestra be? The second fiddlers provide the steady, consistent background for the music of life.

The apostle Paul made the same point, using a different metaphor. Likening the church to a body, he said, "The eye cannot say to the hand, 'I don't need you!' And the head cannot say to the feet, 'I don't need you!' On the contrary, those parts of the body that seem to be weaker are indispensable, and the parts that we think are less honorable we treat with special honor" (1 Cor. 12:21-23, NIV).

And after all, isn't the modern American obsession with winning foolish and self-defeating? How many teams can be number one? How many people can play first violin? How many church members can be the elders and deacons?

Rather than striving to be number one for ourselves, how much better to strive to make Christ number one in our lives and service. Why not enjoy the game of life in itself, why not listen to the music and forget ourselves?

Jesus, in fact, upended modern scales of values. Although He was number one, He became number two—or number 99. And to us who would be His disciples He says, "Whoever wants to become great among you must be your servant, and whoever wants to be first must be your slave" (Matt. 20:26, 27, NIV).

*March 11*

# THE DEMONS OF DOUBT

*Art thou he that should come, or do we look for another? Matt. 11:3.*

This is the same John the Baptist who only a few months before had seen Jesus passing by and proclaimed to the world, "Behold the Lamb of God!" (John 1:36). Now he wonders if he had been mistaken; he sends his disciples to Jesus to ask Him if He is *really* the Messiah.

What had happened to John? How had the demons of doubt crept into his soul?

*First*, John was low, physically. He was a prisoner of King Herod Antipas, incarcerated in his dungeon, cut off from the sweet air and the wide open spaces that he loved.

*Second*, John's disciples had spread misgivings about Jesus. They had been unhappy over the swing in the pendulum of popularity from John to Jesus. Now they resented the fact that Jesus, who could raise the dead to life and untie the bonds of blindness and paralysis, did nothing to set John free.

*Finally*, Jesus wasn't acting the role of Messiah. He wasn't mobilizing the nation to drive out the detested Romans. He was wandering about the countryside, talking, eating and drinking with tax collectors.

The demons of doubt creep into our souls in similar ways. When we become tired or sick, when we feel worn down. When we give place to rumors and innuendos-even from our friends. When God seems silent in our lives, as though He has forgotten us.

But Jesus can drive the demons of doubt away. He didn't argue with the messengers from John: "Of course I'm the Messiah! Is John going crazy?" He apparently didn't make any reply at first; He simply carried on healing the sick and giving sight to the blind. Then He said, "Go back and report to John what you have seen and heard" (Luke 7:22, NIV).

That is still the best way to deal with doubt. "There is an evidence that is open to all—the most highly educated, and the most illiterate—the evidence of experience," wrote Ellen White (*Steps to Christ*, p. 111). As we fix our minds on what Jesus has *done for us*, God can lift us out of the slough of despondency.

*March 12*

# THE SILENCE OF GOD

**And his disciples came, and took up the body, and buried it, and went and told Jesus. Matt. 14:12.**

The greatest religious question of the twentieth century is the seeming silence of God. When evil appears to reign unchecked on every side—robberies, shootings, rapes, tortures, drugs—why doesn't God do something?

After Auschwitz, after the gas chambers of Adolf Hitler's "final solution," thousands of Jews no longer believe. The silence of God has destroyed their faith.

And hasn't each of us at times felt that silence? Haven't we wrestled in prayer, wondering if the heavens merely bounced our words back to us? Haven't we wondered why God didn't intervene to save a dear one from tragic accident or crippling disease?

Take heart, friend of mine—God is not dead! Although He appears to be silent, God is there. Even in the silence. Working through the silence.

John the Baptist died alone. He went to his execution because of a foolish promise made by a weak and drunken monarch. There were no crowds, no friends, at John's death. No one wept. Just John and the executioner—that is how John died.

Jesus didn't intervene. Jesus didn't break the silence.

John already had languished for months in Herod's jail. Jesus didn't come to him, even once. Not one personal word from the Lord broke the silence.

Why? Because John's sufferings and death would be an example to thousands of God's followers in later years. They too would languish alone in dungeons because of their witness for God. They too would meet an untimely end. But they too would find courage in John's fortitude in his supreme test.

God suffers with us. In the silence He weeps. He takes our place, hears our griefs.

In a world gone wrong, love suffers before the onslaughts of evil. But that is how love conquers evil—not by force, but by suffering.

At the center of our faith stands a cross. From that cross a wrenching cry pierces the silence: "My God, my God, why hast thou forsaken me?" (Matt. 27:46).

*March 13*

# FOLLOW DUTY, NOT INCLINATION

**Then Jesus came from Galilee to the Jordan to be baptized by John. Matt. 3:13, NIV.**

For some Christians, loyalty, duty, and obedience are suspect terms. They think they suggest a legal religion, a falling back into the bondage of works. Give us love, they say, and that will be enough.

I am puzzled by this sort of reasoning. Did not God teach His people in the Old Testament, "To obey is better than sacrifice" (1 Sam. 15:22)? And did not Jesus follow duty rather than inclination, submitting to His earthly parents, Joseph and Mary (see Luke 2:51), and also to His heavenly Father? "If you obey my commands, you will remain in my love, just as I have obeyed my Father's commands and remain in his love," He told His friends on that final Thursday night before the cross (John 15:10, NIV).

Christianity is a transforming relationship. The love of Jesus woos and wins our hearts; we fall in love with Him. Then we delight to do what pleases Him.

When two people love each other, marriage isn't a burden. To remain faithful to each other doesn't weaken or destroy love.

To me, loyalty, faithfulness, and obedience are still good words. They capture the response of my heart to those I love most—my wife, children, and friends; and also Jesus.

And so, long ago, Jesus came down from Galilee to the river Jordan. He presented Himself before John as a candidate for baptism. He was the obedient servant, walking in the path of the Father's will.

"Be thou faithful unto death, and I will give thee a crown of life," promises the Lord in the book of Revelation (Rev. 2:10). Jesus was faithful—from boyhood to adult life. And even unto death: a cross at the end of the road that He began that day when He came to John. When that moment came He would shrink from it, but then go forward—following duty to the end.

*O Master whose faithfulness to Your Father's plan won my salvation, lead me today. Whether by still waters or through the valley of the shadow of death, guide me in ways of righteousness.*

*March 14*

# DOORWAY TO NEW LIFE

**And Jesus answering said unto him, Suffer it to be so now: for thus it becometh us to fulfil all righteousness. Then he suffered him. Matt. 3:15.**

I stood by my wife, clenching her hand as she writhed in pain. They had wheeled her into this cold room more than six hours before; now she lay weak, exhausted from the effort and the long struggle.

"Keep trying, darling," I urged. "Push!" cried the nurse. Deep from within she summoned hidden reserves of strength, gritted her teeth, and with a convulsion and a shout gave birth to our firstborn.

"You have a boy," said the nurse. She held him up. We waited. For a heart stopping moment he was silent—alive but silent. Then the nurse slapped his back, and he let out a plaintive wail.

Welcome to the world!

Our son was ugly, as I expect all newborn babies are. The long time in the birth canal had elongated his head (within a day it was back to normal), and with hardly any hair he looked like a little old man. But he was beautiful to me. I was overjoyed.

And also deeply moved. For a few moments time had stood still. I had looked through a doorway to the Great Beyond, seen myself and my own coming into the world, seen the line of human ancestry of birthing and coming, caught a glimpse of the mystery of our existence. My son's birth—like my daughter's, three years later—was a spiritual experience to me.

I recommend the experience to every husband—if you can take it! It may also cause you to reconsider who is really the "weaker" sex!

But I recommend another type of birthing experience to both men and women—baptism. Just as we pass from the cramped, confined, dependent existence of our mother's womb to life on our own with all its incredible opportunities, so through baptism we pass from existence at the earthly, physical level to fullness of life in Jesus Christ.

Our baptism tells the world that we believe in Jesus, that we have turned from a life of sin, that God has touched our hearts. It's a public ceremony, a demonstration of our commitment to Christ, a doorway to new life.

That doorway leads further—it introduces us to the church. We become part of a family, a fellowship of believers that transcends differences of age, sex, race, culture, wealth, or social status. By baptism we all become sons and daughters of the one God, Paul tells us (Gal. 3:27-29). We become members of the spiritual body of Christ, linked to Him by ties that He designs will never be severed—now or forever.

*March 15*

# BAPTISMAL TRINITY

*And straightway coming up out of the water, he saw the heavens opened, and the Spirit like a dove descending upon him: and there came a voice from heaven, saying, Thou art my beloved Son, in whom I am well pleased. Mark 1:10, 11.*

When Jesus was baptized, the heavenly Trinity was present. There in the water is the Son; the Spirit descends like a dove; and from the heavens comes the Father's voice in benediction.

We understand so little about the Trinity that we can scarcely grasp the loneliness of Jesus for His heavenly home. Men wise and not so wise can argue as they have for centuries over the mystery of the God-man—How much did He remember of His life before the Incarnation? How much did He know? But these debates profit little. We can be sure that Jesus was limited by humanity, but He knew that He was God's Son.

See Jesus praying. Sometimes He spent entire nights in prayer. For Him, says Ellen White, prayer was "a necessity and a privilege" (*Steps to Christ*, p. 94). No fact from the Gospels reveals to us more clearly the full humanity of Jesus and His dependence on the Father. And His longing for home.

At least three times during Christ's ministry the Father spoke audibly to the Son—at the baptism, on the Mount of Transfiguration (Matt. 17:5), and in the Temple a few days before the Crucifixion (John 12:28). Twice the Father said, "This is my Son, whom I love." As Jesus longed for His Father, so the Father longed for the Son, and sought to make that plain to disbelieving people.

The Spirit, who descended upon Jesus at His baptism, continued with Him to empower His ministry. "God anointed Jesus of Nazareth with the Holy Ghost and with power: who went about doing good" (Acts 10:38).

The heavenly Trinity is still present at baptisms. Whenever a person turns from his or her own ways, accepts Jesus, and declares that public commitment by baptism, the Father looks down in blessing. "This is My beloved son or daughter," He assures. "In you I am well pleased."

And the divine Dove comes to bring new life and new power. He comes to abide with us—God dwelling within.

So far from home, Jesus wasn't alone. And neither are we.

*March 16*

# JESUS IN WASHINGTON, D.C.

***News about him spread all over Syria, and people brought to him all who were ill with various diseases, those suffering severe pain, the demon-possessed, those having seizures, and the paralyzed, and he healed them. Matt. 4:24, NIV.***

Washington, D.C., is my favorite city. Come in April and see the cherry blossoms and the forsythia and you'll see why. Join the crowds on the Mall for the Fourth of July concerts and fireworks and you'll likely agree. Interested in politics, in the movers and shakers of the United States or the Seventh-day Adventist Church? Or in arts and festivals? Washington has them all.

But a blight rests on this lovely city. As I write, the year is but 40 days old and already 48 people have died violent deaths here. Many of them are young people, one 12, one only 9. Some were killed by other young people—the 12-year-old by his uncle. These teenagers have guns, and they have been turning them on one another, sometimes over possession of a jacket, often over drugs.

If Jesus came to Washington, D.C., what would He do?

There's disease here: people are blind, crippled, and in pain. All the scourges He met in ancient Galilee are here, plus a terrible new one—AIDS. Wouldn't Jesus spend much of His day bringing relief, hope, healing?

In Palestine long ago men and women were victimized by the religious establishment. They are victimized today in Washington, D.C.—not by men of the cloth, but by the dope peddlers and the gun people. Many are out of work, feel frustrated and helpless, and turn to drugs. In the midst of affluent America they are walled in by the ghetto of circumstance.

Jesus took on the religious establishment. Would He take on the drug peddlers? The crime lords? The gun industry? The corrupt politicians? I think so.

Meanwhile, thousands sleep on the streets—in alleys and parks and the stations of the rapid transit system. When the mercury falls down into the teens and the cold January winds blow, they huddle over heating grates on the sidewalk.

Jesus often slept outside. He had no roof to call His own. Would He join Washington's homeless?

Jesus came to Galilee. They didn't know who He was. Would we recognize Him in Washington, D.C.?

*March 17*

# THE BROTHER—ONE WITH US

*For he who sanctifies and those who are sanctified have all one origin. That is why he is not ashamed to call them brethren. Heb. 2:11, RSV.*

We need to see Jesus as the New Testament portrays Him—tempted, dependent, praying, needing to pray, supplicating, crying out, agonizing. Then we will realize how real and how near to us His humanity is.

Dr. Frank Boreham, a great preacher and writer, relates in one of his books an experience from his early ministry. In southern New Zealand, where he had just taken up his parish, he encountered an old Christian named David. David had a problem. "Pastor,

I'm embarrassed to tell you. Every night when I kneel to pray I fall asleep before the Lord. What can I do about it?"

Boreham thought for a moment and replied, "David, you don't always have to kneel in prayer. Why don't you try putting a chair beside yours and speak to the Lord as though He were sitting right next to you?" The old man tried it out and delighted in the new meaning he found in prayer (and he no longer fell asleep).

Eventually David grew feeble and was confined to bed. But always—so the pastor noticed—he kept a special chair by the bedside. It was his prayer chair. The Lord sat there, and no visitor could use it.

One day David's daughter sent an urgent call to the minister. "Come quickly! Father is sinking." But it was too late—he knew as he met her at the door that David had gone to his rest. Then she said, "When I went in to see him and found he was gone, do you know what I saw? His hand was stretched out, touching *the chair*. You understand, don't you?"

Even so does the Son, He who became our brother, draw near to us. An appreciation of His full humanity leads us to a new understanding of the Gospel accounts and to a closer walk with Him. A realization of His humanity leads to absolute confidence in Him.

No one ever doubted Jesus' full humanity when He lived among us. No one ever came up and pinched His flesh to see if it were real. Men and women saw Jesus hungry, weary, thirsty; they saw His struggles.

He was one with them.

And He will be one with you and me today—our Brother!

*March 18*

# PLAYING RUSSIAN ROULETTE WITH THE DEVIL

***Then was Jesus led up of the spirit into the wilderness to be tempted of the devil. Matt. 4:1.***

From ancient times legends told of people who made a pact with the devil. One of these tales became the subject of a drama—Faust, the old philosopher who sold his soul to the devil in exchange for knowledge and power.

But anyone who plays Russian roulette with the devil can be sure of the outcome: the devil will get the gun and that person the bullet. We can't play games with the devil, venturing into his kingdom and attempting to fool him, and survive unscathed.

Jesus didn't invite temptation when He went into the wilderness. He went there to fast and pray, to contemplate His mission, to dedicate Himself to the task. He certainly didn't go there to play games with the devil!

Yet the devil came to Him even there. Even in the quiet surroundings of nature. Even after the spiritual "high" of His baptism and the 40 days of earnestly seeking His Father's will.

I taught for five years at the SDA Theological Seminary at Andrews University. One day a young seminarian blurted out, "You won't find God in this place!" But God *was* there, as other students could testify.

What happened to the seminarian? He had arrived on campus full of expectations. The classes from the church's finest scholars, the resources of the James White Library, the chapel exercises, the privilege of full-time study—surely he would enjoy an uninterrupted spiritual experience.

But Christianity doesn't work like that. No place—no Christian campus, no retreat amid nature—guarantees immunity from temptation. The devil came to Jesus in the wilderness, and he came to the young man at Andrews University. Jesus was ready for the devil and met him; but the seminarian thought the environment would protect him, and he fell. "Wherefore let him that thinketh he standeth take heed lest he fall" (1 Cor. 10:12).

*O God of all our victories and our solace in distress, send us out this day armed with Your Spirit. And when the test comes—as it surely will—keep us safe in Your love.*

*March 19*

# THE BEASTS OF TEMPTATION

**But each one is tempted when, by his own evil desire, he is dragged away and enticed. Then, after desire has conceived, it gives birth to sin; and sin, when it is full-grown, gives birth to death. James 1:14, 15, NIV.**

In his epic work *The Divine Comedy*, Dante graphically portrays the nature of our battle with evil. He is 35, and finds himself in a gloomy forest. Ahead he sees a mountaintop, a vision of the life he seeks. He eagerly turns his steps toward its sunshine.

But suddenly three beasts rush upon him from out of the forest. The first is a leopard, "nimble, light, and covered with a speckled skin." Then a lion leaps upon him, "with his head held aloft and hunger-mad." A gaunt she-wolf follows: "In her leanness [she] seemed full of all wants."

These fierce animals that challenged Dante's ascent of the sunlit hill represent the varieties of temptation.

"The Leopard represents lust, a besetting temptation of youth. The poet loved the beauty of the Leopard. He was entranced by the 'gay skin of that swift animal in the [morning] dawn, and the sweet season.'

"The sins of youth have their own enchantment, the blandishments of beauty. These glamorous temptations are hard to define and still harder to resist, for they are overlaid with youthful idealism and innocence."

The lion represents the sin of pride—the temptation of our years of maturity. Achievement and success make us vulnerable to this new approach of the evil one.

"Finally, the She-wolf of avarice creeps up behind us, persistently stalking us. She comes not precisely with age but just after our zenith is past. Now self-interest and covetousness close our hands and hearts. It seems ironic that a man who has survived his struggle with the beautiful Leopard and the powerful Lion should at last succumb to the wiles of the Wolf, but such are the pitfalls of later life" (Dorothy Minchin-Comm, "Three Beasts," *Adventist Review*, May 7, 1987).

We too wander in the gloomy forest. We constantly are victims of wild animals. We lift our eyes to the mountaintop and know that we cannot attain it alone. But One takes our hand. He will be our Guide today.

*March 20*

# HELP FOR THE TEMPTED

*For in that he himself hath suffered being tempted, he is able to succour them that are tempted. Heb. 2:18.*

Several passages in the book of Hebrews specifically mention the temptations of the incarnate Son. Because of their explicit language they have captured the attention of Christians throughout the centuries and frequently surface in discussions of the Christian life today.

Hebrews 2:18 tells us that, because Jesus Himself has suffered and been tempted, He is able to help us in our temptations. Jesus' temptations were real. If it had been impossible for Him to fail, if His temptations were only an illusion, how could He help us in ours—for we know ours are deadly real.

The word for "temptation" here, as elsewhere in the New Testament, has the essential idea of *testing*. Nothing in Jesus' nature was enticed by sin—He wasn't tempted because He had an appetite for evil. Rather, submission to His Father's will led Him to ever deeper experiences of submission and trust.

So He can help us. Jesus gives us *victorious* help, fortitude to endure the test, as He in the days of His flesh endured. "Let us therefore come boldly unto the throne of grace, that we may obtain mercy, and find grace to help in time of need" (Heb. 4:16).

Bishop Westcott, in his commentary on Hebrews, reminds us that the person who falls prey to temptation never knows its full force, since he falls before the test ends. So Jesus is the only one who has ever lived who has known the extremity of temptation, for only He stayed without sin throughout. Temptation at length succumbed to Him, not He to it.

At the center of our faith stands One who came from heaven to earth to live our life and to die our death. Jesus, the Overcomer, triumphed over sin, the devil and death. He is our Saviour and our Helper for every need this day may bring.

*Jesus, Overcomer, grant me grace to overcome today in Your strength. And should I stumble and fall, take me by the hand and lift me up to Your side again.*

*March 21*

# SUPERMAN OR SUPER SAVIOUR?

*During the days of Jesus' life on earth, he offered up prayers and petitions with loud cries and tears to the one who could save him from death, and he was heard because of his reverent submission. Heb. 5:7, NIV.*

As we contemplate the life of Jesus, it's easy to fall into the pattern of seeing the outcome as inevitable: since Jesus was God in the flesh, He *knew* the end from the beginning. He *knew* that He would triumph in the struggle with the devil. He *knew* that He would win back a fallen world.

The story of Jesus begins to look like a drama. He strides onto center stage before our eyes, playing His appointed role. He looks human and His temptations look real, but He knows how the script will end. For if He is a man He is a superman, whose word commands the stormy wave and whose eye impales the demons.

That's the way we tend to view the drama of Jesus. We see Him in light of the ancient creeds of Christendom—very God of very God, light of eternal light.

But that is not the way the New Testament writers saw Him. Jesus' contemporaries had no doubt as to His full humanity. No, the issue in Jesus' day wasn't whether He was human—no one questioned that—but whether He was *more* than human. Whether He was what He claimed to be, the Son of God.

So the New Testament portrays in graphic and even shocking specificity the fierce reality of Jesus' struggles. They show Him lying prostrate, beseeching deliverance from the cup He was being asked to drink. They record that bone-chilling cry from the cross—that moan of dereliction—"My God, my God, why hast thou forsaken me?" (Matt. 27:46).

Although we today often think of Jesus as a superman, He wasn't. He was vulnerable. He could have fallen. God "permitted Him to meet life's peril in common with every human soul, to fight the battle as every child of humanity must fight it, at the risk of failure and eternal loss" (*The Desire of Ages*, p. 49).

But He won the battle—not a superman but a super Saviour!

*March 22*

# THE TWO ADAMS

***And he was in the wilderness forty days, tempted by Satan; and he was with the wild beasts; and the angels ministered to him. Mark 1:13, RSV.***

Mark alone of the Gospel writers tells us that Jesus was with the wild beasts during His temptations. What did Mark intend to convey by including this detail?

Could it remind us of one who, long before the incarnate Son met the devil in the wilderness, also dwelt in the wilds among the animals? Genesis 2:19 says: "So out of the ground the Lord God formed every beast of the field and every bird of the air, and brought them to the man to see what he would call them; and whatever the man called every living creature, that was its name" (RSV).

And to that man, that first man, the tempter came with his allurements. "Did God say," he questioned, challenging the word of the Almighty, insinuating doubt. "*If* you are the Son of God," he approached Jesus, again calling into question divine facts.

Two Adams, one father of us all, one Saviour of the human race! Two Adams, how similar and how different!

The first Adam stood tall, magnificent in stature, with rippling muscles and unblemished skin. No wart, no pimple, no cough, no sneeze, no limp, no myopia detracted from the perfection of his body. He stood erect, godlike, a worthy specimen, molded fresh by the Creator's hand.

The Second Adam came with the frailties of our fallen human condition. "Jesus accepted humanity when the race had been weakened by four thousand years of sin. Like every child of Adam He accepted the results of the working of the great law of heredity" (*The Desire of Ages*, p. 49).

See Jesus in the wilderness by the Jordan, as Satan comes to Him. No towering giant He, no specimen of physical perfection. And now He looks gaunt, His cheeks sunken from the 40 days of fasting and earnest prayer. He looks vulnerable. He *is* vulnerable.

But the Second Adam will pass over the same ground, meet similar tests to the first. And He will win where the first Adam failed, and thereby secure our salvation and show us the way to triumph when the devil comes to us.

*March 23*

# FEASTING WHILE BABIES STARVE

**And the devil said unto him, If thou be the Son of God, command this stone that it be made bread. Luke 4:3.**

From the time you start reading this page until you finish it, somewhere in the world 50 people will have starved to death. About 38 of them will be infants.

If a gas tank exploded at a chemical factory and a deadly gas leaked out (as it did in Bhopal, India, several years ago), killing masses in its progress, the news media would trumpet the event and the world would be horrified.

But day after day, every day, people starve to death. Every minute of every hour of every day of every year another 24 die, 18 of whom are babies. So every day 35,000 more die; in only two days more starve to death than died in the atomic holocaust at Hiroshima.

Meanwhile, we in the West feast on. Jesus predicted that before the Second Coming men and women would be "eating and drinking" (Matt. 24:38). He even told a parable about the church before His return. In it the "evil servant" begins to "eat and drink with the drunken" (verses 24:48, 49).

Now let's be quite sure—Christ didn't advocate an ascetic religion. He enjoyed a good meal and was so much in demand as a dinner guest that His enemies accused Him of being a glutton and a drunkard (Matt. 11:19). When the devil came to Him suggesting that He turn the stone into bread, He didn't rebuff him because He preferred to go hungry.

But let's remember this: Christ gave much of His time and Himself to helping the poor and the hungry. He rebuked those who trusted in wealth and those caught up in the pleasures of this life.

I think that if Jesus came to the West today He would blast our sensual indulgence. While 35,000 people starve to death every day—12 million every year—we are preoccupied with food. Our rash of books, magazines, articles about cooking, dining, eating; our obesity; our extravagance; our waste—they constitute a moral outrage in view of the starving millions.

The human family's first test focused on appetite. So did Jesus' first temptation in the wilderness. On this point, where humanity first failed, God's people in these last days must overcome like Christ—by the Word of God.

*O God of the human family, forgive us for our indulgence and our waste. Open our eyes to the starving multitudes and show us how to live today as responsible citizens of the kingdom of heaven.*

*March 24*

# VOICES

***The tempter came to him and said, "If you are the Son of God, tell these stones to become bread."** Matt. 4:3, NIV.*

Whose voice is this—God's or Satan's? And how shall we tell?

See these two figures in the wilderness by the Jordan. One is a glorious, handsome, angelic being; the other is emaciated, weak. Surely God is on the side of the glorious being.

Wrong. Appearances can deceive us. "Satan himself masquerades as an angel of light" (2 Cor. 11:14, NIV), and his henchmen still come to us in attractive guise. Conversely, Christ may be among the weak, despised things and bypassed people.

And those voices! Don't be deceived by the mellifluous tones, the persuasive logic. The voice you hear may be the voice of the devil.

Son of Sam, the notorious New York killer, heard voices. The messages they spoke to his inner ear led him to stalk and murder young women.

Not a year passes but at least one story appears in the news about someone who kills another, or several people, because "God told me to do it."

Christians also hear voices, or think they do. Didn't God promise, "Whether you turn to the right or to the left, your ears

will hear a voice behind you, saying, 'This is the way; walk in it' "
(Isa. 30:21, NIV)? Isn't conscience God's voice speaking to our
hearts?

Yes, God does speak to us through the "still small voice" of the
Holy Spirit, the inner revelation of His will. But not only God
speaks—the devil also speaks, and so do our own fantasies and
desires. We can persuade ourselves that God is telling us to do
something when we are merely playing out our own wishes.

Then how shall we distinguish among the voices? In the same
way that Jesus did: He tested the voice by Scripture, and it came up
wanting.

So must we. God will never command a person to murder
another. He will never instruct us to act in a manner contrary to
His law and the teachings of Jesus. Any voice, from within us or
from another, telling us otherwise isn't from God.

So subtle will be the temptations of the last days that only those
who have fortified their minds with Scripture will be able to stand.
Have I fortified myself today?

*March 25*

# THE ORBIT OF TRUST

*And he that doubteth is damned if he eat, because he
eateth not of faith: for whatsoever is not of faith is sin.
Rom. 14:23.*

On at least two occasions Jesus created bread to feed the
hungry. Then what was wrong in turning the stone into bread
when He was starving?

Two reasons made it wrong. First, such an act for His own
benefit would have removed Jesus from the arena of our common
humanity. The miracle would have shown that Jesus really wasn't
like us, wasn't truly human, could call on resources in Himself that
we don't have.

We could think of it this way. Suppose a group of academy
students are playing baseball and the principal joins them. They
choose sides, and the principal plays along with the others.
Everything goes fine until the principal comes to bat. He lets a
pitch go by and hears the umpire call "Strike!" What if he says
"That wasn't a strike! You'd better change the call—I'm the
principal and if I say it wasn't a strike, it wasn't"?

What happens to the game? It dissolves in confusion, because
one player doesn't abide by the rules.

And if Jesus had listened to the tempter and made the stones into bread, He would have destroyed His mission as the God-man, the one who would walk in our moccasins, facing our tests, and relying only on the power—the Holy Spirit—that is available to us.

Second, it would have been wrong because it would have proceeded from doubt, not faith. "If you are the Son of God . . . ," said the devil, calling into question the deity of Christ. To perform the miracle would show that Jesus believed Satan rather than God, that He needed a spectacular act to reassure Himself.

That was the way in which the serpent came to Eve in the Garden *"Has* God said. . . . ?"* Christianity is a relationship—a transforming love affair with Christ—and like all relationships is founded on trust. Whatever is outside of the orbit of trust—whenever doubt or suspicion intrude—weakens that relationship.

Paul aimed always to have a conscience free of offense toward God and man. Let us do likewise today!

*March 26*

# PUTTING THE DEVIL IN HIS PLACE

*Then the Lord God said to the woman, "What is this you have done?" The woman said, "The serpent deceived me, and I ate." Gen. 3:13, NIV.*

Once Ellen White's sister Sarah felt discouraged. She had a dream in which a tall man appeared at the doorway of her room. As she looked up at him he seemed to grow bigger and bigger until he filled the entire space from the floor to the ceiling, while she felt herself shrinking smaller and smaller before him.

But then Sarah said, "I have Jesus; I am not afraid of you!" And the giant began to shrink and shrink until she could hardly see him, and he went out the door.

She said to her sister, "Ellen, we talk a great deal more of the power of the devil than we have any right to. It pleases him, and his satanic majesty is honored; he exults over it, and we give him honor in doing this; but I am going to talk of Jesus, of His love, and tell of His power."

Isn't that still true? Some Christians seem to be more aware of the devil than of Jesus. They speak more about his power and deceptions than they do of the marvelous promises God has put in His Word. Small wonder that when they fall prey to temptation they say, "The devil made me do it!"

Look at Christ's assurances for us as we go out into this day:

"My grace is sufficient for you, for my power is made perfect in weakness" (2 Cor. 12:9, NIV).

"The Lord is my shepherd; I shall not want" (Ps. 23:1).

"But now, this is what the Lord says—he who created you, O Jacob, he who formed you, O Israel: 'Fear not, for I have redeemed you; I have summoned you by name; you are mine. When you pass through the waters, I will be with you; and when you pass through the rivers, they will not sweep over you. When you walk through the fire, you will not be burned; the flames will not set you ablaze' " (Isa. 43:1, 2, NIV).

"To him who is able to keep you from falling and to present you before his glorious presence without fault and with great joy" (Jude 24, NIV).

Today, let's *think* Jesus. Let's *talk* Jesus. Let's *live* Jesus.

*Educate my heart and lips to tell of Your power and love, dear Master. Fix my eyes, my mind, on Your goodness and victory.*

*March 27*

# SPECTACULAR RELIGION

*"If you are the Son of God," he said, "throw yourself down. For it is written: 'He will command his angels concerning you, and they will lift you up in their hands, so that you will not strike your foot against a stone.' " Matt. 4:6, NIV.*

When we lived in India, for some years a miracle worker named Sai Baba made headlines. He claimed to be able to create, making even watches appear in the palm of his hand.

His growing fame led to an editorial in one of the country's leading newspapers. Why is it, the writer asked, that the watches "created" by Sai Baba come complete with Swiss markings? Why is it that the objects he produces are always small enough to be concealed up his sleeve—why doesn't he ever "create" something large, like a pumpkin?

But the editorial did little to quench popular enthusiasm for the miracle worker. Then one day Sai Baba announced what would be his most spectacular feat yet—he would walk on water!

The crowds bought their tickets; 20,000 people jammed the arena around the swimming pool where Sai Baba would walk on water. At the time specified by the astrologers and after chanting *mantras*, Sai Baba stepped off the diving board.

But it was a bad day for walking on water. Sai Baba sank to the bottom of the pool and, emerging from the water, fled the stadium pursued by angry hoards demanding their money back.

Foolish people? Yes; but don't Christians sometimes crave spectacular religion? Don't we long for signs and wonders, for evidence before our eyes and ears to prove that God is with us?

During Jesus' ministry the scribes and Pharisees demanded a sign. He did no sign for them. When Jesus was hauled before King Herod, the dissolute monarch was pleased: he'd heard of Jesus the miracle worker, and expected "a good show." But Jesus did no miracle.

Nor would He cast Himself down from the pinnacle of the Temple. His trust was in His Father, not in spectacular demonstrations of supernatural power.

And we today are to live by faith, trusting Jesus, claiming the promises of the Word. The devil can counterfeit miracles; he cannot counterfeit Scripture.

*March 28*

# THE SECRET OF OVERCOMING

***And they overcame him by the blood of the Lamb, and by the word of their testimony; and they loved not their lives unto the death. Rev. 12:11.***

Could anything be more important than life itself? Isn't death the ultimate enemy? Most people today would answer these questions without hesitation—life at all costs. But the Bible gives us a different perspective, one that pulls us up short in these self-centered times.

The Bible affirms that life is good—we were made to live, and to live forever. Death, it tells us, is an enemy. But then it goes further: it teaches that faithfulness to God is more important than hanging on to this life.

Our text for the day gives us the threefold secret of overcoming—the blood of the Lamb, the word of testimony, and loyalty that is prepared to go even to the death.

Victory begins with the blood of Jesus. Because He gave His life for us, we love Him. He owns us; we belong to Him. His blood has set us free to be sons and daughters of the heavenly king.

Victory springs from the word of our testimony. We confess Christ: we aren't ashamed to let the world know who we are. We know our God and will witness to Him. No hiding of our Bibles when we walk to church. No hurried prayer in a restaurant, trying to avoid being noticed. Our witness is natural, unaffected, spontaneous, bold.

Victory looks death in the eye and doesn't blink. It knows that if our earthly tenthouse should be taken away, our eternal future is secure. The Father holds us by a hand that will never let go. "He who has the Son has life" (1 John 5:12, NIV).

This text—Revelation 12:11—found literal fulfillment many times in the century after John penned it. The annuls of early Christianity glow with the stories of followers of Jesus who went to the beasts or to the stake rather than renounce Christ. The noblewoman Perpetua went hand in hand with the slave girl Felicitus, united in faith, united in love, united in death. The aged bishop Polycarp told his captors not to tie him to the stake. Christ would enable him to bear the flames.

How much do we love Jesus today?

*March 29*

# SHORTCUTS CAN BE DANGEROUS

*And [the devil] saith unto him, All these things will I give thee, if thou wilt fall down and worship me. Matt. 4:9.*

For 40 days Jesus had agonized in prayer, seeking to see clearly the Father's plan for His life and mission. We are born to live; He was born to die. A world gone wrong would be won back to God by God's taking upon Himself its sin and woe.

But then the devil came—and offered Jesus a shortcut.

In April 1846 a wagon train led by George Donner left Illinois for California. On July 20 Donner led 20 wagons onto the untried Hastings Cutoff around the south side of the Great Salt Lake. But that route, instead of speeding their journey, delayed them. By the time they arrived at Truckee Lake in the eastern Sierras, it was October 31, and snow blocked the pass. They were forced to camp. One group built cabins at the lake; the others, including the Donners, settled in at Alder Creek, five miles distant.

By now, with food running low, their plight was desperate. In December, 17 people attempted to cross the Sierras on snowshoes; only seven made it. Eventually relief parties found the remaining survivors, who had averted death by resorting to cannibalism. In all, only 40 of the 87 pioneers survived the ordeal.

Shortcuts, which appear so attractive, can be dangerous. And in spiritual matters shortcuts can lead to eternal loss.

The devil offered Jesus a shortcut—the kingdom without the cross. At the close of His ministry Judas would make a similar attempt—to force Jesus' hand into exerting His power and taking up the crown.

But any path, no matter how inviting, that does not follow the arrow of God's will leads only to ruin. The end never justifies the means; in God's kingdom the process is as important as the goal.

Let's take a long, hard, prayerful look at shortcuts—today!

*Lord of the straight and narrow way, help me today to look straight ahead and walk the path without shadow of turning. May I fix my eyes on Jesus—He who overcame and who now cheers me on the way.*

*March 30*

# HOW JESUS OVERCAME

**God is faithful, who will not suffer you to be tempted above that ye are able; but will with the temptation also make a way to escape, that ye may be able to bear it. 1 Cor. 10:13.**

In two thrilling chapters in *The Desire of Ages*, "The Temptation" and "The Victory," Ellen White sets out for us how Jesus overcame Satan in the wilderness. These principles can help us in our struggles to remain faithful to God, no matter how severe the test.

1. The devil cannot *force* us to yield to him. "The tempter can never compel us to do evil. He cannot control minds unless they are yielded to his control. The will must consent, faith must let go its hold upon Christ, before Satan can exercise his power upon us" (p. 125).

2. If we venture on Satan's ground, we place ourselves at risk. "If he can cause us to place ourselves unnecessarily in the way of temptation, he knows that the victory is his. God will preserve all who walk in the path of obedience; but to depart from it is to venture on Satan's ground. There we are sure to fall" (p. 126).

3. We cannot overcome in our own strength. "In our own strength it is impossible for us to deny the clamors of our fallen nature. Through this channel Satan will bring temptation upon us. Christ knew that the enemy would come to every human being, to take advantage of hereditary weakness, and by his false insinuations to ensare all whose trust is not in God" (p. 122).

4. We must keep our eyes fixed on Jesus. "Let him who is struggling against the power of appetite look to the Saviour in the

wilderness of temptation. . . . He has endured all that it is possible for us to bear. His victory is ours" (p. 123).

5. We overcome by submission and faith. "Jesus gained the victory through submission and faith in God, and by the apostle He says to us, 'Submit yourselves therefore to God. Resist the devil, and he will flee from you. Draw nigh to God, and he will draw nigh to you.' James 4:7, 8. . . . Satan trembles and flees before the weakest soul who finds refuge in that mighty name" (pp. 130, 131).

6. We overcome by the Word of God. "By what means did He overcome in the conflict with Satan? By the word of God. Only by the word could He resist temptation. 'It is written,' He said. . . . When assailed by temptation, look not to circumstances or to the weakness of self, but to the power of the word" (p. 123).

*March 31*

# THE HIDDEN WORD

*Thy word have I hid in mine heart, that I might not sin against thee. Ps. 119:11.*

The apostle Paul tells us that the sword of the Spirit is the Word of God (Eph. 6:17). We probably like that picture—the Scriptures as an offensive weapon, strong in the Christian's hand to cut and to slay.

Unfortunately, that is how some people, especially preachers, see the Bible—as something *they* use, as a tool to defeat opponents in debate, to advance their careers, even to build their television empire.

But God's Word must be hidden in the heart before it is used on others. It must find lodging in our own souls, instructing, rebuking, correcting, guiding, transforming us. Unless we are broken first by the Word, we will misuse it on others.

Thus, the cause of Christ has been wounded by the revelations of recent years. Televangelists whose preaching reached millions every week, who thundered against the sins of others in huge public meetings, have been exposed. The apple looked bright, attractive; but inside was a worm. These famous preachers secretly practiced the sins they vehemently condemned in others.

When we take God's Word into our hearts—when we receive it, cherish it, feed on it—it is the greatest bulwark against temptation. When the devil comes with his insinuations, doubts, and allurements, God already has the answer—"Thus saith the Lord."

We cannot bring out what we have not put in. We cannot find defense in what is written in Scripture if we do not know what is written. The Holy Spirit can bring to our remembrance only what we first have read in the Bible.

Long ago, when I was just a young Christian, a pastor spoke on "Bible Before Breakfast." Feed on spiritual food before physical food, he advised. *Always* start the day with the Scriptures. That was some of the best counsel I ever heard; it has nourished my spiritual life as I made it a habit.

*Dear Father, teach me to daily feed on Your Word. In the midst of all the cares and calls of this day, may the indwelling Word speak Your will to me, giving me strength in the hour of temptation and guidance for my feet.*

*April 1*

# PORTRAITS OF JESUS

**That which was from the beginning, which we have heard, which we have seen with our eyes, which we have looked upon, and our hands have handled, of the Word of life. 1 John 1:1.**

When a four-foot bronze statue of Jesus on the cross was unveiled several years ago in the Episcopal Cathedral of St. John the Divine in Manhattan, worshipers gasped. The Christus was a Christa, with undraped breasts and rounded hips.

When Africans portray Jesus, He looks like an African. When Koreans paint His picture, He looks like an Oriental. When Indians depict Him, He is at home in a saffron robe.

Six centuries before Jesus, the Greek philosopher Xenophanes observed: "If oxen and horses, and lions, had hands or could draw with hands and create works of art like those made by men, horses would draw pictures of gods like horses, and oxen of gods like oxen. . . . Aethiopians have gods with snub noses and black hair; Thracians have gods with gray eyes and red hair."

So why not contemporize Jesus? Isn't He the universal man—or person—whose portrait we each may color in according to our culture and environment?

No. Jesus of Nazareth was a Jew of first-century Palestine.

So color Jesus a Jewish male. Not a Greek or a Roman. Not a woman. Not as White or as Black or as Oriental, even though we might wish Him to be.

Color Him from Palestine. Not from Alexandria (more learned) or from Rome (more sophisticated). Carpenter. Rural. Provincial.

But what does He look like? We don't know. The New Testament writers gave no space to describing Jesus. Under the impress of the Holy Spirit they wrote about something more important.

They gave us four portraits of Jesus, amazingly similar, but also amazingly different. There is variety in a tree, with scarcely two leaves just alike, and in the same manner each Gospel writer gave a distinctive, individual picture of Jesus.

Over the next six months we shall look at these compelling portraits, one by one. No single portrait exhausts the subject, nor do all four together. Together they show us the Man for us, God our Friend, our Saviour, our Lord.

*April 2*

# THE NEW MOSES

*Now when he saw the crowds, he went up on a mountainside and sat down. His disciples came to him, and he began to teach them. Matt. 5:1, 2, NIV.*

Throughout the months of April and May we will meditate on the ministry of Jesus as Matthew presents it in his distinctive portrait of Jesus. We will see Jesus as a king in this Gospel; also as the personification of wisdom. But above all we will find that Matthew paints Jesus as the Great Teacher, the new Moses.

Each Gospel writer selects a different incident to highlight the commencement of Jesus' ministry. Each closes his Gospel in a manner that rounds out the portrait he has developed.

The first act of Christ's ministry that Matthew underscores is the Sermon on the Mount. He devotes three whole chapters—and what chapters they are!—to giving us the instructions of the Master Teacher. This is the longest single block of Jesus' teachings that we find anywhere in the New Testament.

Further, Matthew's Gospel is structured around five sermons, just as Moses wrote five books. After the Sermon on the Mount (chapters 5-7), we find the Sermon on Discipleship (chapter 10), the Parables of the Kingdom of Heaven (chapter 13), the Sermon on the Church (chapter 18), and the Sermon on the End (chapters 24, 25).

And the last scene in the Gospel is a teaching one. The risen Christ, armed with all authority, gives His parting instructions from a mountain in Galilee (Matt. 28:16-20). He commands His followers to go into all the world and make disciples of all nations, "teaching them to obey everything I have commanded you" (verse 20, NIV).

In this intriguing Gospel Jesus is the new Moses, the one greater than Moses, the lawgiver in person. What a Teacher! What teaching! May we open our hearts to receive His words.

*O Divine Teacher, speak to me Thy will and Thy way. As Thou didst show the path to men and women by the sea and on the mountain, lighten my footsteps this day.*

*April 3*

# THE CALLING

*And he saith unto them, Follow me, and I will make you fishers of men. And they straightway left their nets, and followed him. Matt. 4:19, 20.*

*Crunch, crunch, crunch.* Someone is coming along the beach through the early-morning light. Two men are standing in the shallows, gentle waves breaking over them as they throw small nets out into the water and haul them in.

*Crunch, crunch, crunch.* The footsteps are getting close. They stop. And then a voice: "Come, follow me, and I will make you fishers of men."

At once, says the Scripture, they left their nets and followed Him. Why? What magnetism, what charisma, flowed from the person of Jesus, winsome attractiveness strong enough to cause fishermen to abandon their nets and join His mission? First Andrew and Peter, an older person and owner of a small fishing business, and then further along the beach the young man John and his brother James left all—at once.

Fishing in Lake Galilee was hard work, but it was a secure livelihood. People had to eat; and the waters provided a major source of food for the population. Peter, Andrew, James, and John gave up the only work they knew—gave it up on the spot. And for what?

Men and women still do it today, still drop their nets to follow Jesus. "He comes to us as one unknown, without a name, as of old, by the lakeside, He came to those men who knew Him not. He speaks to us the same word: 'Follow thou me!' and sets us to the tasks which He has to fulfil for our time. He commands. And to those who obey Him, whether they be wise or simple, He will reveal Himself in the toils, the conflicts, the sufferings which they shall pass through in His fellowship, and, as an ineffable mystery, they shall learn in their own experience who He is" (Albert Schweitzer, *The Quest of the Historical Jesus*, p. 403).

Dr. Schweitzer would have to be included in any list of the 10 greatest people of the twentieth century. With doctorates in theology, music, and medicine, famous for both his interpretation of the Jesus of the New Testament and the music of Bach, Schweitzer abandoned the comforts of Europe for the life of a missionary doctor in Lambarene (now in Gabon). In spite of floods, pestilence, and lack of trained assistants, he built a hospital equipped to provide care for thousands of nationals, including 300 lepers. He received the 1952 Nobel Peace Prize.

*Crunch, crunch, crunch.* Someone is coming along the beach of our lives. Jesus of Nazareth is walking by. He stops. And we hear His voice: "Come, follow me, and I will make you fishers of men."

*April 4*

# MAGNA CHARTA

**Blessed are the poor in spirit: for theirs is the kingdom of heaven. Matt. 5:3.**

Jesus' words exploded like a hand grenade tossed into the crowd gathered around Him on the mountainside. They hadn't expected this sort of program from the Messiah!

The setting was right for a major pronouncement from the rabbi. A short time earlier He had quit the sheltered life of Nazareth, had walked to the Jordan to identify Himself publicly with the Baptist's movement, had begun to preach and to heal, and had already gathered a band of disciples. Everywhere He went now the people came out: "Large crowds from Galilee, the Decapolis, Jerusalem, Judea and the region across the Jordan followed him" (Matt. 4:25, NIV).

But so far He hadn't announced His strategy. He surely had formulated a secret plan to galvanize the nation for action against the hated Romans. Perhaps on this day, as He is preparing Himself for a major address to the crowds, He will reveal how He intends to lead Israel to victory.

"Blessed are the poor in spirit, for theirs is the kingdom of heaven."

Shock, disbelief, amazement, incredulity—the faces of the listeners register their disappointment. Peter, Andrew, James, and John, who only a short time before had abandoned their fishing business to follow the Rabbi from Nazareth, can hardly believe their ears.

The kingdom—yes! The kingdom—now!

But how? "Blessed are the poor in spirit."

Jesus did announce His program as Messiah. The sermon that these stunning words introduced was in fact the Magna Charta of His kingdom. That unknown mountain in Galilee was the Runnymede for Christians.

Those words still shock and divide—even Christians. Who are His happy ones, His blessed ones? Those who abandon self-sufficiency, the proud ego; who feel their need of God; who cast their lives upon Jesus.

Yes, even you and I. Today.

*April 5*

# BETTER RIGHTEOUSNESS

*For I say unto you, That except your righteousness shall exceed the righteousness of the scribes and Pharisees, ye shall in no case enter into the kingdom of heaven. Matt. 5:20.*

There was another side to the Pharisees. True, they were picky, scrupulous about religion; but they were attempting to preserve the law. They had a passion for righteousness—for the Sabbath, for instance. So they drew up lists of regulations in an endeavor to ensure that the Sabbath would be maintained secure. Eventually their lists of Sabbath do's and don'ts numbered 654.

The Pharisees prayed regularly. They fasted. They gave generously. They called God's people to a higher standard and endeavored to live themselves by that standard.

Righteousness! That was the key word of their religion.

Imagine the shock among those hearers on the mountainside that day when Jesus said, "For I say unto you, That except your righteousness shall exceed the righteousness of the scribes and Pharisees, ye shall in no case enter into the kingdom of heaven." Righteousness that went beyond the Pharisees' earnestness? Sabbath observance that exceeded even their 654 rules? Who could possibly hope to attain that! Who could have a chance to enter the kingdom of heaven?

Let's make no mistake here: Jesus calls His followers to more righteousness than the Pharisees', not less. He doesn't abolish righteousness; He lifts the standard so high that it seems no one now can make it.

Precisely! For in the kingdom of God a new order comes into being. The Pharisees strove and struggled and multiplied rules in a fruitless endeavor to please God. *They were trying to make it on their own.* They believed that in the judgment they would be saved if their good deeds outweighed their bad deeds.

But Jesus Christ brought better righteousness, a higher standard. A standard that searches even our thoughts and motives. But a standard wherein Jesus Himself is the law—and wherein He lives within us to give us power to live for Him.

*April 6*

# THE EVIL EYE

***But I tell you that anyone who looks at a woman lustfully has already committed adultery with her in his heart. Matt. 5:28, NIV.***

"The woman you put here with me—she gave me some fruit from the tree, and I ate it," said Adam after God caught him hiding in the garden (Gen. 3:12, NIV). Men have been doing the same ever since—trying to blame women for their problems.

In the Hindu religion a woman must be reborn—in the scheme of reincarnation—as a man before she can find release from the dreary cycle of life and death. In the Jain religion woman is called the greatest source of temptation against godly living.

The rabbis of Jesus' time taught likewise. If a good man sees a pretty woman coming down the street, better, they said, that he avert his gaze and even stumble and hurt himself than that he should risk being led astray by her.

How radically different the religion of Jesus Christ! Instead of being concerned with male righteousness as opposed to Eve the temptress, Jesus emancipated women. In Jewish society the woman stood to suffer far worse consequences from a sexual dalliance than the man. The law provided for a husband to divorce his wife on grounds as trivial as her cooking; a wife could not divorce her husband for any reason.

So here in the Sermon on the Mount Jesus turns on its head the thinking of the rabbis. He reaches out to protect women from men, rather than men from women.

Although times have changed, in many ways a woman caught up in an "affair" still fares worse than the man involved. Society still has a double standard of social mores.

In today's world, the rule is "If it feels right, it is right." But citizens of the kingdom of heaven live by principle, not inclination.

That means keeping an eye single to the glory of God—and to the honor of members of the opposite sex.

# THE CHRISTIAN'S SPEECH

*But I tell you, Do not swear at all. Matt. 5:34, NIV.*

When God's sweet Spirit takes control of our lives, He puts new thoughts in our minds and new words on our tongues. Profanity and pure speech belong in separate camps—the first to the old life, the second to the new.

Our Saviour was a person of pure speech. " 'He committed no sin, and no deceit was found in his mouth.' When they hurled their insults at him, he did not retaliate; when he suffered, he made no threats. Instead, he entrusted himself to him who judges justly" (1 Peter 2:22, 23, NIV).

The people who stayed around Jesus began to speak like Him. Although Peter, Andrew, James, and John had been fishermen and knew language that could turn the air blue, knew coarse jests and crude expressions, being with Jesus slowly changed them. When they spoke to the crowds in Jerusalem, people were astonished that "unschooled, ordinary men" (Acts 4:13, NIV) could be so persuasive.

I have heard—with distaste—the speech of people whose every second or third word seemed to be a profanity. Swearing shows that a person has a limited vocabulary—the English language, with its hundreds of thousands of words, can adequately convey, without profanity, all we wish to express. And when *we ourselves* are true and honest, when we mean what we say and stand by our promise, we don't need an oath to confirm it. Interposing the oath indicates that our word is shaky.

We all battle poor speech, sub-Christian speech. James tells us that the person who can control the tongue has reached perfection (James 3:2)! The way to pure speech is the same for us as it was for foulmouthed Peter: stay around Jesus. The more time we spend with Him, the more our words will be like His.

"No one ever spoke the way this man does," the guards who came to arrest Jesus declared (John 7:46, NIV).

Once Peter's speech made him an object of embarrassing attention (Matt. 26:73). After Jesus changed him, Peter's speech again aroused curiosity—but because of its power.

May our speech today give evidence of the transforming friendship of Jesus.

# THE CHRISTIAN IN THE AGE OF DISBELIEF

*Simply let your "Yes" be "Yes," and your "No," "No"; anything beyond this comes from the evil one. Matt. 5:37, NIV.*

"This is what modern people have sadly concluded: Greed is the universal motive, sincerity is a pose, honesty is for chumps, altruism is selfishness with a neurotic twist, and morality is for kids and saints and fools."

These words come from a 19-page section of the *Washington Post Magazine*, December 27, 1987, devoted to one topic—remarkably, lying. The cover of the magazine showed "Joe Isuzu" (who advertises Isuzu cars on television by making patently false claims, for instance, that a car can get 112 miles to the gallon). Joe is shown smiling and saying, "1987 was the best year mankind ever had—and next year's going to be even better." Underneath we read in parentheses: "He's Lying." Articles in this section are entitled "Revenge of the Dupes," "According to Our Poll, You're Lying," and "The Academy Awards of Untruth."

Lying usually seems the easiest way out of a problem or an embarrassing situation. In fact, lying exacts a high price—from both the liar and the person lied to.

Liars lose friends. It's impossible to have a close relationship with someone you don't trust—and lying destroys trust. Ninety-four percent of Americans say they value honesty in a friend more than any other quality—no other trait comes even close (just as they place "honesty and integrity" far above any other quality in a president).

So the liar, who takes the easy way out, finds himself alone, the victim of his own folly. He pays a high price.

The person who is lied to also pays a price. Every time someone deceives us, we feel duped; we grow a little more skeptical, a little less trusting, a little less inclined to form a close relationship.

At such a time as this—the age of disbelief—Adventists, like all Christians, can have but one standard—absolute truthfulness. If morality is "for kids and saints and fools," so be it—but the Good Book tells us that no one who practices falsehood will enter God's new society (Rev. 21:27). We are to be men and women who keep our word even when it hurts us financially (Ps. 15:4), who do not slander (Eph. 4:31), who "stand for the right though the heavens fall" (*Education*, p. 57).

How do Adventists measure up? Probably well—and not so well. How about gossip? Rumormongering? Our readiness to believe the worst about the world—or the church? Our hunger for the sensational?

We also need to "clean up our act" at the corporate level. In this age when people distrust government and all institutions of society, we must be open and aboveboard. We should be upbeat about the church, but not try to pretend that the church is perfect or doesn't face big problems, or that leaders never make mistakes. We must take extra care with the way the church's moneys are handled, and give an accounting to the members. We should be ready to apologize when our actions call for it.

When Christ returns to earth He *will* have a people who reflect His character, His truthfulness. Even in the age of disbelief.

*April 9*

# THE OTHER CHEEK

***Ye have heard that it hath been said, An eye for an eye, and a tooth for a tooth: but I say unto you, That ye resist not evil: but whosoever shall smite thee on thy right cheek, turn to him the other also. Matt. 5:38, 39.***

Jesus said many things hard to follow, but this is one of the hardest. Ever since the Sermon on the Mount Christians have been trying to explain it. They usually end up explaining it away.

The Old Testament law about an eye for an eye and a tooth for a tooth seems brutal to our sensibilities. In actual fact the provision was humane, marking a distinct moral advancement over the customs of the times. Supposing a peasant was out hunting and his arrow went astray and took out the eye of a nobleman. The latter, with his wealth and influence, might want to have the peasant hung, drawn, and quartered; but the law laid down the upper limit of vengeance—no more than an eye.

Jesus, of course, went much beyond Moses' law. "But I tell you," He said. In His kingdom men and women, boys and girls, keep no score of wrongs and hurts. They don't lie awake plotting revenge or calling down a curse on their enemies.

Some years ago I spent many hours in conversation with a man who, according to his story, had been unjustly treated some 30 years before. That wrong, actual or imagined, had eaten away like a canker in the soul. Every time we talked he would bring it up. Whatever the facts of the original situation, his brooding over it had multiplied the hurt a hundredfold.

In these strange, hard words of Matthew 5:38-42, Jesus shows us the path to true freedom. The Jews were subject to the Romans, who might at any time strike them or compel them to carry their armor for one mile. But when the Christian exposed the other cheek or offered to carry the load for a second mile, he turned the tables on the oppressor. By taking the initiative, he showed that his freedom—an inner strength and peace—could surmount any outer circumstance.

*O Jesus, who stayed calm in the midst of revilings and beatings, give me freedom—that inner peace and strength—to meet every event of this new day.*

# WHY WE BREAK THE GOLDEN RULE

**Whatsoever ye would that men should do to you, do ye even so to them. Matt. 7:12.**

We have probably read how these words of Jesus are superior to anything that can be found in the great religions of the world, how Jesus turned a negative saying of the rabbis into a positive injunction of golden beauty. Unfortunately, it's easier to praise the golden rule than to practice it. In fact, of all Jesus' words this is the one that Christians most fail at. Why?

When our existence is threatened, we tend to fall back on brute self-preservation. When we find ourselves caught in a traffic jam, inching forward as we dutifully keep in our lane, our blood boils at the sight of the driver who races down the shoulder and forces his way into line. When we wait in a crowded airport lounge to board a long-delayed flight, we feel the urge to push and shove with the others when at last the gate is opened.

The rule of our life is: People should do unto *us* what we want. They should cater to our feelings, our drives, our wishes. So, when we feel tired, or pressed, or anxious, or threatened, we tend to revert to basic, raw existence.

What about Jesus' rule—is it a grand ideal but hopelessly impractical? Does it run against the very grain of our human nature?

Indeed. But isn't that true of the whole Sermon on the Mount?

One "if" makes us stand back and wonder if maybe—just maybe—the Sermon on the Mount, including the golden rule, might really be possible. That "if" is the "if" of Jesus—if Jesus said it (and He did), and if Jesus lived it (and He did), then maybe His ideal can be our ideal also.

Not in our own strength. That will never work. When pressed, we'll simply fall back into the dog-eat-dog, survival-of-the-fittest, looking-out-for-ourselves pattern that the rest of the world follows and that continually pulls us from within like a magnet.

Would it help if, in any given situation, we'd picture Jesus in our place? Caught in rush-hour traffic? Waiting in a crowded airport lounge?

And then—ask Him for power *at this moment* to act as He would act.

*April 11*

# BLESSED ARE THE MEEK

***Blessed are the meek: for they shall inherit the earth. Matt. 5:5.***

Are the meek the doormats of society, the nobodies, the faceless people who have no spirit, no assertiveness? Could this beatitude of Jesus set forth the least attractive ideal of all?

Not so. Consider one of the meanings of the original Greek word for meekness. Here is a colt, full of energy and spirit, galloping free in the wilds, snorting, its neck stretched out. All that power is undirected; the colt hasn't been broken. But one day a man catches the colt, puts a saddle on its back and a bridle and bit between its teeth, mounts it, and subdues it. The colt learns to go or to stay at the master's bidding.

Note that the colt's energy and spirit have not diminished one whit. It has all the restless fire that it once had. But now the colt is meek—its powers are focused, submissive to a higher authority.

Meek Christians are like that. They are spirited for God, but not for themselves. They don't burn up their energies in personal frustration, pride, and wounded feelings; they instead give their all to God and His bidding.

Because God directs their lives, focusing their powers, they accomplish much for Him—like Moses, who was called "very meek, above all the men which were upon the face of the earth" (Num. 12:3), but who brought God's people from Egypt to the borders of Canaan. He was the greatest leader in the Old Testament.

And like Jesus. He was a Man of tremendous strength of purpose. He knew He was born to die. When near the end of His ministry He foresaw betrayal, rejection, and a cross awaiting Him in Jerusalem, He nonetheless set His face like a flint (Isa. 50:7) to go up to the beloved city.

But all His energy was directed toward God's holy purpose. He came to do not His own will but the Father's. So when He was reviled, He reviled not again; when He was struck, He did not retaliate. He was the meekest Man of the New Testament and of the whole Bible. And He was the greatest: Jesus, who by His meekness won our salvation!

*April 12*

# ANTIDOTE TO WORRY

*Therefore do not worry about tomorrow, for tomorrow will worry about itself. Each day has enough trouble of its own. Matt. 6:34, NIV.*

Worry is the besetting sin of a host of Christians. Good men and women who would never rob a bank, run off with someone else's spouse, lie, cheat, or curse, who love Jesus and go to church and pay tithe, over and over fall into the slough of worry.

We worry because we care: worry is the trial of those who care. The more deeply we care—the more we love—the more likely we are to worry. Parents who don't care what happens to their children can sleep through the wee hours when the kids are still out, but those who love them with a fierce love will awaken, check to see if they have come home, and then toss in the darkness with fear gripping their hearts.

Worry over people is the most intense sort. Anxiety about food, clothing, and shelter can sap our energies, as Jesus realized in His counsel in the Sermon on the Mount (Matt. 6:28-32). But we usually can do something to relieve this worry—we can work, build, lay in store. People are different—we can't control them. We have to hand over the reins of their lives.

I remember well the wonderful, tumultuous teen years of our children; remember the struggles, the tears, the pain; remember at last Noelene and I reaching the point where we let go and turned them over to God alone. Parents have to learn to grow every bit as much as their children!

That's still the antidote to worry: let go and turn it over to God. Your spouse, your child, your friend over whom you fret—turn them over to God.

If we care about them, how much more does our heavenly Father! If we love them so, how much more does Jesus! If we would woo them to ourselves and to the right path, how much more does the Holy Spirit!

They are safe in the arms of Jesus. But God cannot compel their will; nor can we.

A friend of mine tells of meeting some parents who were wracked by remorse for their son. As a teenager he had run wild; one night he became drunk and was killed in a car wreck. As this friend listened to their anguish, he thought the tragedy must have recently happened. But then he learned that the boy had died nearly 20 years before! Twenty years—and the parents were still blaming themselves for his decision!

*O God of all our cares, who loves our dear ones even more than we do, we give them to You. Take them, keep them, woo them to Yourself and to us by Your Spirit.*

*April 13*

# HELP FOR THOSE NAGGING ANXIETIES

*Therefore I tell you, do not be anxious about your life, what you shall eat or what you shall drink, nor about your body, what you shall put on. Is not life more than food, and the body more than clothing? (Matt. 6:25, RSV).*

The little foxes, said the wise man, spoil the grapes (S. of Sol. 2:15). Not wild beasts such as bears and leopards, not hailstorm or drought, but the little foxes. And medical researchers now tell us that it's the little tensions and worries—those nagging anxieties—that clog our arteries and predispose us to heart disease.

For years scientists had recognized that crises such as a death of a loved one, a divorce, a job loss, threaten the body's defenses and make it vulnerable to the onslaught of sickness. They had also shown that high stress levels on the job—such as air traffic controllers experience—take a toll of our physical resources. But now they have discovered that the *little* foxes—those daily worries and anxieties—are also deadly.

Nothing—*nothing*—is too big or too small to take to Jesus. If it threatens our peace of mind, He wants to deal with it. Never will He turn us away because something that bothers us is too trivial to warrant His attention.

My prayer daily is that, in the midst of cares and decisions, I might be kept within the cocoon of Jesus' love. That moment by moment I might know His serenity. That I might find abiding joy, whatever the circumstances. That the little foxes might not spoil the grapes of the Spirit.

"He who has given you life knows your need of food to sustain it," wrote Ellen White. "He who created the body is not unmindful of your need of raiment. Will not He who has bestowed the greater gift bestow also what is needed to make it complete?" (*Thoughts From the Mount of Blessing*, p. 95).

Then she quotes this verse:
"No sparrow falls without His care,
    No soul bows low but Jesus knows;
For He is with us everywhere,
    And marks each bitter tear that flows.
And He will never, never, never
Forsake the soul that trusts Him ever."

*April 14*

# WHERE THE HEART IS

*For where your treasure is, there will your heart be also. Matt. 6:21.*

I hesitate to tell the following story, lest any reader should feel I am holding up our family members as paragons of virtue; please indulge me.

When I married Noelene and we started life together as missionaries in India, we had precious few possessions. Nevertheless, among them was a piano—one of our first purchases. Noelene had studied music at Avondale College, along with elementary education, and she taught piano classes for the first 13 years of our married life. In fact, years later piano lessons helped pay the bills during my doctoral studies.

The piano—we had a succession of them—was strictly for her. I don't play at all. But I do like to sing, and one of the loveliest memories of worship together was our sitting at the piano, working our way through the hymnal, singing every hymn in the book.

From India we moved to Andrews University in Berrien Springs, Michigan. Once again, the piano. In fact, we eventually had three pianos in the home. One was a baby grand; we bought it locally, and worked on it together as a family, refinishing it—stripping off the old finish, sanding, staining. We also had an upright, painted blue, that came with the basement. And we had a lovely Yamaha grand, left in our keeping by friends who departed the United States for service abroad.

Then came 1980 and we moved again, to our work at the General Conference. With both our children having to go into boarding school, plus the Washington, D.C., area's higher cost of living, we suddenly found ourselves without a piano. After 20 years, no piano in the home!

As soon as our youngest had finished graduate school and we had paid all our bills, we bought another piano, on Labor Day, 1987. Only the Lord knows how much my wife must have missed the piano during those seven years, but she not once uttered a word of complaint. And neither of us regretted a single cent of the money we put into educating our children.

Now at family worship time we are working our way through the new *SDA Hymnal*, enjoying both the piano and the new tunes.

*April 15*

# MY FAVORITE THINGS

***See how the lilies of the field grow. They do not labor or spin. Matt. 6:28, NIV.***

Every Saturday night for 13 years, millions of Americans turned on their radio—even in the age of television. They tuned in to two hours of folk music on the *Prairie Home Companion* broadcast. The high point every week came during the third half hour, when Garrison Keillor, the tall, lanky compere, strolled out, stood at the microphone, looked up into the lights of the World Theater in St. Paul, Minnesota, and began a monologue.

His tales were about life and people in small-town America. One of them, "State Fair," tells about riding the Ferris wheel and ends thus: "This vision is unbearably wonderful. Then the wheel brings me down to the ground. We get off and other people get on. Thank You, dear God, for this good life, and forgive us if we do not love it enough."

Jesus loved this good life. He who had made "all things bright and beautiful, all creatures great and small," had an eye for the wild anemones (probably the meaning of "lilies" in our text for the day), the sparrow on the wing, the plowman in the field. He saw all, noted all, loved all.

Do we?

In *The Sound of Music,* a celebration of the Von Trapp family singers, who fled for their lives from the Nazi regime, Maria sings about her favorite things: raindrops on roses, kittens' whiskers, kettles, mittens, and so on.

I have my own list: the smell of newly mown grass, the first crocuses of spring, the beach (at any season), Mozart's music (all of it), the *National Geographic,* arriving home to the aroma of fresh-baked bread, family worship singalongs, little children, the satisfaction of a job well done, the sense of the goodness and leading of the Lord. And people—above all, people; but here the list gets too long to include.

Do you have a list?

*Thank You, dear God, for this good life, and forgive us if we do not love it enough.*

*April 16*

# THE LEGACY OF A LIFE

*Do not store up for yourselves treasures on earth, where moth and rust destroy, and where thieves break in and steal. Matt. 6:19, NIV.*

When Jesus died, He left almost nothing of value. The soldiers who sat at the foot of His cross distributed the few items of clothing that He owned. Just one piece was worth something—the long, seamless robe that was His outer garment and that could serve as a blanket when He slept. That was too good to rip into segments, so the soldiers rolled dice for it.

But what a legacy Jesus left! No will, no bank account, no houses and lands—but a life! A life of peerless purity, an example of service and unselfishness, a model of obedience to the Father's will! And a life that, coupled with His substitutionary death, won our salvation.

Mahatma Gandhi also left almost nothing of material value. A pair of sandals, a rice bowl, a pair of spectacles—nothing else. This man who had studied law in England, who had argued before the bar of justice, who once had dressed in Europe's finest fashions, who had stood before monarchs and prime ministers, died penniless, clad in *khadi*—white, homespun cotton cloth.

But the legacy of his life was a free nation, an independent India. By identifying with the poor peasants and by adopting a resolute strategy of nonviolent resistance to the British ruling powers—a strategy derived from the Sermon on the Mount—Gandhi rallied a people and led it to freedom.

If I should die today, what would be the legacy of my life?

It's good to make provision for our loved ones, especially for any dependents—it's good and necessary. But would that be the only treasure that I would leave behind?

What would I be remembered for? Would I have made any difference? Would the world be a little better, the misery of humanity a little less, the church a little stronger, the coming of the Master a little nearer?

*April 17*

# THE SINGLE EYE

*The light of the body is the eye: if therefore thine eye be single, thy whole body shall be full of light. Matt. 6:22.*

What did Jesus mean by the "single" eye? The context probably gives us the clue: "No man can serve two masters: for either he will hate the one, and love the other; or else he will hold to the one, and despise the other. Ye cannot serve God and mammon" (verse 24).

The problem of most Christians is that we try to do what Jesus has said is impossible—we want to serve two masters. We cling to God, and we cling to the world. We are spiritual schizophrenics. Our eye looks to Jesus, but then roves afar. We don't have a "single" eye—an eye fixed unwaveringly on the kingdom of heaven.

"Let your eyes look straight ahead," counseled the wise man (Prov. 4:25, NIV). My father liked to quote that verse. His own gaze was straight, direct—no shiftiness or averted eye. And that is how he walked with God. My earliest memory of him is the same as the last—early in the morning, while the house was still quiet, sitting alone in the living room with the Bible open before him, meditating on the Word.

God can do great things with men and women, or boys and girls, whose eye is single for His glory. When we no longer care about who gets the credit, the work of the church leaps ahead. A person may not have great talent or have amassed a stack of sheepskins, but the single eye is more than sufficient. When the eye is single God finds a Joseph, a Daniel, a Paul. Or a David Livingstone, a William Booth, a J. N. Andrews.

"There is no limit to the usefulness of one who, by putting self aside, makes room for the working of the Holy Spirit upon his heart, and lives a life wholly consecrated to God" (*The Desire of Ages*, pp. 250, 251).

*O God who reads our inmost thoughts, give us this day an eye single to Your glory, a heart that loves You truly and that serves You faithfully.*

# THE RECONCILERS

*Blessed are the peacemakers: for they shall be called the children of God. Matt. 5:9.*

In a quiet, flower-decked cemetery on the edge of the city of Uppsala, Sweden, I stood by the tomb of Dag Hammarskjold, one of his country's most illustrious sons. High born, a deep thinker, Hammarskjold gave himself to the mission of peace. He was the second secretary-general of the United Nations, and died in the line of duty when the plane that was carrying him on a flight to the troubled Congo crashed.

This quiet, unassuming bachelor was a deeply spiritual person. Jottings from his writings, published posthumously as *Markings*, reveal his thirst for God and his desire to be of service to his fellows:

"Never measure the height of a mountain until you have reached the top. Then you will see how low it was."

"The dust settles heavily, the air becomes stale, the light dim in the room which we are not prepared to leave at any moment."

"If only I may grow: firmer, simpler—quieter, warmer."

The entire mass of humanity belongs to one of two basic groups—the dividers and the reconcilers. Some people forever are fomenting discord; they see enemies behind every bush, they sow suspicion and doubt. Australians have an interesting term for them—stirrers.

The reconcilers are the peacemakers. They look for areas of common ground rather than emphasizing differences. They put a positive rather than a negative construction on events. They place a premium on relationships, and work to bring and keep people together.

By far the most important type of peacemaking, however, is reconciling men and women to God. Our Master calls every Christian to this work: "God was in Christ, reconciling the world unto himself, not imputing their trespasses unto them; and hath committed unto us the word of reconciliation. Now then we are ambassadors for Christ, as though God did beseech you by us: we pray you in Christ's stead, be ye reconciled to God" (2 Cor. 5:19, 20).

115

Divider or reconciler—which am I? What is my influence in the church? Today, on the job, in school, at home, what will I be?

*O Prince of Peace, who lived and died to bring us back to God and to each other, make us today reconcilers for Your glory.*

*April 19*

# THE BLESSING NOBODY WANTS

*Blessed are those who are persecuted because of righteousness, for theirs is the kingdom of heaven. Matt. 5:10, NIV.*

This is the blessing nobody wants—persecution. How often do you hear a Christian pray, "Lord, please bring persecution on us"?

It's probably right *not* to want persecution. People who delight in personal suffering or who have a martyr's complex are sick emotionally. Then why did Jesus pronounce this strange beatitude?

Because God's people *will* at times suffer for Him, not because they seek it or delight in it, but because they live in a world gone wrong. "Yea," says Paul, "all that will live godly [lives] in Christ Jesus shall suffer persecution" (2 Tim. 3:12). And when that happens, Jesus has a special blessing waiting for them.

In 1987 the government of Fiji was overthrown by a military coup. For a time strict Sunday laws were enforced; people were forbidden to work on that day. Seventh-day Adventists were permitted to worship on the Sabbath, but when some of them attempted to work the following day, they found themselves under arrest.

Then something interesting happened. As word of the arrests spread around the island, former Seventh-day Adventists and backslidden SDAs began to come back to church; some wanted to be rebaptized.

A little persecution woke them up, shook them out of their spiritual lethargy.

Persecution brings a blessing in other ways as well. As we suffer for our faith, we enter into a deeper relationship with the Master. We become sharers in His sufferings, joined with Him in the ill treatment meted out by the ancient enemy.

For Jesus Himself knew persecution. Not only in Pilate's judgment hall, not only on Golgotha; but as a young man growing up in Nazareth, and as bearer of an unpopular message concerning the Messiah and the nature of His kingdom.

The blessing nobody wants—and that nobody *should* want! But it is a real blessing, a blessing that God gives to comfort our hearts when we most need it. "For unto you it is given in the behalf of Christ, not only to believe on him, but also to suffer for his sake" (Phil. 1:29).

# WHEN WORDS HURT US

*Blessed are you when people insult you, persecute you and falsely say all kinds of evil against you because of me. Matt. 5:11, NIV.*

I once read about a man who was falsely accused. As the vicious rumors circulated, his standing as a leader in the town and in the church was threatened. The man's son, who wrote up the story, was troubled by the unjust attack on his father. But he was even more troubled by his father's reaction. He refused to defend himself, refused to get involved in a slugging match with his chief accuser. "Now I'll see who my true friends really are," said his father. "They know me well enough to recognize that these charges are untrue."

Some friends stood by him, but alas! some whom he thought were friends joined the ranks of the accusers. But in time he was vindicated: he had the truth on his side, and truth won the day.

The greater victory, however, was a personal one. His father had weathered the storm without embitterment and without descending to the level of his attackers.

Words hurt—especially false charges. They make us want to fight, to reply in kind.

But if we are true to God, no person or circumstance in life can hurt us. If we *know* we are in the right, they bounce off us like paper darts.

We can hurt ourselves, however. By harboring thoughts about the unfairness of life, the injustice of our treatment, the fickleness of our friends, we become cynical and calculating. By taking our defense into our own hands instead of letting God and His truth defend us, we run the risk of a wounding of our spirit that will leave lifelong scars.

"While slander may blacken the reputation, it cannot stain the character. That is in God's keeping. So long as we do not consent to sin, there is no power, whether human or satanic, that can bring a stain upon the soul. A man whose heart is stayed upon God is just the same in the hour of his most afflicting trials and most discouraging surroundings as when he was in prosperity, when the light and favor of God seemed to be upon him. His words, his motives, his actions, may be misrepresented and falsified, but he does not mind it, because he has greater interests at stake" (*Thoughts From the Mount of Blessing*, p. 32).

# FACE INTO THE WIND

*Look at the birds of the air; they do not sow or reap or store away in barns, and yet your heavenly Father feeds them. Matt. 6:26, NIV.*

"Of all the wild birds in existence," writes Dr. Virchel E. Wood, "the black-capped chickadee ranks number one with me. When I walk through the woods, this little bird always flits about my path. The plump little wide-eyed bundle of black, white, and gray feathers, loaded with energy and cheer, perches on a branch from which it chants its clear 'dee, dee, dee, chickadee, dee.' . . .

"This little dynamo, because of its confident air and unending resourcefulness, lives in places where other birds fail. It is found on the sunniest days and amid the most relentless storms. At the first hints of autumn, the fair-weather birds flee the cool air to enjoy more comfortable climates, but the chickadee remains. Its courage enables it to face the coldest, most blustery winter the north can hurl. It does not flee the wintry blasts, but revels in blizzards, sings in sleet, and sweeps the snow-covered fields in revenge of the coldest weather. It awakens in me feelings of admiration. The chickadee stays by. . . .

"Resting on some frosty limb, the chickadee remains prepared for life or death, sleeping or eating, or sudden flight. Its courage in emergencies is a marvel. The mixture of simplicity and action, its adaptation to any situation, is the most enduring characteristic of the chickadee. It hints of how we should live. . . .

"The black-capped chickadee can withstand the hard northern blasts because its instinct is to face the wind. Like the feathers of all birds, the chickadee's feathers point toward the tail. The close matting of the feathers seals out the cold flurries, holding in the bird's body warmth.

"If the bird turns its back to the cruel winter, snow blows in among the feathers, carrying the bitter cold next to its body. Once the warmth of the bird escapes, the chickadee freezes to death. The only way it survives is by facing into the wind.

"We all dislike the frigid winds. Hardship and struggle seem severe. The cold realities of life are stern and cause us to turn our backs to the storm. But we must meet our limitations with courage and face into the wind. Each cruel blast can serve some useful purpose or produce a joyful experience. No disaster need destroy us" ("Face Into the Wind," *Adventist Review*, May 19, 1988).

*April 22*

# THE MEANING OF RIGHTEOUSNESS

*Beware of practicing your piety before men in order to be seen by them; for then you will have no reward from your Father who is in heaven. Matt. 6:1, RSV.*

The entire Sermon on the Mount is about righteousness. Here Jesus shows His followers in all ages that the way of righteousness lies between two extremes; it is a channel like that of the ancient Greeks between the rocks of Scylla and Charybdis.

On one side lies "Scylla"—the rock of Pharisaical self-righteousness. Here good deeds are tallied up so that the person can feel superior to his fellows. Here it's important that others see our righteous acts so that they will think how "good" we are.

But, says Jesus, the only reward such righteousness brings is the praise of men—the heavenly Father certainly cannot commend it. Why not? Because it springs from motives of self-glory and influencing others.

On the other side of the channel of righteousness lies "Charybdis"—the teaching that good works are of no significance. Because the Pharisees in Jesus' day paraded their righteousness, and because some Christians in our day aren't very loving, you'll find people who don't want to hear any talk about righteous living. "I won't go to church and be like those hypocrites," they complain.

Even some Christians have overreacted to the pharisaical perversion of righteousness. They're deathly scared of being labeled legalists; they prefer to think of righteousness as only a relationship with Christ.

Now, at its heart righteousness is relational—it centers in our relationship with God first, then with other people. But Jesus' teaching in the Sermon on the Mount makes clear that these relationships produce *action*. The righteous man or woman—that is, the citizen of the kingdom of heaven—*lives*, *does* righteous deeds. Profession without practice is as bad as profession for pride.

*O Master, lead me this day in the paths of Thy righteousness, in a life of unstudied, unselfish, unremembered acts of kindness and of love.*

119

# THE PURE IN HEART

*Blessed are the pure in heart: for they shall see God.*
*Matt. 5:8.*

The pure in heart will see God because they are like God. The Holy Spirit has transformed their thinking, renewed their motives, changed their desires. They love what God loves; they think His thoughts after Him.

An interesting letter, which sheds light on the attitudes of the early Christians, has come down to us from the third century. In it a pagan makes fun of the Christians because of their gullibility. Christians were easy prey, a sort of "soft touch," he mocked, for anyone who wanted to sponge off them. They were so trusting that they readily could be taken in by a clever pretender.

What a compliment! How much better to be trusting and to be deemed gullible than to be suspicious and worldly-wise! Said Paul: "To the pure, all things are pure, but to those who are corrupted and do not believe, nothing is pure" (Titus 1:15, NIV). When Mother Teresa, of Calcutta fame, was criticized for being "used" by politicians, she replied that she would gladly be "used" if out of it all some needy person was benefited.

The purity of heart of which Jesus spoke in the Sermon on the Mount goes beyond sexual purity, although it includes that. He referred to the heart that above all else is devoted to God, that loves to feed on His Word and to do His will, that longs for Him more and more—a heart like His!

"The pure in heart live as in the visible presence of God during the time He apportions them in this world. And they will also see Him face to face in the future, immortal state, as did Adam when he walked and talked with God in Eden" (*Thoughts From the Mount of Blessing*, p. 27).

Revelation 22:4 sums it up: "They will see his face, and his name will be on their foreheads" (NIV).

"Rejoice, ye pure in heart!
Rejoice, give thanks and sing;
Your festal banner wave on high,
The Cross of Christ your King.
Rejoice! Rejoice! Rejoice, give thanks, and sing!"
—Edward H. Plumptre

# THE MERCIFUL

*Blessed are the merciful: for they shall obtain mercy.*
*Matt. 5:7.*

When I stand before God's judgment bar, I hope my case will be decided on the basis of mercy, not justice alone. If justice is to be the only measure, I have no hope. My hope is in God's amazing grace, manifested supremely in the gift of His Son Jesus Christ, as an offering for my sin and for the sins of the world.

The sense of God's mercy transforms us. It makes us like Him—merciful.

The clearest parable of Jesus that teaches this truth is found in Matthew 18:23-35. The story has two parts, the first one incredible, the second altogether credible.

In the first half of the parable we hear about a servant who owes the king a massive amount—10,000 talents. That would be equivalent to millions of dollars in today's money, but Jesus wasn't attempting to specify an amount. He combined the largest number in the Greek language with the largest unit of money in the accounting system. If He were giving the story today He'd tell us to put in the largest sum of money we can think of. A million dollars? 10 million? 100 million? Whatever the number, insert that into the story.

Now comes the incredible part: because the servant cannot pay (who could?), the king freely forgives him this huge debt. Without obligation. Instantly. Simply because of his need.

Now comes the altogether credible part. This servant who has been forgiven so much goes out and oppresses a fellow servant who owes him a paltry sum. The first servant has been shown great mercy, but he doesn't act accordingly.

So he loses the great gift. His huge debt rolls back upon him. His actions showed that he didn't belong in the presence of the merciful king, because he hadn't been transformed by the king's generosity.

Jesus made exactly the same point in the Lord's Prayer: "Forgive us our debts, as we also have forgiven our debtors" (Matt. 6:12, NIV).

Yes, I hope for mercy when I stand before God. But God will ask if I have shown mercy. The besetting sin of many "good" people, church-going people, is their lack of compassion.

*O merciful Saviour, as You have shown compassion to me, make me compassionate to others today.*

# BASSET HOUND CHRISTIANS

***Blessed are they that mourn: for they shall be comforted. Matt. 5:4.***

Is Jesus here advocating that we go around with long faces like basset hounds? Should children of the kingdom of heaven be known for their gravity?

Some texts of Scripture seem to suggest it. "It is better to go to the house of mourning, than to go to the house of feasting," counseled the wise man (Eccl. 7:2). He also wrote that laughter is like the crackle of thorns under a pot (verse 6). And was not Jesus Himself a man of sorrows, acquainted with grief?

But other passages teach differently. The wise man also said, "A merry heart doeth good like a medicine" (Prov. 17:22). Jesus spoke of joy that no one could take from us; of grief being turned into joy (John 16:20, 22). And at times He made humorous statements that must have made His hearers smile—such as about people who strained out a gnat but who swallowed a camel (Matt. 23:24).

In the world laughter is a commercial property. Gag writers, comedians, and cartoonists make their living from it. The world seeks to cover its hurt by laughing. And in doing so it often blocks out the call of God to the soul.

During the twelfth century a courtier, Rahere, entertained the royal family of England. Rahere was a good fellow to have around—he could make clever conversation interspersed with witticisms. But then tragedy struck: the king's son and heir was lost in a shipwreck. Rahere turned to serious matters—he set out on a pilgrimage. Along the way he fell sick and began to contemplate the legacy of his life. Returning to his native London, he built a church—St. Bartholomew's—and a hospital. Both continue to this day.

Often the only time God can get through to us is when our hearts are breaking. When we turn from our self-sufficiency, when we mourn for our sins, when the Holy Spirit convicts our hearts, we are more ready to give God a chance. And when we do, we find His comfort.

# BRILLIANT!

*Blessed are they which do hunger and thirst after righteousness: for they shall be filled. Matt. 5:6.*

Have you been troubled because so few of the leading people of society confess Jesus as their Saviour and Lord? Have you wondered why comparatively few men and women of towering intellect—the Nobel laureates, the giants of science—are practicing Christians?

As a young man I was bothered at times by such questions. But one day I came across this statement, and it helped me greatly: "Call no man brilliant who has not the wisdom to choose Jesus Christ—the light and life of the world. The excellence of a man is determined by his possession of the virtues of Christ" (*Counsels to Writers and Editors,* p. 175).

I grew up in Australia, where the British system of education is followed. "Brilliant" was a word we often heard in the public high school I attended—a "brilliant" solution to a math problem, a "brilliant" performance on an examination. We sat at assigned desks in strict order according to our academic performance: the weakest student under the teacher's nose, the most "brilliant" pupil at the back in the far corner. The teachers worked to prepare us for examinations set and administered by the state.

But Ellen White's penetrating analysis upends the scale of brilliance. Not those with a genius-level IQ, not those who carry away the trophies for academic excellence, not those lauded for their discoveries or achievements, are the truly "brilliant." The measure is now Jesus Christ—the humblest of men, the best of men. And only as we partake of His character do we share in true greatness.

If we love Jesus, we will never be satisfied with our spiritual growth or condition. We shall ever be hungering and thirsting, ever seeking by His grace to be more like Him. How far short of the ideal we are! How frequently we let Him down! How shallow is our profession!

But day by day He is changing us. As we behold Him, seeking to be like Him, He molds us after the divine similitude, refashioning His image within us (2 Cor. 3:18). Already we are the children of God (1 John 5:1), and the best is yet to be!

# POINTING THE FINGER

*Judge not, that ye be not judged. Matt. 7:1.*

Every time we point the finger at someone, do we realize that four fingers are pointing back at ourselves?

Have you noticed that we usually are more demanding of others than we are of ourselves? With us it is different—what we can't abide in another we excuse, rationalize, or make an exception when it comes to us. And often we are most critical of others for faults that we also struggle with: perhaps we seek to cover up our own shortcomings—even to ourselves—by pointing the finger at someone else.

An Adventist academy once had a demoralizing problem —someone in the girls' dorm was a thief. One of the senior girls was certain who it was—another student who was not wealthy and dressed simply. But the girls' dean couldn't act merely on the basis of suspicion, despite the accusations of the senior.

The stealing continued, however, and at length the senior girl came to the dean with a plan. "Let's set a trap," she said. "I'll leave out some money on my dressing table; we can mark it so that when the thief takes it we can catch her. And I know who that will be!"

So they set the trap. The girl and the dean noted the serial number of the bill, and the girl left it lying on her dressing table. It lay there all day and the next, but the third day it disappeared. The senior came running to the dean with the news: "The money is gone! The thief has struck! Now you'll catch her!" So the dean called the principal, and together they commenced a search of the girls' rooms. And they found the missing money—in the purse of the plainly dressed girl!

An open-and-shut case; mystery solved. Except for one hitch: the thief refused to confess. They questioned her for hours, till late at night, but still she asserted her innocence. The next day they sent her home—branded a thief.

Several months later the senior girl came to the Bible teacher. "Something is bothering me," she said. "You remember when we had the stealing problem in the dorm? I was so sure that _____ was the thief that when nothing happened to the money for two days, I took it and put it in her purse."

Things aren't always what they seem. Said the apostle: "Judge nothing before the time, until the Lord come, who both will bring to light the hidden things of darkness, and will make manifest the counsels of the hearts: and then shall every man have praise of God" (1 Cor. 4:5).

# THE CHRISTIAN HAS NO ENEMIES

*Love your enemies, bless them that curse you, do good to them that hate you, and pray for them which despitefully use you. Matt. 5:44.*

A man waiting in line at the registration desk of a hotel was amazed at the courtesy of the desk clerk. She had an especially unpleasant person to deal with—rude, demanding, demeaning. But to every complaint she responded with: "Yes, sir"; "I'm sorry, sir"; "We'll take care of it, sir." The man waiting behind noticed that as she spoke she would scribble occasional notes on her desk pad.

At last the obnoxious character moved away, and the observer himself stood before the gracious clerk. She smiled sweetly and took care of his needs. As she was doing so he happened to glance at the desk pad. It was filled with swear words! While she had been outwardly so courteous, inside she had been boiling with resentment!

Only Jesus can change our hearts. Only His Spirit can take us beyond appearances and conformity and make us *love* our enemies.

Jesus had no enemies—although the religious leaders hated Him, He *loved* them. As they nailed Him to the cross He prayed: "Father, forgive them; for they know not what they do" (Luke 23:34).

Corrie Ten Boom, that marvelous Dutch woman whose book *The Hiding Place* recounts how she and her sister hid Jews from the Nazis during World War II, later described one of the most difficult tests of her life. After the war, when she was speaking at a Christian meeting in West Germany, she recognized one of the guards from the prison camp where her sister lost her life. When this former guard put out his hand in greeting, Corrie Ten Boom froze. She could not bring herself to take it. But then silently she called upon the Lord—and the Lord worked a miracle. He took away the hatred, took away the bitterness; He put in love and acceptance. Corrie Ten Boom reached out and grasped his hand—no longer an enemy, but a brother!

The Christian has no enemies. People may hate us, but the Spirit of Jesus makes us love them.

# THE QUEST FOR PERFECTION

*Be ye therefore perfect, even as your Father which is in heaven is perfect. Matt. 5:48.*

Ah, perfection! We live in a world where all is flawed, where our achievements never quite match our dreams, where the ideal is a shining star that we stretch to grasp but that always eludes our fingertips. Strange creatures, we humans—we can *visualize* the perfect, but we cannot realize it!

And here is Jesus, in the climax of His teaching on the "better righteousness" in Matthew 5, telling us to be perfect! What shall we make of His words?

First, we note the context. In verses 44-47 Jesus has been giving the sixth and last of His "You have heard it said . . . but I say unto you" illustrations that explain how the Christian is to live. These verses go beyond all the others: we are to love even our enemies! Remember, says the Master, that your heavenly Father loves all people without discriminating—He sends His rain and sunshine on the good people as well as the bad—and so should you. "Be ye therefore perfect, even as your Father which is in heaven is perfect."

Second, the perfection Jesus here describes centers in our relationships with others. He is not advocating the life of a religious recluse, who shuts himself or herself away from the world to follow a life of prayer and fasting. No; perfection will be shown by the way we treat others, the way we feel about them. And not just our friends, but even those who hate us, call us bad names, and accuse us falsely.

Third, Jesus has raised the goal so high that we can never hope to attain perfection in our own strength. The pharisaical checklist approach has collapsed—we may be able to discipline our acts (difficult) and even our words (more difficult), but who can force himself to love someone who ill-treats him? This sort of perfection can come only from God, who is perfect Himself, who loves His enemies. This perfection must be a gift, not an achievement.

*O Master, who loved Your enemies and who now calls us to perfection, change this hard, proud heart into one like Yours. During the stresses and hurts of this day be always with me, giving peace, love, and the sense of Your abiding presence.*

# WHAT A FATHER!

*Which of you, if his son asks for bread, will give him a stone? Or if he asks for a fish, will give him a snake? Matt. 7:9, 10, NIV.*

"Father" was Jesus' favorite designation for God. And what a Father! In the Sermon on the Mount we find a threefold description of our heavenly Parent.

God is the heavenly lover, said Jesus. He sends His sunshine and rain alike on the righteous and on the unrighteous. His love knows no bounds, no discrimination. Because God *is* love, He loves and keeps on loving, and always loves (Matt. 5:44-48).

God is the heavenly provider, Jesus said. He cares for the sparrow and the raven. He sees the wildflowers, bringing every spring the recurring miracle of resurrection. So why be anxious about what you will eat and drink, or what you will wear? Why worry about tomorrow? If God cares for the birds and the flowers, how much more will He provide for you (Matt. 6:25-34)?

And God is the heavenly giver, according to Jesus. He loves to give good things to His children. Look at earthly parents, how we love to buy presents for birthdays, Christmas, and other special occasions. See how we are concerned to see that our children get adequate food, that they lack nothing to help them grow up strong, healthy, and happy. In the same way, our heavenly Father will give to us as we pour out our petitions before Him. We don't have to beg and plead; we don't have to ring a bell as in a pagan temple; we don't have to try to manipulate Him. Just ask, that's all; for He delights to give.

All religion and all theology begins with a concept of God. Jesus gave us a concept of God as heavenly Father that transforms all our living. And what Jesus taught, He lived—for He was God made flesh.

What a God! What a liberating concept! What a life-transforming religion! The God on our side, the God who is for us, the God who is with us, the God who died for us! Now we have reason for living; now we have grace for today!

# THE SACRED AND THE PROFANE

*Give not that which is holy unto the dogs, neither cast ye your pearls before swine, lest they trample them under their feet, and turn again and rend you. Matt. 7:6.*

In my judgment, the biggest problem with the entertainment industry, so far as the Christian is concerned, is its consistent failure to acknowledge the sacred. In television and movie productions, characters use the names of God and Christ thoughtlessly —as exclamations or oaths. They treat what is most holy as common, everyday property.

For a short period I once found myself in an environment where the workers on the job used foul language. They cursed and swore; they used the name of the Lord profanely. I didn't like the situation, but it wasn't one of my choosing.

However, when we leave the television turned on a particular program, we make a choice with regard to what we see and hear. I do not think that we can continually listen to people using the name of God or Christ in jest or oaths without being affected. What causes us to wince the first time gradually becomes acceptable. Before we know it, we have conformed to Hollywood's standards.

Alexander Pope said it well:

"Vice is a monster of so frightful mien

As to be hated needs but to be seen;

Yet seen too oft, familiar with her face,

We first endure, then pity, then embrace" *(An Essay on Man).*

In the book of Leviticus we read about Nadab and Abihu, sons of Aaron the high priest. The Israelites had just built the sanctuary to the precise specifications laid down by the Lord, and Nadab and Abihu, along with their father and brothers, had been consecrated to offer sacrifice. But Nadab and Abihu apparently took their sacred responsibilities lightly. Their spirits buoyed by alcohol, they blundered into the sanctuary with unauthorized fire.

"So fire came out from the presence of the Lord and consumed them, and they died before the Lord" (Lev. 10:2, NIV). And the Lord through Moses instructed Aaron and his remaining sons: "You must distinguish between the holy and the common, between the unclean and the clean" (verse 10).

That is still important counsel for Christ's followers today.

*O holy Master, give me the grace today to change the channel or to pull the plug lest I dishonor Thy name.*

# THE PARABLE OF THE CAMELIA

*By their fruit you will recognize them. Do people pick grapes from thornbushes, or figs from thistles? Matt. 7:16, NIV.*

"This camelia may have a hard time surviving the winter," said the clerk at my favorite nursery. "Its level of hardiness is just marginal for this area."

The Washington, D.C., area has hot, muggy summers, and a mild winter. But during January, February, or March a bitter north wind sometimes pierces through, dropping the wind chill factor to 20 or 30 degrees below zero degrees Fahrenheit. A wind like that could freeze the camelia.

Nevertheless, I decided to take the risk. I brought home the camelia with its shiny green leaves and fat buds already formed, ready for a February burst of color. On a warm September afternoon I dug a hole close to the house (camelias like shade), protected from the wind, and planted the camelia.

Fall came; then winter. The buds of the camelia swelled; a tinge of pink began to appear at their tips. Their rendezvous with February was about to arrive.

But in February a fierce, freezing, dry wind from the north hit. All night it blew, and all the next day. The camelia's buds, about to burst open, turned an icy brown; the flower children were aborted.

In the spring I watered and fertilized the plant, and by August it had ready another crop of fat buds. They developed throughout the fall and into winter—but something was different this time. Not till March did they begin to show the pink tip that presaged the blooming. However, once again as the camelia was about to burst open, the north wind struck—in mid-March. The buds again were burned brown, but two survived.

I am writing on a lovely spring morning. The camelia outside my door has come through its third winter. This year it produced a full display of lovely pink blossoms—in mid-April! They have beautified our garden for two weeks already.

That camelia, it seems, refuses to accept the inevitable. It has adjusted to the Washington winter; it keeps coming back year after year, trying again. If it "knows" anything, it is to bear flowers and to keep on bearing them, whatever the circumstances.

My camelia is a living parable of the Christian's life. Life or death, concentration camp or affluence, cannot stop the fragrance of the life hid in Jesus. When we love Jesus and walk with Him, our roots reach down deep, drawing on never-failing springs.

*O God of the camelia, keep me this day in living connection with Your power. May the beauty of Christ be seen in me.*

# ONE MAN WIDE

**But small is the gate and narrow the road that leads to life, and only a few find it. Matt. 7:14, NIV.**

The gate to life is narrow—just one Man wide. Jesus Christ is that gate.

He said, "I am the way, the truth, and the life: no man cometh unto the Father, but by me" (John 14:6). Peter reiterated this eternal fact: "Neither is there salvation in any other: for there is none other name under heaven given among men, whereby we must be saved" (Acts 4:12).

The history of humanity is strewn with religious theories and claims. Jesus of Nazareth is but one leader among a host who have founded world religions or local sects.

But Jesus stands unique. He *is* the Way: He does not simply *teach* the way, like Buddha. He is the Gate because He alone could provide the solution to the terrible dilemma of mankind's sin.

There was no other good enough
To pay the price of sin;
He only could unlock the gate
Of heaven, and let us in.
　　—Cecil Frances Alexander

This claim of Christ and the Christians—the claim to uniqueness—was a scandal in the ancient world. How could a crucified teacher be the Jews' Messiah and the Saviour of the world!

If anything, that claim is even more of a scandal today. In these "enlightened" times people don't fight and kill over religion. Tolerance instead is the key word. Accept one religion as good as another.

But the gate is still small and the path to life is still narrow. Every person who will be saved will be there by virtue of the life and death of Jesus.

We who profess to follow Jesus—we too need to remember the narrow Gate. We tend to fall back to other routes; to enter the kingdom through other gates. These gates and paths are as many and as varied as human devising, but they all have one name—Salvation by Human Effort. Having begun well—having entered through the narrow Gate—we somehow think that we now will make the rest of the journey on our own. But the way we *live* for Christ is the same as the way we *become* Christian: through the narrow Gate.

*O divine Redeemer, keep me today on the narrow path that leads ever upward. Keep me looking to You, living by Your power, abiding in You.*

# PRAYER THAT WORKS

*Ask and it will be given to you; seek and you will find; knock and the door will be opened to you. Matt. 7:7, NIV.*

We need to learn again the power of prayer. "More things are wrought by prayer than this world dreams of," said the poet Tennyson. We need to know our God and be confident that He hears and answers us.

Can you point to any prayer God has answered for you this week? this year? Are you afraid to claim the promise of Jesus in this passage?

I too long for a deeper, richer prayer life. Here are a few hints that I have found helpful:

*1. Tell God just how you feel.*

You don't have to bring yourself into a particular state of feeling before you pray. Look at the prayers in the Bible: see how Job, David, Habakkuk, spoke to God. They brought Him their questions, their doubts, their concerns, their worries.

Think how free you can be with a close friend. "John, I feel terrible today." "Laura, I just can't understand how you could say that." "Did you really mean that?" You can be just as open with God. He's your best Friend.

*2. Be specific.*

Christians oftentimes pray so generally that they have no way of knowing if God has granted their requests. If we ask Him to "bless" Henry, what do we expect to happen? Why not petition God to help Henry find a job, or to quit smoking, or to overcome a bad temper, or to find a new experience in Christ?

Try keeping a prayer list. Write out names and specific requests for each. But keep your list private, a confidence shared by just God and you.

*3. Keep on asking.*

I am fully convinced that we quit too soon. We give up too early; we should keep on praying. Some prayers will be granted immediately (as for forgiveness of our sins), but others take much longer because they involve changing attitudes.

I may be the one whom God wants to change! Prayer will mold me, shape me into the divine will for me. I may find that something I've wanted badly isn't right for me after all. By praying enough I will come to realize that.

If we're praying for someone else, God can't simply change them unless they're willing to be changed. He can woo them by the Holy Spirit, but the process of change may be long—a year, 10 years, 40 years.

But claim God's promise. Keep on hoping. Keep on praying.

*May 5*

# ORGANIZING OR AGONIZING?

*For everyone who asks receives; he who seeks finds; and to him who knocks, the door will be opened. Matt. 7:8, NIV.*

We need to spend more time agonizing with God in prayer, and less time organizing. The great men and women of the past who shaped the Christian church invariably were people of prayer. How much we today need to discover the secret of their power!

As a teenager Ellen Harmon (later Ellen White) learned the effectiveness of intercessory prayer. She began to pray for a group of young friends, and to talk to them individually and in small groups. All except one were converted (*Testimonies*, vol. 1, p. 34).

Later she wrote: "God will make them [your words] a healing flood of heavenly influence, awakening conviction and desire, and Jesus will add His intercession to your prayers, and claim for the sinner the gift of the Holy Spirit, and pour it upon his soul" (*Sons and Daughters of God*, p. 274). And again: "I have been shown angels of God all ready to impart grace and power to those who feel their need of divine strength. But these heavenly messengers will not bestow blessings unless solicited. . . . Often have they waited in vain" (*Our High Calling*, p. 129).

Joe Engelkemier quotes a young pastor, the speaker at a Bible camp: "'After graduating from college, I spent my first year pastoring a small church. During that time only one person made a decision for Christ and baptism—and that individual came from a Bible study already in progress when I arrived. It seemed that I had almost nothing to show for a year's work.

"'I had gotten so busy that I neglected to pray. So I decided to spend 10 minutes a day in intercessory prayer for specific people.'

"There is no merit, Pastor Jim pointed out, in merely 'putting in time.' But as he took time, his prayers became more earnest. Soon 10 minutes passed very quickly, and he started spending more and more time on his knees in intercessory prayer. 'I began to notice a change in my ministry,' he told the delegates. 'The people I studied with began to respond. Lives changed; they made decisions. At the end of my second year I could look back on 13 baptisms'" ("Become a Mighty Petitioner," *Adventist Review*, Dec. 25, 1986).

*May 6*

# THE SET OF THE SAIL

*Enter through the narrow gate. For wide is the gate and broad is the road that leads to destruction, and many enter through it. Matt. 7:13, NIV.*

One ship drives east,
Another drives west,
By the selfsame winds that blow.
'Tis the set of the sail and not the gale
That determines the way they go.
—Ella Wheeler Wilcox

And from the same family one person grows into a strong Christian, while another leaves the church. All the prayers, all the efforts of godly parents, can't determine the destiny of the child. Each of us sets the sail of our life: we are free creatures, with the power to choose our ultimate destination.

So we should quit blaming someone else or some circumstance for what we are, for our failures, for our unrealized dreams. No, life isn't fair—some people get the breaks—but in the final analysis *we* set the sail that determines our port of call. In Shakespeare's play *Julius Caesar*, Cassius says: "The fault, dear Brutus, is not in our stars [that is, don't blame your horoscope!], but in ourselves, that we are underlings."

Which set does our sail have? Or do we even know?

Every now and then it's well to stop and consider where we're headed. The *direction* of our life is far more important than where we happen to be right now.

Do you think that a person who kills another in cold blood decided suddenly to do it? Or that the hardened criminal arrived at that state of mind overnight?

Neither do people slip away from Christ and His church because they one day decide, "I'm going to quit being a Christian today!"

Instead, they gradually drift away; they slide back—they become backsliders. They find themselves one day at a point that years before they thought could never be possible for them.

Let's take a moment to pause and consider the direction of our lives. Right now—am I on the broad way, or am I on the narrow road that leads to life?

The marvelous hope from the Scriptures is that *it's never too late!* Regardless of where we are, no matter in which direction we're headed, God can turn us around. All we have to do is to ask Him.

*O Lord of the narrow road, show me just now where I am, and where I'm going. And Lord, if I am in the broad way that leads to destruction, turn me round and point me home.*

*May 7*

# KNEE POWER

*If you then, who are evil, know how to give good gifts to your children, how much more will your Father who is in heaven give good things to those who ask him! Matt. 7:11, RSV.*

Recently I have been reading *The Kneeling Christian.* This little book was written by an unknown Christian and published in England by Marshall Pickering. In 1945 P. J. Zondervan obtained the rights to print and publish it in the United States, and since then it has gone through 56 printings with a circulation of more than 400,000 copies.

Although the author did not identify himself, he writes personally of his struggles and victories; so devotional is this book that it is better that he give no occasion to draw attention to himself.

"All real growth in the spiritual life—all victory over temptation, all confidence and peace in the presence of difficulties and dangers, all repose of spirit in times of great disappointment or loss, all habitual communion with God—depends upon the practice of secret prayer," writes this unknown Christian.

He goes on to say that the devil's great concern is to keep us from praying. He doesn't mind if we plunge into Christian labor, provided we don't pray. He doesn't fear even if we study the Bible—so long as we neglect prayer.

When we need prayer so much and God is so ready to answer, why do we pray so little? How can we find a richer, more constant life of communion with the Master?

The answer may be surprisingly simple: *why not ask the Lord to help us in our prayer life?*

One man I know wanted to rise early so he could spend time alone talking with God. Trouble was, he couldn't wake up. So what did he do? He asked God to help him by waking him early.

God did. He still does.

Now this friend advises that we each had better be ready to act on God's answer before we pray for His help!

Only the work accompanied by much prayer will accomplish lasting good, and it will endure forever. All fruitfulness in service, all labor that glorifies God, springs from the life of secret prayer.

Sometimes we look for big things—for mass revivals, for large public conversions. But give me a band of praying men and women, unitedly calling down God's Spirit for the conversion of hearts, for the renewing of His people. They are more important than money, talented singers, or famous preachers.

Today we can be part of such a band.

*May 8*

# HOW TO BECOME A CHRISTIAN

*Therefore everyone who hears these words of mine and puts them into practice is like a wise man who built his house on the rock. Matt. 7:24, NIV.*

*The first step* is to recognize that we are lost. For much of our lives we think that we are pretty good—oh, we may have a few faults and foibles, but all things considered, we are as good or better than the average.

But one day God through His Spirit speaks to us and says that all our righteousness is as "filthy rags"; that we must be "born again" (Isa. 64:6; John 3:3). And we begin to see ourselves as we *really* are. We see how far short of the divine standard we fall, how twisted and warped are our motives and desires, how much evil lurks within us.

*The next step* is to see Jesus. God has offered Him as our Saviour from sin. He sent Him to earth to die the death that was ours, that we might live the life that was His. "For God so loved the world, that he gave his only begotten Son, that whosoever believeth in him should not perish, but have everlasting life" (John 3:16).

He is our hope—now and eternally.

He is the door to new life.

He is the rock that will not fail.

Have you seen Jesus, your lovely Lord? Have you heard His sweet voice: "Come unto me, all ye that labour and are heavy laden, and I will give you rest. Take my yoke upon you, and learn of me; for I am meek and lowly in heart: and ye shall find rest unto your souls. For my yoke is easy, and my burden is light" (Matt. 11:28-30)?

*The third step* is to accept Jesus' invitation. Believe His words. Hand your life over to Him. Say, "Lord Jesus, I come to you. Take me, accept me just as I am. I need You. I cannot change myself. But You can, and right now I take You as Lord of my life and my Saviour from sin."

*The final step* is to believe that Jesus has answered your request. You may feel different, or you may not. How you feel doesn't really matter—you are dealing with the King of the universe, who keeps His word. He promised: "If we confess our sins, he is faithful and just to forgive us our sins, and to cleanse us from all unrighteousness" (1 John 1:9). You have confessed; He *has* forgiven. You *are* His. You *are* a new person in His love.

You have built on the Rock. And that Rock will never fail you.

*O God of our salvation, we look to You. We come to You. We place this day in Your hands—the hands nailed to Calvary's cross for us.*

*May 9*

# HOW TO REMAIN A CHRISTIAN

***The rain came down, the streams rose, and the winds blew and beat against that house; yet it did not fall, because it had its foundation on the rock. Matt. 7:25, NIV.***

To start is good; to finish is better. Many people accept Christ, but some do not stay Christians. Like the seed that fell on stony ground, they give up when trouble comes; or like the seed that fell among thorns, their experience in Christ is slowly choked out by the cares and pleasures of life.

Jesus is our best friend. Christianity is knowing Him; it's a transforming relationship. That relationship may become so deep, so intimate, that these words will be true: "If we consent, He will so identify Himself with our thoughts and aims, so blend our hearts and minds into conformity to His will, that when obeying Him we shall be but carrying out our own impulses" (*The Desire of Ages*, p. 668).

But like any relationship, our Christian experience isn't static —we're either drawing closer to Christ or moving apart from Him. How can we keep that precious friendship on track?

1. Spend time with Him. Friends have to be together to talk, to share. And we have to talk with Jesus—that's prayer. The more time we spend in prayer, not only talking but listening, the more our friendship with Him will deepen.

2. Make Him your first thought in the morning. As soon as you wake up, say, "Thank You, Lord, for giving me another day of life. I give myself to You for this day. Keep me in Your love and show me Your plan for me." Before you listen to the news, to music—especially to television!—talk with Jesus.

3. Study His Word. The Bible is Jesus' counsel to you, His love letter. Read it every day; read it quietly, alone; read it and apply it to yourself.

4. Tell someone about Jesus. The telling may not be in words; the life we live speaks more powerfully. Put yourself in the stream of the Spirit, ready to have God place you in just the right time and place to lend the helping hand or to speak the saving word.

By following these simple steps we build on the Rock. Our foundation will stand firm, no matter what storms may burst upon it.

*May 10*

# MOUNTAINS IN MATTHEW

***Then the eleven disciples went to Galilee, to the mountain where Jesus had told them to go. Matt. 28:16, NIV.***

Mountains seem to have a special place in the Gospel of Matthew. Only Matthew tells us that Jesus gave the famous sermon, the Magna Charta of the kingdom of heaven, on a mountain (Matt. 5:1). This was the Mount of Blessing, the Mount of Inauguration. In Matthew's Gospel, early on we see Jesus on a mountain.

The last picture of Jesus we find in this Gospel again has Him on a mountain. The Risen Lord, conqueror of death, commands His followers to go into all the world with the good news of the kingdom. His words come with *authority*: "All authority in heaven and on earth has been given to me" (Matt. 28:18, NIV). They ring also with a divine *imperative*: "Go . . . make disciples . . . baptizing them . . . teaching them." But they also throb with assurance: "And surely I am with you always, to the very end of the age" (verses 19, 20, NIV).

This is the Mount of Commissioning.

We find two other mountains mentioned by Matthew. Unlike the first two, these are mentioned also by other writers.

Late in Jesus' ministry He took Peter, James, and John apart to a "high mountain" (Matt. 17:1). There He was transformed before them, His face shining like the sun and His clothes becoming as white as light. Moses and Elijah talked with Him about His coming Passion. This scene was a foreshadowing of the cross and a preparation for it.

That was the Mount of Transfiguration.

One mountain remains—Calvary. "They came to a place called Golgotha (which means The Place of the Skull)" (Matt. 27:33). There He died—He who had healed the people by word and deed, He who was the Son of God.

Calvary's mournful mountain climb
There adoring at His feet
Mark that miracle of time
God's own sacrifice complete.
                    —James Montgomery
Today, let us go to the mountain with Jesus.

*May 11*

# THE LORD OF THE MISSION

***And as ye go, preach, saying, The kingdom of heaven is at hand. Matt. 10:7.***

The Great Teacher whose Sermon on the Mount will ring to the end of time is also Lord of the mission. He sent out His disciples to preach the same message He preached and to do the same deeds He did—healing the sick, raising the poor, the fallen, and the downcast. He still sends them out today.

March 16, 1988, Peter Knopper, a Seventh-day Adventist missionary from Australia, was shot by assailants lying in wait outside his home at Homu, in the highlands of Papua New Guinea. The shotgun blast at short range struck him in the head. His wife called for help—they got Peter in his car and they set out on the dark, slippery road to medical aid 90 minutes away. Mrs. Knopper held her husband close to her. But by the time they reached Goroka, Peter was dead.

He left three young children. He was only 32.

What about Peter Knopper's life—was it wasted? What about his death—was it meaningless?

138

From a worldly viewpoint, the answer to both questions must be yes. But not for the Christian. For us the ultimate value is not life—precious and beautiful though it is—but Jesus, our Saviour and Lord.

Peter Knopper directed the Adventist work in the Homu area, administering a fast-growing church of some 7,000 believers. He also directed the Homu Laymen's Training Institute and in the three years prior to his murder had helped train 400 lay members in Christian service.

He died at 32; but Peter's Lord lived only one year longer.

From its inception the Christian church was nurtured by sacrifice. Jesus' own followers—those to whom He gave the instruction on mission in the sermon of Matthew 10—followed in His train. James, brother of John, was first to go, beheaded by Herod Agrippa. Peter eventually was crucified, but upside down. But the more the enemies of the cross sought to snuff out the young faith, the more it flourished.

Peter Knopper did not die in vain. Nor does any person who casts his or her life upon the Lord of the mission live in vain.

*May 12*

# THE PURPOSE OF MY LIFE

*Heal the sick, cleanse the lepers, raise the dead, cast out devils: freely ye have received, freely give. Matt. 10:8.*

A dear friend describes the purpose of life this way—"to reduce the sum total of human misery in the world."

My wife and I sailed for India just three weeks after our marriage. We ended up staying for more than 15 years, with periodic breaks for furlough to our homeland. On one of those return visits someone asked us, "What's the use of trying to help those people in India? Any good you can do will be like a drop in the bucket."

True—a drop in the bucket. In fact, when you see the extent of human suffering and need in India, not even a drop!

But that isn't the point. God doesn't call us to help the whole world, but *our* world—the world where we live, the world of our street, of our family.

We don't have to go to India. We don't have to become a Mother Teresa, giving hope and love to the dying on the streets of Calcutta.

I am more and more convinced that what counts most for good are the *little deeds by the little people*—the acts of kindness and thoughtfulness, the unstudied courtesies, the works of grace and generosity that never make the evening news or the pages of the *Adventist Review*.

If we could but open our ears and hear—which means, if God could but open our ears—we would catch something of the still, sad music of humanity; of the secret, silent cry of woe hidden in hearts all around us.

One of the sharpest criticisms of us Christians by those who are hurting is that often we are so caught up in *our* blessings that we can't see those who are hurting. Too often the church is a lonely place for the divorced person, the single, the handicapped, and the aged.

Human misery isn't confined to India. And here is the sharpest cut of all—can we bear to receive it?—the misery may be within our own home. We may be so caught up in our work, our church, our reputation, that we fail to "hear" the silent language of our child or our spouse!

*O God of tender mercies, open my eyes today that I may see, my ears that I may hear. Make me sensitive to the cry of woe that I may, like the Lord of the mission, relieve the sum total of human misery.*

May 13

# THE MAN WHO WAS CONVERTED BY HIS BOOTS

***Whosoever therefore shall confess me before men, him will I confess also before my Father which is in heaven. But whosoever shall deny me before men, him will I also deny before my Father which is in heaven. Matt. 10:32, 33.***

Did you ever hear about the man who was converted by his boots?

It was the first night in Army camp. The raw recruits were settling in for blessed rest after a day of being shouted at, marched up and down in the rain and the mud, ordered here and there. As they undressed, they chatted about the day; someone attempted a few bars on a harmonica.

But one soldier was silent, contemplating what he would do. So far as he knew he was the only Christian in the long hut, and would he . . . ?

The talking slowly died; the music stopped. All eyes turned in one direction, where the Christian knelt by his bed.

Directly opposite, a burly fellow was in the act of pulling off his boots—heavy, muddy boots. He glanced up to see why the hut had suddenly become silent. Seeing the kneeling soldier, he let out an oath and flung his left boot, striking the Christian on the back.

The soldier went on praying.

The big fellow wrenched off his other boot and threw it with all his might. And his aim was good.

The soldier went on praying.

Soon the sergeant barked "Lights out!" and before long everyone was asleep. The next sound they heard was the bugle's reveille with its call to line up outside the hut. The soldiers scrambled to meet the roll call.

As the big fellow hurried to dress, he reached for his boots. With a stab of conscience he remembered the previous night's events and started across the hut.

But there at the foot of his bunk stood his boots. Only they weren't muddy any longer—someone had scraped them clean and polished them.

In time, the big guy became a close friend of the Christian. In time, he too became a Christian.

He was converted by his boots.

Or was it by someone else?

*May 14*

# A CUP OF COLD WATER

***And whosoever shall give to drink unto one of these little ones a cup of cold water only in the name of a disciple, verily I say unto you, he shall in no wise lose his reward. Matt. 10:42.***

God has helpers in the unlikeliest of places. Even in "heathen" lands or the cold, impersonal city streets He touches men and women and they become ministers to His followers in their time of need.

Some years ago our family was traveling by car from southern India to our home at Spicer Memorial College in Poona. We had been on vacation, but had had a series of problems with the old car we were driving. We were still some 250 miles from home and almost out of cash. And credit cards hadn't been introduced yet!

We drove at night to avoid the scorching sun (no air-conditioning!). But what we didn't know was that when we'd had the car serviced 400 miles down the road, the mechanic, in checking the oil in the differential, had failed to replace the plug.

In the middle of the night we heard a grinding sound from under the car. It woke the children and scared the parents.

We pulled off the road and spent a cramped night in the car, waiting for the dawn.

When morning came, we discovered we had broken down opposite a little car repair garage. The young man who ran it proved to be our "cup of cold water." He and I rode a bus to the nearest city, where we scoured the *chor bazaar* (literally, thieves' market) looking for a new differential. The most remarkable part of the incident was not merely the finding of a used differential for a 1948 Chevy, but getting the merchant to let us have it on credit! The young mechanic was a persuasive fellow who simply trusted our word to send him payment in due course.

That wasn't the last of our adventures on that trip, but at every point when we were absolutely helpless someone showed up to help.

When the books are opened and the great Judge of all hands down the verdicts, men and women from the unlikeliest of places will receive their reward. He who does not forget His followers will not forget their helpers.

*O Lord of the mission, may I today be not only a disciple but also a helper.*

*May 15*

# THE REST JESUS GIVES

*Come unto me, all ye that labour and are heavy laden, and I will give you rest. Matt. 11:28*.

When we take Jesus at His word, laying all our burdens at His feet, He keeps His promise. He gives us rest.

The rest that Jesus gives, however, isn't a state of passivity. It isn't the rest of the ignorant, the gullible, or the naive. The rest of Jesus is the peace that comes from finding the Center of existence. "Thou hast made us for Thyself," said Augustine, "and our hearts are restless until they find rest in Thee."

The Sabbath exemplifies that rest. Hebrews 4:9 tells us that our rest in Christ is a *sabbatismos*—a Sabbath-ish rest.

But the Sabbath may be busy. Jesus' Sabbaths often were. Notice that the verses immediately following our passage for today describe several Sabbath incidents.

In the first incident, the Pharisees accused Jesus' disciples of Sabbathbreaking because they plucked some heads of grain from a wheatfield and began to eat them. Jesus replied that "the Son of

Man is Lord of the Sabbath" (Matt. 12:8, NIV). He, not the Pharisees, would decide what was lawful and what was not.

Immediately afterward, Jesus went into a synagogue. A man with a shriveled hand was present, and the Pharisees, seeking a reason to accuse Jesus, asked Him, "Is it lawful to heal on the Sabbath?" (verse 10, NIV). But He replied that it is lawful to do good on the Sabbath, and He healed the man's hand.

The rest Jesus gives is peace in the midst of cares. It is the calm certainty of knowing He is with us, no matter how pressed with work we may be, no matter how hard we may have to work.

Jesus, Lord of the Sabbath, wants to be Lord of our lives—today and every day.

In Him—and Him only—we find rest unto our souls.

*May 16*

# CRYSTAL

*So they are no longer two, but one. Therefore what God has joined together, let man not separate. Matt. 19:6, NIV.*

I don't like to sit in the center seat on airplanes. My long legs never find quite enough room, and I get a feeling of being hemmed in. But one Sunday I sat next to Crystal, and she gave me one of the pleasantest trips ever.

"Must be a full plane," I mused to myself as I squeezed into seat E on Delta's Flight 585 from Portland, Maine, to Boston. The window seat was unoccupied—and inviting. But just before take-off, a man hurried on board with a little girl. He showed her her place. "Give Daddy a kiss," he said, and he was gone.

Crystal.

All of 5, perhaps 6. White dress with purple ribbons. A colored bow on one shoe. Long dark hair. Sad eyes. A little bag with dolls and books sticking out.

Crystal fastened her seat belt. Then she began to stuff her dolls under the belt as well.

"What's his name?" I asked, pointing to a pink doll.

"Panther." She held up the doll.

"Of course. The Pink Panther."

"I have some books, too." She opened up her bag. That's when I saw the name in large, uncertain block letters: CRYSTAL.

"Can you read, Crystal?"

"No. I'm too young."

By now the wheels were racing faster and faster and the engines were roaring and we were up in the sky.

"Look at the big lake down there—such a big lake," Crystal said.

"That's the ocean, Crystal."

So we talked about the ships down below and the clouds and how Crystal was on her way to Georgia, because every summer she came back to Maine to stay with her father. I read stories to her from her mouse book, and all too soon the wheels touched the runway at Boston's Logan Airport.

I gathered my coat and bag and began to make my way down the aisle. I looked back at a little girl in a pretty white dress with purple ribbons. The eyes were very sad. She waved.

Crystal.

Suddenly I felt angry. I felt angry that a little girl has to travel alone hundreds of miles every summer, angry that she sees her mother part of the year, her daddy another part. After meeting Crystal, I could readily become a crusader for children's rights.

Crystal didn't ask to come into this world. Crystal's *right* is a home where she can be loved by both parents and not have to shuttle back and forth alone.

Adventists, are you listening?

*May 17*

# BABES OR ADULTS?

***I thank thee, O Father, Lord of heaven and earth, because thou hast hid these things from the wise and prudent, and hast revealed them unto babes. Matt. 11:25.***

Does God want us to be spiritual babes or adults? How do we weave together the different strands of Scripture on this topic?

In Matthew's Gospel we find strong encouragement in favor of spiritual infancy. Today's text tells us "babes," rather than those who consider themselves mature and wise in religious matters, receive the divine revelation.

That, of course, was the case with the people of Jesus' time. The intelligentsia—the scribes, Pharisees, and Sadducees—largely rejected Him. Just a few, such as Nicodemus and Joseph of Arimathea, had eyes to recognize who He was. It was common folk—fishermen and farmers—who accepted Jesus as the Messiah.

Elsewhere in Matthew's Gospel Jesus says: "Except ye be converted, and become as little children, ye shall not enter into the kingdom of heaven" (Matt. 18:3). And He calls His disciples "little ones" (Matt. 10:42; 18:6).

144

Elsewhere, however, the Bible strongly encourages spiritual growth. Peter says: "Grow in grace, and in the knowledge of our Lord and Saviour Jesus Christ" (2 Peter 3:18). And in the book of Hebrews the early Christians are rebuked because they have failed to mature: "We have much to say about this, but it is hard to explain because you are slow to learn. In fact, though by this time you ought to be teachers, you need someone to teach you the elementary truths of God's word all over again. You need milk, not solid food! Anyone who lives on milk, being still an infant, is not acquainted with the teaching about righteousness. But solid food is for the mature, who by constant use have trained themselves to distinguish good from evil" (Heb. 5:11-14, NIV).

Which, then, is God's ideal for us—babes or maturity?

Perhaps there isn't a contradiction after all. God wants us to stay babes in some respects but not in others.

When we first came to Jesus, we came trusting, taking Him at His word, claiming His promise to forgive. We realized our weakness, our desperate need of Him. We should always have this attitude, no matter how long we remain Christians. We should be "babes" in our dependence on Him and childlike trust in His love and strength.

But while we maintain this attitude, God wants us to grow in grace. He designs that the power of the Spirit daily shall transform us more and more into the image of Christ.

*May 18*

# PERSPECTIVE

*Peter took him aside and began to rebuke him. "Never, Lord!" he said. "This shall never happen to you!" Jesus turned and said to Peter, "Get behind me, Satan! You are a stumbling block to me; you do not have in mind the things of God, but the things of men." Matt. 16:22, 23, NIV.*

As I found my place for a flight from Ontario in southern California to Dallas-Fort Worth, I noticed two little girls seated in the row immediately behind mine. The younger girl sat next to the window. She was probably about 4, and had braids and big dark eyes. Clutching a rag doll and holding her "security blanket" close to her face, she looked scared. The girl next to her, apparently her sister, was a few years older but only slightly more self-possessed. The girls were traveling alone; the flight attendants came by periodically to reassure them.

I smiled at the younger and, pointing to the doll, asked, "What's his name?" She lowered the blanket and was about to reply when the seriousness of her undertaking took over, and she quickly turned her head. I decided any conversation would have to wait awhile.

At last the pilot started the engines and we lumbered down the runway. Faster and faster the plane rolled, trembling with energy and excitement, and then we were flying through the air. Soon we were up above the houses and the trees, up among the clouds and looking down on mountains and deserts.

Then I heard the 4-year-old, her seriousness momentarily overcome, burst out: "Look! That's Africa down there!" We were just leaving California.

If we could see as God sees, we would have an entirely different perspective on reality. No longer would we fall into Peter's error of reasoning on a purely human basis, trusting our own views as to what God's will is.

Nor would we be like the young man who accompanied the prophet Elisha. When the young man saw the city where they were dwelling surrounded by soldiers who had been sent to arrest Elisha, he was scared. "Oh, my lord, what shall we do?" he wondered. "Don't be afraid," the prophet replied. "Those who are with us are more than those who are with them." Then the Lord opened the young man's eyes, and he saw the hills full of horses and chariots of fire (2 Kings 6:13-17, NIV).

How do we get a new perspective—God's perspective? Only by taking time with Him, listening to His voice through prayer and through His Word.

# THE PEOPLE OF NAZARETH

*And they were offended in him. But Jesus said unto them, A prophet is not without honour, save in his own country, and in his own house. Matt. 13:57.*

How could the people of Nazareth be so blind? They who could have claimed Jesus with pride as their native son—how could they have taken offense at His popularity in the rest of Galilee?

Was it because of the sermon He gave in their synagogue at the commencement of His ministry? They hadn't received it well, when He had claimed to be the fulfillment of Isaiah's prophecy in chapter 61:1-3, and especially as He had rebuked their skepticism.

In fact, the sermon had ended with attempted violence; those who came to worship that Sabbath were ready to kill Him! (see Luke 4:16-44).

They thought they knew all about this Jesus. Weren't His brothers and sisters still in the town? Hadn't Jesus grown up there among them? Why did He think He was so smart? He was setting Himself up as someone big—someone better than they. Well, *they* knew all about Him, and *they* weren't going to let Him parade before them with a swelled head.

So Jesus didn't spend much time in Nazareth. Matthew tells us that He did no miracle there because of His home folks' unbelief (Matt. 13:58). He simply withdrew; He made Capernaum rather than Nazareth home base during His work in Galilee.

It still happens—a prophet is not without honor except in his own country. Some of the world's leading artists have scant acclaim in their own village or country, or win grudging acceptance from the down-home people only after they have established a national or international reputation.

May God save us from the small-mindedness of the men of Nazareth! Their fault—envy, the desire to cut down to size—raises its green head even in the church. Anyone who would do anything, who seeks to be an agent of change for the advancement of the Lord's work, will meet opposition from the Nazareth mind-set. He may expect rumors, even accusations, from some small-minded individuals.

Years ago I learned this simple truth: someone else's success is not my failure. His advancement or promotion does not diminish me; so may I have the grace to congratulate him sincerely rather than feel as though he has robbed me of something.

*O Lord of the church, deliver me today from small-mindedness. May I be generous of others' success and humble in my own.*

*May 20*

# THE COST OF FOLLOWING JESUS—I

*And a certain scribe came, and said unto him, Master, I will follow thee whithersoever thou goest. And Jesus saith unto him, The foxes have holes, and the birds of the air have nests; but the Son of man hath not where to lay his head. Matt. 8:19, 20.*

Discipleship costs. While many people make a profession of Christianity, only the Lord knows those who are His. And He says: "Many be called, but few chosen" (Matt. 20:16).

A modern-day scandal of Christianity are the huge salaries and opulent living of some television evangelists in the United States. The American public was first dismayed then sickened by the revelations of the lifestyle of Jim and Tammy Bakker of the PTL ministry. Jimmy Swaggart, who built up a huge complex and an international TV network and who thundered against Bakker's sexual lapses, was himself caught in a moral fall. Oral Roberts, against the advice of leaders in Tulsa, Oklahoma, built a big new hospital, couldn't find patients for it, and went on the air with ridiculous public appeals for money, claiming that the Lord would take his life if he couldn't raise the millions of dollars needed.

How far have we come from the ministry of Jesus of Nazareth! As He traveled about Palestine, He didn't even know where He'd sleep at night. And sometimes He slept outside. No mansions with gold-plated bathroom finger, no private swimming pools, no air-conditioned doghouse for Him!

But it's easier to point the figure at such blatant denials of discipleship than to look at ourselves. The fact is, discipleship still costs. When any man or woman gets rich *from Christian ministry* (not from business ventures) he or she perpetrates a massive denial of the gospel.

Most of us aren't rich and never will be. Jesus' warning to the lawyer still touches us, however. Are we ready to suffer hardship for Christ? Are we fairweather followers, glad to be part of the acclaiming crowds but quick to fall away when these same crowds in their fickleness shout, "Crucify Him! Crucify Him!"?

To share a hovel with Jesus is better than a palace without Him. To sleep under the stars in His company is better and worth more than a Jacuzzi or a private golf course.

*May 21*

# THE COST OF FOLLOWING JESUS—II

*And another of his disciples said unto him, Lord, suffer me first to go and bury my father. But Jesus said unto him, Follow me; and let the dead bury their dead. Matt. 8:21, 22.*

Are not these words of the Master unnecessarily harsh? Shall we let our dear ones go to their rest without regard for their burial and proper leave-taking?

We need to remember that it was Jesus who proclaimed the moral law from Mount Sinai, and that law requires: "Honour thy father and thy mother: that thy days may be long upon the land which the Lord thy God giveth thee" (Ex. 20:12).

In another context Jesus rebuked the religious leaders of the Jews because they encouraged people to neglect the care of their parents. They taught that if a person dedicated his possessions to the Temple, he no longer had an obligation to provide for his needy parents out of his wealth. "Thus you nullify the word of God by your tradition that you have handed down," He said (Mark 7:13, NIV).

So whatever Jesus meant in His teaching about discipleship in Matthew 8:21, 22, He certainly didn't intend for us to forsake our parents in their need. Jesus provided for His mother as He hung upon the cross, and we as His followers likewise will show more care for our dear ones than do non-Christians.

Nor can we suggest that the dead in sins—that is, nonbelievers—should bury our dead. This would mean that we turn over the funeral arrangements to non-Christian relatives—an incredible idea!

What could Jesus have had in mind, then, by those cryptic words?

I think He is setting forth the priority of His kingdom. Jesus' call to discipleship is to take precedence over ties of family and home, over the associations and security of the hearth.

Notice that the man to whom Jesus spoke these words didn't say that his father already was dead. When Jesus called him to discipleship, he replied, in essence: "Not now, Jesus. Let me wait awhile." And that "awhile" might have entailed years.

When Jesus called Peter, Andrew, James, and John as they were mending their nets by the sea, they immediately rose up and followed. That is still the pattern for discipleship today.

Jesus comes first.

*May 22*

# THE COST OF FOLLOWING JESUS—III

***And when he was entered into a ship, his disciples followed him. Matt. 8:23.***

"Follow" is the operative word in discipleship. It binds together the various strands in the passage we have been contemplating for the past three days.

In Matthew 8:19, the lawyer presents himself to Jesus and says: "I will follow you wherever you go" (NIV). But Jesus tells him that discipleship means hardship.

In verse 21, another man comes and asks that he first be permitted to bury his father. Jesus replies: "Follow me, and let the dead bury their own dead" (verse 22, NIV). Jesus' call and His kingdom must take priority.

Now, in verse 23, Jesus gets into the boat and His disciples *"follow."* We are about to find out what happens to disciples.

Without warning, a furious storm sweeps over the lake. In fact, Matthew uses the Greek word *seismos,* corresponding to our "earthquake," to describe it. The disciples are terrified, but Jesus, exhausted from a heavy day, keeps sleeping!

Often our lives run a similar course. We set out in the Christian way, ready to follow Jesus wherever He leads. "I'll go where You want me to go, dear Lord, o'er mountain, or plain, or sea," our hearts sing. But suddenly we find ourselves caught up in problems and trials that threaten to engulf us.

Have you noticed how our day can change without warning? The morning that started so confidently collapses in a maelstrom of pressures, frustrations, insoluble questions. "Let him that thinketh he standeth take heed lest he fall" (1 Cor. 10:12).

And Jesus sleeps on.

But He is still the Master of ocean and earth and sky. Just as soon as we cry out to Him, "Lord, save us! We're going to drown!" He rebukes the wind and the waves, and a great calm settles over our lives.

To follow Jesus in the midst of cares—this is discipleship. To turn to Him in every test—this is discipleship. To know His power to rebuke the fearful heart and to calm the angry sea—this is discipleship.

*O Master of the sea, empower me today to follow You.*

*May 23*

# THE DRAGNET

**Again, the kingdom of heaven is like unto a net, that was cast into the sea, and gathered of every kind. Matt. 13:47.**

When I was a boy, I spent many hours by the seashore. A relative owned a dragnet, and often my brothers—all older than I—would organize a netting trip to the ocean.

We would carry the net out to sea in a rowboat, feed it into the water, and then wade ashore, hauling in the net by each end. Dragging the net up on the beach, we would stoop over the harvest of the sea.

As more and more of the net came from the water and only a few yards were left, excitement would mount. What strange sights, dredged from the ocean bed, would meet our eyes?

Indeed, we often found a strange and marvelous conglomeration of animal and vegetable life. Crabs and fish, shrimps and octopuses, slimy creatures and oozy leaflike streamers, along with sand, seaweed, and mundane objects such as an orange or a piece of wood—the dragnet gathered them all in.

For many years now I have been "catching" people instead of fish, but how like the harvest from the sea is the church of the living God. Adventist Christians come off no production line; they bear no common stamp to set them apart from the rest of humanity. They are Black, Brown, and White; they are rich, poor, and middle-class; they are laborers, professionals, and businesspeople; they are young, middle-aged, and old; they are female and male. And they come from every continent, from "every nation, and kindred, and tongue, and people."

We must jealously preserve this individuality. We are strong collectively as we are strong separately. Some Adventists emphasize one aspect of healthful living; some stress a particular facet of doctrine. This variety is good—as long as we refrain from a spirit of judgmentalism and pull together in the task God has assigned us.

My brothers and I used to sort out the good fish from the bad by the sea, but in the church that work is assigned to the angels, not to us. Jesus said at the end of the parable: "So shall it be at the end of the world: the angels shall come forth, and sever the wicked from among the just, and shall cast them into the furnace of fire: there shall be wailing and gnashing of teeth" (Matt. 13:49, 50).

In Revelation we read that waters are a symbol of "peoples, multitudes, nations and languages" (Rev. 17:15, NIV). The net of God's last message is dredging these waters. From them will emerge at last the people of God who will dwell with Him forever. That will be the glorious harvest of the sea.

*May 24*

# THE TEMPLE TAX

*But so that we may not offend them, go to the lake and throw out your line. Take the first fish you catch; open its mouth and you will find a four-drachma coin. Take it and give it to them for my tax and yours. Matt. 17:27, NIV.*

In the time of Jesus, every Jew was expected to pay a two-drachma tax for the support of the Temple. When Jesus and the disciples arrived one day in Capernaum, the tax-collectors asked Peter, "Doesn't your teacher pay the temple tax?"

"Yes, He does," Peter replied, quick to defend Jesus against any slander.

Once again Peter spoke before thinking. Later, Jesus pointed out that in fact He was exempt from the tax. He was One greater than the Temple (Matt. 12:6). One to whom all its services pointed.

Nevertheless, so as to avoid offense, Jesus told Peter to pay the tax. The first fish he caught in the lake would have a four-drachma coin in its mouth—payment for both Jesus and Peter.

Although Jesus was in the right, He chose not to make an issue of it. He did not see every situation in life as something He should fight for. He reserved His effort for what *really* counted—and for that He went to the death.

"So what is the lesson here for us and Peter? Simply this: *Be careful when you are right,* for there is something dangerous about being right.

"Being right can create a selfish sense of superiority. It can lead to righteously robed lawyers manipulating religious words and texts with their legalese. When being right is more important than being sensitive to human needs; when holding to right church policies is more important than people; when being right is more important than being righteous—then we have traded the good news of Jesus for the bad news of His enemies.

"Jesus was right! He was not obligated to pay the Temple tax. 'But so that we may not offend them,' He had Peter go and pay it. He chose not to hasten His trip to the cross by making an issue of something when it wasn't necessary. Jesus didn't sacrifice principle; *He simply avoided controversy.*

"So while we must not sacrifice principles of truth, we need not force controversy either. We must be careful when we are right. We have the right church, the right day of worship, the right diet, the right schools, and we believe the right things. But there is danger in being right. . . .

"It is one thing to believe right doctrine. It is another to allow right doctrine to be a wall, rather than a bridge, between us and others. It is one thing to be right. It is another to use 'rightness' as a ticket to superiority. There is nothing so obnoxious as a religious superiority complex.

"Be careful of the feeling of being right. The more you need to prove to others that you are right, the less your ability to prove your love to them. Being right in the theory is a long way from being right in the practice. Being right in the doctrine is a long way from being right in the life. Being right is a long way from being righteous" (Gordon Bietz, "The Danger of Being Right," *Adventist Review*, Jan. 8, 1987).

*May 25*

# BEWARE THE SPIRITUAL VACUUM!

*Then it goes and takes with it seven other spirits more wicked than itself, and they go in and live there. And the final condition of that man is worse than the first. Matt. 12:45, NIV.*

Nature, said the ancients, abhors a vacuum. That is true also for the spiritual life.

Matthew records a curious parable Jesus told. It's about an evil spirit that leaves a man and goes elsewhere. Eventually it comes back and finds the house unoccupied, swept clean and put in order. Then the evil spirit takes seven other spirits—even more wicked than itself—and they take up dwelling there. "And the final condition of that man is worse than the first," says Jesus.

There's no point in telling our children to turn off the TV unless we're prepared to help them find something else to do. And the church that instructs its young people not to go to the movies had better suggest or provide an interesting alternative. Simply to *condemn*, or to *take away* without providing a substitute, invites a condition that will be worse than the original.

Nonbelievers often look upon Christians as killjoys. The Australians have an interesting word—"wowsers." Originally it stood for "We only want social evils removed," but long since it passed into the language as a pejorative designation of Christians.

Sad to say, we often come across—to our own young people as well as to the world—as those who suck the fun out of life.

"Thou hast conquered, O pale Galilean.
The world has grown cold at Thy breath,"
wrote the poet Swinburne. He was absolutely wrong—Jesus *gives* joy and color to life; He raised men and women and boys and girls to fullness of joy.

We who profess His name often don't do as well. Probably Swinburne was seeing our Master through the defective lens of His followers.

Jesus' parable about the empty house applies individually also. It gives a foundation principle for changing habits. Whether we're trying to lose weight, fight alcohol, or be victorious over anger, we overcome evil with the good. "Something better" is our watchword.

# TAKING UP THE CROSS

*Then said Jesus unto his disciples, If any man will come after me, let him deny himself, and take up his cross, and follow me. Matt. 16:24.*

Saint Francis of Sales said, "To take up one's cross cannot mean anything else than that we should receive and suffer all the pains, contradictions, afflictions, and mortifications that happen to us." People still speak about the difficulties they have to bear—a physical ailment, a social hardship, a longstanding problem—as their cross.

But is my cross to be understood as a rheumatic back or a weak digestive tract? Is it even a nagging wife or husband or an unpleasant boss? No, indeed. Paul speaks about these sorts of problems, but he does not call them the cross. He referred to his physical affliction as a "thorn in the flesh" (2 Cor. 12:7ff), not as a cross.

What then does it mean to take up the cross?

First, the cross points to *conflict*. Between Jesus and the world there can be no quarter. The world despises the cross, as it always has and ever will. Now, most of us don't like conflict; we would rather have those "flowery beds of ease" that the poet sings about. But this saying reminds us that conflict is inevitable, if we are followers of Jesus the Christ. If there is no conflict, there are but two possibilities—either the world has ceased to be the world, having been won to the lordship of Jesus, or else the world has taken over the church.

"In the acceptance of the cross we are distinguished from the world, who love us not and ridicule our peculiarity," writes Ellen White. "Christ was hated by the world because He was not of the world. Can His followers expect to fare better than their Master?" (*Testimonies*, vol. 1, p. 525).

Second, the cross is *uncompromising*. The cross is radical: it stands for death. It calls us to cast ourselves totally upon the work of Christ. It humbles us, putting our pride in the dust, exalting only the Lord. This is why Paul says: "I am crucified with Christ:

nevertheless I live; yet not I, but Christ liveth in me: and the life which I now live in the flesh I live by the faith of the Son of God, who loved me, and gave himself for me" (Gal. 2:20).

# THIS ABOVE ALL

*For whosoever will save his life shall lose it: and whosoever will lose his life for my sake shall find it. For what is a man profited, if he shall gain the whole world, and lose his own soul? or what shall a man give in exchange for his soul? Matt. 16:25, 26.*

This passage points to three dimensions of genuine selfhood —confrontation, consecration, and concern.

*Confrontation.* The true self stands over against the false self. Jesus is about to go up to Jerusalem to lay down His life for the salvation of the world. For Him, Jersualem will be the place of suffering, betrayal, and rejection. But Peter opposes Him: "God forbid! This mustn't happen to You!"

For each one of us the confrontation continues. The true self constantly faces the possibility of the false self. Compromise, dishonesty, and cowardice mark that self—yes, and littleness and pettiness of spirit; and beyond that, baseness and grossness in the seemingly unlimited possibilities of the self for good or for evil.

Shakespeare, that incisive student of human nature and human dealings, saw well the nature of this confrontation. In Act I, scene 3, of *Hamlet,* Polonius says: "This above all: To thine own self be true, and it must follow, as the night the day, thou canst not then be false to any man."

*Consecration.* For some people, self-honesty requires that we set aside all presuppositions, lay aside the past, and start from ground zero.

But for the Christian, there is no desire to do so. Jesus Christ is our foundation, and we hold that only in Him can we find our true selves. We were made for God, and our hearts are restless until they find rest in Him.

Honesty does not equal repudiation of the past.

*Concern.* Jesus said: "Verily, verily, I say unto you, Except a corn of wheat fall into the ground and die, it abideth alone: but if it die, it bringeth forth much fruit" (John 12:24).

Some people think that finding your true self means always to be "agin the government." They are compulsive mavericks. Perhaps they confuse self-honesty with eccentricity. Christian selfhood is never an end in itself, but is always for the other. It issues in a life of giving, a life of concern. Its ideal is the Carpenter of Nazareth, who came not to be served but to serve, and to give His life a ransom for many. As He once gave His all for us, so now we give our all for others.

*May 28*

# CUT IT OFF!

*And if your eye causes you to sin, gouge it out and throw it away. It is better for you to enter life with one eye than to have two eyes and be thrown into the fire of hell. Matthew 18:9, NIV.*

These are radical words. And those that come immediately before are no less severe: Jesus calls His followers to cut off the hand or foot that causes us to sin.

Over the course of the centuries some Christians have done just that. Burdened with a sense of guilt, they have maimed themselves. One, the scholar Origen, who was born near the end of the second century and lived into the third, allegedly castrated himself in an endeavor to gain victory over sexual sin.

Did Jesus intend us to take these words literally? If He did, the churches should be full of people with one eye, one foot, or one hand!

But consider the ministry of Jesus: He spent His time making men and women whole—physically, emotionally, spiritually. He restored withered hands and crippled legs; He made the blind to see and the deaf to hear. He was the healer, not the maimer!

Nor did He call upon His followers to cut off their actual hands and feet or to gouge out their actual eyes. He didn't tell Peter to cut off his tongue because he denied Jesus, or Judas to cut off the hand that had taken the 30 pieces of betrayal silver.

By these radical words Jesus wants us to catch a sense of the seriousness of sin. He calls us to break with any habit, any practice, that is antithetical to our profession as Christians.

It's still true—what we do not overcome by Christ's indwelling strength overcomes us. One sin cherished will eventually neutralize all the power of the gospel, Ellen White tells us.

We each have cherished sins. Some are of the eye—perhaps magazines or books or TV programs or movies that dishonor Christ. Some are of the hand—practices that we know are wrong but that we rationalize. Some are of the foot—places we like to go, or that we refrain from going to, when we should.

Sin is a disease, but Jesus is the physician. Sin calls for radical treatment, but He is the divine surgeon. By His grace we shall be made whole.

# THE PRIVILEGE OF CHURCH MEMBERSHIP

*And I will give unto thee the keys of the kingdom of heaven: and whatsoever thou shalt bind on earth shall be bound in heaven: and whatsoever thou shalt loose on earth shall be loosed in heaven. Matt. 16:19.*

For increasing numbers of Christians today, the church is like a social club. Depending on how they feel on any given day, they may or may not show up. It's as though they decide whether to renew their membership for another year, or take a year off.

Some clubs are more demanding than the church. Members of the Rotary Club, for instance, are expected to attend the weekly meeting no matter where their travels may take them. A series of absences leads to automatic loss of the privilege of membership.

We Christians value the church all too lightly. Although each person must accept Christ individually, after that he no longer stands alone. He becomes part of something much bigger than himself—the church. So as Christians we have a corporate identity as well as an individual identity.

Scripture uses many metaphors to explain the nature of the church and the privilege of membership. The church is the body of Christ, a temple, a household, an army, a new race, a community, a family.

Ellen White also employs a host of graphic figures. The church is a case that contains God's jewels (*Testimonies*, vol. 6, p. 261). It is Christ's channel of communication (*The Acts of the Apostles*, p. 122), His fortress in a revolted world (*Medical Ministry*, p. 89), His representative on earth (*The Acts of the Apostles*, p. 122), the dearest object on earth to God (*Christ's Object Lessons*, p. 166), God's city of refuge (*The Acts of the Apostles*, pp. 9, 11), the theater of God's grace (*The Acts of the Apostles*, pp. 9, 12).

During the Middle Ages the church abused its high calling—it took Jesus' words in Matthew 16:18, 19 as warrant for high-handed treatment of monarch and common man. It was in this spirit that the German emperor Henry IV was kept waiting in the snows as the pope made a point of his authority. Ordinary men and women feared excommunication most of all, for it meant denial of burial in consecrated earth and so hope of everlasting life.

Our problems today are just the opposite. We want to denude the church of authority, turn it into a social center, make it subject to our whims.

But Jesus is still Lord of the church. It's still His body. We treat church membership lightly at our eternal peril.

*May 30*

# PROTECTING THE "LITTLE ONES"

*Woe unto the world because of offences! for it must needs be that offences come; but woe to that man by whom the offence cometh! Matt. 18:7.*

Nothing makes my blood boil so much as crimes against children. Yet such crimes happen every day in our sick society. Children are battered and bruised in body and psyche. Some will die; all will be maimed. And other adults drag children into the maw of their perverted sexual fantasies, sometimes within their own families, sometimes for profit.

The Master reserved His strongest words for such offenders. His words reach beyond child abuse and perversion, however. In the "little ones" He included those spiritually immature, His newly won disciples. They too need protection from those who would cause them to stumble.

Many years ago, as a young man growing up in Australia, I saw how Satan works to turn the "little ones" out of the straight path. A divisive movement arose, an offshoot. It attracted two types of people—disgruntled longtime members, and new Christians. The latter, sincere and zealous, lacked maturity. Some were drawn into the vortex of dissent, criticism of leadership, defiance of church structure.

After a while, the offshoot withered away. Many of those who had been attracted to it returned to the parent church. But some of the "little ones," embittered and disillusioned, did not come back.

I have observed the same pattern over the years. Every now and then a new movement arises. It centers in a charismatic leader and concentrates on the shortcomings of the church. While professing to preach Christ, it attacks His body. It eventually passes away, but some "little ones" lose their way because of it.

And so, while my blood boils when I read or hear about crimes against children, I also get angry when I see attacks on the church that weaken those who are new in the faith. God intends the church to be a haven, a home for His children—especially the little ones.

*Jesus, Lord of the church, help me today to build up Your people. Keep me from any word or act that would weaken Your body.*

# THE CALL OF THE KING

*The kingdom of heaven is like unto a certain king, which made a marriage for his son. Matt. 22:2.*

The empty can came flying through the door. It fell with a clatter among the bottles and empty beer containers. Two chickens pecked amid the debris.

Where was this? The Florida Keys, those islands in the sun fabled for their sparkling water and pristine charm. Jogging along a path, I had come upon a cluster of broken-down trailers and rough huts half hidden among the trees. As I passed one of these trailers, someone threw the empty can outside.

Now, opportunities certainly aren't equal in life. Some of us are born to a mansion; some of us have to settle for a trailer. But even if our lot is the latter, we can keep it clean; we can plant flowers; we can dispose of our garbage.

Jesus' kingdom lifts its citizens. I have seen dozens of lives raised, changed, transformed. During the 12 years I taught at Spicer College in India I saw dramatic growth. I saw young people from a far-off village (and there's nothing wrong with the village!) arrive on campus unsure of themselves, struggling to frame one sentence of correct English. Some of those students blossomed—they earned Ph.D. degrees, became leaders of the church and society. Some conduct radio and TV talk shows in the United States!

Eric B. Hare used to tell a story about a hermit and a king. The old hermit lived alone on the top of a mountain. Dirty and bedraggled, he slept on a heap of rags and subsisted on whatever scraps of food he could find.

But one day a man came galloping, galloping, up the mountain—it was the king! The poor old hermit felt so ashamed—of himself and of his dwelling, and because he had nothing to offer the king.

But the visit of the king changed the hermit's life. Because he expected his king to come back, he washed his clothes, shaved his face, cleaned out the spring, prepared a bed, and gathered food to welcome the king.

The kingdom calls us. More than this, the King calls us. He calls us away from the garbage heap and up to the mountain. He who now rules in our hearts is coming back for us!

*June 1*

# STRONG SON OF GOD

***The beginning of the gospel of Jesus Christ, the Son of God. Mark 1:1.***

June has come! Throughout the northern climes summer is bursting out all over—lawns grow lush, robins sing merrily, warm mellow days stretch out into evenings of cool relaxation.

During this month we will concentrate on the Gospel of Mark. As the sun surges higher in the heavens (and as it falls to its lowest point in the Southern Hemisphere) we will be probing this shortest of the four biblical portraits.

And we will see day by day different aspects of the strong Son of God. Matthew's story of Jesus focuses on the Master's teachings, but Mark's concentrates on His actions. Throughout this book Jesus is continually *doing*—casting out demons, healing the sick, calming the tempest. He is powerful, He is mighty; His acts evoke wonder. "Who is this?" we hear the people say. "What sort of new teaching is this?" they ask in amazement.

Mark's emphasis on Jesus' deeds reminds us that God does not call us to a life of contemplation. He calls us to active service, to involvement in the pain and sickness of humanity. "Faith without works is dead," James tells us (James 2:20). And four times in the book of Revelation God says: "I know your works" (Rev. 2:19; 3:1, 8, 15). He knows and records our deeds—good and bad. He knows what we have done as well as what we might have done. "To him that knoweth to do good, and doeth it not, to him it is sin" (James 4:17).

Recently I have been reading *City of Joy*, by Dominique Lapiene. It's an amazing, moving book. The "city of joy" is a suburb of Calcutta—an overcrowded, stinking place lacking elementary sanitary and health facilities; a place where the city's artisans too poor to afford better quarters live in tiny huts alongside lepers and vermin. Through June's scorching heat they live together; through the monsoon's storms and floods, when the drains overflow and the putrid waters lap into the rough dwellings, they live together.

Into this morass came a man—a Christian priest. By dwelling there, by working there, by *doing* there, he gradually brought hope and healing. One man made the difference.

*O God of the summer, God of the winter, long ago one Man made the difference. The strong Son of God changed the world and wrought salvation. Make me strong in His strength that I too may make a difference in my world.*

# LIVING WITH THE PLAGUE

*And there came a leper to him, beseeching him, and kneeling down to him, and saying unto him, If thou wilt, thou canst make me clean. Mark 1:40.*

Recently I attended a seminar on AIDS hosted by the U.S. Centers for Disease Control, based in Atlanta, Georgia. The center, which is responsible for tracking patterns of disease, is the source of the grim statistics on AIDS that alerted the West to the enormity of the pain and the problem of this modern plague.

The most moving episode in the two-day meeting, which was provided at government expense for editors, involved a middle-aged couple telling of their son's death from AIDS. Patients with AIDS die terrible deaths—emaciated, discolored, disfigured. In the case of this boy, the worst pain was the social rejection. In the hospital where he lay dying, nurses refused to answer his call for a drink of water. They left his food tray outside the door of the room. He was shunned—cut off, isolated, unclean.

Victims of any new plague suffer the same sort of rejection. When the Black Death decimated the population of Europe 600 years ago, when the influenza epidemic ravaged the world following World War I, those afflicted and their families faced not only the trauma of the disease but ostracism from neighbors and friends.

The lepers of Jesus' day knew that rejection. "Of all diseases known in the East the leprosy was most dreaded. Its incurable and contagious character, and its horrible effect upon its victims, filled the bravest with fear. Among the Jews it was regarded as a judgment on account of sin, and hence was called 'the stroke,' 'the finger of God.' Deep-rooted, ineradicable, deadly, it was looked upon as a symbol of sin. . . . Away from his friends and his kindred, the leper must bear the curse of his malady. He was obliged to publish his own calamity, to rend his garments, and sound the alarm, warning all to flee from his contaminating presence" (*The Desire of Ages*, p. 262).

Sound like AIDS? Yes—in almost every point.

But Jesus did not shun the leper. He reached out and touched him, and healed him.

Nor should we shun people with AIDS today. Instead of joining the mass hysteria, we should accept AIDS victims in the love and spirit of Jesus, bringing hope to the hopeless.

*June 3*

# CLEANSING FROM DEFILEMENT

*And Jesus, moved with compassion, put forth his hand, and touched him, and saith unto him, I will; be thou clean. Mark 1:41.*

Jesus broke the law. By touching the leper, He defiled Himself—the law required that He wash His clothes and bathe with water; He would be unclean until the evening (Lev. 15:7). Although Jesus commanded the leper whom He had just healed to offer the sacrifices required for cleansing (see Lev. 14:1-32), He did not abide by the same law's provision.

This wasn't the only time that Jesus disregarded the ceremonial law. When He was on the way to Jairus' house, a woman with a problem of bleeding came up behind Him in the crowd and touched Him (Mark 5:22-29). Because of her discharge she also was unclean according to the Levitical law, and by touching Jesus she made Him unclean. But as before, Jesus shrugged off the law's demands.

Have you ever wondered why we as Christians no longer feel bound by those laws of defilement and purification? According to them, any woman who is menstruating should be separated from the congregation—she shouldn't come to church! Likewise a man who has a discharge in the night, or a woman who has recently given birth. Nowhere in the New Testament do we find an abrogation of the ceremonial laws, but Christians don't observe them. Why?

Because of Jesus. He is the ultimately pure One, the One in whose presence defilement vanishes and death flees away. He could touch the leper or the woman with the hemorrhage and not be polluted because He is not only the author of the Old Testament laws but their fulfillment.

Defilement is still a problem—for us. No, not ceremonial defilement associated with menstruation or childbirth or bleeding. Our problem is something much worse. We are morally defiled; we are stained and polluted in our minds, desires, and motives.

But Jesus offers cleansing. "If we confess our sins, he is faithful and just to forgive us our sins, and to cleanse us from all unrighteousness" (1 John 1:9).

"In laying His hand upon the leper, Jesus received no defilement. His touch imparted life-giving power. The leprosy was cleansed. Thus it is with the leprosy of sin—deep-rooted, deadly, and impossible to be cleansed by human power. . . . Whoever will fall at His feet, saying in faith, 'Lord, if thou wilt, thou canst make me clean,' shall hear the answer, 'I will; be thou made clean' (Matt. 8:2, 3, RV)" (*The Desire of Ages*, p. 266).

*June 4*

# WHERE HAVE ALL THE HEROES GONE?

*People were overwhelmed with amazement. "He has done everything well," they said. "He even makes the deaf hear and the mute speak." Mark 7:37, NIV.*

We live in the age of the anti-hero. People have become cynical of leadership at all levels and in every sphere—government, business, the police, even the clergy.

The media is relentless in sniffing out a whiff of scandal. Once the press covered up the indiscretions and moral lapses of presidents; now they revel in them. The result? The public has become ready to believe the worst. We *expect* rumors to be true.

The heroes have gone. Those men and women who loomed larger than life, who could be held up as role models to the youth—they have fallen. They've been shown to have feet of clay.

But thank God we still have a Hero!

Where have all the heroes gone?
Those men of courage, wealth, and fame?
It seems like only yesterday
That neon lights displayed their name.
We held in awe their stand for right,
Applauded when they stood so tall,
And cheered them as they fought the wrong,
Assured that they would never fall!
But then, as idols often do,
They disappoint us, let us down,

And frantically we search to find
Another king to wear our crown.
And then one day with weary heart
We turn our gaze to Calvary,
And there, beholding, change our mind
Of what a hero ought to be!
—Gloria Wilde

*June 5*

# BATTLING DEMONIC FORCES

*Just then a man in their synagogue who was possessed by an evil spirit cried out, "What do you want with us, Jesus of Nazareth? Have you come to destroy us? I know who you are—the Holy One of God!" Mark 1:23, 24, NIV.*

Have you noticed how often in the Gospels Jesus confronted demonic powers? Mark in particular records these battles—it's as though the hosts of darkness assembled their might in an effort to thwart the mission of the Son of God.

In the wilderness after the baptism, Satan in person tempted Jesus. Defeated, he withdrew for a time, but his emissaries were never far from the Master. The rude interruption of Jesus' teaching in the synagogue that Sabbath morning was reminder enough!

Although few men and women recognized Jesus for who He was—only after a couple years would Peter articulate the great confession, "You are the Christ, the Son of the living God" (Matt. 16:16, NIV)—the demons knew. The powers of evil marshaled to find a way to defeat Him.

In modern times belief in Satan and his minions has greatly diminished. What was formerly attributed to evil spirits is now explained away by psychology. Satan is banished to the realm of superstition or jests.

But evil remains a frightening reality. Our vaunted twentieth century, which has seen such a cloudburst in knowledge and technology, also has brought the bloodiest wars and the most monstrous crimes in the history of the human race. Men and women have become skilled in evil. They haven't just acted like animals—their behavior would be an insult to the animals!

The human mind—marvelous ground for beautiful and noble deeds, or for greed and lust! The checkered history of our times demands an adjective commensurate with its evil—demonic. If the devil no longer exists, someone or something else is carrying on with full force the schemes of his satanic majesty!

"Our struggle is not against flesh and blood, but against the rulers, against the authorities, against the powers of this dark world and against the spiritual forces of evil in the heavenly realms" (Eph. 6:12, NIV).

And those forces are gathering—gathering for the climax of the age just as they did at Jesus' first coming. We may expect to see not only increasing lawlessness and diabolical deeds, but also spiritistic phenomena—miracles, communication with the dead, predictions from the world of the occult.

At such a time as this Jesus will be our strength. He who defeated the hosts of darkness—first in heaven, then on earth—is still the mighty Conqueror. In Him we too shall overcome.

*June 6*

# PETER'S MOTHER-IN-LAW

*But Simon's wife's mother lay sick of a fever, and anon they tell him of her. And he came and took her by the hand, and lifted her up; and immediately the fever left her, and she ministered unto them. Mark 1:30, 31.*

She is the only mother-in-law mentioned in the New Testament. Even then we don't know her name, and the Scriptures give only two verses to her. But those two verses speak to Christian mothers-in-law for all time.

Mothers-in-law have a difficult role to fill. If they exert themselves they run the risk of being thought meddlers. If they stand back they can be thought of as uncaring. With marriage, the balance of relationships and responsibilities changes, and the mother-in-law may find herself feeling on the outside.

I'm not sure what it would be like to have Peter as a son-in-law. Impulsive, quick to make promises he couldn't keep, used to taking charge—he probably was both an inspiration and a trial, lovable and frustrating.

And now she is sick—in bed with a fever. That's not where we usually find mothers-in-law. Mothers-in-law are in the kitchen, helping with the food preparations, or washing or ironing. Mothers-in-law are active, busy. They don't get sick, or if they do they keep on working. They go to bed only when everyone has left, when the work is finished.

So Peter's mother-in-law was really sick. Even mothers-in-law can get so sick they have to go to bed. The fever was raging; she was too weak to get up to welcome the honored guest.

But the Guest came to her. As soon as He heard about her sickness, Jesus went to her bedside. He took her by the hand, and helped her up. And the fever left her.

The strong Son of God, who banished Satan in the desert and cast out demons in the synagogue—the fever could not stay in His presence. The Healer, the Life-giver—sickness and death fled when He drew near.

Jesus still draws near to mothers-in-law. He still takes them by the hand, and helps them up. They stand on their feet again, and carry on.

"And she began to wait on them." Mothers-in-law have learned to take second place, to let the spotlight fall on others. They are content to serve quietly.

No, we don't know her name. Scripture gives only two verses to her. But Jesus knows, notices, cares.

*June 7*

# THE SECRET OF HIS POWER

*And in the morning, rising up a great while before day, he went out, and departed into a solitary place, and there prayed. Mark 1:35.*

No one ever lived like Jesus, because no one ever prayed like Him. If we would learn the secret of His abiding trust in the Father, of that life of unbroken communion with God and unswerving adherence to the divine will, we will find it in the place of quiet prayer.

"In a life wholly devoted to the good of others, the Saviour found it necessary to withdraw from the thoroughfares of travel and from the throng that followed Him day after day," writes Ellen White. "As one with us, a sharer in our needs and weaknesses, He was wholly dependent upon God, and in the secret place of prayer He sought divine strength, that He might go forth braced for duty and trial. . . . Through continual communion He received life from God, that He might impart life to the world. His experience is to be ours" (*The Desire of Ages*, pp. 362, 363).

When I entered the ministry, my first assignment was to be dean of boys and Bible teacher at Vincent Hill School, a boarding academy on a spot cut from the Himalayas in northern India. At an elevation of nearly 7,000 feet, we lived where the clouds formed—it was a rugged, beautiful place. In those days my wife and I were exceedingly busy—I taught a full load of classes, was in charge of the boys (they ranged in age from 8 to 18), and supervised two of their work details. We lived in a corner of the boys' dormitory and were always with them—classes, play, work, worship, town trips. In fact, my wife and I went many months before we had our first weekend away from the dormitory.

How did the Lord hold our lives together during those packed days and nights? We were young—that helped. But more than that, I found a secret place of prayer, a quiet grove in the woods, a trysting place known to no one but God and me. I would go there when I could find a break, just to be quiet, alone with God.

Those woods are gone now—cut away by timber hunters—and the school long since has been sold. But that quiet place of prayer will always be with me.

The old saying still holds true: Much prayer, much power; little prayer, little power; no prayer, no power. Only the work consecrated by communion with God will last—and it will last forever.

*June 8*

# RAISING THE ROOF

*Since they could not get him to Jesus because of the crowd, they made an opening in the roof above Jesus and, after digging through it, lowered the mat the paralyzed man was lying on. Mark 2:4, NIV.*

This story of the paralyzed man lowered through the roof (Mark 2:1-13) is one of the most delightful, even humorous, incidents of Jesus' ministry. At its close the people say, "We have never seen anything like this!" (verse 12, NIV), and neither have I.

The room was crowded, bodies pressed one against another; even the doorway was choked. Outside, heads bobbed up and down to see what was happening inside. And inside it was hot and stuffy; the teachers of the law were feeling decidedly uncomfortable. They weren't used to being pushed and shoved and having to fight for a few square inches of floor space.

Now, what's happening? Why are bits of debris falling from the ceiling? What sort of man is this Jesus, who has such followers and submits to such undignified surroundings? What's that noise above? Oh no! Don't tell me! They're tearing the roof off!

And down into that overcrowded room comes a bed, with a man lying on it! Since no one wanted the bed to land on him, they pressed back even closer together, making a place on the floor for the newcomer—a paralytic, of all people!

His was a desperate act, the paralytic's. So was the act of the four men who had carried him—they literally tore the place apart to get to Jesus.

Deeds like this offend the religious establishment, those institutional leaders whose humbug and pretense must have every *i* dotted and every *t* crossed, whose God cannot be shaken out of the routine they have established for Him.

They are offended as the bishop of Bristol was offended by John Wesley's preaching about the Holy Spirit: "To pretend to extraordinary revelations from the Holy Ghost is a horrid thing, a very horrid thing."

They are offended as Amaziah, the paid puppet priest of Bethel, was offended by the preaching of the rugged prophet Amos: "Go back south," he said. "Do your prophesying there; go anywhere, but get out of Bethel. Don't you realize that this is the king's court? We don't do that sort of thing here!" (Amos 7:12, 13, paraphrased).

But the kingdom of heaven has come, and the violent take it by force (Matt. 11:12). People tear off the roof to get to Jesus, and He welcomes them home.

Oh, that we might be shaken out of our stuffiness and lethargy and be energized with the presence of the kingdom!

*June 9*

# POWER TO FORGIVE

***But that ye may know that the Son of man hath power on earth to forgive sins, (he saith to the sick of the palsy,) I say unto thee, Arise, and take up thy bed, and go thy way into thine house. Mark 2:10, 11.***

Have you wondered about Jesus' question—"Which is easier: to say . . . , 'Your sins are forgiven' or to say, 'Get up take your mat and walk'?" (Mark 2:9, NIV).

We would probably think that it's easier to heal than to forgive, but Jesus' reasoning demands just the opposite. If forgiving were more difficult than healing, then Jesus' healing the paralytic would still leave unproved His claim to forgive. Jesus did the more difficult—healing—to show that He could do the easier—forgiving.

Of course, He did so because of the doubts of the religious leaders who were present. Although they hadn't uttered a word, He discerned their thoughts. They had been silently reasoning: *So He says He can forgive sins. That's an easy claim to make, because no one can check it out! Only God knows if He has that*

168

*power. Let Him do something that we can see, that we can test.* For them, "easier" meant something that couldn't be established one way or the other.

In fact, the power to heal is the same as the power to forgive (see *The Desire of Ages*, p. 270). Both involve making people whole—the one physically, the other spiritually.

And Jesus, author of life, brought immediate wholeness. He not only cared for people's pain and distress; He also gave the assurance of reconciliation with God.

That was a startling idea to the rabbis.

Some Christians need that good news today. They go through life in a cloud of self-doubt, always wondering if their sin has been *really* dealt with by Jesus.

But it has! Just as surely as the paralytic received the power to stand up and walk as a whole man, so we who have confessed our sins in Jesus' name have received the power of new life. We already are whole—we are new men and women.

My sin—O the bliss of the glorious thought!
My sin—not in part but the whole,
Is nailed to His cross and I bear it no more;
Praise the Lord, praise the Lord, O my soul!
    —Horatio P. Spafford

# THE CAT AND THE GRACKLE

**He did not say anything to them without using a parable. But when he was alone with his own disciples, he explained everything. Mark 4:34, NIV.**

Jesus, the master teller of parables, often drew from everyday things to convey His teachings. Here is the story of the cat and the grackle, which we observed when we lived in Berrien Springs, Michigan. Our daughter, Julie, is the teller.

The cat was a mighty hunter, lord of the yard and nearby fields. With gleaming white hair and golden tail, the cat looked regal, aristocratic.

The cat was usually a benevolent ruler. However, if you were small and easily eaten (a field mouse or rabbit), the cat became fangs, claws, and danger. The birds eyed him at a distance, chiding him but always wary.

The cat roamed his kingdom by night and slept much of the day. He returned home each sunrise to lovingly leave for us a remnant of his kill—ears, maybe a tail, or feathers—on the front porch. All he expected in return from us was a bowl of milk and a place in the sun for his nap.

But one morning at dawn we found him mewing weakly on the front porch. He had blood on his fur, and his dignity was in tatters. With torn ear, cuts, and scratches, he could barely limp.

For days he lay in the sun. Every step to the bowl of milk and the pills provided by the veterinarian was an effort. The mighty hunter had fallen.

This gave the grackle the opportunity it wanted. Each day it grew bolder, taunting the sick king, mocking him first from a nearby branch, then swooping closer and closer. He laughed at the cat, dared the cat, challenged the cat.

The sick king never moved. Occasionally his fur would twitch as the grackle screamed into his ear, or a shudder would run the length of his body. Only his eyes showed the irritation and frustration that the grackle inflicted.

Day after day the cat lay in the sun, occasionally moving ponderously to the milk bowl. Day by day the grackle grew bolder.

One day when we returned home we found the cat purring to meet us. He walked stiffly but confidently. The glazed look had gone from his eye—did it have a gleam?

And the grackle had gone also. On the front porch we found a heap of blue-green feathers.

Jesus sometimes left His parables unexplained. However, if you would like some suggestions for the story of the cat and the grackle, look up 1 Corinthians 10:12 and 1 Peter 5:8.

*June 11*

# THE PERSONS JESUS CHOSE

***And he goeth up into a mountain, and calleth unto him whom he would: and they came unto him. Mark 3:13.***

To:
   Jesus, Son of Joseph
   Woodcrafters Carpenter Shop
   Nazareth 25922
From:
   Jordan Management
   Consultants
   Jerusalem 20544
Dear Sir:

Thank You for submitting the résumés of the 12 men You have picked for management positions in Your new organization. All of them have now taken our battery of tests, and we have not only run the results through our computer but also arranged personal interviews for each of them with our psychologist and vocational aptitude consultant. The profiles of all tests are included, and You will want to study each of them carefully.

As a part of our service and for Your guidance, we make some general comments, much as an auditor will include some general statements. This is given as a result of staff consultation and comes without any additional fee.

It is the staff opinion that most of Your nominees are lacking in background, education, and vocational aptitude for the type of enterprise You are undertaking. They do not have the team concept. We would recommend that You continue Your search for persons of experience in managerial ability and proven capability.

Simon Peter is emotionally unstable and given to fits of temper. Andrew has absolutely no leadership qualities. The sons of Zebedee, James and John, place personal interests above company loyalty. Thomas demonstrates a questioning attitude that would tend to undermine morale.

We feel that it is our duty to tell You that Matthew has been blacklisted by the Greater Jerusalem Better Business Bureau. James, the son of Alphaeus, and Thaddaeus definitely have radical leanings, and they both registered a high score on the manic-depressive scale.

One of the candidates, however, shows great potential. He is a man of ability and resourcefulness, meets people well, has a keen business mind, and has contacts in high places. He is highly motivated, ambitious, and responsible. We recommend Judas Iscariot as Your controller and right-hand man. All the other profiles are self-explanatory.

We wish You every success in Your new venture.
Sincerely Yours,
Jordan Management Consultants

---

This letter is reprinted by permission from the *Baptist Messenger,* September 27, 1984.

# TWELVE TO CHANGE THE WORLD

*And he ordained twelve, that they should be with him, and that he might send them forth to preach, And to have power to heal sicknesses, and to cast out devils. Mark 3:14, 15.*

When God wanted to change the world, He chose people. He entrusted the most important task in the world to human beings. Do we think we can improve on God?

The computer is revolutionizing society. Writers can buy software that will check their spelling, correct their grammar, throw an instant thesaurus on the screen. But these aids don't produce good writing, any more than a new hoe and rake grow a beautiful garden. Good writing comes from a good writer, not from a computer (Shakespeare isn't in danger!).

When Chrysler Corporation was in deep financial trouble in the early eighties—trouble so deep that economists despaired for its survival—the United States government came to the rescue by providing massive loans. The company eventually turned around —but not principally because of the government's financial under-girding. One man at the helm, Lee Iacocca, saved Chrysler.

The greatest want of the world isn't more dollars or more programs or more education. It's people—men and women.

"The greatest want of the world is the want of men—men who will not be bought or sold, men who in their inmost souls are true and honest, men who do not fear to call sin by its right name, men whose conscience is as true to duty as the needle to the pole, men who will stand for the right though the heavens fall" (*Education*, p. 57).

And they are the greatest want of the church, also. Anciently, 12 men changed the world (and one of them was a bad apple in the barrel). They can do it in our day.

What about those 12—were they people of outstanding gifts, standouts in the crowds?

No. But they were men God could use. They were earnest, dedicated. They loved Christ. They lived for His mission. And so they accomplished much.

That's still the way God changes the world.

*O Master of the mission, make me a person You can use to change the world. Help me to learn that Your work goes forward as silently as the dawn, as quietly as the stars of heaven. Wherever You put me today may I glorify Your name.*

# DOGS EAT THE CRUMBS

*"Yes, Lord," she replied, "but even the dogs under the table eat the children's crumbs." Mark 7:28, NIV.*

Jesus was traveling outside His native Galilee, journeying near Tyre. He sought to keep a low profile, but a woman, mother of a little girl possessed by a demon, sought Him out.

Consider how great was her faith:

*She believed despite the barriers of ethnic pride.* The Jews had a superior, condescending attitude toward other nations. In their sight, God had divided the world into Jew and Gentile. Converts to Judaism had to undergo a long process before they could be accepted into the congregation. And this woman, this Greek born in Syrian Phoenicia, wasn't even a convert.

*She believed despite the barriers of gender.* A morning prayer of the rabbis went like this: "I thank Thee, Lord, that I am not born a Gentile, a slave, or a woman." Even in Jewish society women had second-class status—they were chattels who could be divorced at the whim of their husbands.

An apocryphal writing from the second century, the so-called Gospel of Thomas, perpetuates this denigration of women. In it we find Jesus telling women that they must become men in order to enter the kingdom of heaven!

*She believed despite the apparent rejection of Jesus.* The Master seemed to turn a cold shoulder to her pleas for help. "First let the children eat all they want," He said, "for it is not right to take the children's bread and toss it to their dogs" (Mark 7:27). "Dogs"! That attitude was just what she might have expected.

But the woman persisted. She clung to the Master in faith; she refused to give up.

Something in Jesus' manner surely encouraged her. Although the words sounded harsh, faith heard the tone of love and pity in His voice. And faith persisted until it gained the victory.

Jesus, in fact, was teaching the disciples a lesson. He reacted just as they—and the Jews—would react to this foreign woman. He revealed their prejudices by playing their role.

But dogs eat the crumbs, and sometimes dogs appreciate them more than the children who sit at the table.

# A DEAD GIRL AND A SICK WOMAN

*He took her by the hand and said to her, "Talitha koum!" (which means, "Little girl, I say to you, get up!").* **Mark 5:41, NIV.**

In Mark 5:22-43, we read about a double miracle of Jesus, a miracle within a miracle. The main plot centers on a little girl, daughter of Jairus. Most of the Jewish religious leaders had scant regard for Jesus, and Jairus was one of the synagogue rulers. But now his daughter, the light of his eyes, was desperately ill. In his extremity Jairus cast aside prejudice and begged Jesus to come heal her.

But Jesus' progress to Jairus' home was interrupted. An anonymous woman came up in the crowd and touched his garment. Hers was no ordinary touch: it too was a cry of desperation. For years this woman had been subject to bleeding—bleeding that defied the efforts of the physicians, drained her strength and emptied her purse.

She touched Jesus in faith ("If I just touch his clothes I will be healed" [verse 28, NIV]), and she was healed. But Jesus knew what had happened, and called her aside from the crowd. He made a public example of her faith.

All this delayed Him, and now a message came from Jairus' home—it was too late, the girl had died. As Jairus broke down Jesus reassured him, "Don't be afraid; just believe."

When they arrived at the home, He saw a commotion—crying, wailing, the professional mourners already taking over. They ridiculed Jesus' statement that the little girl wasn't dead, only asleep.

But He put them all out, and taking with Him Jairus and his wife, and Peter, James, and John, He went to the girl's room. How still she lay—the stillness of death! But the Life-giver took her hand and commanded, "Little girl, time to get up!"

And at once she stood up!

Two miracles, one telescoped within the other. Two miracles, so very different. Or are they?

Notice how the number 12 ties together these stories: the older woman had suffered from bleeding for 12 years (verse 25); Jairus' daughter is 12 years old. The first stands at the end of her biological cycle, the second at the beginning. The first represents womanhood at its close, the second at its beginning.

And for both, Jesus is the Healer, the Life-giver, the Raiser of women to fullness of life.

# TOUCH HIS GARMENT

*And he said unto her, Daughter, thy faith hath made thee whole; go in peace, and be whole of thy plague. Mark 5:34.*

Every miracle of healing by Jesus, the strong Son of God, opens a window in our salvation. Over and over the Gospel writers use the same word, *sozo*, for healing of the body and healing of the soul. For Jesus makes men and women *whole*—He is the author of life.

"Money cannot buy it, intellect cannot grasp it, power cannot command it; but to all who will accept it God's glorious grace is freely given. But men may feel their need, and, renouncing all self-dependence, accept salvation as a gift. Those who enter heaven will not scale its walls by their own righteousness, nor will its gates be opened to them for costly offerings of gold or silver; but they will gain an entrance to the many mansions of the Father's house through the merits of the cross of Christ" (*Sons and Daughters of God*, p. 233).

"If I but touch his clothes, I will be healed," the woman with the 12-year bleeding said to herself. She came behind in the crowd, pressed forward, and, unnoticed, touched Jesus' cloak. And she was made whole.

We too may touch and be healed. The Life-giver isn't present in person to banish our bodily aches and scourges, but He is just as real today. Jesus is alive—and we may know the power of His life.

Our only recommendation is our need. Every person who feels the need of help from outside himself, every man or woman who renounces self-sufficiency and leans wholly on the merits of Jesus, everyone who comes and touches in simple faith—every such soul finds wholeness.

And listen! Jesus makes us whole not just once, but over and over. He provides new life not just at our conversion but every moment that we reach out to touch His garment. We touch Him in life's throng and press, and we are whole again.

Today we may touch Him and be made whole. When we are broken, when we feel a failure, when we struggle with pain and scourges that have devastated us for years, we may reach out and touch His garment.

# THE SHINING MOUNTAIN

*Then Jesus beholding him loved him, and said unto him, One thing thou lackest: go thy way, sell whatsoever thou hast, and give to the poor, and thou shalt have treasure in heaven: and come, take up the cross, and follow me. Mark 10:21.*

He is youth embodied, this young man who comes running to Jesus. He is the shining mountain, the dream, the potentiality, the future. He comes bursting with opportunities.

How *enthusiastic* he is! No dignified carriage befitting status. No concern for social niceties. He wants to meet Jesus, and he *will* meet Him. That's all that matters. He arrives at a gallop, catching his breath as he speaks.

How *polite* he is! He falls on his knees before the Galilean. His first words show the deep respect in which he holds Jesus: "Good teacher . . ."

How *talented* he is! Although but a youth, he already carries heavy responsibilities. No squandering of his wealth, no careless playboy activities for him. He is serious; he has learned to wear the yoke of service in his youth.

How *earnest* he is! One concern fills his being—the religious quest. "What must I do to inherit eternal life?" he asks the Master.

"Jesus looked at him and loved him" (Mark 10:21, NIV).

He looks at every young man and loves him, at every young woman and loves her. Jesus has big hopes for every young person. He sees the shining mountain, the dream, the potentiality, the future.

A marvelous story—at the beginning. A sad story—at the close. The rich young ruler didn't run away. He slunk away.

Jesus had given him a glimpse of the person he might be—but also what it would cost. The rich young man caught that glimpse —but turned away from the cost.

To each of us, as the poet says, there opens a way, and ways, and a way. But which one will we choose?

Today we will make that choice again—inevitably we will make it. Whether we are a housewife or the president of the General Conference, we will make it. Will we be big or will we be petty? Noble or base? The high road or the low?

*O Lord of the morning, I commit myself into Your hands. In every situation of the new day give me grace to choose the better way, the way of Your kingdom.*

# THE ANGRY CHRIST

*He looked around at them in anger and, deeply distressed at their stubborn hearts, said to the man, "Stretch out your hand." He stretched it out, and his hand was completely restored. Mark 3:5, NIV.*

What happened to the gentle Jesus, meek and mild? Isn't anger a sin?

No—at least, not all anger. Sometimes it's a sin *not* to be angry! When we see the poor and the weak treated unjustly and we don't get angry, that's a sin.

When we hear God's name dragged into the dust and don't feel moved, that's a sin.

When we meet people tearing apart the church and don't get angry, that's a sin.

Most often, we get angry because somebody steps on our pride or because we don't get our own way. Our supersensitive ego always looks out for number one, always wants the best for itself; and it pouts and fumes when life isn't served up on a silver platter.

Jesus got angry because men of religion were making religion a sham. Under the guise of superior piety they stalked the footsteps of Jesus, notepads at the ready to record every word, compiling a list of accusations. Their religion was so ingrown and rulebound that they couldn't see the raw human need before them in the person of the man with a withered hand—they could only see an opportunity to trap Jesus for "Sabbathbreaking."

This wasn't the only occasion when Jesus got angry. Religious pride and hypocrisy called forth divine wrath within Him. His most scathing rebukes—and He could be cutting when the situation demanded it—fell on the scribes and Pharisees for the games they played in the name of God.

He got angry too when He saw God's house of worship turned into a bazaar. He made a whip out of cords, turned over the tables, drove the money changers and the merchants outside. "To those who sold doves he said, 'Get these out of here! How dare you turn my Father's house into a market!' " (John 2:16, NIV).

For many Christians today, our fault may be less a fiery temper than our inability to get angry for a righteous cause. We have become so complacent, so peace-loving, that "anything goes" without moving us.

Perhaps we need a dose of the anger of the Lord Jesus.

# THE CRY OF A TORTURED SOUL

*He shouted at the top of his voice, "What do you want with me, Jesus, Son of the Most High God? Swear to God that you won't torture me!" Mark 5:7, NIV.*

He had had enough of torture. His body, slashed with stones and bleeding and bruised from chains and fetters, housed a tormented mind. No wonder he cried out, "Swear to God that you won't torture me!"

When your body is wracked with pain, when the circuits of your mind have arced out, when society has rejected you and hunts you down because you are a madman, a wild man of the tombs and the mountains, existence becomes torture. The metronome of life swings its relentless beat of pain and the sudden coming of another person on the scene, even Jesus, means only more torture.

Tortured souls walk the streets of our cities. They have no address; they have no home. The government has Social Security checks made out for them, but since they have no address the government doesn't know where to send them, or if perchance they receive their checks they fall easy prey to street thugs. Some of these suffering people once were housed in hospitals, but under "enlightened" welfare programs they have been cast upon the streets.

The street is hard. The street is ice-cold in December. Only a hostel (if there's still a vacancy) or a heating grate in the sidewalk offers hope.

How shall we modern followers of Christ—we who are well-fed, clothed, and in our right minds—react to the cry of these tortured souls?

Members of the Belvedere SDA Church in Atlanta, Georgia, were shocked one wintry Sabbath morning to see police carry the body of a man from the woods near their church. He had frozen during the night.

Members rallied to build an extension for the church, put in showers, buy a truck. They organized a pickup service for the homeless on Atlanta's streets, developed a food supply in cooperation with local supermarkets. On winter nights homeless now find a shelter, food, warmth, and a chance to start over. Even the children get involved—every Friday they pin messages of encouragement to the lockers for the homeless.

A far cry from Gadara?

Yes. But maybe not. The Son of God has set us free; now we seek to extend that freedom to others.

# RELIGION BEGINS AT HOME

*Howbeit Jesus suffered him not, but saith unto him, Go home to thy friends, and tell them how great things the Lord hath done for thee, and hath had compassion on thee. Mark 5:19.*

It often seems hardest to share our faith with those who are closest to us. We feel more comfortable talking about our religion with a neighbor or even a total stranger than with a brother or sister. Why?

Because accepting Jesus threatens the network of relationships that the family has built up. Religion—heart religion—is deeply personal and arouses powerful emotions in both the new Christian and other family members who have not said yes to Christ. Sibling rivalry, perhaps long dormant, rises up. Brothers, sisters, parents may feel as though the convert—in a manner that they can sense but not articulate—has abandoned them, or at least weakened his ties of blood.

Jesus recognized that His call inevitably would strain family ties and sometimes sever them. He said: "Do not suppose that I have come to bring peace to the earth. I did not come to bring peace, but a sword. For I have come to turn 'a man against his father, a daughter against her mother, a daughter-in-law against her mother-in-law—a man's enemies will be the members of his own household' " (Matt. 10:34-36, NIV).

Yet religion begins at home. Every Christian has various spheres of influence, but the first circle is home.

The demon-possessed man whom Jesus had just healed begged to accompany Him. Jesus told him, "Go home!"

What about those of us who have the blessing of a Christian home? What does this text tell parents?

That we should tell our family members *what Jesus has done for us*. We mustn't take for granted that they already know.

I am a minister of the gospel. I have preached thousands of sermons. I have told audiences large and small how much the Lord has done for me.

My children have heard me preach publicly many times. But that doesn't meet the need of Jesus' admonition in Mark 5:19. I

179

must tell my children personally, tell them in the context of the family, tell them in words that come from the heart to the heart.

We have too much "canned" religion. We need to get back to basics—which is testifying to one another how much the Lord has done for us, how He has had mercy on us.

And that sort of religion begins at home.

*June 20*

# BEWARE THE CROWD!

*And from Jerusalem, and from Idumaea, and from beyond Jordan; and they about Tyre and Sidon, a great multitude, when they had heard what great things he did, came unto him. Mark 3:8.*

Throughout Mark's Gospel the crowds follow Jesus. They come to Him from town and village, from Judea and outside, from Jerusalem and Tyre. They press upon Him as He teaches by the lake, so He has to teach from a boat (Mark 4:1). They jam a home He enters, and even break up the roof (Mark 2:1-4). Eventually Jesus no longer enters a town openly, but still the people find out His lonely places and come to Him (Mark 1:45).

But the crowd is fickle. The crowd that hung upon His every deed and word in Galilee would turn against Him in Jerusalem. Some of those who shouted "Hosanna!" and "Blessed is he who comes in the name of the Lord!" (Mark 11:9, NIV) on Palm Sunday would chant "Crucify him! Crucify him!" on Good Friday.

Crowds become mobs. Cool reason gives way to passion. Mobs lynch. Mobs crucify.

If we follow the crowd, we will acclaim Jesus one day but crucify Him the next. Religion at times is popular (whoever heard a presidential candidate mock God?), but popular religion has no place for a cross.

"We should not wish to invent something to make a cross; but if God presents to us a cross, we should cheerfully bear it," writes Ellen White. "In the acceptance of the cross we are distinguished from the world, who love us not and ridicule our peculiarity. Christ was hated by the world because He was not of the world. Can His followers expect to fare better than their Master? If we pass along without receiving censure or frowns from the world we may be alarmed, for it is our conformity to the world which makes us so much like them that there is nothing to arouse their enmity or malice; there is no collision of spirits" (*Testimonies*, vol. 1, p. 525).

Throughout history the men and women who have shaped events have been prepared to stand alone. They have been confident enough of their convictions to march to a different drummer, letting the crowd go on its way without them. Thoreau in jail. Churchill banished to England's political wilderness. Florence Nightingale with her lamp.

And Jesus, Man of Calvary.

*June 21*

# MEN AS TREES WALKING

*And he looked up, and said, I see men as trees, walking. Mark 8:24.*

By any reckoning this is a strange miracle. Jesus has come to Bethsaida, a little town on Lake Galilee, home for Philip, Andrew, and Peter (John 1:44). Some people bring a blind man to Jesus, begging Him to touch him. Jesus takes the blind man by the hand and leads him outside the village. He spits on the man's eyes and puts His hands on him.

So far the story follows a predictable pattern. Mark doesn't tell us why Jesus didn't heal the man in Bethsaida itself, but presumably Jesus was trying to avoid the popular acclaim that His miracles was attracting. Nor does His spitting on the man's eyes mark a departure—He acted similarly on at least two other occasions (Mark 7:33; John 9:6), reinforcing faith by using a physical medium.

Now, however, we meet two startling differences. After Jesus has touched the man, He asks him if he sees anything. That is a "first" among Jesus' many miracles—everywhere else Jesus simply commands and healing follows immediately.

Further, the man isn't fully healed! He looks up and sees the vague forms of people, but they are blurry like trees. The miracle is only half baked.

Once more Jesus puts His hands on the man's eyes. He doesn't ask him anything now—the man's sight is wholly restored.

What are we to make of this two-stage miracle, unique among the Gospel stories? Didn't Jesus have quite enough power the first time around—did He have power sufficient to restore only partial sight? Did Jesus Himself doubt (after His first attempt) that the healing had been successful?

Or could the explanation be just the opposite—that the blind man's lack of faith hampered the free flow of Jesus' healing power? Do we see here a ready but doubting soul whose faith progresses

181

as we watch? Unlike others, he doesn't cry out for Jesus—someone else brings him. Unlike at other times, Jesus doesn't speak the healing word on the spot—He leads him aside, and then puts His hands on the blind eyes. The Master is dealing gently with him, not rebuking but guiding him from doubt to faith and from darkness to light.

Do you see men as trees walking? Sometimes I do. I believe in Jesus, profess Him, preach Him, write about Him. But sometimes my trust is feeble and I clog up the channel of His power.

But He leads me by the hand, deals gently with me, and leads me on to faith and light.

*June 22*

# THE QUIET PLACE

*Then, because so many people were coming and going that they did not even have a chance to eat, he said to them, "Come with me by yourselves to a quiet place and get some rest." Mark 6:31, NIV.*

When we are too busy to eat, we are too busy.

A curse of our late-twentieth-century lifestyle is the way we eat on the run. We crush our food rather than chew it; we shovel it down, talking all the while, our minds anxious about business and work. If eating is a mark of advanced civilization, then fast-food joints highlight the decline and fall of our society! In this respect the Europeans, with their outdoor cafés and relaxed dining, leave Americans in the dust.

The disciples of Jesus were too busy even to eat. They had become caught up in a round of duties, ministering to people, doing good. Their fault was the fault of conscientious Christians today—the tendency to overwork, to think that we are indispensable, that we must be constantly engaged in activity.

But activity isn't necessarily action. We need to set our priorities straight.

"In the estimation of the rabbis it was the sum of religion to be always in a bustle of activity. They depended upon some outward performance to show their superior piety. Thus they separated their souls from God, and built themselves up in self-sufficiency. The same dangers still exist. As activity increases and men become successful in doing any work for God, there is danger of trusting to human plans and methods. There is a tendency to pray less, and to have less faith. Like the disciples, we are in danger of losing sight of our dependence on God, and seeking to make a savior of our activity. We need to look constantly to Jesus, realizing that it is His power which does the work. While we are to labor earnestly for the salvation of the lost, we must also take time for meditation, for prayer, and for the study of the word of God. Only the work accomplished with much prayer, and sanctified by the merit of Christ, will in the end prove to have been efficient for good" (*The Desire of Ages*, p. 362).

Jesus puts our priorities straight. By taking time to be quiet, to be still long enough that our mind can get away from its anxious quest to accomplish our tasks, we can hear His voice setting our house in order.

God meant food to be enjoyed—to be chewed, not crushed on the run. And He provides spiritual food the same way.

*June 23*

# A TREASURE OF LESSONS

*And when he had taken the five loaves and the two fishes, he looked up to heaven, and blessed, and brake the loaves, and gave them to his disciples to set before them; and the two fishes divided he among them all. Mark 6:41.*

"The simple food passed round by the hand of the disciples contained a whole treasure of lessons," comments Ellen White on Jesus' miracle of feeding the 5,000 (*The Desire of Ages*, pp. 366, 367). Here are some from that precious horde:

1. *The simplicity of the fare Jesus provided.* Here is the Creator of the universe at work, feeding a crowd of hungry humans. He could have made caviar; He gave them fish. He could have created croissants; He provided barley bread.

But never were bread and fish as tasty! Plain, simple, wholesome food, well cooked and well served, still satisfies the most.

2. *Jesus cares for all the needs of His children.* He who fed the multitude on the mountainside long ago still provides even for the robins and the sparrows. Every good thing comes from His hand—and the best of all is His presence. "Never will I leave you; never will I forsake you," He promises (Heb. 13:5, NIV).

We are complete in Him. "My God shall supply all your need according to his riches in glory by Christ Jesus" (Phil. 4:19).

3. *God calls us to cooperate with Him.* Jesus performed the miracle of multiplying the loaves and the fish, but the disciples first brought the five and the two to Him; the disciples also distributed the food to the crowd. Jesus didn't create the banquet on a zero base, nor did He put it in the mouths of the people.

4. *Gather up the fragments*. He who had infinite resources at His right hand told the disciples to pick up the fragments, that nothing should be lost.

When Rajneesh, the guru of Antelope, Oregon, was at the height of his popularity, he owned more than 60 Rolls Royces! For him, religion meant *getting*. What a contrast with the Son of God, who left heaven for us! As He lived to impart life to others, so are we to feed His fragments to men and women today.

*June 24*

# THE RELUCTANT KING

*And straightway he constrained his disciples to get into the ship, and to go to the other side before unto Bethsaida, while he sent away the people. Mark 6:45.*

After a hearty meal, guests rise up and bless the host. And when the host has created the food for them, multiplying five loaves and two fish to feed thousands, they are ready to entertain dreams of grandeur.

This peasant from Nazareth—could He be the long-awaited Deliverer? Could He really be the Messiah, and we failed to recognize Him? If He can provide food for so many, His armies won't lack provisions. Nor need any soldier be afraid, because He can heal the wounded and even raise the dead to life. He will lead the nation to liberation from the despised Roman occupying forces. We will be free!

Interesting—Jesus had given transparent evidence of His divinity. He had healed thousands; His word had brought peace, forgiveness, and hope; people had found new life in Him; His character was without spot or blemish. The men of Galilee had seen it all, but still they doubted. They couldn't get beyond His humble origins, His unpretentious bearing, His gentle approach. Only when their bellies were full, filled by the food He provided, were they to acclaim him king.

Scripture tells us that Jesus "made" His disciples get into the boat and leave. The language of the text is strong—the Master *compelled* them to be on their way. They too had been caught up in the spirit of the crowd. They applauded the mass movement to crown Jesus. Jesus as king? Great, and they would be the chief officers in the Messiah's government.

But Jesus said no. Firmly, decisively, He dismissed the crowd and ordered the disciples to take the boat at once. He turned aside their arguments, poured cold water on their enthusiasm.

It was a turning point. That mountain in Galilee was the high point of the Saviour's popularity, the moment when events came together for a mass movement, a people's uprising. But the king refused the crown, and expectations would never reach that zenith again. His followers would gradually melt away, until one day, on Calvary's hill, He would be totally alone.

Jesus chose the cross that day, chose it when the crown was but a grasp away.

And so must we.

# THE FAMILY CONNECTION

*And he looked round about on them which sat about him, and said, Behold my mother and my brethren! For whosoever shall do the will of God, the same is my brother, and my sister, and mother. Mark 3:34, 35.*

A few years ago I visited the state penitentiary in Nashville, Tennessee. It's a grim, forbidding, castlelike structure, where men convicted of murder and other crimes are confined under maximum security, some awaiting execution. Drugs, homosexual rape, and killings are common.

Yet Seventh-day Adventists have a church inside the prison walls. Started by Conn Arnold when he was youth director for the Kentucky-Tennessee Conference, the church now meets under the direction of laypeople from the Nashville First Seventh-day Adventist Church.

Because my visit was arranged on short notice, only about 20 inmates, instead of the usual 70 or so, could attend. We gathered in a stark, windowless room; we had exactly one hour for the meeting.

The prisoners wanted to talk, to ask questions. After about 40 minutes a tall, lean man who had been looking at me intently spoke up.

"Mr. Johnsson, I've wanted to meet someone like you for a long time. I first met Conn, and he was different from anyone I'd ever met. Then Doug [one of the church elders] came along, and he somehow was different also, somehow like Conn. I used to wonder to myself: What is it about them? I used to wonder, if a Seventh-day Adventist came from somewhere else—from California, say, or New York—would he have this same sort of difference?

185

"And now I've met you today. You've come from a long way away, from Washington, D.C. You're different from Conn and Doug, and yet somehow you're just the same."

He paused. His eyes looked straight into mine. And I felt both proud and humble. He had paid me one of the greatest compliments I had ever received.

The family connection—although skin, people, faces, are different, we are connected to one another. We are brothers and sisters of Jesus.

What a family!

*June 26*

# THE GIVER

*And wherever he went—into villages, towns or countryside—they placed the sick in the marketplaces. They begged him to let them touch even the edge of his cloak, and all who touched him were healed. Mark 6:56, NIV.*

Jesus lived to bless others. His life was a constant outflowing of mercy and compassion. Imagine! After He had passed through a village, not one person remained sick, not one cry of pain could be heard. If Jesus were here today, He'd put hospitals and funeral parlors out of business.

But it all seems so far away, so remote from us—His ministry of unceasing love. What can we do today?

Greg was about to turn 16. For two years he hadn't received a birthday present—his mother was struggling to bring up Greg and his young sister, Linda, on her own. But at last she had gathered together money this year. Greg would enjoy a gift.

Greg, however, had a different idea. He'd noticed the look on Linda's face every time the kids rode by on their bicycles. Linda simply sat on the porch and watched. She had no bicycle, and there was no money for her to get one.

So Greg went to his mother and said: "Mom, for my present this year let's put the money into a bicycle for Linda." Mother and son bought the bicycle, and Greg stayed up late assembling it. On his birthday he received his gift—a bicycle for Linda!

It was hard to tell who was happier that day, Linda riding her new bicycle up and down the street, or Greg as he watched her.

The path of everyday living can be bathed in beauty as the Master's love awakens our hearts. Regardless of age, we may bless others. Our lives may be an unbroken paean of praise to God.

And that is the greatest power for change, for the transformation of society today. More than money, education, power, or title, *lives* make a difference.

*O divine Redeemer, lead me this day in the path of Your unselfish life. May I too live to bless others.*

# THE CLEAN AND THE UNCLEAN

*He went on: "What comes out of a man is what makes him 'unclean.' " Mark 7:20, NIV.*

The Pharisees were sticklers for cleanliness. For them, cleanliness wasn't just next to godliness—it *was* godliness.

Mark tells us about their scruples in chapter 7, verses 1-4. When they came from the marketplace, they wouldn't touch a piece of food unless they first went through a ceremonial washing. Tradition had laid out its forms in detail: "The washing here referred to was strictly ritualistic, not sanitary. This rite is said to have consisted of pouring a small quantity of water upon the fingers and palm of first one hand and then the other with the hand tilted so that the water ran from the palm to the wrist, but no farther (all the time care being taken lest the water run back into the palm), and then alternately rubbing one hand with the palm of the other hand. The minimum amount of water prescribed was that which could be contained in one and a half egg shells" *(The SDA Bible Commentary*, vol. 5, p. 622).

No wonder Jesus thundered against such trivializing of religion. He refused to abide by the traditional rules for cleansing, and also encouraged His disciples to ignore them. When the Pharisees and lawyers accused the disciples of setting aside the law, Jesus replied: "You have let go of the commands of God and are holding on to the traditions of men" (verse 8, NIV).

Later, Jesus explained the true difference between the clean and the unclean: "What comes out of a man is what makes him 'unclean.' For from within, out of men's hearts, come evil thoughts, sexual immorality, theft, murder, adultery, greed" (verses 20, 21, NIV).

Of course, people today wouldn't fall into such distorted thinking as the Pharisees. Or would they?

Americans have a passion for cleanliness. The bathroom has become the stellar attraction in new homes—large, elaborate, costly (and may come equipped with TV and telephone!). We spend billions annually on shampoos, lotions, perfumes, deodorants, powders, and potions designed to make us feel clean and to look clean to others. We despise "ring around the collar" and a waft of body odor.

But out of our washed and rinsed and scrubbed and Jacuzzied bodies come the same things that Jesus rebuked in the Pharisees. A beautiful, clean mouth, flossed and waterpicked, utters hate, pride, selfishness, lust.

Would that we'd spend as much time on cleaning up the inner man as we devote to the outer!

*June 28*

# BARTIMAEUS

*And Jesus answered and said unto him, What wilt thou that I should do unto thee? The blind man said unto him, Lord, that I might receive my sight. Mark 10:51.*

How long had he sat there begging? When every day is night because you are blind and you never see the sun come up and go down or the leaves falling or the snow, one day blends into the next until another year has come and passed. All you know is that you are still alone and that life consists in finding your spot by the Jericho road and crying out for alms from the people who walk by, day after day, day after day.

One day Bartimaeus, the blind beggar of Jericho, hears the sound of many feet. Who is it? Has the governor arrived on an official visit? A religious procession? But he'd have known about that already.

Someone tells him: "Jesus of Nazareth is passing by" (Luke 18:37, NIV). *Jesus of Nazareth! The healer from the north! They say He has fed a crowd of thousands from only five loaves and two fish. They say that when He speaks, even the storm subsides. They say He can raise the dead. They say—He can open eyes even blind from birth!*

"Jesus, Son of David, have mercy on me!" (verse 38, NIV). *On* me, *on poor blind Bartimaeus. If you gave blind people sight in Galilee, do it in Jericho—and do it for* me!

"Be quiet, old man!" "Hold your tongue!" "Sit down and shut up!"

But louder now, insistently, plaintively: "Son of David, have mercy on *me*!" (verse 39, NIV).

And above the voices rebuking him, another, sweet, compassionate: "Call him."

Bartimaeus casts off the rags in which he wraps himself and pushes toward that inviting voice. Grudgingly the people let him through.

"What do you want me to do for you?" It's that voice again.

"Lord, I want to see."

"Receive your sight; your faith has healed you" (verse 41, 42, NIV).

And immediately Bartimaeus receives his sight and follows Jesus along the road.

*O Master, we sit alone in our rags, but pass by just now and call us to Yourself. For we cry to You, "Jesus, Son of David, have mercy on me."*

June 29

# CHRIST OF THE COMMON MAN

*And the common people heard him gladly. Mark 12:37.*

The twentieth century is the era of the common man. Man in his individuality, his uniqueness, his essential humanity; man in himself regardless of bloodline or title or race—this is one of the crowning social movements of our time, be it still poorly achieved.

Whereas 200 years ago composers such as Bach and Mozart sought patrons of the arts and dedicated their music to kings and counts, in our day Aaron Copland writes *Fanfare for the Common Man*.

In fact, all along Jesus has been Christ of the common man. In His own day the common people heard Him gladly, while Pharisees and Sadducees ignored Him or looked upon Him with contempt. After His death and resurrection the new faith in His name spread far and fast—but largely among ordinary people. "Brothers, think of what you were when you were called," wrote Paul to the Corinthian believers. "Not many of you were wise by human standards; not many were influential; not many were of noble birth" (1 Cor. 1:26, NIV). Christianity spread rapidly among the slaves—just as it did in modern times.

The pagan Celsus, a critic of Christ and the early Christians, tried to disparage Jesus. He is the strangest of teachers, said Celsus, "for . . . while all the others cry, 'Come unto me, you who are clean and worthy,' this singular master calls, 'Come to me, you who are down and beaten by life'; and so, being taken at his word by these impossible people, he is followed about by the rag, tag, and bobtail of humanity trailing behind him."

The Christian scholar Origen replied: "Yes, but He does not leave them the rag, tag, and bobtail of humanity; but out of material you would have thrown away as useless He fashions men, giving them back their self-respect, enabling them to stand up on their feet and look God in the eyes. They were cowed, cringing, broken things. But the Son has made them free!"

And Jesus still makes men and women free. He is the Christ of the common man, not because He passes by the rich, the proud, and the powerful, but because they pass by Him.

But everyone who feels his need and comes to Jesus, casting his life upon Him, will know that He is the Christ. This simple Galilean, the carpenter, is Saviour and Lord, in whom we find forgiveness and newness of life.

*June 30*

# HE WAS TRANSFIGURED

*And after six days Jesus taketh with him Peter, and James, and John, and leadeth them up into an high mountain apart by themselves: and he was transfigured before them. Mark 9:2.*

Looking on Jesus, who would have thought that this carpenter from Nazareth was the Son of God? This man in peasant dress, untutored, unlettered—how could He be God in the flesh?

Yet He was. Veiling His deity, He had become one with us, born as we are born, raised as we are raised, subject to the human lot of suffering, pain, and trials.

Where you hear "God," what comes to mind? Blinding light? Ten thousand times ten thousand angels singing? Thunderclaps from Sinai? Lightning bolts of retribution?

Jesus spoke a great deal about God, but almost nothing about this side—the power and the majesty—that we most associate with deity. Instead, Jesus revealed the *character* of God—His compassion and care for us, His great love that longs to welcome us home.

So if people could only have looked closer at Jesus, could have put aside their prejudices and preconceptions, they'd have recognized a character utterly extraordinary in this man from Galilee. Such purity of life, such love, such unselfishness—this could only be God!

Occasionally, however, the light of deity flashed through Christ's humanity. Its supreme display came to just three of the twelve—to Peter, James, and John—on a lonely mountain in Galilee. There, as He prayed through the night, He was momentarily transformed in the blinding glory of His heavenly home. "His clothes became dazzling white, whiter than anyone in the world could bleach them" (Mark 9:3, NIV). And Moses and Elijah left heaven to talk with Him about His approaching death.

It was a foretaste of Jesus' triumph. After He would fight and win the decisive battle with the enemy in Jerusalem, when the agelong controversy between good and evil should be resolved, He would be surrounded by the redeemed in heaven's glory. Elijah represented His followers who would be translated at His second coming, having never seen death; Moses represented those faithful ones who died in Him and who will be raised to never-ending life at His coming.

The glory soon faded, but Jesus was no less Son of God when it did. And so may we, in the ordinary tasks of the day, bring to them the glory of the Saviour's character.

# FRIEND OF SINNERS

*Then drew near unto him all the publicans and sinners for to hear him. And the Pharisees and scribes murmured, saying, This man receiveth sinners, and eateth with them. Luke 15:1, 2.*

July—and we turn now to Luke's Gospel.

Luke differed from the other Gospel writers in two important respects: he was not a Jew, and he was a physician. We know little about him except that he was a friend of Paul, who accompanied him on some of his travels. Luke suddenly appears in the account of Acts as the narrative changes from "they" to "we" (Acts 16:10). Paul called him "the beloved physician" (Col. 4:14).

Matthew and John were apostles and included firsthand reports in their writing. Mark wasn't one of the twelve, but according to early traditions, he heard Peter preach about Jesus and based his Gospel on those reminiscences. Luke tells us that as he wrote he had before him other accounts of the life and ministry of Jesus (Luke 1:1, 2). The Holy Spirit guided in his selection of material.

Unlike the other Gospel writers, Luke addressed his story of Jesus to a notable person, Theophilus (Luke 1:3; Acts 1:1). Obviously Luke wanted his Gospel to circulate in the Roman world—and this was a way of commending it to others.

What portrait of Jesus emerges from the hand of this Gentile physician? A Christ who, as Saviour of the *world,* brings hope and new life to everyone, regardless of social status.

Perhaps Luke's medical background made him sensitive to those who were less fortunate in society. Perhaps being a Gentile helped him to appreciate the universality of Jesus' message —maybe he had suffered at the hands of Jewish exclusiveness and prejudice. At any rate, his Gospel stands apart from the others in its concern for the downtrodden, the lowly, the despised, the outcast. Here Jesus isn't just "son of David," "son of Abraham" (Matt. 1:1)—He is Son of Adam (Luke 3:38), friend of everyone.

"Friend of sinners!" they hurled at Him. Oh, what a compliment! Because no one was too weak or too helpless or too poor for Jesus, *we* have hope and new life in Him!

*Jesus, friend of sinners, be my friend today.*

*July 2*

# REMEMBER STEPHEN HAWKING

*The Spirit of the Lord is upon me, because he hath anointed me to preach the gospel to the poor; he hath sent me to heal the brokenhearted, to preach deliverance to the captives, and recovering of sight to the blind, to set at liberty them that are bruised. Luke 4:18.*

When you feel that you aren't worth much because you don't have a beautiful body, remember Stephen Hawking.

Stephen Hawking is Lucasian Professor of Mathematics at Cambridge University in England—the chair once held by Sir Isaac Newton. Born on the anniversary of Galileo's death, Hawking is widely regarded as the most brilliant theoretical physicist since Einstein. He seeks a theory to link the two greatest intellectual achievements of the twentieth century: relativity and quantum mechanics. The former deals with the structure of the universe, the latter with forces that operate at the atomic scale and below. Even Einstein could not reconcile the two theories.

Hawking is best known for his work on black holes. These—if in fact they exist—are regions of extremely dense matter. Gravity is so strong that nothing, not even light, can escape. Surrounding a black hole is the event horizon—a sort of trapdoor through which matter passes into the black hole.

Stephen Hawking, still in his 40s, is world-famous. He has a brilliant mind; he has published groundbreaking books and articles; he holds the world's most prestigious chair of physics.

So he has everything on his side? Wrong.

Stephen Hawking cannot stand or walk. He cannot even speak. Paralyzed by the progressive and incurable disease amyotrophic lateral sclerosis—better known as Lou Gehrig's disease—he communicates with the world by a twitch of his fingers, generating one computer-synthesized word every six seconds. A 10-page lecture takes an entire day to prepare.

But Stephen Hawking does "speak"—and the world waits for his words. He travels the world, attended round the clock by three nurses and a graduate student who looks after his elaborate communications equipment.

Sometimes we look in the mirror and worry because we have lost a few strands of hair or because our hips are too big. "The heartbreak of psoriasis," a crass TV ad used to whine. Let's remember Stephen Hawking!

Jesus looked beyond outward appearances. He saw the person within. That's hard to do in our media-slick age. But Jesus can give us the heavenly eyesalve to make it possible.

*July 3*

# PROCLAIM THE JUBILEE

*He hath anointed me . . . to preach the acceptable year of the Lord. . . . And he began to say unto them, This day is this scripture fulfilled in your ears. Luke 18:21.*

In Old Testament times God made specific provision for people who had fallen on hard times. In the predominantly agricultural economy of Israel, land was life: to lose one's land meant poverty and slavery. So God decreed that every 50 years all debts should be canceled and all land returned to the original owners.

We have no indication that God's people carried out His instruction. Presumably greed edged out the year of jubilee.

But Jesus proclaimed it. In His inaugural sermon in His hometown synagogue, He proclaimed deliverance to the captives, release to the poor, and liberty to the broken. He, Messiah, proclaimed it—proclaimed deliverance from the tyranny of social structures that grind down the poor and from the tyranny of sin and shame.

"The words of Jesus to His hearers in the synagogue struck at the root of their self-righteousness," notes Ellen White, "pressing home upon them the bitter truth that they had departed from God and forfeited their claim to be His people. Every word cut like a knife as their real condition was set before them" (*The Desire of Ages*, p. 239).

Luke alone records this sermon of Jesus. He highlights it as the first major event of His ministry; it sets the direction of Luke's presentation of Jesus as He who has particular concern for the weak of society. Gentiles, Samaritans, tax collectors, women, the poor—in Luke's Gospel Jesus declares the jubilee for all.

But all this has nothing to do with us, you say. There aren't any Samaritans or Romans around here—and tax collectors (the IRS) today are feared rather than despised.

As I write, I have before me a weekly news magazine. The cover layout features a woman holding a young girl. Both look scared; their eyes spell fear. The cover copy reads: "Mothers on the Run." Inside, the story tells about women who take their children and run, breaking the law, when judges require that fathers charged with being sexually abusive be granted visitation rights.

The measure of any society is its justice toward its weakest elements. The measure of the church is the concern it shows for those among it who wield the least power. The measure of my Christianity is the degree to which I can help captives go free today.

*July 4*

# OF FIREWORKS AND FLAGS

*For the Son of man is come to seek and to save that which was lost. Luke 19:10.*

It's the Fourth of July, and I'm sitting here thinking about two incidents etched in my memory.

The first happened many years ago when we lived in India. One Sabbath morning as usual I taught students in a baptismal class at Spicer Memorial College in Poona. When it was over, a student came up to me looking agitated.

"Sir," he said, "there's a rumor going around the campus that President Kennedy has been assassinated."

"That's surely only rumor," I replied. "I don't see how it could be true."

But it was. Within a few minutes I knew the worst: John F. Kennedy, shot and killed in Dallas on that fateful Friday, November 22, 1963.

The second incident occurred much more recently. On a Monday morning just before noon, Aileen Sox, who worked in the ADRA office next door to the *Adventist Review*, came running into my office.

"Bill, something terrible has happened to the space shuttle," she said. "They're showing it on TV."

I ran with her to a nearby room where people were crowded around a TV set. Silent. A few dabbed their eyes.

And again and again the same sequence: bright-blue sky, liftoff, fireball, ribbons of white cutting the blueness to shreds, bright-blue sky.

Noelene and I were to leave Washington, D.C., on a four-week itinerary in South America. As we drove to National Airport that evening, we heard President Ronald Reagan on the radio: "We will never forget them nor the last time we saw them this morning as they prepared for their journey and waved goodbye and 'slipped the surly bonds of earth to touch the face of God.' "

January 28, 1986—the *Challenger* is lost, and with it beloved elementary school teacher Christa McAuliffe and the other six members of the team.

Why on this Fourth of July do my thoughts turn toward John F. Kennedy and the *Challenger*? Is it because this day of all days in the year is a day of fireworks and flags, a day to lift the eyes to something bigger than the little world with which we fill our days?

Many readers will share my feelings on this day. Others will associate them with another anniversary of freedom and patriotism. And all of us who believe in Jesus will breathe a prayer of thanksgiving for the One who came to set us free.

*July 5*

# THE SCHOOL OF SUFFERING

*Those on the rock are the ones who receive the word with joy when they hear it, but they have no root. They believe for a while, but in the time of testing they fall away. Luke 8:13, NIV.*

A friend sent me the following quotation from an unknown source: "The present circumstance which presses so hard against you is the best-shaped tool in the Father's hand to chisel you for eternity. Do not push away the instrument lest you lose its work. The school of suffering graduates rare scholars."

"The trials of life are God's workmen," writes another Christian, "to remove the impurities and roughness from our character. Their hewing, squaring, and chiseling, their burnishing and polishing, is a painful process; it is hard to be pressed down to the grinding wheel. But the stone is brought forth prepared to fill its place in the heavenly temple. Upon no useless material does the

Master bestow such careful, thorough work. Only His precious stones are polished after the similitude of a palace" (*Thoughts From the Mount of Blessing*, p. 10).

Recently I have begun to see problems in a new light. Instead of seeking to be free from difficulties, instead of bemoaning hardships and tough situations, I am learning—by God's grace—to *welcome* them.

Every problem is an opportunity for growth. Every difficulty suggests possibility. We can strive and struggle to maintain the status quo, longing for the "good old days" and bemoaning the factors that have brought change, or we can go forward in faith. We can think new thoughts, try new ways. We can smell adventure again, feel the call of the untried. We can risk for God.

If God didn't permit problems and difficulties, most of us would be too lazy to try the new. We'd be content to stagnate. So I thank Him for the tough decisions and perplexities He sends my way.

I thank Him too for the school of suffering. In that house of learning we draw closer to Jesus, the Man of sorrows. We draw closer to our fellowmen. Our sympathies deepen. We tap resources of the human spirit that can only be located in that school.

Rare scholars! The Lord designs that we shall come forth as gold, graduating with distinction.

*O God, teach me today to welcome every difficulty. And may I not push aside Your instrument with which You chisel me for eternity.*

*July 6*

# THE FORGOTTEN WOMEN OF GALILEE

*And the twelve were with him, and also some women who had been healed of evil spirits and infirmities: Mary, called Magdalene, from whom seven demons had gone out, and Joanna, the wife of Chuza, Herod's steward, and Susanna, and many others, who provided for them out of their means. Luke 8:1-3, RSV.*

This is a startling passage. It opens a window on Jesus' itinerant ministry.

**1. Jesus had women disciples who traveled about with Him.**

The paintings and movies of Jesus in Galilee are inaccurate. We see Jesus walking along the road, accompanied by Peter, James, John, and the other nine apostles. But Luke tells us that there were women in the group. He names three—Mary Magdalene, Joanna, and Susanna—and says there were "*many* others."

What did the Jewish leaders think about this arrangement? The rabbis must have been shocked; they viewed women as a temptation.

**2. Among the women who accompanied Jesus were notable people.**

Luke mentions Joanna, wife of Chuza, steward of King Herod. Apparently Susanna, whom he also lists, was another well-known person since she also was singled out from the "many."

**3. These women who traveled around with Jesus had wealth.** They "provided for them out of their means"—that is, they helped finance the ministry of Jesus and the apostles.

So while Jesus was a poor man from an infamous town, He attracted women of social status and wealth, and admitted them into the inner circle.

The King James Version translates Luke 8:3—"which ministered unto him of their substance." Perhaps we have thought the women's duties centered in cooking and waiting on Jesus and the twelve. *That* is not the meaning of the text. The women who accompanied Jesus handled the treasury for Jesus' Galilean ministry.

The women of Galilee—how important to Jesus' work, but so soon forgotten! As the church after the time of the apostles became increasingly centered in a priesthood, which was male, the early role of women faded.

We find one more reference to these women—at the cross. "And all his acquaintances and the women who had followed him from Galilee stood at a distance and saw these things" (Luke 23:49, RSV). They stuck with Jesus not only in days of acclaim in Galilee, but to the bitterness of Calvary.

*July 7*

# JESUS AND THE ELDERLY

*There was also a prophetess, Anna, the daughter of Phanuel, of the tribe of Asher. She was very old; she had lived with her husband seven years after her marriage, and then was a widow until she was eighty-four. She never left the temple but worshiped night and day, fasting and praying. Luke 2:36, 37, NIV.*

It's nice to see Luke give the elderly a place in his Gospel. He alone mentions several senior citizens with whom Jesus was involved. After what we've seen already of Luke's sensitivity to all classes of people, his interest in the elderly doesn't surprise us quite as much.

Anna, the subject of our text for today, was a very old woman. The text can be understood in two ways: either Anna was 84 when she saw the baby Jesus or she had been a widow for 84 years, making her more than 100—an extraordinary age for those times.

Whether she was 84 or more than 100, this prophetess spent all her time in the Temple worshiping, praying, and fasting. With divine insight, she recognized in Mary's child the Deliverer of the nation, Israel's star of hope. Age had not dimmed her faculties or blunted her spiritual perceptions.

Luke mentions Simeon in the same chapter. He doesn't tell us his age, but he notes that this devout man, filled with the Holy Spirit, had been shown by the Lord that he would see the Messiah before he died (Luke 2:25-32). After he saw and acknowledged the baby Jesus as the long-awaited light of Israel, he said, "Now dismiss your servant in peace" (verse 29, NIV). He was ready to die now. Apparently he also was advanced in years.

Elsewhere Luke relates incidents that suggest Jesus' involvement with the elderly. He shows the Master's compassion for a woman who had been crippled up, totally bent over, for 18 years. Jesus put His hands on her, saying, "Woman, you are set free from your infirmity" (Luke 13:12, NIV). And immediately she straightened up and praised God.

Never did people in the West have greater need to share Christ's love for the elderly. In previous generations old people were cared for at home. The extended family surrounded them with love and goodwill; their light slowly faded in dignity and peace.

But today many elderly spend their days alone in a vacuous existence in front of the TV. Modern medicine sustains life even though the mind has atrophied. Many old people today are shells, sunken images of the men and women they once were, bereft of dignity.

Jesus loves them. He sees them as they were and as they will be in the resurrection morn.

So must we.

*July 8*

# SHORT SALVATION

*He wanted to see who Jesus was, but being a short man he could not, because of the crowd. Luke 19:3, NIV.*

The last discrimination that awaits removal is height, claims an article in the Washington *Post*. Tongue-in-cheek, the writer argues that statistics prove his point—in United States presidential elections during the past 40 years, the taller candidate won almost every time!

When you are 12 and male, an inch can seem like a mile. Boys struggling to make the football team, with girls their own age looking down their noses at them—literally—long for a growth spurt. I remember our own son and daughter—pencil marks on the door frame, book on head for an accurate measure, arguments as to who had grown the most, stretching tall for maximum effect.

Zacchaeus was a little man. Not just short—little in mind, mean. He was a cheat, a rogue. He made up for his lack of height by gaining power, more and more power, until he was chief tax collector of Jericho. That made him one of the wealthiest citizens, although he was feared and hated.

Zacchaeus was a doer. He had learned well what it takes to get on in the world, what you have to put out to get to the top. He could fend for himself, and he did.

Now he wanted to see Jesus. He'd heard about the Teacher from the north but had never met Him. But today Jesus was passing through Jericho. As always the crowds thronged Him. Poor Zacchaeus—no way to see over them and no way to get through them; no one was about to give *him* a front seat. But not to worry: his resourcefulness clicked in, and running ahead, he climbed a sycamore tree along the way. He would get the best view in town—even if it was a little undignified.

But events took a turn that upended this carefully crafted scheme. Meeting Jesus, the Master's request to stay with him, his quick consent, the confession of his crookedness, his promise to pay back fourfold anyone he'd cheated—it all happened so fast.

And the bottom line was this: "Today salvation has come to this house, because this man, too, is a son of Abraham" (Luke 19:9, NIV).

We are all Zacchaeuses. But when Jesus finds us, we grow to the stature of sons and daughters of the King.

*July 9*

# JESUS IS WORTH IT

*Suppose ye that I am come to give peace on earth? I tell you, Nay; but rather division. Luke 12:51.*

Mohammed was a soldier in the Indian Army. Wounded in battle, he was sent to a hospital in Poona, in central India, to recuperate. Then facing discharge, he spent several months in a training school to learn a trade. Mohammed learned electrical wiring.

Sabbath afternoons young men and women from Spicer College in Poona fan out into the neighboring suburbs to conduct branch Sabbath schools for the children and to study the Bible with anyone who may be interested. Thus it came about that Mohammed met Manzoor, a ministerial student at Spicer.

After several weeks of study, Mohammed was close to becoming a Christian. The Lord was tugging at his heart, but he wasn't quite ready to make the break.

"Don't put off the day of decision," urged Manzoor. "Life hangs by a slender thread!"

But Mohammed could not bring himself to choose Jesus. He completed his training and left Poona for a city in the north of India, many hundreds of miles away. We lost all contact with him.

One day we received a letter. "I want to be a Christian; I want to be baptized," wrote Mohammed. He decided to come to Spicer College, enroll for a semester of schooling, and be baptized there. He gathered together his fees and told us the train on which he would arrive.

The train pulled in, but Mohammed was not on it. We wrote back to him, but received no reply. We wrote again, but Mohammed seemed to have vanished.

Then several weeks later, out of the blue, we received a hastily written note from him. "I've had such trouble," he said. "The night before I was to leave to come to Spicer College, my uncle found out my plans. When I came home from work that evening, he locked the door, took down the rifle from the wall, pointed it at me, and said, 'If you become a Christian, you are a dead man!' "

"While I slept, they took away my clothes. They took my money and my train ticket. When I woke up, I found myself a prisoner in my own home.

"At last they let me go back to work. I'm writing this letter from work. What shall I do?"

We wrote back immediately, sending the letter to his workplace. "Mohammed, come to us at once. We'll send you a money order through the mail. When you receive it, get on a train and come to Poona."

And that is how Mohammed came to Spicer College. After further studies, he was ready to follow his Lord in baptism. As I baptized him, I said to myself, "Here is a person who truly loves the Lord. Mohammed is no rice Christian!"

Few if any of us will ever face a situation that compares with Mohammed's. But everyone who chooses Jesus will be tested. We will have to decide—again and again—if Jesus and His call are more important to us than anything else in this life.

# GOOD NEIGHBORS

*But he, willing to justify himself, said unto Jesus, And who is my neighbour? Luke 10:29.*

Which is your favorite parable of Jesus? I am not aware of any survey data on the topic, but I expect that most people would choose either the prodigal son or the good Samaritan.

Both parables are found only in the Gospel of Luke. While both illustrate God's love and salvation for the lost and the broken, the good Samaritan highlights His embracing of those on the social fringes.

The Jews despised the Samaritans. They had as little to do with them as possible; they snubbed them; they wouldn't talk to them. That's why the Samaritan woman by the well was amazed when Jesus struck up a conversation (John 4:7-9).

Samaria lay between Galilee in the north and Judea in the south. The situation was similar to the modern Israeli-Palestinian problem: two peoples, ethnically distinct, living side by side, but separated by centuries of smoldering resentment.

The Samaritans were a people of mixed blood. They originated from the time of the captivity of the 10 northern tribes of Israel in 722 B.C.; the Assyrian conquerors imported other peoples to occupy the land (2 Kings 17:23, 24). These new inhabitants developed a religion that was an amalgam of the worship of Yahweh with idolatry. When later the Jews returned from the Babylonian exile that followed the fall of Jerusalem in 586 B.C., the Samaritans wanted to have a part in rebuilding the Temple. But the Jews flatly turned them down (Ezra 4:1-3). So the Samaritans built their own temple on Mount Gerizim, and offered sacrifices in it.

What a shocker Jesus' parable must have been to His hearers! The good guy turns out to be a Samaritan!

In Charles Dickens' great work *David Copperfield*, one of the characters states: "Other things are all very well in their way, but give me blood!" Many people still operate on the same philosophy. When the chips are down, they revert to family, caste, ethnicity—to blood.

But the gospel makes good neighbors. It breaks down the barriers, even of blood, even of longstanding suspicion and resentment. It calls a people out of every nation, kindred, tongue, and people, and makes them one in Jesus Christ (Rev. 14:6, 7).

# ON THE JERICHO ROAD

***Which now of these three, thinkest thou, was neighbour unto him that fell among the thieves? Luke 10:36.***

Did you notice how Jesus turns the lawyer's question on its head in the parable of the good Samaritan?

The lawyer asked Jesus: "Who is my neighbour?" (Luke 10:29). But after telling what happened on the Jericho road, Jesus asked the lawyer: "Which now of these three [the priest, the Levite, the Samaritan] . . . was neighbour unto him that fell among the thieves?" (verse 36). That is, instead of Who is *my* neighbor? the issue becomes Who *acts* as neighbor? Thereby hang two worlds of religion.

The first world, like the lawyer, seeks to justify itself. It wants to put faith in a box, to spell out duty, to define the correct response to every situation in life. It will tell you what to do in every circumstance, and because it hopes to measure up to the law itself, it will justify itself. God will *have* to welcome into His eternal home citizens of this world, because they have been so "good."

Trouble is, the Jericho road messes up the plan. Religion on the Jericho road doesn't fit neatly into boxes. The Jericho road is a world of thieves and robbers, of muggings and murders. It's an ugly road, and the lawyer's religion wishes it could close its eyes and find out that the Jericho road was only a bad dream.

But the Jericho road is real, not a dream. Then the lawyer's religion, trying to come to terms with it, asks: Who is my neighbor? Whom should I help? How far—if at all—should I get involved?

The Samaritan's world doesn't ask that question. It sees raw human need, not color, race, bank account, or education.

In the parable, the good Samaritan stands for Jesus. Secondarily, he stands for everyone who follows in the steps of Jesus on the Jericho road.

I suspect that most people still find the lawyer's religion more comfortable, because they want to justify themselves. Have you seen Alan Collins' life-size sculpture of the Good Samaritan, located on the campus of Loma Linda University in Southern California? It's striking—and shocking. Collins gave the Samaritan the features of a Black man. One night several years ago someone defaced the Good Samaritan.

*O Jesus, Lord of the Jericho Road, help me to respond to the cry of need today.*

# THE RICH FOOL

**But God said to him, "You fool! This very night your life will be demanded from you. Then who will get what you have prepared for yourself?" Luke 12:20, NIV.**

Jesus' parable of the rich fool (Luke 12:13-21) speaks to our day with special power. In this age of getting and spending, in our rush and nervous haste, are we gathering up riches for eternity?

**SEVEN** Days

"On the **First** Day

"He was 3. His mother had told him about prayer. So he prayed for candy. By a long coincidence some friends came for an unanticipated visit and brought him some gumdrops.

"On the **Second** Day

"The desire of his life was a bicycle, just as the other fellows had. He prayed so hard. God was equal to a young man's faith.

"On the **Third** Day

"He hadn't studied as hard as he should, but he prayed for a good grade that would permit him to go to college. He did not deserve it, but God answered anyway.

"On the **Fourth** Day

"She was so popular that he probably did not have a chance. But he prayed, 'Please, God, just this once.' Another prayer and another miracle.

"On the **Fifth** Day

"A baby was due. The outcome was not certain. Again a prayer, and again God smiled.

"On the **Sixth** Day

"If the deal went through, he'd be set for life. Success, security—everything for him, his children, and his grandchildren. 'Please, God, and I'll never bother You again.' It worked.

"On the **Seventh** day

"Only 60 years, but they were hard lived. But even with all manner of assets, he had only a shaky hold on the future. The prospect was bleak, and he regarded the hereafter as the dreadful unknown. 'Please, God, just a few more years—for my family's sake.' But on the seventh day God rested" (Bill Iles, in *Adventist Review*, June 9, 1988).

*July 13*

# IN THE STREAM OF THE SPIRIT

*How God anointed Jesus of Nazareth with the Holy Ghost and with power: who went about doing good, and healing all that were oppressed of the devil; for God was with him. Acts 10:38.*

Luke underscores the role of the Holy Spirit in the ministry of Jesus. Anointed at His baptism with the Spirit, the Master returned from the Jordan filled with the Holy Spirit (Luke 3:22; 4:1). In His keynote sermon at Nazareth, Jesus quoted Isaiah: "The Spirit of the Lord is upon me" (Luke 4:18).

How can we be led of the Spirit today? What difference might it make if we were prepared to put aside our own timetables so the Lord could use us for His?

In his book *Christian Excellence*, Jon Johnston tells of a recent event involving the head of a Christian denomination. He was scheduled to give the keynote address at a large function one Sunday morning in Dallas, Texas. But on the day of the big event he failed to appear. The church was filled; people were dressed in their finest; those in charge paced back and forth, looking at their watches.

At last he arrived—late! Without a word of explanation or apology, he joined the platform party and went ahead with his address.

Highhanded? Uncaring? Arrogant? What sort of leader was he?

A few days later his critics heard the rest of the story. A woman telephoned the church office to thank "the unknown gentleman" who had come to her aid the previous Sunday. Her car had quit, and she'd tried in vain to flag down someone from the stream of traffic. No one wanted to stop. No police car appeared. She began to feel desperate.

But then she noticed a car pulling over. The driver had passed her, seen her distress, and had exited the freeway to get back to her. A fine-looking man in a suit got out, inquired about the problem, and looked under the hood. After ascertaining that the car needed major repairs, he took the woman to a service station and arranged for a tow truck.

And of course, he was late for the big meeting.

Perhaps the Holy Spirit can't use us as often or as powerfully as He'd like because our appointment book gets in the way.

Are you ready for spiritual adventure? Then pray this prayer—and mean it: *"Lord, put me today in the stream of Your Spirit, ready to go or come, to speak or be silent, as You choose."*

# THE SERENITY OF JESUS

*And when his disciples James and John saw this, they said, Lord, wilt thou that we command fire to come down from heaven, and consume them, even as Elias did? But he turned, and rebuked them, and said, Ye know not what manner of spirit ye are of. For the Son of man is not come to destroy men's lives, but to save them. And they went to another village. Luke 9:54-56.*

Those foolish Samaritans! Jesus is passing through. He's on the way to Jerusalem, and He wants to spend the night in their village. He won't pass this way again; the opportunity will be the last they'll ever have to entertain the Master. And they turn Him down; their narrow prejudices, fostered by 500 years of animosity, drive them to narrow, petty behavior. No wonder James and John are ready to call down the fire, as Elijah did. No one will insult Jesus and get away scot free!

But Jesus rebuked James and John. He led His disciples right past that village. They went on to another for the night. Those ungracious people received fit punishment—they lost their chance of receiving the Lord of glory.

It's the small mind that is forever jealous for its rights, forever sensitive to slights and breaches of protocol. The big mind, serene in its self-assurance, trusting in the Father's will, goes on to more important things.

William Ellery Channing sums up Christian living like this:

I will seek elegance rather than luxury,
    refinement rather than fashion.
I will seek to be worthy more than respectable,
    wealthy and not rich.
I will study hard, think quietly,
    talk gently, act frankly.
I will listen to stars and birds,
    babes and sages, with an open heart.
I will bear all things cheerfully, do all things
    bravely, await occasions and hurry never.

In a word I will let the spiritual, unbidden
and unconscious, grow up through the common.

*O Jesus, serene under every provocation, grant me grace on this day for a life of unruffled tranquility. Grant me Thy mind, which looks beyond little hurts and protocols. Lift up your countenance upon me and keep me in peace.*

*July 15*

# COOKING THE BOOKS

**And the lord commended the unjust steward, because he had done wisely: for the children of this world are in their generation wiser than the children of light. Luke 16:8.**

The parable of the unjust steward, found only in Luke's Gospel (Luke 16:1-9), is one of the most puzzling teachings Jesus ever gave.

Here is a manager who has been wasting his boss's possessions. Called to account, he knows he faces firing. So what does he do? He cooks the books. He calls in each of his master's debtors and changes their accounts—to their advantage. One debtor owes 800 gallons of olive oil; the manager crosses out 800 and writes in 400. Another owes 1,000 bushels of wheat, but has the number reduced to 800.

Now comes the amazing part: Jesus seems to praise the fellow for what he has done! After the Ivan Boeskys have manipulated the stock exchange, trading on inside information for personal gain of millions; after revelations of high priced scandals in the Pentagon over defense weapons contracts; after the Jimmy and Tammy Bakkers' have exploitated religion for personal gain; after the politicians have been caught with their hands in the till—we don't need advice like this! The *last* sort of teaching we need from Jesus is commendation for cooking the books.

Look again at the parable. Who is "the lord" in verse 8? Familiar with this term for Jesus, many Christians think immediately of Him. But remember, *lord* can mean "master" or even a term of respect such as "sir."

In fact, verse 8 doesn't refer to Jesus at all. Note that Jesus speaks *throughout* verses 1-9 without a break (actually, right through verse 13). The "lord" of verse 8 is the boss. Such modern translations as the New International Version rightly capture the sense: "The master commended the dishonest manager because he had acted shrewdly."

So the commendation for cooking the books comes not from Jesus, but from the boss in the parable. Apparently he also was used to financial sleight of hand; maybe that's how he'd gained his wealth. One crook praising another for his shrewdness!

Then why did Jesus tell the story? The punch line comes in the last part of verse 8 and following: "For the people of this world are more shrewd in dealing with their own kind than are the people of the light. I tell you, use worldly wealth to gain friends for yourselves, so that when it is gone, you will be welcomed into eternal dwellings" (verses 8, 9, NIV).

As children of the King, our destiny is heaven. God designs for us to live forever with Him. Since that is our goal, that is where our heart should be—and our money.

Trouble is, we often act out of a divided heart. We have one foot in this world and one in heaven. We hedge our bets: we use *part* of our wealth as a heavenly insurance policy, but most we lavish on this life.

*July 16*

# CREDIT LINE

***But the tax collector stood at a distance. He would not even look up to heaven, but beat his breast and said, "God, have mercy on me, a sinner." Luke 18:13, NIV.***

It's amazing how much can be accomplished when we no longer worry about who gets the credit. And there's no limit to what Christ can do in and through and for us when the Holy Spirit cleanses our hearts from the desire to have some of the credit.

How we want to have a credit line! At the end of the show when the tributes fly, if we can't be the producer or the director, at least put our name *somewhere*! Even if it's in fine print, give us a credit line.

"Man must be clothed with Christ's righteousness," wrote Ellen White. "Then he can, through the righteousness of Christ, stand acquitted before God. . . . Here is our strength, Christ our righteousness. . . . Is that not enough for us?" (Manuscript 5, 1889).

No, it isn't. Our egos, twisted by sin, want to have *some* part, some merit, some credit. We're like the Pharisee in the parable Jesus told in Luke 18:9-14, reckoning up how much better we are than the tax collector standing alone in the corner as he prays.

Hear Ellen White again: "The Lord Jesus imparts all the powers, all the grace, all the penitence, all the inclination, all the pardon of sins, in presenting His righteousness for man to grasp by living faith—which is also the gift of God. If you would gather together everything that is good and holy and noble and lovely in man and then present the subject to the angels of God as acting a part in the salvation of the human soul or in merit, the proposition would be rejected as treason" (*Faith and Works*, p. 24).

So we will boast in our Christ and in Him alone. We will not take comfort from our faith, for it is a gift of God. We will not pride ourselves in our good works, for they are as filthy rags. We will not wrap ourselves in our knowledge of theology as a security blanket, for knowledge puffs up, and only love builds up.

In Jesus alone is our justification.

*God, be merciful to me a sinner!*

*July 17*

# GOD HUNGER

**And it came to pass in those days, that he went out into a mountain to pray, and continued all night in prayer to God. Luke 6:12.**

Here is Jesus, praying right through the night. Every sound has died away; even the birds have fallen into restless slumber. The moon runs its westward course, the silent guardian of the earth at rest. Lower it sinks, and still the Saviour prays. Now the air turns cool, and dew condenses on Jesus' hands and on the grass on which he kneels. But Jesus keeps praying.

I have never prayed all night. I have taken part in all-night vigils, adding my link to the chain of unceasing prayer, and I have prayed earnestly in the dark alone. But I have always slept and prayed—I have never known the Saviour's night of unbroken communion and petition.

Now, I don't advocate such discipline as an end in itself. Certainly there's no merit in denying our bodies sleep or food, even though some men and women have thought there was. The Sicilian monk Conon existed for 30 years on only one meal a week. Adolus never slept except for three hours before the dawn. Sisoes spent the night in a crag so that if he fell asleep he would pitch to his death. Pachomius never lay down, but slept standing in his cell. Macarius ate nothing cooked by fire for seven years, so that his bones stood out. Simon Stylites dropped vermin as he walked.

Jesus prayed all night because He was hungry for fellowship with the Father. We too may come to know God as our best friend. We know Him now through Jesus, the God-Man who lived and died for us. He rose again; He is alive! He longs to walk with us, to commune with us, to impart the mystery of His presence.

"O God, thou art my God; early will I seek thee," prayed the psalmist. "My soul thirsteth for thee, my flesh longeth for thee in a dry and thirsty land, where no water is" (Ps. 63:1). And again: "My heart and my flesh crieth out for the living God" (Ps. 84:2).

O for such a heart! O for a heart that hungers and thirsts to *know* God—not to *use* God for my plans and petitions, but to commune with Him as friend to friend!

*God, give me today such a heart!*

*July 18*

# ON LETTING GO

*The younger one said to his father, "Father, give me my share of the estate." So he divided his property between them. Luke 15:12, NIV.*

He was a wise father. Although his heart was breaking to see his young son wanting to cut the home ties, he didn't stand in his way.

He had noticed with foreboding the signs that pointed to this day—the restlessness, the complaining, the chafing against the rules. There'd been angry scenes. Somehow his boy—*his* boy—could only find fault. He took kindnesses for granted, but seemed impossible to please.

Looking back, it all seemed inevitable. Despite his prayers and his pleas, his boy had been preparing himself—and the family—for this day. It was as though he *wanted* them to be glad to be rid of him, *wanted* to act so obnoxiously that the final parting would be a relief.

"So he divided his property between them"—between the two sons. He gave the boy what he wanted, stepped back, and let him go.

And he went.

That's the hardest part of parenting—letting go. I remember vividly the tumultuous teen years of our children, when my wife and I shouted and wept and prayed and pled. At last we did what we needed to do—we let go. We turned our children over to the Lord: "Lord, take them, for we can't do anything more!" we begged.

I believe that we who are parents have every bit as much growing to do as our children—maybe more. I believe the more earnest and devoted we are as parents, the more intense will be the struggle to let our children go.

For they will go. They will go one way or another. We can try to grasp our authority, sure that we know what is best for them; but they will go. The only question is whether the parting will be amicable or ugly.

In fact, they must go. If they are to become adults, if they are to realize their potential, if they are to become solid Christians of their own choice, they must go.

And if we can find the grace to let them go gracefully, we may find them again. That's what happened to the father, who was a wise father, in Jesus' famous parable. "When he came to his senses, he said, 'How many of my father's hired men have food to spare, and here I am starving to death! I will set out and go back to my father and say to him: Father, I have sinned against heaven and against you. I am no longer worthy to be called your son; make me like one of your hired men.' So he got up and went to his father" (Luke 15:17-20, NIV).

*July 19*

# THE ELDER BROTHER'S RELIGION

*The older brother became angry and refused to go in. So his father went out and pleaded with him. Luke 15:28, NIV.*

We commonly call Jesus' famous story in Luke 15:11-32 the parable of the prodigal son. That designation misses fully half of the story—and the main half. The parable would better be called the loving father or the two prodigals.

Both sons were lost—that's the point. The older son was as truly lost as his brother. In fact, his case seems worse, because when the story closes, he is still outside and arguing with his father while the younger boy is safe inside.

Both sons were lost. One was lost outside the home; the other lost inside. We can be inside the church *and lost* just as surely as the drunkards and prostitutes outside.

Something was terribly wrong with the elder brother's religion. He'd been a "good boy." He'd never sown wild oats. He'd never disgraced the family's good name. He'd sweated and he'd toiled and he'd never disobeyed.

But something was terribly wrong with his religion. It brings him to the point at which he refuses to go in to the feast. He stands outside arguing. If his brother (note that he calls him "your son" instead of "my brother"!) is there, forget it!

Could it be possible that we might one day find ourselves arguing with God, refusing to go into His kingdom because we think He has messed up the judgment?

Incredible! Yet that's just what this parable suggests.

The story, like the two that precede it in Luke 15—the lost sheep and the lost coin—was meant especially for "good" people. When the tax collectors and sinners gathered around Jesus, intent on His words, the Pharisees and teachers of the law muttered, "This man welcomes sinners and eats with them" (Luke 15:2, NIV). That led Jesus to tell the three "lost and found" parables.

The first two and the first half of the third all have the same focus—the "lost," representing the tax collectors and sinners whom Jesus welcomed. Only in the third story, in the second half, do we see Jesus' thrust. And how powerful it is—the religious leaders are further from salvation than those whom they despised!

Did you notice that Jesus left the parable unfinished? He doesn't tell us whether the older brother softened, whether he yielded to the father's entreaty and went in to the feast. That's because when Jesus told the story, the scribes and Pharisees still had a chance—the door was still open.

It's still open today for "good" people who think they're better than tax collectors and sinners.

# WHEN HEAVEN SINGS

*I say unto you, that likewise joy shall be in heaven over one sinner that repenteth, more than over ninety and nine just persons, which need no repentance. Luke 15:7.*

The three "lost and found" parables of Luke 15 have three elements in common: someone or something valuable is lost, a search, and rejoicing when the lost is found. How these matchless parables speak to our hearts, for who hasn't been lost, who hasn't searched for something precious? And what timeless spiritual lessons they bring us, as fresh as if the Master yet walked among us!

**1. The supreme worth of every human being**

No matter how lowly, how insignificant, a person may be, God values him or her. Everyone is precious in His sight. People—we are the object of God's supreme regard.

"The value of a soul, who can estimate?" writes Ellen White. "Would you know its worth, go to Gethsemane, and there watch with Christ through those hours of anguish, when He sweat as it were great drops of blood. Look upon the Saviour uplifted on the cross. . . . Remember that Christ risked all. For our redemption, heaven itself was imperiled. At the foot of the cross, remembering that for one sinner Christ would have laid down His life, you may estimate the value of a soul" (*Christ's Object Lessons*, p. 196).

## 2. God seeks us out to bring us home

The shepherd left the 99 sheep in the fold and went out on the hillside, looking for the one lost sheep. The woman lit a candle and swept the house in search of the lost piece of silver. And the father waited and prayed and looked and longed for the wayward boy, and when he turned again home, he ran to meet him, throwing his arms about him and showering him with kisses.

O when will we learn that God is on our side in the race of life? When will we grasp how much God wants to have us with Him forever? When will we sense something of the divine heartache for lost men and women?

Preachers and theologians have made God into a heavenly policeman, an absentee Deity, a stern and demanding judge. Only when we contemplate the mission of Jesus—His coming and His dying—can we begin to appreciate the Father's love and desire for each one of us.

## 3. Joy in heaven

When the shepherd found the lost sheep, he called together friends and neighbors to share the good news. When the woman found the lost piece of silver, she just had to tell others about it. And when the father welcomed home the lost son, he threw a party in celebration.

God's invitation to you and me is: Come to My party. My joy won't be complete without you.

*July 21*

# THREE YEARS OF GRACE

*A certain man had a fig tree planted in his vineyard; and he came and sought fruit thereon, and found none. Then said he unto the dresser of his vineyard, Behold, these three years I come seeking fruit on this fig tree, and find none: cut it down; why cumbereth it the ground? And he answering said unto him, Lord, let it alone this year also, till I shall dig about it, and dung it: and if it bear fruit, well: and if not, then after that thou shalt cut it down. Luke 13:6-9.*

This little parable, found only in Luke's Gospel, customarily escapes notice. Did you ever hear a sermon on it, or read an article about it?

The context sheds light on Jesus' meaning. In the verses immediately prior, He has commented on the bloody death of the Galileans slain by Pilate. This particular massacre isn't mentioned by the historians, but they record others by the Roman governor. Apparently the Jews had reasoned that the unfortunate Galileans, being very bad people, had suffered a divine judgment. Jesus scotched this line of thought: "I tell you, Nay: but, except ye repent, ye shall all likewise perish" (verse 3).

Then He told the parable of the unfruitful fig tree. His words pierced home to the nation of Israel. Despite their abundant opportunities, especially since Messiah had been among them for three years, they had failed to bear fruit unto God. Three years of grace!—but they had been squandered.

*We* are in this parable. Let's not point our finger at the Jews. By doing so, we fall into the same trap as the first hearers, whose faulty surmising led Jesus to tell the parable.

Grace! How marvelous, how wonderful! It is the air around us; we live *in* grace. Life comes to us; it is given. God and His universe are on our side. The world is good, not bad. Grace has lifted us when we have fallen and skinned our knees. Grace has brought us safe thus far.

Three years of grace! Opportunity upon opportunity, favor upon favor. "Grace upon grace," says the apostle John (John 1:16, RSV). God's compassions fail not; new every morning, they sustain and keep us.

But what have these years of grace brought? We do not stay the same: the events of life, the years of grace, are changing us. We are writing our future every day, writing it with a pen of iron, writing in stone. Either we are growing more and more into the divine image, or we are defacing that image ever more terribly. "The heart that does not respond to divine agencies becomes hardened until it is no longer susceptible to the influence of the Holy Spirit" (*Christ's Object Lessons*, p. 218).

*O Lord of the vineyard, forbid that I should be a "cumberer of the ground"! By Your sweet Spirit bear fruit in my life today.*

# JERUSALEM'S FAVORITE DINNER GUEST

*The Son of Man came eating and drinking, and you say, "Here is a glutton and a drunkard, a friend of tax collectors and 'sinners.' " Luke 7:34, NIV.*

Jesus was, of course, no drunkard or glutton. But this accusation by His enemies highlights the contrast between Jesus and John the Baptist, between John's asceticism and the social nature of the Master's ministry.

John followed a life of severe self-discipline. He was a man of the desert, living off locusts and wild honey, fasting frequently. But Jesus didn't fast; rather He enjoyed a good meal and often was invited out to eat. He gave many of His most important teachings in a dinner setting.

Jesus must have been good company. People of all strata of society vied to have Him at their table. "This man welcomes sinners and eats with them," grumbled the Pharisees and lawyers (Luke 15:2, NIV). And He did: at least twice He fed a multitude of them. He even sat down at banquets in the home of tax collectors such as Levi Matthew (Luke 5:29) and Zacchaeus (Luke 19:5-7). But Pharisees also invited Jesus home, and He accepted (Luke 7:36; 11:37; 14:1).

Two of Jesus' parables have a banquet setting—the great banquet (Luke 14:16-23) and the king's marriage supper (Matt. 22:1-14). And His most famous parable of salvation, the prodigal son, closes with a party scene (Luke 15:11-32).

Eating! It's nearly our first activity when we come into the world, and it's one of the last pleasures when we are old. Visit the geriatric ward sometime and see the aged men and women—life's satisfactions all but gone—making their way in wheelchairs and on walkers to the dining room.

Jerusalem's favorite Dinner Guest opens up new dimensions in Christian living for us today. Eating together can be a link to unite us with neighbors, breaking down prejudice and introducing Jesus.

Many baby boomers do not spend much time in preparing food; they love to eat out. One couple I know makes friends with new people by inviting them to a meal at a restaurant—that's a wholly nonthreatening location—and no one refuses. Later, of course, we can open our home and provide a simple, tasty meal in Christian hospitality.

Jesus was a sociable person, interesting to be around, fun to have as a dinner guest. No wonder He received so many invitations to meals. If more of us could share His outgoing spirit, His church would have a better name.

*O Master of the table, make me hospitable to men and women of all classes so that I may share with them the beauty of Your life.*

# THE GOD WHO AVENGES HIS PEOPLE

*And shall not God avenge his own elect, which cry day and night unto him, though he bear long with them? Luke 18:7.*

Often Jesus' parables teach by comparison. "The kingdom of heaven is like," said Jesus—treasure hid in the field, a pearl of great price, wheat growing in the field, laborers in the vineyard, a wedding feast, and so on.

But sometimes His parables convey truth by contrast. The story of the persistent widow, found in Luke 18:1-8, follows this form. Here is a widow who keeps appealing to a judge to give her her rights. The judge, however, is unjust. He cares nothing for God or the unfortunate. But the widow keeps coming to him, pleading for justice, and at last the judge, tired of being bothered, decides to act in her behalf.

"And," said Jesus, "will not God bring about justice for his chosen ones, who keep crying to him day and night? Will he keep putting them off? I tell you, he will see that they get justice, and quickly" (Luke 18:7, 8, NIV). That is, if even a crooked judge eventually does what is right, how much more will God avenge His own people!

I know a minister who was once accused of a serious moral offense. After stating his innocence, he refused to debate with his accusers. He simply turned the case over to God, leaving it in His hands.

That was an extraordinary line of defense, given the way the world works. For many people today, the approach would be: get a lawyer, don't make a statement, admit only what others already know. The big concern is to win. "I'll see you in court!"—with its overtones of threat and challenge—sums up the course of action in this litigious age.

Judges can be bought. Lawyers—not all—are more concerned with winning the case than with justice. Widows, the poor, minorities, often cry in vain for someone to avenge them.

But Someone notes all this. "From India, from Africa, from China, from the islands of the sea, from the downtrodden millions of so-called Christian lands, the cry of human woe is ascending to God. That cry will not long be unanswered. God will cleanse the earth from its moral corruption, not by a sea of water as in Noah's day, but by a sea of fire that cannot be quenched by any human devising" (*Christ's Object Lessons*, p. 179).

To whom then may we turn? "Let all who are afflicted or unjustly used cry to God. Turn away from those whose hearts are as steel, and make your requests known to your Maker. Never is one repulsed who comes to Him with a contrite heart. Not one sincere prayer is lost. Amid the anthems of the celestial choir, God hears the cries of the weakest human being" (*Ibid.*, p. 174).

*July 24*

# WHEN JESUS WEPT

*O Jerusalem, Jerusalem, which killest the prophets, and stonest them that are sent unto thee; how often would I have gathered thy children together, as a hen doth gather her brood under her wings, and ye would not! Luke 13:34.*

We read of at least three times when Jesus wept.

Jesus wept at the tomb of Lazarus (John 11:35). Surrounded by mourners, He felt the press of the world's sorrow—so many funerals, so many breaking hearts, so many tears—and wept. He wept with us, and for us.

Jesus wept in the Garden of Gethsemane. "He offered up prayers and petitions with loud cries and tears to the one who could save him from death," the book of Hebrews tells us (Heb. 5:7, NIV). Facing the horror of separation from the Father, He recoiled in tears and supplication as He struggled to submit to the divine will.

And Jesus wept over Jerusalem. Jerusalem the beloved, Jerusalem the golden, Jerusalem the city of God—how He longed to win it for Himself! But in spite of all His teachings, all His miracles, Jerusalem kept her distance. She spurned her God—and Jesus wept.

An ancient Hebrew prayer runs:
From the conscience that shrinks from new truth,
From the laziness that is content with half truths,

From the arrogance that thinks it knows all truth,
O God of truth deliver us.

But the Jews did not hearken to this prayer. Brought face-to-face with the One who is truth embodied, they crucified Him. Jesus had foretold it: "No one after drinking old wine wants the new, for he says, 'The old is better' " (Luke 5:39, NIV).

Does Jesus still weep? Could He weep over you and me?

The "truth" is a tricky thing. "Having the truth" can be dangerous. The question isn't whether *we* have the truth, but whether the truth has *us*. Head knowledge won't save us; it can make us puffed up, arrogant. When the final gun goes off, only heart knowledge will count—knowing the One who is the author of truth, who Himself is truth.

Jesus still longs to gather us to Himself. He wants to enfold us in His arms, protect us, guard us, hold us.

What an invitation as we start this new day!

# EXCELLENCE, ANYONE?

***Indeed there are those who are last who will be first, and first who will be last. Luke 13:30, NIV.***

America at the close of the twentieth century is a society in quest of excellence. Advertisers promise excellence. Politicians pretend to have it. Educators promote it. Athletes seek it.

General Motors—"We're the mark of excellence."

Atlantic Richfield—"We're putting our energy into excellence."

Express Mail—"We deliver excellence 95,000 times a day."

Why this passion for excellence? Because we're tired of faucets that leak, repairmen who've never seen a model quite like ours before, and do-it-yourself instructions that are incomprehensible.

As Christians, sons and daughters of the living God, we are called to excellence. Timidity, halfheartedness, provincialism, shoddiness, slovenliness, shallowness, dullness—they have no part with the Creator who pronounced His own work very good (Gen. 1:31).

The God whom we serve, the Lord who loves us supremely and gave Himself to redeem us, wants to refine our speech, to sharpen our sensitivities, to improve our health and make us like Himself.

"Higher than the highest human thought can reach is God's ideal for His children. Godliness—godlikeness—is the goal to be reached" (*Education*, p. 18). "Have you thoughts that you dare not express, that you may one day stand upon the summit of intellectual greatness; that you may sit in deliberative and legislative councils, and help to enact laws for the nation? There is nothing wrong in these aspirations. You may every one of you make your mark. You should be content with no mean attainments. Aim high, and spare no pains to reach the standard" (*Messages to Young People*, p. 36).

But, said Jesus, some of those who are first—who have achieved dazzling success—will be last; and some of the last will end up first in God's kingdom.

There's the crucial difference: excellence, yes; success, no! As followers of Jesus, we must refuse to be caught up in the mad scramble to be considered successful.

Every one of us, regardless how wealthy or famous or learned people may consider us, may walk the path of Christian excellence. We walk it hand in hand with the One whose name is Wonderful, our Lord Jesus Christ.

*July 26*

# FAITH—AT SUCH A TIME AS THIS

*Nevertheless when the Son of man cometh, shall he find faith on the earth? Luke 18:8.*

According to Jesus, the last days of earth's history will be a crisis hour for faith. At His return our Lord will find few who still hold fast in trust and hope.

Many Christians will be caught up in the pleasures and business of life. Absorbed in buying and selling—in plans for marriages, buildings, and boats—they will be shocked at the Second Coming, just as were the people of Noah's day (Matt. 24:37-39).

Others will be snared by Satan's devices. He knows that his time is short, so he works with doubled energy to win men and women away from Christ (1 Peter 5:8, 9).

Amazing indeed is the net of evil cast for the unwary in today's world. Millions of people—some only children—have become slaves to chemicals. The drug industry in the United States alone grosses a staggering $140 billion. Children see brothers and sisters taking drugs; they see their parents smoking marijuana or snorting cocaine. Sometimes parents even hand their toddlers marijuana joints "for fun." What hope do children have in circumstances such as these?

For people in the ghetto, drugs promise relief from the feeling of being trapped. They offer instant gratification, an immediate sense of achievement. Men and women and boys and girls who see no light at the end of the tunnel, for whom the American dream is a nightmare, can feel as though they count, that they are somebody successful. Drugs offer the devil's counterfeit to the feelings of self-worth that come with hard work and achievement.

And drugs offer the promise of big money, fast money. A youngster peddling dope can earn as much in one hour as he'd take home after a full day's work at a regular job.

Faith on earth—no wonder the Son of man will have to search to find it when He appears. The devil has made this generation chemically dependent—not just on cocaine, PCP, and marijuana, but on the "soft" drugs alcohol and nicotine.

At such a time as this, God looks for people who shine like stars in the midst of a crooked and depraved generation (Phil. 2:15). He wants by His grace to sift us out from the evil of this age.

May we be among His faithful few in earth's last days!

*July 27*

# EDUCATED HEARTS, EDUCATED LIPS

*And all bare him witness, and wondered at the gracious words which proceeded out of his mouth. And they said, Is not this Joseph's son? Luke 4:22.*

I have a cousin with a voice like a nightingale. She is one of the most cheerful people I have ever met. Yet early in life she was struck down by polio, and for years she has struggled to get about, standing with the help of leg braces and crutches as she sings soprano solos.

I have never heard her complain. She is without bitterness, a bright spirit who warms everyone who comes near.

What we choose to focus on makes a vast difference in our Christian experience. By dwelling on negatives we become cynical and supercritical; by concentrating on positives—by telling of God's love and power—we find joy and calm assurance in the midst of hardship.

We desperately need to know the transforming love of Jesus. Naturally we tend toward judgmentalism; we see threats to faith behind every bush. Why? Because we spend too much time talking about the power of the devil, the uncertainty of the future, and the faults of others.

But love can't coexist with suspicion. Trust in God has no truck with apprehension.

*Now* is the day of salvation. *Today* is the only day we have. If we will fill this day with love for Jesus and our neighbor, tomorrow will take care of itself. Who knows if we will see another day? So let us pack every moment with the power and peace of God's grace.

We don't have to defend the truth—it's quite capable of defending itself. Nor do we have to save the church or the world—Jesus is Lord of both.

Praise His name—He's given us a work to do. Cooperating with Him, we serve as agents of His purposes. But He remains in charge; and He who made the universe and gave Himself to win back a lost world can do abundantly above all we ask or think. So let us talk of Christ's love and power; let us fill our days with His praise.

"I wish you would use your hearts and lips to praise Him, to talk of His power and glory," said a fine Christian woman at the close of her sermon. "I wish you would tell of His power."

Educated hearts. Educated lips. Educated to praise.

*O God, give them to us today.*

# ONLY ONE TIME AROUND

*And beside all this, between us and you there is a great gulf fixed: so that they which would pass from hence to you cannot; neither can they pass to us, that would come from thence. Luke 16:26.*

The parable of the rich man and Lazarus (Luke 16:19-31) puzzles many Christians. In it, you recall, Jesus contrasted the fate of the beggar with that of the man who had lived in luxury. Lazarus went to the bosom of Abraham, the rich man to Hades. Does the parable teach that at death a person goes either to heaven or hell?

Not at all. The details of the parable shouldn't be pressed here any more than in the other parables of our Lord. Can the saved see the wicked in torment, for instance? Heaven wouldn't be a very happy place if that were so!

Rather the story, which Jesus took over from Jewish tradition, teaches one central truth: we have only one time around, so we should make the most of present opportunities. In fact, the parable of the rich man and Lazarus is the counterpart of the story of the unjust steward, which we find in the first half of Luke 16. The crooked manager used the time and money in his control to pad his future; whereas the rich man squandered his life and his wealth.

There's no second chance, Jesus is telling us. We have only one life, so we should fill every moment with eternity in view.

That teaching confronts many of the ideas circulating in society today. Some time ago I was involved in the preparation of a video program on death and dying. We interviewed scores of men and women around the United States, asking them, "What do you think happens when you die?" Almost everyone felt free to go on camera with answers—and what answers they were!

"You come back again in another form."

"I have probably lived hundreds of lives already, and I will live many more."

"I may come back again as a stone, a dog, or some other animal."

"It all depends on my karma—that determines the form in which I'll come back."

No, says Jesus in this parable. The rich man couldn't come back—a great gulf separated him from his family, from his past, from eternal bliss.

The Greeks portrayed opportunity as having winged feet, long hair in the front, but bald at the back. Once past, opportunity is gone forever—and so is this life.

*O Lord of the flying minute, fill my life today with the glory and beauty of Your presence.*

# THE WILL TO DISBELIEVE

**And he said unto him, If they hear not Moses and the prophets, neither will they be persuaded, though one rose from the dead. Luke 16:31.**

Jesus' parable of the rich man and Lazarus goes beyond His teaching about making the most of life's opportunities in preparation for eternity. In an uncanny twist the story prepares us for what was about to happen.

The rich man, in torment in Hades, begs Abraham to send Lazarus to dip the tip of his finger in water and cool his tongue. When Abraham denies that request, the rich man has another. "Then I beg you, father, to send him to my father's house, for I have five brothers, so that he may warn them, lest they also come into this place of torment." Abraham replies: "They have Moses and the prophets; let them hear them." Still the rich man pleads: "No, father Abraham; but if some one goes to them from the dead, they will repent." But Abraham remains adamant: "If they do not hear Moses and the prophets, neither will they be convinced if some one should rise from the dead" (Luke 16:29-31, RSV).

That's the end of the parable. And now the real life: someone did rise from the dead, and his name was Lazarus! But the Jewish leaders refused to believe even with this evidence.

The eleventh chapter of John tells the story—one of the most gripping in the entire Scriptures—of Jesus raising Lazarus to life after he had lain for four days in the tomb. The miracle caused a sensation. But how did the religious hierarchy react? "So the chief priests and the Pharisees gathered the council, and said, 'What are we to do? For this man performs many signs' " (John 11:47, RSV). Notice: not "This man must be the Messiah," but "How can we handle Him?"

Later we read this incredible statement: "When the great crowd of the Jews learned that he was there, they came, not only on account of Jesus but also to see Lazarus, whom he had raised from the dead. So the chief priests planned to put Lazarus also to death" (John 12:9, 10, RSV).

The religious leaders had set their minds to disbelieve. They'd made their decision, and neither Scripture nor resurrection would move them.

I find that a chilling thought. Religious leaders, steeped in God's Word, whose minds were set in concrete, whom God could not reach.

May our gracious God deliver us today from the will to disbelieve!

*July 30*

# THE GOOD PART

*But one thing is needful: and Mary hath chosen that good part, which shall not be taken away from her. Luke 10:42.*

What conscientious person hasn't felt like Martha at times? Here she is, slaving away to put on a first-class meal for her honored Guest, anxious to have every detail just right. She's pushed herself to the limit, and when she most needs help to complete preparations, what does her younger sister do? She leaves the work to Martha and sits down by Jesus!

No wonder Martha felt angry with Mary and unhappy with Jesus. Was He so insensitive to what she was trying to do—to please *Him*? At last she could hold back the resentment no longer. "Lord, don't You care that my sister has left me to do all the work? Tell her to come and help" (See Luke 10:40).

Pretty strong words!

Jesus didn't reply in kind. He didn't snap back "Hold your tongue, woman! Who do you think you are, speaking to *Me* like that!"

Instead, He spoke gently, lovingly, winsomely. "Martha, Martha, you are worried and upset about many things, but only one thing is needed. Mary has chosen what is better, and it will not be taken away from her" (verses 41, 42, NIV).

A fine meal, well prepared and presented, is a work of art. But it isn't the most important thing in entertaining guests.

A home—vacuumed, dusted, and polished—in which the silver gleams and every item is in order shows industry and respect, but it isn't the most important way of welcoming guests.

The human dimension—this counts most. Putting guests at ease. Interest and concern for *them* rather than for *my* home.

And the Guest in that home at Bethany was Jesus. Mary had it right: time with Jesus was more important than the meal or the furniture.

It's easy for us males to direct this story exclusively to members of the fair sex. But the lesson is just as much for us. In our work or our play, Jesus is the best part. Yes, even for ministers of the gospel, who can become caught up in the machinery of the church. Jesus is the best part.

Let's sit at His feet today.

# GOD'S ANSWER TO GUILT

*But while he was still a long way off, his father saw him and was filled with compassion for him; he ran to his son, threw his arms around him and kissed him. Luke 15:20, NIV.*

Worshipers arriving one Sabbath morning at Sligo SDA Church in Takoma Park, Maryland, saw graffiti in large letters, defacing windows and stone blocks. "I feel guilty—punish me" someone had spray-painted in the night.

Who had done it? Some crazy person? Teenagers embarked on a Friday evening escapade?

Whoever, the words encapsulate a common reaction to guilt—punish me. By word and action we inculcate this idea in children, and we send the same message through words or body language to adults.

World religions have sprung from it: "I feel guilty—punish me." I will torture my body by fasting and all-night vigils. I will trek to the mountains. I will deny myself pleasures of body and home. I will scourge myself, freeze myself, maim myself. See how I punish myself—surely this will take away my guilt!

But punishment isn't God's answer to guilt. The god who takes pleasure in inflicting pain, the god who has to be appeased before he will forgive, isn't the God of the Bible, the God who came in the flesh, whom we call Jesus.

Here is God's answer to guilt: "But while he was still a long way off, his father saw him and was filled with compassion for him; he ran to his son, threw his arms around him and kissed him." God *runs* to meet us, welcoming us home. God embraces us, receives us as His child, showers kisses upon us.

Two marvelous songs of the Old Testament—Psalm 32 and Psalm 51—convey the same truth. "My bones wasted away through my groaning all day long," "My strength was sapped as in the heat of summer," "My sin is always before me" "Let the bones you have crushed rejoice" (Ps. 32:3, 4; 51:3, 8, NIV)—here is the heart cry of the man or woman who is burdened with guilt.

But when, like the boy in Luke 15, we come to ourselves and turn to God, our guilt rolls away. "Blessed is he whose transgressions are forgiven, whose sins are covered." "Restore to me the joy of your salvation and grant me a willing spirit, to sustain me" (Ps. 32:1; 51:12, NIV).

How foolish to stay among the swine, broken with a sense of our failures! God is calling us home, calling us to the lightness of His love. Let's cast all our guilt on His forgiveness.

*August 1*

# LIFE THROUGH HIM

*But these are written, that ye might believe that Jesus is the Christ, the Son of God; and that believing ye might have life through his name. John 20:31.*

Today we embark on an exciting journey. Throughout this month and the next we will travel through the Gospel of John. As we walk in the footsteps of the Word made flesh, we will find spiritual treasures on every side.

It's deceptively simple, this fourth Gospel. Beginning students in New Testament Greek always start here; the vocabulary and grammar are elementary. But the plain, straightforward language conveys the profoundest ideas of the entire Scriptures—which reminds us that writing needn't be difficult to understand in order to express great ideas.

According to early Christian tradition, John wrote this Gospel after the others. He deliberately avoided repeating what Matthew, Mark, and Luke had included, concentrating instead on comparatively few incidents in the story of Jesus that make plain His message and mission.

If we had only the first three Gospels, we would conclude that Jesus' ministry was basically confined to Galilee and lasted only about 18 months. But John shows that the Saviour's work also embraced Judea and, because it embraced four Passovers (John 2:13; 5:1; 6:4; 13:1), lasted more than three years. As a result of the Gospel of John, we gain a perspective on the Saviour's ministry.

John wants us to find a more important perspective, however. He didn't just write a biography about an interesting person; he didn't write in honor of his dead friend. He wrote with a purpose: "But these are written, that ye might believe that Jesus is the Christ, the Son of God; and that believing ye might have life through his name" (John 20:31).

So this is the Gospel of belief, the Gospel of eternal life. The earlier three also are designed to lead us to faith and to keep us in faith, but in John the material and the appeal are more powerful.

Come with me then, dear reader, on this journey of journeys. During these two months of contemplation on John's simple but profound words, summer days will wax to full heat, then fade toward the fall in northern climes. In India monsoon showers will quench the parched earth as we travel together. Down in Australia the almond will blossom and then the wattle as we follow the footsteps of Jesus.

And may we come to believe, and to believe more fervently, that Jesus is the Christ, the Son of God; and believing, have eternal life through His name.

*August 2*

# DIVINE SYMPHONY

*In the beginning was the Word, and the Word was with God, and the Word was God. The same was in the beginning with God. John 1:1, 2.*

What an entrée! Every bit as dramatic as the *da-da-da-dah! da-da-da-dah!* that rivets our attention at the start of Beethoven's Fifth Symphony.

*Beginning, Word, God*—the three terms rise, intersect, combine, fall in mysterious, majestic symphony.

**The Word was in the beginning.** Before the world was—before the sky turned pink in the first dawning light or a robin sang or a cornflower bloomed—the Word was. Before the sun, before the stars, before time, the Word was.

The Hindu sacred writings affirm: "In the beginning was the deed." From that root springs a philosophical scheme that centers in human works, in the unrelenting law of *karma* that drives us back to earth in countless rebirths to reap the inexorable harvest of our deeds in past existences.

But the Christian scriptures affirm: "In the beginning was the Word," and from that root springs eternal life through faith in Jesus Christ.

**The Word was with God.** When only God was, the Word was. This insight falls like a shaft of light on the mystery of deity. The one God, it tells us, is complex beyond anything that religious aspiration and human intellect have imagined. The Word coexists with God.

**The Word was God!** So the Word isn't a divine power or influence. God is; the Word is. Our salvation is rooted in the Word who became flesh, Jesus Christ, and that means in God. In coming to Jesus we don't just come to an exalted being, the first of God's creation, His preferred or chosen one. No! We come to God Himself. For the Word was God. Is God. Always will be God.

**The Word was with God in the beginning.** So the three statements of verse 1 come together—the Word was in the beginning, the Word was with God, the Word was God. John is reiterating the ideas, changing the combination, but stressing the same three great ideas:

1. The eternity of the Word
2. The deity of the Word
3. The distinctive identity of the Word

Since the Word is God, verse 2 could read: "God was with God in the beginning." Mind-boggling? Indeed! Especially when we remember that the great Old Testament affirmation that there is only *one* God is never denied in the New Testament!

*O eternal Word, who was in the beginning with God, who is God, who became flesh, we worship You, we praise You, we adore You.*

*August 3*

# ETERNAL LIFE—NOW!

*In him appeared life and this life was the light of mankind. John 1:3, Phillips.*

In Jesus Christ everyone may have eternal life—now! The devil hates this fact and has spread two lies to oppose it.

**Lie number one.** "Follow *me,* and you'll really live." He paints Jesus as the one who sucks the life from us, who takes the joy out of living, who puts us in a cage so He can lord it over us. Jesus, says the devil, stifles creativity, kills fun, inhibits our self-expression and development.

The devil uses this lie to entrap and to hold the large body of unbelieving men and women in the world.

But it's a lie. In Jesus alone do we find life—not only physical life, for He is our Creator, but that life which is "the light of mankind." When we take Jesus as Saviour and Lord, we find our true selves. We find the peace that releases our creative energies, our powers of intellect. We are complete in Him.

Who finds freedom—the man who walks out on his marriage because he doesn't want to be restricted, or the man who grows and changes in a love relationship with his wife?

Who finds life—the person who feels compelled to oppose every rule and law, or the one who finds protection and security in just laws?

**Lie number two.** "We can have no assurance now of eternal life." We can accept Jesus, strive to obey Him, walk with Him for years—then blow everything at the end. We can think a wrong thought, be hit by an oncoming car, and miss out on the goal of eternal life.

The devil uses this lie to discourage Christians.

But listen to what the Master says: "Verily, verily, I say unto you, He that heareth my word, and believeth on him that sent me, hath everlasting life, and shall not come into condemnation; but is passed from death unto life" (John 5:24). "He that hath the Son hath life; and he that hath not the Son of God hath not life" (1 John 5:12). "Verily, verily, I say unto you, He that believeth on me hath everlasting life" (John 6:47).

Eternal life—now! Yes, even at this moment, by believing on Jesus, we may have His everlasting life. We may be united with Him in mysterious communion so that the life we live will be by faith in Him. And so whatever may happen to our body—even if we should die—our future is secure. That life of Jesus will bring us back from the grave on the resurrection morning.

Do I have that assurance today?

# TRUTH WITH GRACE

*For the law was given by Moses, but grace and truth came by Jesus Christ. John 1:17.*

Twice in chapter 1 of his Gospel John tells us that Jesus combined truth with grace. He, the Word made flesh, was *"full* of grace and truth" (John 1:14). And through Him grace and truth came upon mankind (verse 17).

That's a combination each of us should aspire toward—truth with grace.

Sometimes we act in un-Christlike ways because we divorce the two. We justify our spreading bad news about someone or the church by saying, "Well, it's true, isn't it?" If it were only rumor, we'd be gossiping, but if we have the facts straight, we can make whatever use of them we please.

Not so. For Jesus, truth alone wasn't sufficient. He combined truth with grace. We need to learn when to hold our tongue. Not everything that we know, not everything that is true, needs to be blabbed to the world.

Think of how much Jesus knew about people! He who could discern the motives, desires, and fantasies of men and women could have exposed them publicly. He could have embarrassed His critics, disarmed any opponent.

But He didn't. He mingled truth with grace.

Only once did He reveal the secret sins of His enemies. When the woman caught in the act of adultery cringed before her accusers, awaiting the death sentence, He stooped down and wrote in the dust. Silently, one by one, beginning with the eldest, they left, until only Jesus and the woman were left. The sand told the story: a few cryptic words showed that Jesus knew the sins of the religious leaders (see John 8:1-11).

Even here Jesus combined truth with grace. Truth in revealing secret sins, but grace for the woman. And perhaps the hope of grace for those who had been exposed, as they might turn to accept Jesus.

Almost every day we confront the question of what is truthful. Do we also try to mingle it with grace?

You have been asked to preach one Sabbath. The soloist tries hard, but slaughters the music. At the door of the church, as she shakes your hand, she beams, "How did you like the special music, Pastor?"

So you're strictly truthful and say, "That was the worst solo I have ever heard in my life."

Or do you remember Jesus and say, "Sister, you put everything you had into that number"?

*Today, O Lord, help me to combine grace and truth as Jesus did.*

# WHAT WILL I DO WITH JESUS?

*He came unto his own, and his own received him not. But as many as received him, to them gave he power to become the sons of God, even to them that believe on his name. John 1:11, 12.*

The first 18 verses of John's Gospel have a majestic, hymnlike quality. In simple language they plumb the depths of deity and eternity, stretching our minds to the limits of comprehension.

The Word is the center of focus in this passage—preincarnate (verses 1-4), and then incarnate, calling men and women to the most important decision anyone must face.

John turned to the Greek word *logos* in attempting to describe the person and work of Jesus Christ. He is the *logos*, the eternal Word.

Already Greek and Roman thought had speculated at length concerning the *logos*. The *logos*, the stoic philosophers had concluded, was the divine reason governing the world. In Jewish speculation the *logos* was viewed as both "pattern" and "instrument" of God in Creation.

But John's Gospel goes beyond such speculation. In soaring thought inspired by the Holy Spirit, the aged apostle states unequivocally what Jew and Gentile would never have dared to utter—the *Logos* is God, and the *Logos* became man. He throws down the gauntlet, challenging Jew and Gentile to confront the question What will *I* do with Jesus?

He who made the world came to His own creation, but His people did not receive Him. They did not recognize Him; they *refused* to recognize Him.

The *Logos* become flesh came for both revelation and judgment. Everyone had preconceptions about God, but those ideas were about to be held up to the light, as God Himself would appear. And when the feebleness and paucity of humanity's ideas would be revealed by God's revealing of Himself, what then? Would mankind receive the correcting, accept the correcting, of religious conceptions?

229

So Jesus, revealer of God, Saviour of the world, is also judge. He divides mankind: will we recognize Him, receive Him; or will we turn away, turn off the Light that exposes the falseness of our piety?

But praise God—"As many as received him, to them gave he power to become the sons of God, even to them that believe on his name"!

When we *see* Jesus, when we *believe*, when we *receive*, we too sing the hymn of John 1:1-18. The soul set free sings of the Eternal Word, God of God, Creator of the universe, incarnate among us, full of grace and truth.

*August 6*

# THE WORTH OF A SOUL

*For God so loved the world, that he gave his only begotten Son, that whosoever believeth in him should not perish, but have everlasting life. John 3:16.*

Yesterday I listened as a friend described the overwhelming impression India had left upon him. He had returned to the West just the day before, and he said he found himself waking up in the night, haunted by the scenes of India still playing in his mind. India assaults your senses and assaults your theology, he said: the smells, poverty, dirt, and raw human need; and also the staggering task of bringing the good news of Jesus to the multitudes who throng her streets and villages.

Already India swarms with more than 850 million people. At present rates of growth her population will soar to 1.2 billion by the year 2000, surpassing even China's.

My wife and I first saw India 30 years ago. We arrived straight out of college, fresh with energy and idealism, confident in our ability to find solutions to the problems of the world—even India's.

We stayed in India more than 15 years, with breaks for furloughs. Both our children were born there; India claimed the best and perhaps happiest years of our lives.

For I should add that India is everything about which one can dream—or fear. She is ugly, but also exceedingly beautiful. She is bowed down with poverty, but also extravagantly wealthy. She is vastly overpopulated, but her sons and daughters are the gentlest, most hospitable souls I have encountered on God's good earth.

At last we left India. We left with tears, wrenching ourselves away from the pleas of students and faculty whom we had grown to love dearly, feeling that we were cutting away part of ourselves.

230

But we left with few answers. We left more convinced that the evangelization of India can come only by remarkable, unmatched power of the Holy Spirit descending to accomplish what cannot be accomplished by human plans and energies.

We left more sure of the worth of a human soul—of *every* human soul. Those men and women who sleep on the sidewalks of Bombay, those children who gaze with forlorn eyes at you when your train comes to a station, those peasants who trudge the unpaved roads of the hundreds of thousands of India's villages—every one is precious in God's sight.

Here is the world's favorite text: "For God so loved the world, that he gave his only begotten Son, that whosoever believeth in him should not perish, but have everlasting life" (John 3:16). And here is a statement almost as remarkable: "The Saviour would have passed through the agony of Calvary that one might be saved in His kingdom" (*The Desire of Ages*, p. 483).

*August 7*

# HOW JESUS TREATED PEOPLE

*Then saith the woman of Samaria unto him, How is it that thou, being a Jew, askest drink of me, which am a woman of Samaria? for the Jews have no dealings with the Samaritans. John 4:9.*

One of the features of John's Gospel is its concentration on encounters between Jesus and various individuals. Instead of describing many incidents in the ministry of Jesus, John selects a few choice meetings and treats them at length—Jesus and Nicodemus, Jesus and the woman by the well, Jesus and the impotent man, Jesus and the man born blind, Jesus and Lazarus.

Although Jesus had come to save the world, He always had time for just one person. He was never too busy or too tired or too much above someone to take time to talk about his or her deepest needs. Jesus seems to have worked on the principle that He would best accomplish His mission by showing an interest in every person He encountered.

What a rebuke to our age! We are caught up in plans, strategies, and goals—even in the church. Sometimes with all our activity for God we're really only spinning our wheels. People are falling between the cracks of our committees and our programs; we're so caught up in schemes that we forget that how we deal with people—*every* person—counts the most in the kingdom of God.

The measure of the greatness of any institution or church is how it treats the weakest elements in its midst. North America's prosperity and military strength make it a modern wonder; but what about the thousands who've been turned out on the street from mental institutions, people who have no political clout because they cannot even cope with the pressures of day-to-day living? What about the unborn? The aged, the infirm, the senile?

And in the church: what about minorities? the illiterate? women? Must the church wait until a group organizes to demand fair treatment? Or will it treat everyone—especially the weak—as Jesus treated people?

I have noticed a curious tendency among Christians (and I include myself). We will form a group and go down to another country—say, to Mexico—to build a church or a hospital. While there we'll mingle with the people as our brothers and sisters. But what happens if Mexicans move into our town or suburb? We keep as far away as we can from them, maybe even calling them names that deny our Master!

*O Jesus, You who love every person, help me today to treat the people in my world like the way You treated them in Yours. Help me especially to regard the weak as Your sons and daughters.*

August 8

# BRIDGES OF GOD

***The first thing Andrew did was to find his brother Simon and tell him, "We have found the Messiah" (that is, the Christ). And he brought him to Jesus. John 1:41, 42, NIV.***

Have you noticed the pattern of experience behind Jesus' first four disciples?

Andrew was first to accept Jesus as Messiah. Already a follower of John the Baptist, he heard John say of Jesus, "Behold the Lamb of God!" (John 1:36). Matthew turned from John and cast in his lot with Jesus.

Immediately he sought out Peter, his brother. "We have found the Messias!" he exclaimed. He brought Peter to Jesus—and Jesus had another disciple, one who in time would become the leader of the twelve.

The third disciple was Philip. John simply tells us: "The day following Jesus would go forth into Galilee, and findeth Philip, and saith unto him, Follow me" (John 1:43).

But like Andrew, Philip could not keep the good news to himself. He sought out his friend Nathanael, "We have found the one Moses wrote about in the Law, and about whom the prophets also wrote. . . . Come and see" (verses 45, 46, NIV).

How quickly the chain of discipleship grew. Of these first four, only one had received a direct invitation from Jesus; the other three accepted Jesus because of the word of another.

That's still the pattern for Christian witness. We don't need elaborate programs and training. We simply start where we are with what we have, telling our relatives, neighbors, friends: "We have found Jesus . . . come and see."

Some Christian leaders call this method "bridges of God." They emphasize that a person who has been converted is immediately at the center of a circle of influence for relatives and friends, with wider potential for bringing new disciples to Christ than at any time in the future.

Bridges of God—He wants to use everyone who names the name of Jesus today.

*Divine Master who has made me new, make me Your bridge today.*

# BURN THOSE LABELS!

**And Nathanael said unto him, Can there any good thing come out of Nazareth? Philip saith unto him, Come and see. John 1:46.**

Nathanael was a good man, but he suffered from a fault that overtakes many good people—he was quick to stereotype others. Nazareth was notorious among the cities of his day, and when Nathanael heard that Jesus came from Nazareth, his immediate response was "Can any good thing come out of Nazareth?"

Labeling people is unfair and unchristian.

It's unfair because labels are inaccurate. No one is conservative or liberal or radical or progressive in all matters. People are complex, and they surprise us by their reactions and positions, their behavior in different circumstances. Some who *sound* liberal are traditional in behavior, while others who have a conservative image are more daring in their practices.

Labels help simplify life—for the labeler. They enable him to reduce highly complex situations and peoples to pigeonholes, to categories. But labels distort reality, fool the labeler, and get in the way of exchange of ideas.

Because of labels we fall into the trap of assessing the value of an idea by referring to its source. We dismiss ideas out of hand that may have great merit simply because we already have attached a pejorative label to the source. Conversely, we give other ideas far more credence than they deserve merely because the person who originates them wears a badge that makes us feel comfortable.

Labeling can be downright vicious with regard to young people. Early in life some children are branded "losers," "dull," "misfits," "troublemakers." Teachers and peers *expect* them to fail; the label becomes a self-fulfilling prophecy. But how far from the approach of Jesus, who saw the best in every person and encouraged them to see it also!

I find it more helpful to think in terms of open- or closed-mindedness, rather than conservative or liberal. The open-minded person is ready to look at new ideas, regardless of his own position; the close-minded person is not. Close-mindedness is just as much a problem of liberals as it is of conservatives.

Fortunately, Nathanael was open-minded. Although he was quick to stereotype Jesus, he reversed his position when confronted by the evidence.

May we today likewise be open to others.

# JESUS AND NATHANAEL

***Nathanael saith unto him, Whence knowest thou me? Jesus answered and said unto him, Before that Philip called thee, when thou wast under the fig tree, I saw thee. John 1:48.***

Jesus adapted His approach and method to every person He met. He read the heart and turned the conversation in a direction best suited to win confidence and acceptance.

Here was Nathanael, a person of unusual spirituality. Although he harbored prejudice toward the inhabitants of neighboring Nazareth (he was from Cana), he sought after God's righteousness. As Jesus saw him approaching, He gave a glowing commendation: "Behold an Israelite indeed, in whom is no guile!" (verse 47). Jesus recognized in Nathanael something more important than the blood of Abraham—a heart devoted to God, a heart pure in its affections.

How would Jesus bring this earnest individual into a saving knowledge of Himself and His work? By referring immediately to a place most precious to Nathanael—the fig tree. That was the scene of Nathanael's secret prayers, the retreat where he poured out his soul in longing for Messiah and His kingdom.

It was enough! Nathanael cast prejudice to the winds and embraced Jesus of Nazareth: "Rabbi, thou art the Son of God; thou art the King of Israel" (verse 49).

If Jesus wished to reveal Himself to you or to me today, would it be by reference to our "fig tree"? Do we even have a "fig tree"?

Which is more precious to us: the fig tree or the TV?

As we study through the Gospel of John, we will notice several accounts of people who met Jesus. None other is as short as this one; some involve lengthy conversations, and even then without a clear-cut decision for Jesus.

But Nathanael lived close to God. No ostentatious street-corner prayers for him, no public recitations in the synagogue. He sought God in secret, under the fig tree. Those times of quiet communion changed Nathanael, molding him after the divine likeness, preparing him for revelation of Messiah that God intended.

God is looking for Nathanaels today! The church needs Nathanaels. The world needs Nathanaels! For Nathanaels are of all people most ready to hear God's message.

*August 11*

# JESUS AND HIS MOTHER

*Jesus saith unto her, Woman, what have I to do with thee? mine hour is not yet come. John 2:4.*

Jesus' reply to Mary falls harshly on our ears. "Woman" instead of "Mother." And "what have I to do with thee?" sounds as if He wasn't interested in her or her problem.

In fact, Jesus' words conveyed no such disrespect toward Mary. Notice how modern translations seek to capture their meaning.

New International Version—"Dear woman, why do you involve me?"

Phillips—"Is that your concern, or mine, Mother?"

*The New English Bible*—"Your concern, mother, is not mine."

"This answer, abrupt as it seems, expressed no coldness or discourtesy," writes Ellen White. "The Saviour's form of address to His mother was in accordance with Oriental custom. It was used toward persons to whom it was desired to show respect. Every act of Christ's earthly life was in harmony with the precept He Himself had given, 'Honour thy father and thy mother' (Ex. 20:12). On the cross, in His last act of tenderness toward His mother, Jesus again addressed her in the same way, as He committed her to the care of His best-loved disciple. Both at the marriage feast and upon the cross, the love expressed in tone and look and manner interpreted His words" (*The Desire of Ages*, p. 146).

Mary and Jesus—what a study in personalities! Mary, full of grace, who trusted the word of the Lord, yielding herself without struggle or doubt to be His handmaiden, the mother of Israel's Messiah. Mary, treasuring in her heart the words and life of her growing son, pondering what manner of Boy He was, what He might be.

And now Mary is solicitous of Jesus' reputation, as is any proud mother. Mary has heard of His baptism in Judea; she sees the bright-eyed young staff members who have joined His traveling ministry; she senses that the time of His recognition by Israel as its deliverer is near.

So she comes to Jesus, nudging Him toward action. The wine at the wedding feast has run out—an acute embarrassment to the host—and she says, "They have no more wine" (John 2:3, NIV). She doesn't tell Him what to do, but she implies it. There's just a hint of mother-knows-best in her words, a flashback to the years when she cradled Jesus in her arms.

Jesus' reply, courteous but firm, reminded Mary that He, not she, must chart the course of His mission. " 'Dear woman, why do you involve me?' Jesus replied, 'My time has not yet come' " (verse 4, NIV). Don't worry—I have matters in hand. Leave everything to Me—in My own time.

And Mary did. "Do *whatever* He tells you," she instructed the servants (verse 5, NIV). Her counsel to Jesus had come in the mildest form; Jesus' correction likewise was gentle. Gentle—but sufficient.

Oh, what a relationship—when merely a hint sufficed to set matters straight! No resentment, no irritation, no strong language; just a few words spoken in love, passing between hearts in communion.

*O Lord, may I today live so close to You that I can receive the softest correction of Your Spirit.*

*August 12*

# JESUS AND NICODEMUS

**Jesus answered and said unto him, Verily, verily, I say unto thee, Except a man be born again, he cannot see the kingdom of God. John 3:3.**

Of all the encounters between Jesus and people in the Gospel of John, He is most direct in dealing with the religious leader Nicodemus.

Nicodemus—Pharisee, teacher, leader—came to Jesus with opening gambit carefully rehearsed. "Rabbi, we know you are a teacher who has come from God," he began. "For no one could perform the miraculous signs you are doing if God were not with him" (John 3:2, NIV).

Jesus cut him off. Slicing through niceties and formalities, He said, "I tell you the truth, no one can see the kingdom of God unless he is born again. . . . *You* must be born again" (verses 3-7, NIV).

*Rabbi, we know . . .* Herein lay Nicodemus' spiritual problem. He knew—or thought he did. Schooled in the writings of the Old Testament and the interpretations and traditions that had grown up around them, he felt secure in his religious heritage. Religion was his bag. His world was the world of theological discussions and arguments, of learned debates that only the privileged few had access to, and further, the world of ecclesiastical hierarchy where the Sanhedrin met in self-righteous deliberation to decide what was best for the souls of the children of Abraham.

Nicodemus knew so much, but knew nothing at all. He hadn't learned the most elementary lesson of the kingdom of God—that one enters there not by virtue of learning or position, but because one has been born again. That the greatest truth, the essence of religious knowledge, doesn't reside in books, but in knowing God. Nicodemus knew *about* God; he didn't *know* God.

So Jesus exposed his need, his lack. Jesus refused to debate—Nicodemus had hoped for that, and would have excelled—and instead cut to the heart with almost cruel sharpness.

Surgery is radical; but sometimes surgery offers the only hope for healing.

Nicodemus came to Jesus with a bag of questions and expectations. He went away with just one question: What would he do with the counsel brought home so bluntly to him?

Nicodemus wasn't converted that night. In time he was, however. Later we find him defending Jesus before the Sanhedrin (John 7:50-52) and finally coming forward openly as a follower of Jesus (John 19:39).

Jesus, the Great Physician, had saved another patient—this one by surgery.

# JESUS AND THE WOMAN BY THE WELL

*He told her, "Go, call your husband and come back." "I have no husband," she replied. John 4:16, 17, NIV.*

If you had suggested to the Sanhedrin colleagues of Nicodemus—not to mention Nicodemus himself—that an illiterate Samaritan woman with a reputation for sleeping around would be a likelier candidate for the kingdom of heaven than they, they would have risen up in horror, gathered their robes around them in righteous indignation, and excommunicated you from the assembly.

See her by the well. She is a lonely and tragic figure. Not for her even the chitchat of women drawing water. She wears a scarlet letter. She comes for water when no one is around to mock her, to cast reproachful glances in her direction.

She came (see John 4:7).

Nathanael came, brought by Philip.

Mary came, anxious for Jesus to act.

Nicodemus came, curious about the Teacher from Galilee.

To Nathanael, Jesus could talk about the place of secret prayer—the fig tree; to Mary, about His mission; to Nicodemus, about the nature of spiritual truth.

But what can He say to this woman of Samaria? Hers is a world of water and one-night stands. She knows nothing of prayer, miracles, or sacred writings.

So Jesus talks to her about water and one-night stands.

We easily forget—we who are nourished and nurtured in the bosom of the church—that the *whole* world is God's. Carrying water is no less dignified than teaching Hebrew.

Nor are sexual relations evil per se. The sensory world, with its emotions, creativity, and vital experiences, is also God's world.

To men of religion the woman by the well would have seemed shallow and sensual. To Jesus she was as much a child of God as Nicodemus or Nathanael.

Jesus spoke to her about the world she knew—water and one-night stands. At the close of the conversation only the woman's waterpot remained by the well. The woman was in the village, no longer ashamed to meet people, telling them, "Come, see a man who told me everything I ever did. Could this be the Christ?" (verse 29, NIV).

In one day—in just a few hours—the woman by the well had found living water, fulfillment for her restless longing, cure for her loneliness.

It took years for Nicodemus to reach that point.

# JESUS AND THE NOBLEMAN

*Then said Jesus unto him, Except ye see signs and wonders, ye will not believe. John 4:48.*

The nobleman's motives were mixed, and so he represents every one of us. We seek the gift; we ought to seek the Giver.

Notice how "believe" frames this story: "Except ye see signs and wonders, ye will not *believe*," Jesus told him as he begged for Jesus to go to Capernaum (Jesus at that time was in Cana) and heal his dangerously ill son.

"The man *believed* the word that Jesus had spoken" (John 4:50). When in desperation the official cried out "Sir, come down ere my child die," Jesus gave the good word: "Go thy way; thy son liveth" (verses 49, 50). And he believed.

"And himself *believed*, and his whole house" (verse 53). He had believed Jesus' word spoken in Capernaum; now he believed at the news that his son had been healed.

Here we see three stages in the growth of faith:

*Stage 1*: A tentative, flickering faith. The nobleman seeks out Jesus because he has a measure of faith in Him—not as Messiah, but that He may be able to perform healings. *If* Jesus will make a miracle and restore his son, he will accept *Him* also—not just His mighty acts.

*Stage 2*: Jesus' words cut to the bone, exposing the shallowness of the nobleman's faith—"Unless you people see miraculous signs and wonders, you will never believe" (verse 48, NIV). Now he realized that Jesus could read his very motives. "His vacillating faith appeared to him in its true character. In deep distress he realized that his doubt might cost the life of his son" (*The Desire of Ages*, p. 198).

But he believed Jesus' words that his son would live. Although up to this time Jesus' miracles had come about by Jesus laying His hand on the sick person, the nobleman accepted that Jesus' power could flash from Cana to Capernaum.

Cana to Capernaum is only about 15 miles. The nobleman met Jesus about 1:00 p.m.; he had ample time to get home that day. But he took his time, only the next day reaching Capernaum. He wasn't anxious; he had faith in Jesus' word.

*Stage 3*: The good word from his servants confirmed and strengthened the nobleman's faith. He and his entire household now believed in Jesus—not just as a miracle worker, but as Messiah.

*O God, You know how mixed our motives are. We seek You, but we seek our own interests also. Lead us to unwavering trust in You.*

August 15

# JESUS AND THE MAN BY THE POOL

*When Jesus saw him lie, and knew that he had been now a long time in that case, he saith unto him, Wilt thou be made whole? John 5:6.*

The story of the man by the pool of Bethesda used to trouble me. It seems straight out of the superstition of the Middle Ages: blind people, lame people, paralyzed people, hobbling to the pool, hoping for a miracle. An angel comes down sometimes and stirs up the waters—and if you can get in first, you will be cured of whatever disease you have!

Is this the way God works? Is His healing reserved for the quickest and the strongest, for the one who can shove others aside and get to the water?

We have seen pictures of them—the blind, the lame, and the paralyzed—pilgrims on their way to Lourdes, where the virgin Mary is supposed to have appeared to a young woman. Other unfortunate folk struggle to a cathedral, to a sacred relic that supposedly will impart power.

Still others, Protestants, seek out faith healers. They become participants on live television, waiting in line to be struck on the forehead by the preacher and pronounced cured.

No, God doesn't work in these ways. He can heal, and does heal, miraculously. But His blessings aren't just for the strongest and the quickest. And God, I think, is furious at religious hucksterism, at any setup that makes money and provides a living in His name from the wretchedness of humanity.

It's significant that the oldest manuscripts of the New Testament omit verse 4—the story about the angel stirring up the water and healing the person who could get in first. This statement probably was added later by someone who held to the superstition.

Of course, the man by the pool believed it. Poor wretched fellow, an invalid for 38 years, it seemed his only hope. But what faint hope! How could he, crippled up as he was, ever get into the water first?

What a life—38 years an invalid! Years of hoping, waiting, grasping at the shadow of healing.

But then Jesus came. "Do you want to get well?" He asked (verse 6, NIV). The man could think only of the pool, of his problem in getting to the water. Was Jesus about to offer to stay by and help him in when the water was stirred?

No, something better: "Get up! Pick up your mat and walk" (verse 8, NIV). And at once the man was cured. He picked up his bed and walked away. Once he had hoped in superstition; this day he took hold of Christ's word in faith.

*Dear Jesus, our souls are palsied. Of ourselves we are no more capable of living a holy life than was the impotent man of walking. But we hear Your word, and today we look up to receive Your healing power, to be set free in Your strength.*

*August 16*

# JESUS AND THE WOMAN TAKEN IN ADULTERY

*"Neither do I condemn you," Jesus declared. "Go now and leave your life of sin." John 8:11, NIV.*

With each of the previous six people we have been noticing in the Gospel of John—Nathanael, Jesus' mother, Nicodemus, the woman by the well, the nobleman, and the man by the pool—Jesus spoke the saving word. But He brought salvation to the woman taken in adultery by remaining silent.

It's early morning in Jerusalem. The long rays of the rising sun sweep across the face of the Temple, flashing from gold ornamentation, lighting marble blocks. Jesus sits teaching in the courtyard, surrounded by a crowd of listeners pressing close to catch every phrase. He rose early and has been here since dawn.

Suddenly the quiet beauty of the morning is interrupted. A group of scribes and Pharisees push their way through the crowd, dragging a woman who looks scared to death. They thrust her before Jesus and say loud enough for everyone to hear: "Teacher, this woman was caught in the act of adultery. In the Law Moses commanded us to stone such women. Now what do *you* say?" (verses 4, 5, NIV).

Of course it's a trap. Whatever Jesus answers, they figure to have occasion to accuse Him. If He speaks in the woman's favor, it will show that He is soft toward the law—as they already claim. If He tells them to execute the woman, they can make capital out of that with the Roman authorities—He's taking the law into His own hands.

And the woman waits, terror-stricken. One word of condemnation from Jesus, and she will die.

What will Jesus answer? He says nothing. He stoops down and begins to write in the dust.

Tension builds. The scribes and Pharisees press Him to pronounce judgment, but He continues to doodle in the sand as though He doesn't hear them.

At last He straightens up. "If any one of you is without sin, let him be the first to throw a stone at her" (verse 7, NIV). They see now what He's been writing, and one by one her accusers begin to slip away. Jesus has written just enough to let them know that He knows *their* secret sins! The tables have been turned. The scribes and Pharisees lie exposed in their hypocrisy.

And the woman? Trembling, she awaits Jesus' word of sentence. It does not come. Finally every accuser has slunk away, and she is left face-to-face with Jesus. Looking her in the eye, He says, "Neither do I condemn you. Go now and leave your life of sin."

*O merciful Saviour, You who read our secret thoughts, before whom our lives lie open and bare, we thank You for accepting us as we are. In the power of Your life we go forward into this new day.*

*August 17*

# JESUS AND THE MAN BORN BLIND

**He answered and said, Whether he be a sinner or no, I know not: one thing I know, that, whereas I was blind, now I see. John 9:25.**

He's one of my favorite Bible characters, this nameless beggar of Jerusalem. The entire ninth chapter of John's Gospel tells his story—how Jesus healed him, and what happened thereafter. In some respects he has more problems *after* he gets his sight back than before. But he exhibits a solid common sense that refuses to bow before the theological humbug of Israel's men of religion.

Even the disciples of Jesus have questions about him. They want to know why he was born blind: did he sin (the rabbis taught that even a fetus could transgress!), or his parents? For them—following current theological patterns—*someone* must have sinned, since God obviously had inflicted punishment in the form of blindness.

Jesus scotches that line of reasoning. No, He says, neither the man nor his parents sinned. Life and theology are more complex than you have thought.

Then Jesus heals the blind man. He spits on the ground, makes mud with the saliva, and puts it on the man's eyes. "Go, wash in the pool of Siloam," He tells him. The man does so—and he sees! For the first time in his life he sees.

Story with a happy ending? Not quite. Our friend becomes the center of a theological controversy.

First, the Pharisees don't like Jesus. They can't bring themselves to accept that He might be the Messiah. This beggar fellow is an embarrassment. He should *not* be able to see now—not if it's Jesus who is supposed to have healed him.

So they put the beggar through a third-degree cross-examination. Maybe he wasn't really blind before? Maybe this isn't the same man who used to sit and beg by the roadside?

They work his parents over also: Is this *really* your son? (*Yes.*) Was he *really* born blind? (*Yes.*) Then how can he see now? (*We don't know—ask him. Leave us alone!*)

Second, Jesus has healed this man on the Sabbath. There, that's the clear proof that He can't be from God—He breaks the Sabbath.

They turn again on this fellow in rags—this embarrassing creature. "What have you to say about him [Jesus]?" they ask. "He is a prophet," the man replies (John 9:17, NIV).

Later they summon him again. " 'Give glory to God, they said. 'We know this man is a sinner' "(verse 24, NIV).

Then his marvelous reply: "Whether he is a sinner or not, I don't know. One thing I do know. I was blind but now I see!" (verse 25, NIV).

They cast him out of the synagogue—excommunicate him. But they cannot cast out his witness—"One thing I do know."

Do we have that witness today?

*August 18*

# LIGHT A CANDLE

*The light shines on in the dark, and the darkness has never mastered it. John 1:5, NEB.*

Outside Bombay, India, I saw streaked in letters two feet high this motto: "It is better to light a candle than to curse the darkness."

Commuters rushing past to the daily grind in some dingy office saw it. Urchins wandering by saw it. People from the country, pressing toward Bombay and the hope of work and new life in the metropolis, saw it.

*There is plenty to curse about.* There is plenty to curse about in Bombay. Bombay, for all its buzzing commerce, is a dark city.

Many voices curse the darkness enveloping society. They give vent to increasing frustration at problems of inflation, crime in the streets, lack of respect for established social institutions. Frustration, fear, bewilderment, anger—these are what these voices utter as they curse the darkness.

Many voices curse the darkness that has enveloped the church. For the church it is the best of times—and the worst of times. The church is big business. Rich and increased with goods, it "never had it so good." More and more its ministers are required to be managers of high finance as well as (or more than) preachers of the simple gospel of Jesus Christ. And so the best of times becomes the worst of times—as an agent of moral force in the life of society, and as a body to which men and women look for guidance and uplift, the church seems more and more to be losing its power. There is plenty to curse about. What shall we do—join those who denounce the rotting away of our society and the encroaching feebleness of organized Christianity?

*It is better to light a candle than to curse the darkness.*

Shall we crawl into our cave and wait for the "big bang"? Shall we smugly count the disaster headlines, muttering, "Of course! Of course!"

No; it is better to light a candle than to curse the darkness. It is better to get up from the cave and get out among the people—to leave our campfire and plunge into the darkness.

As Mahatma Gandhi, father of modern India, lay slain from the bullet of a fanatical Hindu, a broken Jawaharlal Nehru told a broken nation, "The light has gone out!" Fifteen years later another leader was cut down at high noon in the streets of Dallas. To a stunned nation it seemed that a bright new light had suddenly gone out.

We are not Mahatma Gandhis. We are not John F. Kennedys. But we are men and women. Old or young, we have a candle to burn—one life-power long. Let us not doubt its world-transforming power!

One solitary candle breaks the darkness. One solitary life, lit up by love, is irresistible.

# WHATEVER HAPPENED TO TRUST?

*If I have told you earthly things, and ye believe not, how shall ye believe, if I tell you of heavenly things? John 3:12.*

Every autumn a Peanuts cartoon depicts Charlie Brown trying to placekick a football. Just as his foot is about to make contact, Lucy removes the ball, and Charlie falls flat on his face. She is attempting to teach him not to be so trusting. But Charlie keeps falling on his face year after year. Why? Charlie explains that the key is his "undying faith in human nature."

In 1990 Charlie Browns are in a distinct minority in our society.

We retreat into our fortresses in the inner city, walled in by shutters, dogs, chains, and electric-eye systems. "We'll return your call"—but often no one does. "Mr. Brown is not in," lies his secretary. And even Johnny may be instructed by the parents in the next room to tell the caller, "Mommy and Daddy are out."

Cynicism, suspicion, distrust—these are marks of our age. No wonder that alienation abounds. Children are alienated from parents, men from women, Whites from Blacks.

When trust goes, there is great loss. When we lose our basic confidence in our fellow inhabitants of Planet Earth, we become something less than human. Our fabled progress tends toward the barbarism of the jungle.

Julian B. Rotter, a clinical psychologist at the University of Connecticut at Storrs, has developed an instrument for measuring degrees of trust. He is able to classify people as either high or low trusters by analyzing their responses to a 25-item questionnaire (sample: "Given the opportunity, most people would steal if there were no danger of being caught").

But are not high trusters easy prey in our troubled society?

Rotter's studies reveal the opposite. Low trusters, in fact, make readier targets for con artists. He also found that high trusters are no less intelligent than low trusters. However, they are happier, more likable—and more trustworthy. Low trusters, on the other hand, not only are perceived as less trustworthy than others, but are actually more likely to lie, cheat, and steal.

Christians should be high trusters. At the heart of our religion stands faith—and the essence of faith is trust. We trust the God of the covenant, the one who cannot deny Himself (2 Tim. 2:13), though all others prove unfaithful.

And because we profess to know such a God, to serve such a God, we should reflect His character. He has gone, and still goes, to incredible lengths to save human beings, treating us not according to our desserts, but according to grace.

Samuel Johnson said: "It is . . . happier to be sometimes cheated than not to trust." Perhaps that thought also encourages Charlie Brown every autumn.

*August 20*

# LOVE CONQUERS ALL

*And I, if I be lifted up from the earth, will draw all men unto me. John 12:32.*

The high school I attended had as its motto "Labor Omnia Vincit"—work conquers all. From the class assignments it was obvious that the teachers believed it!

Later I was a teacher myself at Spicer Memorial College in India. Here the motto was "Amor Omnia Vincit"—*love* conquers all. And the second motto is correct, not the first.

How does God meet evil? Not by evil, but by love. How does God meet force? Not by force, but by love. And His love will win the day.

The apostle Paul would certainly agree. His most famous words are a hymn to love—1 Corinthians 13.

It's a hymn in four stanzas. The first stanza makes this very point—*love is greater than all.*

"If I speak in the tongues of men and of angels, but have not love, I am only a resounding gong or a clanging cymbal. If I have the gift of prophecy and can fathom all mysteries and all knowledge, and if I have a faith that can move mountains, but have not love, I am nothing. If I give all I possess to the poor and surrender my body to the flames, but have not love, I gain nothing" (1 Cor. 13:1-3, NIV).

Love is greater than money. Greater than cars and clothes. Greater than education. Greater than work. Greater than beauty.

The second stanza describes *what love is like.* In modern terms it goes like this: "Love is patient; love is kind and envies no one. Love is never boastful, nor conceited, nor rude; never selfish, not quick to take offence. Love keeps no score of wrongs; does not gloat over other men's sins, but delights in the truth. There is nothing love cannot face; there is no limit to its faith, its hope, and its endurance" (1 Cor. 13:4-7, NEB).

This leads Paul to stanza 3—*love never fails.* All else fails. Only love abides—and it abides forever. Is there beauty? It will fade away. Is there wealth? It will vanish in inflation. Is there a spiritual gift? It will disappear. Is there knowledge? It will be swallowed up in truth.

But love will abide.

And so to stanza 4—*Paul's appeal to love*: "When I was a child, I talked like a child, I thought like a child, I reasoned like a child. When I became a man, I put childish ways behind me. Now we see but a poor reflection as in a mirror; then we shall see face to face. Now I know in part; then I shall know fully, even as I am fully known. And now these three remain: faith, hope and love. But the greatest of these is love" (1 Cor. 13:11-13, NIV).

Christians have rightly noted that everywhere Paul says "love" in this chapter, we could substitute "Jesus." For Jesus is love personified.

He who was lifted up on Calvary's tree draws the world to Himself. He conquers evil by the winsomeness of His love.

*August 21*

# THE WATER WALKERS

*Verily, verily, I say unto you, He that believeth on me, the works that I do shall he do also; and greater works than these shall he do; because I go unto my Father. John 14:12.*

Recently I read again this precious statement: "Not because we see or feel that God hears us are we to believe. We are to trust in His promises. When we come to Him in faith, every petition enters the heart of God. When we have asked for His blessing, we should believe that we receive it, and thank Him that we *have* received it. Then we are to go about our duties, assured that the blessing will be realized when we need it most. When we have learned to do this, we shall know that our prayers are answered. God will do for us 'exceeding abundantly,' 'according to the riches of His glory,' and 'the working of His mighty power.' (Eph. 3:20, 16; 1:19)" (*The Desire of Ages*, p. 200).

And Jesus said that the person who believes in Him will do the same works that He did—and even greater works.

My friend Henry Wright, preacher extraordinary, has a sermon he entitled "You Too Can Walk on Water." He loves to tell Christians that they can be like Peter and walk on the water. In fact, he says, Christians *already* are water-walkers. Every time we go to church instead of following the crowd to the ball game, every habit of cigarettes or liquor or drugs or casual sex overcome, every turning from foul mouth or foul temper is a walking on water.

He's right. It takes greater power to make a bad person good, to live a life of consistent unselfishness and caring, than to walk on water. After all, bugs can walk on water—it's not such a big deal!

How do we walk on water? Every day—*this* day—we turn our lives over to Jesus. We ask Him for grace to meet every need; we lay before Him every decision, every worry, every task. Then we thank Him for hearing and answering our petition, and we go out into the day, knowing that *already* the blessing is ours. When we need it most, the blessing will be there awaiting our use.

I believe God invites every Christian to a higher calling. We sing, pray, and talk Christ, but most of the time our lives are just like everyone else's—harried, anxious, frustrated. God invites us to the unbroken peace, joy, and assurance that Jesus experienced when He lived among us.

*O God, I turn my life over to You. While the day is still fresh, take every care, every burden. I claim Your promise to supply the answer when I need it most. And thank You for already giving me this blessing.*

*August 22*

# UNDERSTANDING THE CODE

**And when he putteth forth his own sheep, he goeth before them, and the sheep follow him: for they know his voice. And a stranger will they not follow, but will flee from him: for they know not the voice of strangers. John 10:4, 5.**

Some years ago, according to a story I heard, Western Union Telegraph Company advertised for a telegraph operator. Many people applied for the job. When one young man arrived at the office, the room was already full.

As he sat down among them to await his turn to be interviewed, he noticed that a telegraph key was click-clack-clacking.

Suddenly the young man jumped to his feet and disappeared down the hall. A few minutes later he was back. "I got it! I got it!" he yelled.

The others protested, "We've been here all day. How did you do it?"

He'd simply listened to the click-clack-clacking of the telegraph key. It was giving a message: "If you understand this code, come immediately to room 212 for an interview."

If we love Jesus, we know He is our best friend. We know that He knows all about us and wants only what is best for us. We listen for His voice; we understand the code.

"Jesus knows us individually, and is touched with the feeling of our infirmities," writes Ellen White. "He knows us all by name. He knows the very house in which we live, the name of each occupant. He has at times given directions to His servants to go to a certain street in a certain city, to such a house, to find one of His sheep" (*The Desire of Ages*, p. 479).

The apostle Paul understood the code. On his second missionary journey he and Silas were "forbidden by the Holy Spirit to speak the word in Asia." When they attempted to go into Bithynia, "the Spirit of Jesus did not allow them" (Acts 16:6, 7, RSV); so they passed on to Troas.

Old Testament men and women of God also understood the code. Abram, dweller in opulent Ur of the Chaldees, abandoned comforts and security to go to a land he'd never seen. He heard the code—and understood.

The child Samuel, robed in a gown made by his mother, Hannah, understood the code. Three times the Lord came, calling to him in the night—"Samuel, Samuel." And at last the little boy replied, "Speak; for thy servant heareth" (1 Sam. 3:10).

*God, give me ears today to hear Your voice!*

*August 23*

# WHILE THE SUN STILL SHINES

**I must work the works of him that sent me, while it is day: the night cometh, when no man can work. John 9:4.**

Recently my wife got out a folder of my early sermons, and we sat together looking over those old notes. Written out in full, often including several drafts, they brought back the earnestness and the hopes and the exhortations of situations nearly 30 years ago.

Thirty years! Where did they go? I spend very little time looking back. I hadn't seen those yellowing notes in many years, hadn't given a thought of those early days of ministry. I like to keep my head to the wind, to keep moving ahead, to leave the past to someone else. The Lord has been exceedingly kind to Noelene and me, leading us along varied and changing paths, taking us to many lands of earth, continually opening to us new avenues of ministry.

So I looked at those witnesses to messages I gave long ago—I *must* have said what the notes say I intended to say, even if I can hardly recognize myself—with mingled feelings of interest and revulsion. To me, going back, even for an hour, is like throwing in the towel on life. The last use I'd want to make of those sermons is to preach them today!

Night is coming, says the Master, when no one can work. Night is coming for the world—its day in the sun must soon come to an end. And my night is coming. Unless Jesus returns to earth soon, I shall reach the sunset, as did my father and my mother and all others before them.

How fast the flying days, "swifter than a weaver's shuttle" (Job 7:6)! Sunrise, sunset, one day following another, until 30 years have gone, until 50, until 70.

But the sun still shines. It shines no more for the billions who have gone to their long rest, but it shines for me. It shines for you. It shines today.

So like Jesus, let us do the will of Him who has called us to His love. Let us fill this day with the joy of His presence.

*August 24*

# JESUS MEANS FREEDOM

*If the Son therefore shall make you free, ye shall be free indeed. John 8:36.*

Let's think of two men from our generation.

For the first, picture a sunless, timeless room. The heavy shades are drawn—as always. It's always day in this room—and always night. This room is a penthouse apartment in Acapulco, but it could be anywhere, or nowhere.

A man lives in this room. Lives? He exists. His frame, once a lofty six feet three, has shrunk by inches. Once he could win the favor of any movie star his gaze rested upon; now he weighs a mere 90 pounds. His hair is long, down to his waist; his nails have grown out; his toenails have grown till they look like corkscrews.

For years he has lived like this, in apartments such as this. He sits or lies on his bed, naked or almost naked. He runs movies; one, *Ice Station Zebra,* he has seen 150 times. Aides wait on him. They bring him whatever he wants—but he doesn't want much. He sits for hours, gathering up his long hair, letting it fall, gathering it up, letting it fall. Sometimes he picks up the telephone—"Bob, I'm lonesome."

Now he is sick, very sick. In his last moments his hand reaches out for the hypodermic that is always by his bedside. He inspects it, puts it to the vein, and tries to press down the plunger. But he's too weak—he cries out for an aide to help him.

Looking at that wraith, that pathetic skeleton, who could have thought that he was one of the world's richest men? But he was—both rich and powerful, worth billions of dollars. But soon only the money would remain. His aides would put him on the plane, in secret and with subterfuge as ever, but Howard Hughes would die before reaching Dallas.

With all his riches, all his power, was he a free man?

Now for the other man's story. He is a Russian artillery officer on the German front; it is a few months before the end of World War II. One day the military police suddenly seize and arrest him. His offense? In a private letter he has been so indiscreet as to refer slightingly to Stalin, and the Russian censors have caught it.

So he is now on his way out of Germany—back to Russia. He will spend the next 11 years in prison, labor camps, and exile. He will lose all his possessions, each badge of office, every right.

But by losing everything, he would find freedom. He would write of the blessed experience of that prison cell as "the heavenly kingdom of the liberated spirit," as "gulping down the elixir of life." To the world Aleksandr Solzhenitsyn would become a symbol of the liberated spirit—a spirit that bars and walls, forced labor and starvation, bad names and deprivation, cannot take away.

Strange, isn't it? The prisoner found true freedom—by losing everything. And that's the way we find freedom in Jesus.

*August 25*

# THE FREEDOM JESUS OFFERS

*Jesus then said to the Jews who had believed in him, "If you continue in my word, you are truly my disciples, and you will know the truth, and the truth will make you free." John 8:31, 32, RSV.*

Recently someone said to me: "When you meet an atheist and he says he doesn't believe in God, ask him which god he doesn't believe in!" There are gods I don't believe in also. But the Jesus of the Gospels is the liberator—for the people of His time and for every age.

The freedom Jesus offers is freedom *from*, freedom *to*, and freedom *in*.

He reminds us of that little loaded word *sin*. Everyone who commits sin is a slave, He says. "Truly, truly, I say to you, every one who commits sin is a slave to sin" (John 8:34, RSV). But He has come to break sin's bonds, to burst its yoke.

251

I don't know just which bonds you may have. They may be vicious habits that shame you in the silent hours. Or they may be "respectable" vices. Some of us have our special bonds, you know. We tend to be cold and aloof, setting ourselves apart from other people, retreating into our little cave in which we use the same jargon and eat the same foods. We're afraid to get involved in the world, in which men and women are desperate and dying. We tend to distance ourselves from humanity, and try to perfect character by looking at ourselves.

But Jesus had a larger vision. He had left behind Nazareth, home, and work to do the work of God. He who offered freedom —freedom from sin, from the bonds of habit, from fear, from old ways—knew and lived it Himself.

It was not merely freedom *from*—it was also freedom *to*. So often we think of all the things we give up as Christians. Jesus calls us to a freedom of *becoming*, of a *life*. Instead of the bonds of slavery, He wants us to enjoy a new status—sons and daughters of the living God. "And the servant abideth not in the house for ever: but the Son abideth ever" (John 8:35).

Jesus can make us free. Free to set aside pride and prejudice, barriers of race and wealth. Free to take another by the hand and say from the heart, "My brother! My sister!" Free to love, free to laugh, free to share, free to work together.

But this freedom to which He calls us is a freedom *in*—in Him. "If the Son sets you free, you will be free indeed" (John 8:36, NIV). He is the Liberator, our Liberator. He frees us—only He.

This is why we need to keep our eyes fixed on Him. Not a Jesus of our prejudices, not a Jesus of centuries of ecclesiastical tradition, not a remote, inaccessible Jesus. But the Jesus of the Gospels. Jesus the Liberator. The living Jesus.

*August 26*

# WHAT GOD IS LIKE

*Jesus said to him, "Have I been with you so long, and yet you do not know me, Philip? He who has seen me has seen the Father; how can you say, 'Show us the Father'?" John 14:9, RSV.*

One day while in a large city in an Eastern land, I saw a strange sight. A group of men were lining up for a religious parade. Each year on the anniversary of a famous teacher of their faith, they assembled to march through the town. They carried sacred objects from the shrine with them, and musical instruments to announce their coming.

Then the musicians began to play. The music grew louder and faster, and some of the young men began to dance as the procession moved down the street. Louder and faster, louder and faster—the dancing became frenzied. The dancers would pause, one by one, and make their way to the priest. Their faces were flushed; their eyes burned brightly. I was amazed to see what the priest had in his hand—metal skewers, at least six inches long. The dancers would take a skewer and force it through one cheek and out the other, or through the nose, or the lobes of the ear, or the skin of the torso. Some had several piercing their flesh. They uttered no cry, made no grimace, showed no sign of pain; nor did I notice any bleeding. Then back to the procession, to dance with even wilder frenzy.

It was not a pretty sight to me, and I turned away from it. But it has remained sharp in memory and has caused me to reflect on this question: What idea of God did those people have?

History tells us that religion has called forth the most bizarre acts. Wars have been fought in the name of God, babies slaughtered, populations decimated. People have starved themselves, flogged themselves, left parents, spouses, children—all because they thought God demanded it of them.

So it is supremely important to know what God is really like. We cannot trust our impressions, our imagination, our inner voices, what others might tell us. The matter is too important to be left to chance.

And Jesus, to whom we are looking in every reading this year, is the supreme revelation of God. He shows us what God is really like. "No one has ever seen God; the only Son, who is in the bosom of the Father, he has made him known" (John 1:18, RSV).

We don't know the actual word Jesus used when He told us to call God our Father, since He was speaking in Aramaic and the New Testament is written in Greek. But in two places Paul goes back to an Aramaic word, *Abba* (Rom. 8:15; Gal. 4:6). This word is a term of deep affection, one that we could translate as "Daddy."

When my son was just a little fellow and was learning how to put sounds to words, he would call me "Dadden." In the middle of the night we would hear the young voice from the crib: "Dadden! Dadden! Dadden-adden!" Even at midnight those words were precious to me.

This, Jesus was telling us, is how we should think of God. Think of Him as our Dad, as One who cares for us supremely.

What a God!

# STINGERS

*For God sent not his Son into the world to condemn the world; but that the world through him might be saved. John 3:17.*

I have a file of unsent letters. Occasionally I feel compelled to write a "stinger" to someone, but my practice is *never* to mail it the same day. I let it sit for at least one night. The next morning, or several mornings later, I deal with it—it usually goes into the unsent file!

Now, at times I have mailed a stinger. After letting it sit for a night or even longer, I have decided to let it fly. Usually the stinger was in response to something that came in my mail.

I'm getting to the point of concluding that all stingers would be better left unsent. Regardless of how much the person addressed deserves to be set straight, regardless of what he or she may have written, regardless of all the reasons I can muster to justify—even to demand—firing off the stinger, the truth is that the stinger contains too much of my pride and too little of the spirit of Christ, no matter how many references it may make to Him.

But, you may say, didn't Jesus at times speak harshly? What about His series of woes on the scribes and Pharisees? (See Matt. 23:13-36.) Hypocrites, He called them, and blind guides, snakes, a brood of vipers!

Yes, but Jesus always rebuked in love. Even when He exposed and denounced religious cant and hypocrisy, tears were in His voice. He hated the sin but loved the sinner.

Nor did Jesus seek to justify Himself. He left His case in the hands of His Father. "The one who sent me is with me; he has not left me alone, for I always do what pleases him" (John 8:29, NIV). And again: "I am not seeking glory for myself; but there is one who seeks it, and he is the judge" (verse 50, NIV).

It isn't our place to condemn. Jesus came, not to condemn the world, but to save it.

It isn't our place to judge others. We are too flawed for that task. Unlike Jesus, we love the sin and hate the sinner.

It isn't our place to defend ourselves. If we cast our lives wholly over to the Father as Jesus did, He will take care of us. And if we have His approval, why worry about what others say?

*Dear Lord, teach me today to live by the power of the Christ-life. I turn my life over to You. Make me patient, slow to anger, slow to judge; quick to forgive, quick to forget.*

# GROWING OLD GRACEFULLY

*I tell you the truth, when you were younger you dressed yourself and went where you wanted; but when you are old you will stretch out your hands, and someone else will dress you and lead you where you do not want to go. John 21:18, NIV.*

In this passage Jesus predicted the manner of Peter's death. At the end of his road he would hang, like his Master, from a cross. Tradition has it that when that day came, Peter, perhaps recalling his threefold denial of Jesus, requested that he be crucified upside down.

Peter, always active, quick to take the lead, ready to rush in where angels feared to tread, would find himself in the hands of others, taken where he did not want to go. Thereby he becomes typical of us all as we grow old.

To grow old gracefully—that is the goal. Many people, I have noticed, fall into a negative mind-set as they come to retirement. *Aprés moi le déluge* ("After me the flood"), they seem to think with Louis XV. The business or the company won't be as good anymore; everything has started to fall apart already; the old days were better.

It's hard to hand over the reins of control to younger hands. It's hard to hand over the reins of our own lives to someone else. We need much of the Lord's grace to grow old gracefully.

Paul found the secret of eternal youth. Although his outer man—the body—was wearing out, he said, the inner man—his spirit—was renewed every day (2 Cor. 4:16). He had learned to look away from others and to keep his eyes fixed on the Lord Jesus. "For our light and momentary troubles are achieving for us an eternal glory that far outweighs them all," he said. "So we fix our eyes not on what is seen, but on what is unseen. For what is seen is temporary, but what is unseen is eternal" (verses 17, 18, NIV).

My favorite Christian author puts it this way: "When we submit ourselves to Christ, the heart is united with His heart, the will is merged in His will, the mind becomes one with His mind, the thoughts are brought into captivity to Him; we live His life" (*Christ's Object Lessons*, p. 312).

Jesus was "full of grace and truth" (John 1:14). Every stage of His life—childhood, teen years, adulthood, carpentry, ministry—was marked by grace.

May that be said also of us today, no matter what our age.

# JESUS AND THE GREEKS

*And there were certain Greeks among them that came up to worship at the feast: The same came therefore to Philip, which was of Bethsaida of Galilee, and desired him, saying, Sir, we would see Jesus. John 12:20, 21.*

At the birth of Jesus, Wise Men came from the East to worship Him. Now, toward the close of His ministry, men came from the West to learn more about Him.

Strange, isn't it, that those closest to Christ appreciated Him the least. The teachers of Israel, whose whole lives were bound up with the law, who looked for the Messiah, failed to recognize the One to whom the law and the prophets pointed. They did not acclaim His birth, though foreigners did; and now, near the end of Christ's mission, their hearts remained sternly set against Him. But those outside the pale, those denied the opportunities and privileges of the religious hierarchy, would come, saying, "Sir, we would see Jesus."

Christianity spread rapidly among the slaves of the Roman Empire. In India it took root among the untouchables of Hinduism—those whom Mahatma Gandhi later would call *Harijans*, "children of God." In country after country it has been embraced by the poor and the broken, rather than by the wealthy, the highborn, and the comfortable.

What encouragement these Greeks must have brought to Jesus! They reminded Him that His years of labor had not been in vain, that the widespread rejection among His own people would not be repeated everywhere. "When Christ heard the eager request, 'We would see Jesus,' echoing the hungering cry of the world, His countenance lighted up, and He said, 'The hour is come, that the Son of man should be glorified.' In the request of the Greeks He saw an earnest of the results of His great sacrifice" (*The Desire of Ages*, p. 621).

Praise God for the Greeks! And praise God that Jesus welcomed the Greeks into His kingdom!

For I am a Greek—not because the blood of ancient Hellenes runs in my veins, but in that I too am outside the pale of Judaism. If the gospel comes only to those who have the right parents, then I have no hope.

But Paul tells us: "For I am not ashamed of the gospel of Christ: for it is the power of God unto salvation to every one that believeth; to the Jew first, and also to the Greek" (Rom. 1:16).

*Today, dear God, we too would see Jesus. Give just a glimpse of His glory and grace to make the things of earth grow strangely dim.*

# THE LAW OF SELF-PRESERVATION

**Verily, verily, I say unto you, Except a corn of wheat fall into the ground and die, it abideth alone: but if it die, it bringeth forth much fruit. John 12:24.**

God's universe runs on principles that are just the opposite of the way most people approach life. Only when the Holy Spirit opens our eyes do we see as God sees.

Take happiness, for instance. Everybody wants to get it—but happiness doesn't come by getting. Just the reverse: as we forget ourselves and seek to make someone else happy, happiness comes to us.

For most people, success in life comes from acquiring, and the greater the acquisitions, the more the success. Long ago a wise king who in some respects also was very weak discovered the fallacy of that line of reasoning. The book of Ecclesiastes recounts the barrenness of his quest. He sought after pleasure, building enterprises, gardens and orchards, swimming pools; acquired servants, silver and gold, choirs and orchestras, but in the end all was vanity, emptiness (see Eccl. 2:1-11).

Perhaps that led Solomon to formulate the proverb: "There is that scattereth, and yet increaseth; and there is that withholdeth more than is meet, but it tendeth to poverty" (Prov. 11:24).

Are we ready for the ultimate reversal of human values? "The law of sacrifice is the law of self-preservation. The husbandman preserves his grain by casting it away. So in human life. To give is to live. The life that will be preserved is the life that is freely given in service to God and man. Those who for Christ's sake sacrifice their life in this world will keep it unto life eternal" (*The Desire of Ages*, pp. 623, 624).

Christianity offers life—but its supreme symbol, the cross, stands for death! In Jesus we see God's grain of wheat cast into the furrow of the world's need. By His willingness to go to the death for us, we have hope of eternal life. By His stripes we are healed. Through His sufferings we find comfort.

On a cold November day my daughter, Julie, and I scooped out holes in the dark Michigan soil, dropped in bulbs—daffodils, tulips, hyacinths, crocuses—and ran inside as the snow flurries began to

BHG-9                    257

swirl. For months the bulbs lay buried under three feet of snow. But then March, the snow gone, the good earth emerged again — and trumpets of yellow, cups of red and orange, and bells of blue.

And from our lives, plain and insignificant as they may seem, spring forth divine blossoms as we cast ourselves into God's furrow.

*August 31*

# TO DO HIS WILL

*If any man will do his will, he shall know of the doctrine, whether it be of God, or whether I speak of myself. John 7:17.*

There is no part of the brain that neurosurgeons can point to and say "That is the will." Rather, willing is an activity of the whole person, a mysterious ability of our mysterious minds.

Indeed, such behaviorists as B. F. Skinner, who wrote *Beyond Freedom and Dignity*, dispute that "will" describes anything significant. They hold that rather than our deciding or choosing, we really *respond* to stimuli and situations. They say that our heredity and past experiences condition us, that what we think is a choice is really an inevitable reaction from all that has gone before.

The biblical view of humanity directly opposes this concept. No, we don't have *absolute* freedom—heredity, environment, and past experiences do influence us in every situation. Further, we have a bent toward evil, an appetite for evil, as a result of the fall of our first parents. But we have *sufficient* freedom—we ultimately are masters of our own fate, captains of our own destiny.

The Holy Spirit makes the difference. Adam and Eve, before their sin, could choose freely; we cannot. Left to ourselves, we will turn always to the wrong, because that is the bent of our natures. "I was shapen in iniquity, and in sin did my mother conceive me" (Ps. 51:5). But the Holy Spirit restores freedom of choice to us; He activates our conscience, creating the desire for God and His purposes for our lives. But finally *we* make the decision.

"Everything," wrote Ellen White, "depends upon the right action of the will" (*The Ministry of Healing*, p. 176). As I understand Christianity, its essence is a series of choices, of continually saying yes to God as the Holy Spirit offers to us the way of life.

Some days it's easy to say yes to God. Our whole being yearns after Him, like the psalmist, who cried out: "As the deer pants for streams of water, so my soul pants for you, O God. My soul thirsts for God, for the living God. When can I go and meet with God?" (Ps. 42:1, 2, NIV).

But some days are much harder. Some days we feel like turning our back on God, blocking out the invitation of the Spirit to walk in the good way. What will we do then—follow duty or follow inclination?

Make me a captive, Lord,
And then I shall be free;
Force me to render up my sword,
And I shall conqueror be.
I sink in life's alarms
When by myself I stand;
Imprison me within Thine arms,
And strong shall be my hand.
—George Matheson

# WHO ARE YOU?

*"Who are you?" they asked. "Just what I have been claiming all along," Jesus replied. John 8:25, NIV.*

Jesus has made the cover of *Time* magazine 16 times, most recently in 1988, when the August 15 issue ran a long story, "Who Was Jesus?" In an ingenious cover, the portrait of Jesus was composed of details from 17 images of Jesus, ranging from a sixth-century Italian mosaic to a 1980s painting by Englishman Curtis Hooper.

What led to the *Time* cover? Release of a controversial movie, *The Last Temptation of Christ.* In it Jesus is married to Mary Magdalene, Judas is a hero, Paul a hypocrite and liar, and Jesus on the eve of His crucifixion doesn't know whether to preach love or murder to the Romans.

In an effort to block showing of the movie, an evangelical leader offered to buy it for $10 million—so that he might burn it. Other Christian leaders picketed the home of Lew Wasserman, chairman of Universal Studios, makers of the film. But *The Last Temptation of Christ* went to the public nonetheless.

Jesus remains the great unsolved question of the ages: "Who are You?" He intrigues men and women today as He intrigued them 2,000 years ago.

Scholars argue over His person. Some set Him forth as a wandering wise man, others as a revolutionary, still others as a brilliant rabbi. They dispute over His words, arguing as to which are authentic, at times displaying amazing lack of historical perspective—because eyewitnesses were still living when the Gospels were penned and could quickly have called foul if Matthew, Mark, Luke, and John had falsified the accounts.

But to us who believe, Jesus is not a question. He is an answer, God's answer to all our needs, all our worries, all our questions. In Him we find our all—our true selves, our life.

Back of all our problems lies that little, powerful, loaded word—*sin*. And only Jesus can take away our sins. No one else. Nothing else. Apart from Him we will die—and do die—in our sins.

I believe that Jesus was who He claimed to be—God's Son, the Messiah, the Saviour of the world. I believe not merely as a wish that it might be so, but because I know *Him*—know Him as friend, as brother, as Lord of my life.

Friend, who do *you* think He is?

September 2

# THE BREAD OF LIFE

*And Jesus said unto them, I am the bread of life: he that cometh to me shall never hunger; and he that believeth on me shall never thirst. John 6:35.*

This saying of Jesus was a turning point in His ministry. On the previous day the people of Israel had flocked around, attempting by force to crown Him king. Fed on the barley loaves and fishes, they acclaimed Him as Messiah. But after this saying and its elaboration, they turned from Him in disappointment. So great was the falling away that Jesus would ask the twelve, "You do not want to leave too, do you?" (John 6:67, NIV).

Jesus fed the multitude on the mountainside in Galilee. He fed them because they were hungry. He feeds us also. Every slice of bread we eat comes from His hands of love. The air we breathe, the sunlight and the rain, the snow and the harvest, are gifts of His goodness. He upholds all things by the word of His power (Heb. 1:3). "He's got the whole world in His hands."

The crowds, their bellies filled, wanted more the next day. They sought out Jesus, and eventually found Him in the synagogue at Capernaum. They sought the gift rather than the Giver. Do we?

Jesus spoke straight to them: "I tell you the truth, you are looking for me, not because you saw miraculous signs but because you ate the loaves and had your fill" (John 6:26, NIV). What would He say to us? We're all glad for the good times: "The Lord has really

260

blessed me," we say. What would we say if the bad times rolled in—if we lost our health, lost our job, lost our farm, lost our business?

Job, who owned much and who had been blessed by God, lost all—even his sons and daughters. But his trust in the Lord didn't flinch: "Naked came I out of my mother's womb, and naked shall I return thither; the Lord gave, and the Lord hath taken away; blessed be the name of the Lord" (Job 1:21).

Jesus is the bread of our life. He Himself, not His gifts, not His blessings. Just Jesus alone.

"Christ became one flesh with us, in order that we might become one spirit with Him. It is by virtue of this union that we are to come forth from the grave—not merely as a manifestation of the power of Christ, but because, through faith, His life has become ours. Those who see Christ in His true character, and receive Him into the heart, have everlasting life. It is through the Spirit that Christ dwells in us; and the Spirit of God, received into the heart by faith, is the beginning of the life eternal" (*The Desire of Ages,* p. 388).

*September 3*

# WAITING TO BE GATHERED IN

*All that the Father giveth me shall come to me; and him that cometh to me I will in no wise cast out. John 6:37.*

Often the work of the gospel seems slow and difficult. But every now and then we come across someone who is "waiting only to be gathered in"—one of those souls who are "looking wistfully to heaven" (*The Acts of the Apostles*, p. 109). Like Suresh.

Suresh was born a Brahmin—the highest caste of Hinduism. Further, his relatives were members of a sect that strongly opposed Christianity. They'd break up evangelistic meetings and try to persuade converts from Hinduism to renounce Christianity.

Suresh—an unlikely candidate for Jesus' kingdom? Look again.

As a high school student, Suresh one day saw an ad for correspondence lessons. He enrolled, began the course, but didn't finish it because of the pressure of other studies. After high school, he went on to university and earned a degree in meteorology. This led him into the Indian Air Force, in which he worked as a part of a ground crew.

He was a serious-minded young man. A clean liver, he didn't waste his time and money on carousing when he went on leave. Instead, he continued to read and to study, eventually gaining two master's degrees.

One evening he was listening to the radio. The program from Radio Ceylon (now Sri Lanka) switched to religious music. A man with an American accent began to speak, in a voice that was earnest, sincere, and kind—the voice of H.M.S. Richards, Sr. Suresh was hardly listening, but the voice impressed him. At the close of the program he heard the name of the sponsor—the Voice of Prophecy.

The Voice of Prophecy! He remembered the correspondence lessons, never completed, from years before. Quickly he noted the address from the radio announcer and wrote away for more information.

Some time later he visited Bombay. His parents had arranged a bride for him, and he wished to meet her. But he had a second purpose: he hoped to make contact with Seventh-day Adventists, who he now knew sponsored the Voice of Prophecy.

Now, Bombay is a city of more than 8 million people. Adventists have few members there, just a couple of churches. What were the chances of Suresh's meeting an Adventist? From human statistics, remote; but not when God's Spirit is at work.

As Suresh checked into a hotel, he noticed a foreigner in the lobby. He approached him and asked, "Would you happen to know where the Seventh-day Adventist mission is in this city?"

"Indeed," replied the stranger. "I am president of the mission!" It was Pastor Robin Riches. He took Suresh to the mission, and for four hours they studied the Bible together, going over Suresh's questions.

Later I met Suresh. We studied some more, and eventually I had the great privilege of leading him into the waters that Jesus had entered long ago—baptism.

In Isaiah 43:12 the Lord tells us: "I have revealed and saved and proclaimed" (NIV). That word is as true today as it has ever been.

September 4

# A SYMBOL TRANSFORMED

*Then Jesus said unto them, Verily, verily, I say unto you, Except ye eat the flesh of the Son of man, and drink his blood, ye have no life in you. Whoso eateth my flesh, and drinketh my blood, hath eternal life; and I will raise him up at the last day. John 6:53, 54.*

Do you find these words mysterious? So did the people who first heard them. John records: "Many therefore of his disciples, when they had heard this, said, This is an hard saying; who can hear it?" (verse 60).

Jesus was speaking to Jews, and Jews carefully avoided ingesting blood. The prohibition went back to God's covenant with Noah after the Flood: "But you must not eat meat that has its lifeblood still in it" (Gen. 9:4, NIV). It was repeated to Israel at the founding of the nation: "Any Israelite or any alien living among them who eats any blood—I will set my face against that person who eats blood and will cut him off from his people" (Lev. 17:10, NIV).

Conscientious Jews today still observe this stipulation. They eat only meats from which all the blood has been removed. But here is Jesus in the synagogue of Nazareth saying: "Drink My blood." No wonder His hearers bristled and His disciples cringed.

Now, if Jesus had said "Eat My flesh and pour out My blood," or even "Eat My flesh and sprinkle My blood," the people wouldn't have been nearly so offended (although human flesh was considered unclean). The concept would have conformed to the Jewish sacrificial system.

But Jesus radically transformed the symbol of blood by saying, "Drink my blood." God told the children of Israel: "But be sure you do not eat the blood, because the blood is the life, and you must not eat the life with the meat" (Deut. 12:23, NIV).

Jesus died on our behalf, God's sacrifice for our sins. But He does even more: He gives us His life.

It is still true—the life is in the blood. People whose blood seeps away because of accident or disease will die; they cannot live without blood. And a person who does not receive Christ's "blood" will die spiritually. We cannot live without the nourishment His life provides.

Now we begin to understand the deep import of these mysterious words of Jesus. They give us added insights into the meaning of the Lord's Supper. The Supper reminds us of His death for us, but it also speaks of life—His life imparted to us. "This is my blood of the covenant," said Jesus. And He also said: "Drink from it, all of you" (Matt. 26:28, 27, NIV).

What mystery is here! No, not, as some say, because the bread and wine become the *actual* body and blood of the Lord. But a greater miracle: the Lord of the universe, Creator of heaven and earth, gives us *Himself.*

He gives us not just an example of life, but life itself!

September 5

# POWER IN THE BLOOD

*He that eateth my flesh, and drinketh my blood, dwelleth in me, and I in him. John 6:56.*

In Jesus' sermon on the bread of life recorded in John 6, He shows our utter dependence on Him by using two symbols: one homespun, the other startling.

The first symbol is bread. "I am the bread of life," He tells us (verse 48, NIV). He further elaborates: "I am the living bread which came down from heaven" (verse 51).

Bread—simple, basic, elemental food. We are as dependent on Jesus for our spiritual life as we are on our daily bread for physical life.

The second symbol startles us: He tells us to eat His flesh and to drink His blood. But the meaning is the same as the first: "The bread that I will give is my flesh, which I will give for the life of the world," Jesus says (verse 51).

Bread, flesh, blood—Jesus is our life, our power.

Dr. Paul Brand, who pioneered restorative surgery for lepers, tells of an epidemic of measles that struck Vellore in south India, where the Brand family was then living. The Brands had an infant daughter, Estelle, and because of her age she was exposed to high risk.

The pediatrician explained that convalescent serum—serum from a person who had contracted measles and overcome it —would protect the little girl. Word went around Vellore that the Brands needed the "blood of an overcomer."

"It was no use finding somebody who had conquered chicken pox or had recovered from a broken leg. Such people, albeit healthy, could not give the specific help we needed to overcome measles. We needed someone who had experienced measles and had defeated that disease," writes Brand in his book *In His Image*. The Brands located such a person, took out some of his blood, and injected their daughter with the convalescent serum. Armed with the "borrowed" antibodies, their daughter fought off the invading disease. The injected serum gave her body time to manufacture its own antibodies. Estelle overcame measles—not by her own body's strength, but as the result of a battle that had taken place previously within someone else.

And Jesus, who has suffered and overcome, gives us His life. We today may supplicate His throne of grace for strength to overcome.

264

# LIFE MORE ABUNDANT

*The thief cometh not, but for to steal, and to kill, and to destroy: I am come that they might have life, and that they might have it more abundantly. John 10:10.*

Even without hope of the afterlife, Christianity is the best, the happiest, the most fulfilling life we can enjoy on this earth.

Now, the world portrays Christ and Christians as killjoys. They say following Jesus drains the color from life—makes us weak, dependent wimps. That's a lie.

They say also that Christians can only long for "pie in the sky by and by" because they don't have fun here. That too is a lie.

When Jesus is our best friend, heaven begins right here, right now. We find our true selves. We feel wholly complete, fulfilled. We have peace. And at His "right hand there are pleasures for evermore" (Ps. 16:11).

"Heaven is to begin on this earth," wrote Ellen White. "When the Lord's people are filled with meekness and tenderness, they will realize that His banner over them is love, and His fruit will be sweet to their taste" (*Testimonies*, vol. 7, p. 131). And again: "The life on earth is the beginning of the life in heaven; education on earth is an initiation into the principles of heaven; the lifework here is a training for the lifework there" (*Education*, p. 307).

Confucius is supposed to have remarked that the loveliest sight in the world was a little child walking down the path hand in hand with an adult. I can think of a lovelier one: a child, a teenager, or a young adult who decides he or she doesn't have to waste time sowing wild oats, but instead turns life and energy over to Jesus.

In adult life also Jesus gives us life more abundant. Those years of building the nest; of school days, camping trips, ball games; of putting down roots and shaping character; of struggling to pay the bills and fighting problems and establishing oneself in a lifework—He walks by our side every day. He's with us every moment, in every care, in laughter and in heartache.

And when the nest once again is empty, He continues to pour His life upon us. Even when we stand alone—children gone, life's companion gone—His life is more abundant. "Hearken unto me, O house of Jacob, and all the remnant of the house of Israel, which are borne by me from the belly, which are carried from the womb: and even to your old age I am he; and even to hoar hairs will I carry you: I have made, and I will bear; even I will carry, and will deliver you" (Isa. 46:3, 4).

# ETERNAL LIFE—NOW!

*Verily, verily, I say unto you, He that believeth on me hath everlasting life. John 6:47.*

As a teenager growing up in Adelaide, South Australia, my best friend was Bill Marr. Although he was a couple years older, we shared common interests—motorcycles and the Lord.

With thick black hair, dark bright eyes, and Scottish brogue and humor, Bill Marr was liked by everybody. Bill was in love with life and in love with the Lord.

In his 20s Bill felt a tug from the Lord and went off to study theology at Avondale College. I chose chemistry and, after completing a degree, joined a large chemical manufacturer. But after a few years I too felt the Lord's tug and left for Avondale.

Bill Marr had completed his studies by several years before I enrolled there. Students and faculty still talked about him, however—especially how his energetic, excitable nature led him to stutter at times. But the problem left him whenever he stood up to preach.

Bill's life had taken an abrupt turn before I ever met him. Back in Scotland he and his family had dabbled in the occult. As a boy there, early one morning Bill woke up and saw a green woman sitting on his bed. He threw his pillow at her—and it went right through her!

By the time the family decided to emigrate to Australia, they had become ardent spiritualists. Bill could snap his fingers and make a table or a chair move across the room.

But in Australia they were confronted by One who has greater power than the spirits. They met Jesus, and after a fierce battle, He became their Lord.

Many times I heard Bill tell his story. "I have seen the power of the spirits and I have seen the power of Jesus, and I know who is the best Lord," he would tell audiences.

Bill became a powerful preacher. People loved him. Many considered him one of the most promising young evangelists in the land.

And then—leukemia. Bill Marr was cut down at the height of his powers, dead in his mid-30s.

But he will live again. On earth he already *had* eternal life. He knew Jesus, and Jesus' life had become His. That life guarantees that Bill Marr will rise from the grave to live forever with his Lord.

# BREAD OF HEAVEN

*Jesus said to them, "I tell you the truth, it is not Moses who has given you the bread from heaven, but it is my Father who gives you the true bread from heaven. John 6:32, NIV.*

Bread! Jesus could have employed no more arresting symbol to His hearers. Bread! That one word brought together the struggle for existence, the day-to-day quest to sustain life.

We who live in the West are accustomed to such abundance that we scarcely grasp the struggle for existence of the rest of the world. Many of us spend more money on our dog or cat than millions of people have to live on day by day.

For the most part, the Israelites at the time of Christ ate sparingly. Their basic food was bread. In Hebrew "to eat bread" meant "to have a meal," just as in the Greek poet Homer's writings, a "breadeater" meant "a man," notes Henri Daniel-Rops. "Bread, then, was to be treated with respect: it was forbidden to put raw meat on top of a loaf, to set a pitcher of water upon it or a hot plate against it, and it was forbidden to throw away the crumbs, which, if they were 'as large as an olive,' were to be gathered up. And bread was not to be cut, but broken. . . .

"The poor ate barley-bread, the rich the bread of wheat. The corn was ground between two millstones, almost always by the women, and at home: more than usually careful work produced the particularly fine flour that was used for cakes and certain liturgical purposes. The dough was worked in kneading troughs, and these homely objects are to be found as early as Exodus" (From *Daily Life in the Time of Jesus*, by Henri Daniel-Rops, pp. 229-232. Published in 1980 by Servant Publications, P.O. Box 8617, Ann Arbor, Michigan 48107. Used with permission.).

In view of the common people's battle for daily bread, we understand better why they were so impressed by Jesus' miracles of mass feeding. Although the food He provided—bread and fish—was simple, that was their usual meal. And now One had come who could by a word create bread and fish! With Him as leader of the nation, they would have a secure food source—no more empty bellies and crying children!

Food meant much to them. It still means much to people with empty bellies and crying children, who exist on a day-by-day basis. But Jesus pointed the Jews, as He points us all, to bread that is even more important. When Jesus Himself was hungry and the tempter urged Him to turn stones into bread, He replied, "Man does not live on bread alone, but on every word that comes from the mouth of God" (Matt. 4:4, NIV).

To *know* God—this is bread from heaven.

To *know* Jesus as our best friend—this is the true bread.

To *know* the Spirit as indwelling guide and power—this is living by the word of God.

# THE LIGHT OF THE WORLD

*Then spake Jesus again unto them, saying, I am the light of the world: he that followeth me shall not walk in darkness, but shall have the light of life. John 8:12.*

Oh, the creative genius of the human mind! Marvelous in its complexity, its intricacy, it dwarfs any computer man might construct. For computers, after all, derive from that same fertile mind.

In Dr. Oliver Sach's fascinating book *The Man Who Mistook His Wife for a Hat*, he describes cases of troubled genius that came to his attention. Here is a parade of men and women whose brains had developed in irregular ways. Some of these people were idiots if measured by the yardstick of normality, but in one field or another they displayed astonishing powers.

One man with low IQ knew by heart Grove's massive encyclopedia of music. He knew the entire scores of some symphonies.

Two others, identical twins, were withdrawn social misfits, society's rejects. But their eyes would light up and their faces shine as they communicated with each other—by numbers. In that world of pure thought they could calculate beyond the ability of any computer yet devised.

It's a great book, and the finer for the compassion with which Sachs handles the subject matter. The procession of "unfortunates" opens a window on the untapped potential of our minds.

And look at the parade of men and women whose powers have lifted and ennobled the race, forging into new mental territory —creating, inspiring: Einstein, Newton, Plato, Buddha, Mozart, Bach, Beethoven, Shakespeare, Gandhi, Lincoln.

The greatest of all is Jesus Christ. He is the light of the world. Every gleam of light in the past or today, every flash of brilliance from the mind, every act of goodness, every ray of truth—derives from Him.

"We can trace the line of the world's great teachers as far back as human records extend; but the Light was before them. As the moon and the stars of the solar system shine by the reflected light of the sun, so, as far as their teaching is true, do the world's great thinkers reflect the rays of the Sun of righteousness. Every gem of thought, every flash of the intellect, is from the Light of the world. In these days we hear much about 'higher education.' The true 'higher education' is that imparted by Him 'in whom are hid all the treasures of wisdom and knowledge.' 'In Him was life; and the life was the light of men' (Col. 2:3; John 1:4). 'He that followeth me,' said Jesus, 'shall not walk in darkness, but shall have the light of life' " (*The Desire of Ages*, pp. 464, 465).

*O Jesus, light of the world, shine in this heart today. Chase away the gloom, the shadows; lead me into the sunlight.*

# LOVING JESUS TOO MUCH

***Then said Jesus to those Jews which believed on him, If ye continue in my word, then are ye my disciples indeed. John 8:31.***

Christians delight in conversion stories. We like to contrast the life that was with the one that is; we rejoice in the changes that come when a person connects his or her life to Jesus.

Unfortunately, we often pass over the process. We tend to forget that the Christian life is a battle and a march, that conversion must be new every day, that the changes Jesus brings become part of the life only as they become habitual. We must *continue* in Christ's word if we would be His disciples.

Some years ago we visited friends in Pennsylvania. They owned a Mercedes-Benz, a diesel model. On that particular model the preignition switch and the ignition switch were joined together and locked into the steering column. One day their son, playing cars, broke off the ignition key in the lock. The car wouldn't warm for starting, wouldn't turn on, and wouldn't steer. It had to be towed into a repair shop in a nearby town.

After a day or two the mechanic had it ready. He showed us the big, complicated switching mechanism that he'd had to take out and fix. The job had meant eight hours on his back, his feet up on the front seat, working under the dashboard in close quarters, wrestling the broken part off and getting a new one on.

We admired his work. We admired also the calm way in which he described the difficulty of the job. We talked about cars and how complicated some repair work can be.

Then he said, "One day a man came to the shop and said to me, 'Here, I want you to curse this part on for me.' I turned to him and said, 'I'll fit the part for you, but I won't curse it on. *I love my Lord too much*!' "

Here was someone who continued in Jesus' word. Covered in grease, sweating with effort, his knuckles skinned from scrapes with sharp metallic edges, he loved his Lord too much to curse like the other mechanics.

Do we love Jesus too much? Too much to dishonor Him by our words? Too much to follow the ways of the world? Too much to follow our selfish, petty panderings and pleasures?

*Dear Jesus, teach me to continue in Your word. Give me grace to love You too much ever to deny You.*


*September 11*

# NOT WHAT, BUT WHOM

**Jesus saith unto him, I am the way, the truth, and the life: no man cometh unto the Father, but by me. John 14:6.**

In eight dramatic sayings, all in the Gospel of John, Jesus centers Christianity in Himself. Religion ceases to be a "what" and becomes a "whom."

"I am the bread of life" (John 6:48).

"I am the light of the world" (John 8:12).

"I am the good shepherd" (John 10:11).

"I am the door of the sheep" (verse 7).

"I am the way" (John 14:6).

"I am . . . the truth" (verse 6).

"I am . . . the life" (verse 6).

"I am the resurrection, and the life" (John 11:25).

These affirmations are entirely without parallel among the world's religions. Whereas other teachers and founders of the faiths on which men and women hang their lives claimed to be able to show the path from darkness to life, from truth to error, from death to life, Jesus of Nazareth set forth Himself as the *way,* the *truth,* the *life* personified.

These eight unique affirmations, which would be the height of hubris if they weren't true, all rest on the foundation of another "I am" saying of Jesus. "Jesus said unto them, Verily, verily, I say unto you, Before Abraham was, I am" (John 8:58).

No wonder, as John tells us, His hearers took up stones to kill Jesus (verse 59). What He had said was blasphemy to them: He'd taken to Himself the most sacred name of God in the Old Testament, the personal name by which God had disclosed Himself to Moses at the burning bush (Ex. 3:14), the designation so revered by the Jews that the scribes left it blank in their copying, that for centuries worshipers refused to sound it aloud, pausing in silence when they came to it in the reading of scripture.

In appropriating the name of Yahweh, the I AM, the eternally self-existing one, Jesus made claim to be the God of the Old Testament, the source and ground of all that is.

So He is the bread of life—sustainer of all.

He is the light of the world—revealer of all.

He is the good shepherd—protector of all.

He is the door of the sheep—enabler of all.

He is the way—guide of all.

He is the truth—judge of all.

He is the life—renewer of all.

He is the resurrection—Re-creator as well as Creator.

Today it's not *what* I believe, but *Whom.* In Christ Jesus are hid all the treasures of wisdom and knowledge. In Him is strength for every trial, victory in every battle. "That I may know him" (Phil. 3:10)—this is my quest for the new day.

*September 12*

# JESUS THE WAY

*And whither I go ye know, and the way ye know. John 14:4.*

Long ago, in the sixth century B.C., a boy was born into a royal family in the land we today call Nepal. The legends say that his father shielded the prince, heir to his kingdom, from the sadness and misery of the human lot. His boy knew only pleasure and mirth, good times and learning.

But one day everything changed. The young man chanced upon a sick man, his face contorted in pain. For the first time in his life he saw the suffering of disease. Then he met an old man, body bent, shuffling along the road—the suffering of old age. After this he came upon a funeral procession, saw the corpse, heard the wailing—the suffering of death.

The prince Gautama was profoundly moved. Leaving his wife and young son, he renounced the throne and became a wandering monk, seeking answers to the suffering of humanity. Eventually he found them, and henceforth was called Buddha, the enlightened one.

In Buddha's analysis of the mystery of life, all existence is suffering. The cause of suffering is desire; when desire ceases, suffering also ceases. So Buddha set forth the way to overcome desire.

The Buddha's teachings, noble as they are, contrast radically with those of Jesus of Nazareth. Gautama claimed to *show* people the way; Jesus claimed to *be* the way. Buddha did not center attention on himself or seek to be worshiped; Jesus said He was the eternal I AM. Buddha saw mankind fallen into the pit of sin and told them how to get out; Jesus got down into the pit and lifted them out on His shoulders.

When Jesus told His disciples that He was the way, He was about to leave them. He'd spoken about going to His Father, going to prepare a place for them.

His words troubled the disciples. Jesus—going away? Jesus—leaving them alone to cope in the world?

No, said Jesus, "you know the way to the place where I am going" (John 14:4, NIV).

Thomas spoke for us all: "Lord, we don't know where you are going, so how can we know the way?"

Then Jesus answered: "I am the way and the truth and the life. No one comes to the Father except through me" (verses 5, 6, NIV).

Today we may not know which way to turn, how to handle the worries and pressures of life—home, kids, job, church. Jesus *is* the way. He doesn't just show us the way; He *is* the way. So let us turn our life over to Him—every care, every heartache, every hope, every fear.

*September 13*

# JESUS THE TRUTH

### *Pilate saith unto him, What is truth? John 18:38.*

"There is one thing a professor can be absolutely certain of: almost every student entering the university believes, or says he believes, that truth is relative," writes Allan Bloom in his best-selling *Closing of the American Mind*. "If this belief is put to the test, one can count on the students' reaction: they will be uncomprehending. That anyone should regard the proposition as not self-evident astonishes them, as though he were calling into question $2 + 2 = 4$. These are things you don't think about. The students' backgrounds are as various as America can provide. Some are religious, some atheists; some are to the Left, some to the Right; some intend to be scientists, some humanists or professionals or businessmen; some are poor, some rich. They are unified only in their relativism and in their allegiance to equality" (p. 25).

Bloom points out that relativism and equality are related in the minds of students: they see relativism as the condition of a free society. Relativism leads to tolerance of others' viewpoints; absolutism brings bigotry and persecution.

How do these ideas measure up against a biblical perspective?

Not well. We hear in modern guise the skeptical question raised by Pilate in the judgment hall: "What is truth?" Who can know what is right or wrong—or why try, if truth is relative?

Remember, those are Pilate's words. Jesus' understanding of truth was far different. He said: "To this end was I born, and for this cause came I into the world, that I should bear witness unto the truth. Every one that is of the truth heareth my voice" (John 18:37).

Jesus speaks not merely of truth but of *the* truth. Truth is not something uncertain, shifting. Truth is rock solid, fixed, sure. Christ came to the world to testify to it, and everyone who is on the side of truth listens to Him.

The night before, Jesus had taken the discussion about truth further. "*I* am . . . the truth," He told His disciples (John 14:6). It was a bold, startling statement, challenging the philosophical speculation of Greece and Rome on the one hand, and the relativism of modern thought on the other.

If God did not exist, truth must be relative. Rightness or wrongness would be defined by each society.

But God does exist. He is the moral arbiter of the universe. Truth resides in Him: what God *is*—His character—defines right and wrong.

And God became flesh—Jesus Christ. That is why, seeing Him, we see the truth.

*September 14*

# JESUS THE LIFE

*God is spirit, and his worshipers must worship in spirit and in truth. John 4:24, NIV.*

Have you ever wondered about the severity of the penalty God meted out to Adam and Eve? Death for taking one piece of fruit—that's a stiffer sentence than any judge would hand down in North America or any country I can think of!

But maybe thinking in terms of penalty and punishment distorts the truth of this matter. By choosing to disobey God, our first parents removed themselves from the orbit of His life. They stepped outside the circle, and death was the inevitable consequence.

The laws of the universe are *descriptive* rather than *prescriptive*. For instance, if you jump from a 20-story building, your body will hurtle through the air, accelerating at the rate of 32 feet per second every second. You will slam into the pavement at high speed, crushing life from the body.

Is this because God laid down a law "Thou shalt not jump from 20-story buildings, and if you do I'll kill you"? Not at all. You will have broken the law of gravity—not something prescribed, but a law that describes the forces of attraction between objects.

Jesus is the life. Our life is only in Him. We are creatures, dependent; He is the source of life. These are the facts; it isn't that He arbitrarily set up the world this way, that His ego demands that people fawn around Him.

The story of the human race records our ongoing attempts to deny or reject this most basic fact of our existence. Our first parents took the step first; multitudes follow behind. Man wants to be *self*-sufficient, not God-dependent.

But when we know Jesus as our best friend, we gain a totally new perspective. God gives us back our sanity. We step back inside the circle of His life. This is where we *belong*, where we find our true self, where body, mind, and spirit achieve rest and integration.

What I'm describing here isn't just a matter of self-preservation, however. Jesus' life isn't merely eternal in time—it's eternal in quality. It's richer, fuller, freer; it's life more abundant!

*Lord of my life, You in whom alone I find my true self, I gladly give myself to You for this day. Take me inside the circle of Your love and grace; keep me by Your life through every moment.*

*September 15*

# COMMANDED LOVE

*A new commandment I give unto you, That ye love one another; as I have loved you, that ye also love one another. John 13:34.*

How can anyone command love? Obedience, yes; but love? Love comes from the heart, from free choice. After all, didn't God set up the universe on the basis of freedom, with all the possibilities it brings for misuse of choice, precisely because He wants us all to love Him and not be mere automatons?

And further, why did Jesus say He was giving a *new* commandment? Fourteen hundred years earlier God had told Israel: "Thou shalt love thy neighbour as thyself" (Lev. 19:18); so wherein is the element of newness in Jesus' command to His disciples on that last Thursday evening?

The original text helps us understand Jesus' words. Translated literally, it reads: "I give you a new command: love one another. As I loved you, so [or so that] you love one another."

"*As I loved you*"—here is the key to grasping the meaning. The root of our action is Jesus' love for us. We love, said John in his first letter, "because he first loved us" (1 John 4:19). We love not only God—we love, period. The power and influence of a loving Christ in our lives makes us like Him; so we love one another.

Jesus loved us *in order that* we might love one another. By gritting our teeth and steeling our will, maybe we can live with one another according to standards of moral rectitude. We don't kill, steal, rape, commit adultery, blaspheme; we're good, law-abiding citizens. Thousands of people live thus. They have high personal standards, and society looks up to them.

But God has a problem with them. The "moral" people, exactly because they appear to be so "good," often don't feel their need of a Saviour. They appear fine to others, but their hearts remain unconverted. They may *do* good, but they cannot love—not until the heavenly Lover makes them over. When His love captures their souls, they love as He loved.

So here is the newness of the new command—new not in time but in *demonstration*. "As I have loved you"—Jesus provides the example and the motivation to love one another.

Love—that's the law of the kingdom of heaven. God's commands no longer are grievous, for they're based on loving hearts.

*O Lord of heaven, who teaches us to love, transform my stony heart today into a heart like Yours.*

# CHRIST'S MOST DRAMATIC MIRACLE

***When he had said this, Jesus called in a loud voice, "Lazarus, come out!" The dead man came out, his hands and feet wrapped with strips of linen, and a cloth around***

***his face. Jesus said to them, "Take off the grave clothes and let him go." John 11:43, 44, NIV.***

Every time I read John 11, shivers run up and down my spine. So many elements in the high drama of this chapter shed light on the Saviour—and on the shared lot of humanity.

*"He whom thou lovest is sick"* (verse 3). Not "Lazarus is sick," not "Our brother is sick, please come at once." No: "He whom *thou* lovest is sick." We see the tender regard of Jesus for Lazarus, His closeness to that family in Bethany. If Jesus hears Lazarus is sick, He'll drop everything and come immediately—so Martha and Mary reason.

But Jesus didn't come immediately. *"Lazarus is dead"* (verse 14). Around the circle of the earth today, Lazarus is dead. Good people have prayed that he might live, but he died. Jesus didn't come to his bed with the healing touch of long ago.

*"Lord, if thou hadst been here, my brother had not died"* (verses 21, 32). Martha and Mary greeted Jesus with identical words. They expressed confidence in Jesus as the author of life, as the one before whom death flees away. But they also carried a rebuke: why *weren't* You here? Why didn't You come when we sent for You?

Why? And we today wrestle, caught up in the same dilemma of faith and doubt. We believe—but we wonder why God doesn't act to protect or to heal.

*"Jesus wept"* (verse 35). The shortest verse in the Bible, but eloquent in its portrayal of the Man of sorrows. Here is our Brother, here is Immanuel—God with us—weeping at the tomb of Lazarus, weeping as we weep at the graveside.

The ground seems so cold, so hard, so lonely. It closes over our dear one, and we feel alone—forsaken. We know part of ourself lies there and will always lie there, that no matter what healing the passing days may bring, they will never restore fully what we have lost.

Jesus weeps with us.

*"Lazarus, come forth!"* (verse 43). Who on earth could be so bold as to attempt this miracle? Lazarus has been dead and *buried* for four days already. Even though Martha claimed to believe in Jesus' life-giving power, she didn't want Him to try this! It was scandalous, a violation of Lazarus' rite of passage, a re-opening of the wounds that were just now beginning to close.

But Lazarus came out! Bound hand and foot in the grave cloths, he came out! Lazarus, dead and buried for four days, came out!

And the enemies of Jesus were beside themselves.

# EXPEDIENCE

***Ye know nothing at all, nor consider that it is expedient for us, that one man should die for the people, and that the whole nation perish not. John 11:49, 50.***

Jesus' raising of Lazarus created a sensation. It was by far the most spectacular of His mighty works, incontrovertible evidence of the validity of His claim to be the Messiah.

True, He had called at least two people from the dead before this—Jairus' daughter and the son of the widow at Nain. But the former act had been done quietly, with only Peter, James, John, and the parents present. The latter had occurred in a little country town off the beaten track.

Jesus raised Lazarus in full view of a crowd of watchers, sophisticates from Jerusalem. He raised Lazarus after he'd been buried for four days. And Lazarus was not your average person. Several lines of evidence suggest that the family was wealthy and prominent in Jerusalem society.

No wonder the miracle led many of the Jews to believe in Jesus. News of it went everywhere. Later, when the children of Abraham gathered for the Passover in Jerusalem from all over the nation, many sought out not only Jesus but Lazarus—they wanted to meet the "miracle man."

And how did the religious leaders react?

Number one: they made plans to put Lazarus away (John 12:10)!

Number two: they made plans to kill Jesus! Instead of admitting that they were wrong in their rejection of Jesus, instead of acknowledging what seemed crystal clear to others, they called a committee to devise a strategy.

Notice their deliberations. Their reasoning sheds chilling light on the manner in which wrong ideas, cherished, pervert moral values and corrupt religion.

"Then the chief priests and the Pharisees called a meeting of the Sanhedrin. 'What are we accomplishing?' they asked. 'Here is this man performing many miraculous signs. If we let him go on like this, everyone will believe in him, and then the Romans will come and take away both our place and our nation.' Then one of them, named Caiaphas, who was high priest that year, spoke up, 'You know nothing at all! You do not realize that it is better for you that one man die for the people than that the whole nation perish' " (John 11:47-50, NIV).

Although they were supposed to be spiritual guides, their chief concern was for their Temple and nation. Guardians of institutions. Institutions that had become the end rather than the means of religion.

So they were ready to let Jesus die so that the nation might be saved. Expedience, not principle, determined their course of action.

Of all people on earth, religious leaders should be men and women of principle. When they reason and act chiefly on the basis of expedience, great evil descends on the human race, evil that most of all offends the Lord, because it blasphemes His name and character.

*September 18*

# TAKE AWAY THE STONE

### *"Take away the stone," he said. John 11:39, NIV.*

"Christ could have commanded the stone to remove, and it would have obeyed His voice. He could have bidden the angels who were close by His side to do this. At His bidding, invisible hands would have removed the stone. But it was to be taken away by human hands. Thus Christ would show that humanity is to cooperate with divinity. What human power can do divine power is not summoned to do. God does not dispense with man's aid. He strengthens him, cooperating with him as he uses the powers and capabilities given him" (*The Desire of Ages*, p. 535).

The interaction of humanity with God remains one of the most important questions of the Christian life. Theological debates go back to the fifth century, when Augustine disputed with Pelagius over the role of the human will.

Each man brought his own personal history to his understanding of the matter—as we still do. Augustine, who had lived a dissolute life before conversion, had a profound sense of the power of grace. It seemed to him that the will was weak, useless; that he had been rescued only because of overwhelming intervention, because God had predestined him for eternal life.

Pelagius, however, had lived a life of moral probity. To him, the will seemed capable of ordering life, of choosing the right way and walking steadfastly in it. Where Augustine's thought had God determining who would be saved or lost, Pelagius' put the responsibility wholly on man.

Our text of the day, although posed in a nontheological setting, sheds light on the debate.

We see first the divine initiative. Jesus is in charge—very much so. If we have a part to play, it will be only because Christ has first acted. Whatever we do will be by His command, working as His agent to effect His will.

In this regard, Augustine rather than Pelagius had matters straight. No one can ever turn to God, ever walk in the good way except God acts first. Our wills, weakened and corrupted by sin, will never choose God unless God the Holy Spirit activates them.

But second, God calls on us to respond to His initiative. "Take away the stone"—we have a part to play. We can refuse His call. Lazarus can stay forever bound in the tomb. Or we can take away the stone that blocks the opening to new life.

We may take away the stone today. Moment by moment we may rely on divine power, turning from our self-sufficiency, resting wholly in His grace and love.

*Dear Father, I hear Your call to new life this day. And gladly I come to You. Loose me and let me go forth in Your new life.*

# JESUS THE RESURRECTION

*Jesus said unto her, I am the resurrection, and the life: he that believeth in me, though he were dead, yet shall he live: and whosoever liveth and believeth in me shall never die. Believest thou this? John 11:25, 26.*

Christ doesn't merely raise the dead to life—He *is* the resurrection. Every person whose life is bound with His life will rise from the grave because of this fact.

Have you ever contemplated the miracle of resurrection? It enfolds all the marvels of creation, and adds some.

According to the Bible, no conscious entity survives when we die. The soul isn't some part hidden in our bodies that continues to exist—the soul is *us*, our personality, our individuality, the sum total of all we are. When the body dies, the soul dies with it.

This would be a grim teaching were it not for the resurrection. Death would be the end, the final gun. But the resurrection assures us that one day God will recreate us, bringing back our individuality in a new, deathless body.

Wouldn't it be simpler for God to start over? Why bother, in the new act of creation, to go back to us?

But God *does* bother. He keeps us in His memory bank, awaiting the time of resurrection. He (in whose presence past, present, and future are one) stores our vital facts in His heavenly computer. Chaplain Larry Yeagley says that when God re-creates us, He will bring us back just as we were except that He'll press the button that says "eternal model"!

Oh, what a marvelous and compassionate God, lover of individuality, lover of us all! The resurrection will be the supreme miracle of His power. It so boggles the mind that philosophers would never have conceived of it.

"In Christ is life, original, unborrowed, underived. 'He that hath the Son hath life' (1 John 5:12). The divinity of Christ is the believer's assurance of eternal life" (*The Desire of Ages*, p. 530).

Jack Provonsha, physician and ethicist, tells of a man thrown from a horse at midday. Knocked unconscious by the fall, he lay beside the roadside. Regaining his senses, he thought of the flying hoofs and thrust his body from the road. Then he looked up and saw the sun—it was setting!

So will be the resurrection. We will sleep in Jesus. The world will go on, but time will stand still for us.

But we are safe in His keeping—in life or in death. He *is* the resurrection and the life.

*September 20*

# JUDGED BY THE LIGHT

**And Jesus said, For judgment I am come into this world, that they which see not might see; and that they which see might be made blind. John 9:39.**

I find this text to be one of the most heart-searching passages of the Bible. It forces me to ask myself: Am I blind, or do I see?

When Joseph and Mary brought their baby Son to the Temple, the devout Simeon had said of Him, "This child is destined to cause the falling and rising of many in Israel, and to be a sign that will be spoken against, so that the thoughts of many hearts will be revealed" (Luke 2:34, 35, NIV).

Jesus revealed "the thoughts of many hearts." Regardless what a person's religious profession might be, no matter how exalted his spiritual office, his reaction to Jesus revealed his heart. Faced with Jesus and His claims, those who saw—or thought they did—became blind, while the blind received sight.

Jesus spoke the words of today's text to a man who, blind from birth, now rejoiced in full vision. What a day that had been—that Sabbath in Jerusalem! A poor blind beggar had been miraculously healed, had stood his ground when scoffed at and scorned, had been cut off from the synagogue, but had come to faith in Jesus.

But on the same day he passed from blindness to sight, from nonbelief to faith, the "lights" of Jerusalem were going out. The religious establishment, confronted with the Light of the world, chose darkness! No greater condemnation could be possible.

Jesus still reveals the thoughts of many hearts. In the final analysis, spirituality is intensely personal. We live and work in the church in a network of relationships and duties. Jesus alone knows our hearts, knows how we will react when the light shines upon us. That's why the final judgment will bring many surprises.

What about those men of religion in Jerusalem—did they know what they were doing? Did they choose darkness rather than light in a carefully premeditated act?

I doubt it. Rather, I think, they had become victims of the greatest deception—they had deceived themselves. To them, light had become darkness and darkness light.

I find that a frightening idea to contemplate. It forces me to look deep into my heart, to examine my motives. How would I have responded if I had been one of those leaders in Jerusalem?

How do I react to the Light today?

*O Lord of the light, shine on my heart and drive out the dark—especially the dark of self-deception.*

*September 21*

# DIG!

**Search the scriptures; for in them ye think ye have eternal life: and they are they which testify of me. John 5:39.**

In August 1860 an expedition set out from the city of Melbourne in southern Australia to attempt the first crossing of the continent from south to north.

Founding the new land in 1788, the first settlers had grouped along the eastern and southeastern seaboard. Gradually they pushed west until they hit the mountains. What lay beyond? Nobody knew. They discovered rivers that flowed west from the mountains, but to what? Did the interior of the land perhaps enfold lakes, valleys, and fertile plains?

In command of the "great northern exploration," as it was called, was an impetuous Irishman, Robert O'Hara Burke. His surveyor and second in command was an Englishman, W. J. Wills. The expedition included 16 others, plus camels brought from India.

After trekking several months, they reached the limits of the map—Cooper's Creek, in the middle of the continent. Burke decided to make a dash for the sea. Taking with him Wills and two other men, Gray and King, he set out into the unknown.

They found no lakes, no verdant valleys; only burning deserts and, as they approached the ocean, swamps. In February 1861, they reached the Gulf of Carpentaria—they had crossed the continent.

But with rations running low, their plight was now desperate. Gray died on the return trip. Finally Burke, Wills, and King staggered into the base camp at Cooper's Creek, many weeks later than they had expected.

They found the depot deserted. In an incredible touch of irony, the others, sick and having given up hope for the survival of Burke and his men, had left for the south. They broke camp on the morning of the very day Burke, Wills, and King returned!

Before leaving, however, they buried a cache of food under a big eucalyptus tree. On the trunk of the tree they emblazoned "DIG." But Burke, Wills, and King, worn and emaciated, did not get the message. They tried to live off the few berries and leaves in the bush, but first Burke died on June 28, and later Wills. King somehow survived. Taken in by the Aborigines, he was rescued—a skeleton of a man—by a search party in September.

Dig! The message of the tree is Jesus' message for us today. Dig in the Scriptures! Search them diligently! In them is life eternal, food to supply our every need.

*Lord of the Bible, living Word, give me grace to keep searching, to keep digging in Your never-failing supply of life in the Scriptures.*

*September 22*

# THE FATHER'S BLESSING

***Father, glorify thy name. Then came there a voice from heaven, saying, I have both glorified it, and will glorify it again. John 12:28.***

"All of us long to be accepted by others," wrote Gary Smalley and John Trent in *The Blessing*. "While we may say out loud, 'I don't care what other people think about me,' on the inside we all yearn for intimacy and affection. This yearning is especially true in our relationship with our parents. Gaining or missing out on parental approval has a tremendous effect on us, even if it has been years since we have had any regular contact with them. In fact, what happens in our relationship with our parents can greatly affect all our present and future relationships" (p. 9).

The authors go on to tell about Brian, who spent a lifetime seeking his father's approval. His father, a career Marine officer, wanted him to be the best and the brightest. Brian tried—how desperately he tried! When his father lay dying, Brian flew across the country to be by his bedside and pleaded, "Please say you love me, please!" But his father died without giving Brian the words he most wanted to hear.

Blessing, in noun and verb forms, occurs frequently in the Scriptures, especially the Old Testament. In their simple but profound and practical book, Smalley and Trent show that the acceptance many people spend a lifetime looking for is none other. than the biblical blessing.

Analyzing the biblical concept of blessing, shown in stories such as God's blessing of Abraham or Isaac's blessing of Jacob and Esau, they identify five basic parts:

1. Meaningful touch.
2. A spoken message.
3. Attaching high value to the one being blessed.
4. Picturing a special future for the one being blessed.
5. An active commitment to fulfill the blessing.

How much our fractured world needs "the blessing" today! With sundered relationships, broken homes, hurting hearts, what a model for life in these times!

And Jesus Himself, the source of all our blessings, received His Father's blessing. Three times during His ministry—at the baptism, on the Mount of Transfiguration, and in the Temple, God spoke words of love and affirmation. By these heavenly interventions, we catch a glimpse of the deep love of the Trinity.

Our mission today? "To turn the heart of the fathers to the children, and the heart of the children to their fathers" (Mal. 4:6). In other words, to spread the blessing.

*September 23*

# THE GOOD SHEPHERD

*I am the good shepherd: the good shepherd giveth his life for the sheep. John 10:11.*

In calling Himself the good (or noble) shepherd, Jesus drew on a wealth of biblical allusions. The patriarchal civilization, and

Israel's after the conquest of Palestine, was largely pastoral. Even when agriculture became dominant, nostalgia remained for the pastoral age.

The patriarchs, Moses and David, were all shepherds. "Shepherd" became a designation for the rulers, with bad kings denounced as wicked shepherds (see 1 Kings 22:17; Jer. 10:21).

In particular, Ezekiel 34 gives us background to Jesus' words about the good shepherd. Here God first rebukes the shepherds, or rulers, who have been more concerned about their own interests than in caring for the flock (verses 2, 5, 6).

God promises to come to the aid of His sheep: "For thus saith the Lord God; Behold, I, even I, will both search my sheep, and seek them out. As a shepherd seeketh out his flock in the day that he is among his sheep that are scattered; so will I seek out my sheep, and will deliver them out of all places where they have been scattered in the cloudy and dark day. . . . I will seek that which was lost, and bring again that which was driven away, and will bind up that which was broken, and will strengthen that which was sick: but I will destroy the fat and the strong; I will feed them with judgment" (verses 11-16).

The chapter climaxes with the prediction of "my servant David," God's true shepherd: "And I will set up one shepherd over them, even my servant David; he shall feed them, and he shall be their shepherd" (verse 23).

Jesus, the good shepherd, fulfilled this prophecy. How tenderly He cared for the lame, the sick, the broken! How He gathered up His flock, leading them beside still waters, in the paths of righteousness—yes, and even through the valley of death!

Jesus is still the good shepherd. "I am the good shepherd, and know my sheep, and am known of mine," He says (John 10:14). He knows us by name, knows where we live, knows the color of our eyes and hair, knows even the number of the hairs on our head. He knows us as a lover knows; He knows us for our eternal welfare.

And we, His sheep, know Him. We recognize His voice—a hireling's we will not follow. We will go where our noble Shepherd leads—even through the valley of the shadow of death.

In one respect Jesus, the good shepherd, goes beyond the prophecy of Ezekiel 34. He says: "The good shepherd giveth his life for the sheep" (John 10:11). Such willingness of a shepherd to die for His sheep is nowhere clearly taught in the Old Testament. Jesus' words go beyond custom or requirement, beyond duty or expectation.

Love that goes even to death for the other, for us—this is Jesus, the good shepherd.

# THE POWER OF ENDLESS LIFE

*No man taketh it from me, but I lay it down of myself. I have power to lay it down, and I have power to take it again. This commandment have I received of my Father. John 10:18.*

Among the many exotic figures we encountered during our 15 years in India, none was more bizarre than Meher Baba. He lived in the city of Ahmednagar, some 70 miles away from Poona, location of Spicer Memorial College, where we taught.

Meher Baba claimed to be an incarnation of Deity—God in the flesh. Men and women flew in from around the world to sit at his feet, to experience his *darshan*—his presence.

But no one heard his voice. Some 30 years before, Meher Baba had taken a vow of silence. He communicated with his followers by writing answers to their questions on a slate. Sometimes he would tell jokes.

And then he announced that he was about to break his silence, setting the date far enough ahead for the believers to gather to hear his first words. The word went out; they gathered from near and far.

They came with eager anticipation. What would his voice be like? And what would he say—divine instruction for world peace? the secret of spiritual life?

They never heard Meher Baba's voice. They did not receive the long-awaited word. *Meher Baba died—of throat cancer*!

His followers milled around, trying to encourage one another, attempting to extract a gleam of hope and meaning out of their devastating loss. But soon they were heading for buses and the airport, wending sad ways home.

Meher Baba's movement collapsed with his death. The "god" had died!

Jesus of Nazareth also died, but His movement lives on. In fact, His death became the capstone of His living, because He broke the bands of the grave.

Can you imagine anyone saying "No one takes it [my life] from me, but I lay it down of my own accord. I have authority to lay it down and authority to take it up again" (John 10:18, NIV)? We have all heard of people who defy death in spectacular stunts. Occasionally we meet someone whose ego is so big that he feels he can outsmart even the Grim Reaper. But who would be so crazy as to claim that he has authority to lay down his life and to take it up again?

Only the One who *is* the resurrection and the life, the One in whom is life original, unborrowed, underived. Then the words aren't crazy, but fact.

By the power of that life we too may live—today!

# THE ONE WHO STANDS BY OUR SIDE

*And I will pray the Father, and he shall give you another Comforter, that he may abide with you for ever. John 14:16.*

The Holy Spirit is the most mysterious member of the Trinity. Although the nature of God forever must remain veiled to our understanding, our everyday associations and relationships help us understand something of the Father and the Son. But what of the blessed Spirit, the God who dwells within us, who can be present everywhere at once and yet is a divine person?

Jesus, who showed us what God is like, helps us understand the Holy Spirit. He calls Him the *Paraclete*—the One called to be at our side. And that means far more than Comforter.

The Paraclete stands as our advocate. In fact, the identical word is used of Jesus in 1 John 2:1—"And if any man sin, we have an advocate with the Father, Jesus Christ the righteous." So the Holy Spirit speaks in our defense; He represents us.

Earlier Jesus had promised the disciples: "But when they deliver you up, take no thought how or what ye shall speak: for it shall be given you in that same hour what ye shall speak. For it is not ye that speak, but the Spirit of your Father which speaketh in you" (Matt. 10:19, 20). So the Christian not only has a Friend in the heavenly court—where Jesus Christ stands as his defender—he has a Friend on earth. The Holy Spirit empowers him, giving him appropriate words, calling to his mind the teachings of Jesus.

The Paraclete stands by our side to teach us, also. "When he, the Spirit of truth, is come, he will guide you into all truth," said Jesus (John 16:13). The things of God require divine illumination if we are to grasp them, and the Holy Spirit opens our eyes. We find treasures in God's Word; we discern His hand in our lives; our affections turn from the world to our heavenly home.

The Paraclete strengthens us for conflict. Sometimes we need comfort: scarred, bruised, broken, we need someone who will listen, who will care. But often we need firm resolve, determination to go forward in faith despite discouragements and obstacles, strengthening of the will to choose the good over against the evil. And the Paraclete, our heavenly helper, supplies that need.

The Holy Spirit is real. Invisible, mysterious, silent, He lives within us if we choose to let Him. He is the Spirit of the Father, the Spirit of Christ. With Him we are in touch with God.

Dear reader, do the words of today's reading seem incredible to you? Then let me invite you to test them for yourself. The truths of which I write cannot be grasped by studying for assignments in a Bible class or the seminary. You can know them in only one way: by *believing* the words of Jesus and *taking* them to yourself.

*Holy Spirit, blessed Paraclete, come stand by my side today. Be my comforter, advocate, helper, guide, and friend.*

*September 26*

# THE THREEFOLD WORK OF THE HOLY SPIRIT

***And when he is come, he will reprove the world of sin, and of righteousness, and of judgment. John 16:8.***

In a statement that boggled the minds of His apprehensive followers, Jesus told them that it was for their good that He was about to leave them. He said that only by His departure would the Holy Spirit be enabled to enter upon His full ministry in the world (John 16:7, 8).

According to Jesus, that work centers in a threefold ministry that embraces sin, righteousness, and judgment.

*First*, the Holy Spirit convicts men and women of sin.

The bad news about *us* comes prior to the good news of God's salvation provided in Christ Jesus: we need help! We can't make it on our own. No matter how wealthy or clever or learned, we have a terrible disease, and it's called *sin*.

Elaborating on the Spirit's work in convicting with regard to sin, Jesus added, "Because men do not believe in me" (verse 9, NIV). Here is the ultimate question, the heart of it all. When we stand before God, the issue won't be what have we *done* (our score of good and bad deeds), but what have we *done with Jesus*. He is our salvation; we have no hope apart from His name.

That was the condemnation anciently. Jesus came, and men of religion chose darkness rather than light. Today the condemnation is no less, as the Holy Spirit perpetuates the ministry of Jesus.

*Second*, the Holy Spirit convicts men and women of righteousness.

Every person has norms for his or her life. Society sets up laws, rules of etiquette, polite behavior. But God alone defines what righteousness is. We dare not substitute our standards for His.

The Holy Spirit convicts in regard to righteousness, said Jesus, "because I am going to the Father, where you can see me no longer" (verse 10, NIV). So long as Jesus walked among us, His words and deeds defined righteousness. He *is* the way, the truth, the life. He *is* the law embodied.

But that voice has gone from us; those hands no more serve humanity. How shall we know righteousness today? Through the Holy Spirit, who points us to Jesus, God's eternal standard.

*Third*, the Holy Spirit convicts of judgment.

"The prince of this world now stands condemned," explained Jesus (verse 11, NIV). In the light of Christ's life, and especially in the light that streams from Calvary, evil is unmasked. Satan, the Spirit shows us, is a liar and a murderer. God's condemnation rests rightly on him and on all who choose to walk in his ways.

Jesus—for our *good* that He should leave us? In light of the Holy Spirit's threefold ministry, yes!

*September 27*

# JESUS THE TRUE VINE

*I am the true vine, and my Father is the husbandman.* *John 15:1.*

This final "I am" saying of Jesus shows our utter dependence on Him.

I grew up in southern Australia. The warm, dry summers and cool, wet winters provide an excellent climate for growing grapes and stone fruits. We had several varieties of grapes in our back-yard—whites and blacks and some tiny currant grapes. But while the apricot, almond, plum, apple, and peach trees stood alone, the vines always had to be supported; we constructed trellises or trailed them over the fence.

We need Jesus to support us. Left to ourselves, trying to get by on our own strength, we will fall like the vine to the lowest point.

But attached to Jesus, we can climb high. We can reach for and attain the heights.

Notice that Jesus calls Himself the *true* vine. Men and women attach themselves to many other vines—to political and social causes; to the pursuit of wealth or learning; to the stars of movies, television, and sports; to religious teachers. For every leader in the world a million people tag along.

But Jesus alone is the true vine. Only in Him can we realize our full potential: achieving the glorious destiny of adoption into the family of God, with its restoration of the image of God.

The book of Ezekiel reminds us that the wood of the vine is useless. "Son of man, how is the wood of a vine better than that of a branch on any of the trees in the forest? Is wood ever taken from it to make anything useful? Do they make pegs from it to hang things on? And after it is thrown on the fire as fuel and the fire burns both ends and chars the middle, is it then useful for anything?" (Eze. 15:2-4, NIV).

And we, attached to Jesus, the true vine, find our worth only in Him. At no point, now or eternally, will it be true that our inherent worth qualifies us to stand alone. Stand? Severed from Him we cannot and do not stand, but flop to the ground like the branch of the vine.

"Abiding in Christ means a constant receiving of His Spirit, a life of unreserved surrender to His service. The channel of communication must be open continually between man and his God. As the vine branch constantly draws the sap from the living vine, so are we to cling to Jesus, and receive from Him by faith the strength and perfection of His own character"(*The Desire of Ages*, p. 676).

*September 28*

# AUTONOMOUS MAN

*Remain in me, and I will remain in you. No branch can bear fruit by itself; it must remain in the vine. Neither can you bear fruit unless you remain in me. John 15:4, NIV.*

In his book *Thus Spake Zarathustra* the German philosopher Nietzsche writes about a hermit who goes into the forest to meditate. When he comes back to society, he bears a startling message: "God is dead. But I give you Superman!"

A straight line runs from Nietzsche's ideas of superman in the past century to the philosophy of autonomous man that dominates our age. Autonomous man, says Dr. Gerhart Niemeyer, is man without a father, man without a Creator, and man without any judge.

"At this time we conclude that the autonomous man is (1) man without a father, having divested himself not merely of his heavenly Father, but also of his early parents, his forebears, and the past in general; (2) man without a Creator, who finds creatureliness something impossible to accept and live with, who, with Marx and Nietzsche, refuses to acknowledge any dependence of his on anyone or anything, particularly for his life; (3) man without any judge, either in heaven, or on earth, who deems himself unaccountable either to his fellowmen, or to a divine judge, or for the meaning of his life, in the moment of death, who has eliminated all potential measures or yardsticks, such as *physis* (nature, in Aristotle's sense) or *nomos* (civil law) or *ethos* (custom)" ("The 'Autonomous' Man," *Intercollegiate Review,* vol. 9, No. 3).

But we who confess Jesus Christ as Saviour and Lord reject this concept. In Him alone we find life; in Him we live and move and have our being. He has made us for Himself; we find our true selves in Him alone. He is our life, our light, our love.

"By faith in Him as a personal Saviour the union is formed. The sinner unites his weakness to Christ's strength, his emptiness to Christ's fullness, his frailty to Christ's enduring might. Then he has the mind of Christ. The humanity of Christ has touched our humanity, and our humanity has touched divinity. Thus through the agency of the Holy Spirit man becomes a partaker of the divine nature. He is accepted in the Beloved" (*The Desire of Ages,* p. 675).

*September 29*

# FRUITBEARING

*Herein is my Father glorified, that ye bear much fruit; so shall ye be my disciples. John 15:8.*

Jesus speaks unequivocally: fruit-bearing is the test of discipleship. God's plan is for us to bear *much* fruit, and so His name will be glorified. Christianity must, and does, make a difference in our lives.

What is the fruit of which Jesus speaks so emphatically? It is the recapitulation of the life and character of the lovely Jesus. Earlier in His discourse Jesus had promised: "Verily, verily, I say unto you, He that believeth on me, the works that I do shall he do also; and greater works than these shall he do; because I go unto my Father" (John 14:12). Paul lists the fruit: "love, joy, peace, longsuffering, gentleness, goodness, faith, meekness, temperance" (Gal. 5:22, 23).

What then is the secret of fruit-bearing? Jesus gives us three principles:

**1. Good fruit comes only from a good tree.**

"Ye shall know them by their fruits. Do men gather grapes of thorns, or figs of thistles? Even so every good tree bringeth forth good fruit; but a corrupt tree bringeth forth evil fruit. A good tree cannot bring forth evil fruit, neither can a corrupt tree bring forth good fruit" (Matt. 7:16-18).

An apple tree will never bear mangoes, no matter how much you work the soil or pour in fertilizer. Apples come only from apple trees, and mangoes from mango trees.

No more can we of ourselves produce the fruit God is looking for. We can discipline ourselves, program ourselves, grit our teeth as we work at it, but all our deeds of piety will be worthless, no better than vain show to convince others and maybe ourselves.

"Ye must be born again," said Jesus (John 3:7). God must give us a new heart—make us into a good tree—before we can bear good fruit.

## 2. We must remain joined to Christ.

"Abide in me, and I in you. As the branch cannot bear fruit of itself, except it abide in the vine; no more can ye, except ye abide in me" (John 15:4).

How often we ignore His words! We *begin* with Christ, looking to Him for forgiveness, and then foolishly we try to make it on our own.

How pathetic is the professed follower of Christ who attempts to live without the Master! He ends up reducing God to the level of his own petty mind.

If we would bear fruit, we must maintain a living connection with the living Jesus. We must *know* Him—know Him personally; we must feed on His Word daily; we must commune with Him; we must speak for Him. Remember that the sterling qualities Paul listed in Galatians 5:22, 23 are all fruits *of the Spirit*.

## 3. We must submit to the Father's discipline.

"Every branch in me that beareth not fruit he taketh away: and every branch that beareth fruit, he purgeth it, that it may bring forth more fruit" (John 15:2).

God works on our characters, pruning off the unfruitful wood. He knows best—He's the master gardener. Sometimes His cutting hurts us, but He has an everlasting future in mind for us. He wants us to bear fruit—to become more and more like Jesus now and eternally.

*September 30*

# SIGNS AND GLORY

*Though he had done so many signs before them, yet they did not believe in him. John 12:37, RSV.*

John's Gospel falls into two distinct parts—"signs" and "glory."

The signs, translated "miracles" in the King James Version, run through the first 12 chapters of the book. Jesus, the Word made flesh, full of grace and truth, manifested His deity by a series of startling deeds.

Jesus turned the water into wine at the wedding feast in Cana; that, says John, was the beginning of His signs (John 2:11). He performed miraculous signs in Jerusalem at the Passover, and many people believed in Him (verse 23). Nicodemus, not yet a believer, was attracted to Jesus by His signs, and sought Him in a night audience (John 3:1, 2). After Jesus healed the nobleman's son at Capernaum, that official and all his household believed (John 4:48-53). And Jesus performed many other miracles—He restored the lame man by the pool of Bethesda (John 5); He fed the multitude on the mountainside (John 6); He gave sight to a beggar blind from birth (John 9).

Many people today don't believe in miracles. Even some Christians have become doubters, dazzled by the achievements of the scientific method and seduced by psychology. But if God *were* to come to earth as a man, we *should* expect miracles.

Jesus' miracles revealed who He was. They were flashes of divinity. Even so, John mournfully notes, "Yet they believed not on him" (John 12:37). People saw the signs but did not read them.

The "signs" motif, which binds together the first 12 chapters, ceases abruptly with this verse. Now a new term will dominate the remainder of the book—*glory*. Already verse 23 of chapter 12 introduces it: "And Jesus answered them, saying, The hour is come, that the Son of man should be glorified."

So we come to the closing scenes of the story of Jesus. Ellen White, who counseled us to spend a thoughtful hour each day meditating on the life of Christ, recommended that we especially dwell on His final days (*The Desire of Ages*, p. 83).

These scenes will preoccupy us during the next three months. We shall go forward, day by day, with Jesus during the Passion Week. We will trudge with Him, lonely and burdened, to the Garden of Gethsemane. We will be taken, bound, with Him to the judgment hall. And at last we will climb the hill of Calvary.

He is taken from prison and judgment. He is cut off out of the land of the living. His death is infinitely sad.

Yet as we trace the steps to it, not confining ourselves to any one Gospel, John's motif of "glory" will inform our meditation. John reminds us that, tragic as these closing scenes are, they are the supreme manifestation of the glory of the Word made flesh.

# THE RESOLUTE CHRIST

*And it came to pass, when the time was come that he should be received up, he stedfastly set his face to go to Jerusalem. Luke 9:51.*

If you want to meet the leanest, clearest, brightest-eyed people, show up at a runner's meet. No potbellies or cigarettes, no slumping shoulders, no sallow faces here. They electrify the air with anticipation and eagerness as they mingle together at the start of a 10-miler or a marathon.

But take a look at those same people three, four, or five hours later after they have forced their bodies to complete the marathon! They sit or lie exhausted. They do not speak. Their faces are gray. Their eyes tell stories of the struggle to conquer the 26.2 miles.

I saw similar faces on Mount Kilimanjaro. In September 1988 six of us climbed the 19,340-foot peak. Many thousands of people have scaled the mountain—it doesn't require sophisticated equipment—but the distance (62 miles round trip), altitude, and cold do not yield easily. Before the climb we saw those who had returned from the grueling five-day trek. They sat, eating in silence. They gave clipped responses to questions about what the climb was like. Their eyes told a story of struggle, pain—and determination.

Four days later we understood—after we had climbed Kilimanjaro!

And Jesus set His face to go to Jerusalem. He had been there before, but this time would be different. He knew it would be His last visit. He knew that betrayal, mocking, scourging, crucifixion, and death awaited Him there.

But He set His face to go to Jerusalem. The book of Isaiah tells us He set it like a flint (Isa. 50:7). He had been born for this: to die.

When He had closed the door on the carpenter's shop in Nazareth some three years before and had set out for the Jordan where John was baptizing, He knew that Jerusalem would lie at the end of the road. He knew that no matter how popular He might become for a time, how successful His ministry would seem to the band of followers who devotedly clustered around Him, it would all end in a cross.

Jesus was a man of velvet and of steel. So meek, so gentle; friend of children, friend of sinners; compassionate, forbearing, gracious—He had a touch of velvet.

But Jesus also had hands and a will of steel. He could lash the money grubbers in the Temple. He could confront the religious establishment's hypocrisy in anger. And when the hour struck, He could set His face to go to Jerusalem.

Velvet and steel—see how they come together in the closing scenes of His life and ministry.

Velvet and steel—we who would follow Him also need that combination.

# SAY IT WITH FLOWERS—NOW

*Then took Mary a pound of ointment of spikenard, very costly, and anointed the feet of Jesus, and wiped his feet with her hair: and the house was filled with the odour of the ointment. John 12:3.*

Twenty thousand dollars for a single gift—what extravagance! Twenty thousand dollars used up in one evening—what waste!

No wonder the followers of Jesus grumbled. They muttered among themselves about all the projects that $20,000 could have funded, all the poor it could have helped.

But Jesus saw matters differently. In Mary's pouring out of the nard—a costly perfume from the mountains of India—in the alabaster box, He recognized the greater gift of herself. Mary's present, worth almost a year's salary, was her way of saying thank you.

After Jesus died on the cross, Joseph of Arimathea and Nicodemus brought expensive spices to anoint His body. But Mary brought her love offering while He was still alive.

Isn't it strange that the occasion when we give the most tributes, floral and spoken, is the one time when they cannot be appreciated—at a funeral!

Why not send the flowers now—especially the spoken ones? We're too quick to judge and condemn, too slow to encourage and commend.

Of Mary and her gift Ellen White notes: "But few appreciate all that Christ is to them. If they did, the great love of Mary would be expressed, the anointing would be freely bestowed. The expensive ointment would not be called a waste. Nothing would be thought too costly to give for Christ, no self-denial or self-sacrifice too great to be endured for His sake" (*The Desire of Ages*, p. 565).

Like Mary's, my heart overflows in appreciation to the Christ who has loved me so unstintingly. His graciousness, His compassion, His patience—in Him I live, and with Him I want to spend eternity. "Love so amazing, so divine, demands my life, my soul, my all."

How long has it been since you gave someone flowers? Since you sent God a bouquet of roses? The word left unspoken, appreciation left unexpressed—spouses and sons and daughters and colleagues and neighbors go through life wondering if we care.

Let's be like Mary and do something beautiful.

Now.

*October 3*

# HAIL TO THE KING

*And the multitudes that went before, and that followed, cried, saying, Hosanna to the son of David: Blessed is he that cometh in the name of the Lord; Hosanna in the highest. Matt. 21:9.*

The Passion Week began with lightning; it ended with the roll of drums.

That final Sunday of Jesus' life Jerusalem went wild. Matthew tells us that "a very great multitude" hailed Him as king. They spread their garments in the way. They cut down branches from trees and laid them along the road, giving to Jesus the homage fit for Israel's long-awaited Messiah.

And Jesus did nothing to discourage them. He set aside the role of quiet servanthood that He had guarded so carefully during the previous three and a half years of ministry. He didn't rebuke the acclamation of royalty as once He had done on the mountainside in Galilee (John 6:15).

Rather, Jesus encouraged the enthusiasm and expectations of His followers. To announce publicly His entrance to Jerusalem, He reached into Israel's past and chose a symbolic act that none could fail to notice. He sent two of His disciples to a nearby village to find an ass and its colt. He simply appropriated them for His triumphal entry. When the owner asked what was going on, the disciples were to reply, "The Lord hath need of them" (Matt. 21:2).

Five hundred years earlier, Zechariah had predicted: "Rejoice greatly, O daughter of Zion; shout, O daughter of Jerusalem: behold, thy King cometh unto thee: he is just, and having salvation; lowly, and riding upon an ass, and upon a colt the foal of an ass" (Zech. 9:9).

Now Jesus of Nazareth consciously acts out the fulfillment of the ancient prophecy. He comes riding into Jerusalem, descending the Mount of Olives, a huge crowd in front and behind, hailing Him as Israel's King.

"Hosanna to the son of David," they shout, "Hosanna in the highest." *Hosanna* is a cry to God for deliverance—"Save, we beseech thee." O Lord, come now and bring the redemption of Your people that prophets have foretold and for which we long.

This itinerant preacher from the north, this miracle worker, this humble teacher, Jesus of Nazareth—*He* is Israel's King. He can feed the hungry; He can heal the sick; He can raise the dead. The nation's armies will be invincible with Him as head; the Roman yoke quickly will be broken.

A day of lightning, that Palm Sunday. But Friday would bring the roll of muffled drums. Israel's Messiah, acclaimed with such widespread enthusiasm on Sunday, would hang from a felon's cross ere the Sabbath would dawn.

And Jesus knew it.

*October 4*

# THE LORD IN HIS TEMPLE

*And Jesus went into the temple of God, and cast out all them that sold and bought in the temple, and overthrew the tables of the moneychangers, and the seats of them that sold doves. Matt. 21:12.*

Twice on that final Sunday of His earthly life Jesus demonstrated His authority as Israel's Messiah. He entered Jerusalem majestically, acclaimed by throngs shouting hosannas and hailing Him as king. Then He went into the Temple and drove out the merchants cluttering its courts. By the first act He claimed His right to rule; by the second, His right to define worship.

Behold Him, angry at the abuse of the Lord's house! No puny visionary here, no meek and mild, gentle Jesus! He looks around in consternation at the buying and selling—the braying of animals, the cooing of doves, the clink of money changing hands. *Bang!* He turns over the tables. *Crash!* The cages for the birds fall to the ground. Money is rolling everywhere. Money changers are scrambling after it and then scrambling in terror to get away as fast as they can.

If we let this scene with its display of raw strength seep through our imagination, the Lord will teach us some unforgettable lessons.

First, unless we can get angry at the abuse of true worship, our religion doesn't count for much.

Love isn't passive—it's the most potent force for change in the universe. Love refuses to sit by idly when God's name is at stake. Love refuses to stay quiet when evil tears apart a society or a soul. Love acts. Love calls sin by its right name. Love rolls up its sleeves and goes to war.

Second, no amount of rationalization can ever justify the compromise of true worship. The Pharisees and Sadducees could give a dozen reasons why it was acceptable for the merchants to be in the Temple courts. Maybe they convinced others and convinced themselves, but they were wrong. And today no amount of fund-raising or financial need or extenuating circumstance can justify our turning the hour of worship into an hour of merchandise.

We need to know the Jesus who cradled the children. We need to know the Jesus who died to save the world. But we also need to know the angry Jesus, Lord in His Temple.

*October 5*

# CURSING THE FIG TREE

*And when he saw a fig tree in the way, he came to it, and found nothing thereon, but leaves only, and said unto it, Let no fruit grow on thee henceforward for ever. And presently the fig tree withered away. Matt. 21:19.*

Is this the one blot on the perfect life of Christ, the one occasion when He yielded to a display of temper?

Throughout the story of Jesus recorded in the Gospels, He refused to exercise His power for His own benefit. When the tempter came to Him after the 40 days of fasting in the wilderness with the suggestion that Jesus turn stones into bread, Jesus thrust him aside. Although He commanded 10,000 angels, although His fingers had shaped the stars and flung them into space, He limited Himself during the period of His earthly sojourn. As the Pathfinder of our salvation, He availed Himself only of those divine agencies to which we His brothers and sisters have access.

So what are we to make of His actions on the final Monday morning of His earthly life? After the tumultuous events of the previous day—the ride into Jerusalem and the cleansing of the Temple—Jesus had gone back to Bethany to spend the night (Matt. 21:17). Now, as He is returning to Jerusalem early in the morning before breakfast, He sees a fig tree in the distance. From afar the disciples can tell that it is in leaf—which means that it should have figs also, since the young figs appear before the leaves. But when they come up to the tree, they're disappointed: it is fruitless.

And Jesus pronounces a curse upon the barren fig tree. Before long the tree withers and dies—from the roots up, Mark tells us (Mark 11:20).

Despite the views of some Bible critics, this was not a mean act on Jesus' part, a temporary display of human passion. His actions corresponded exactly with a parable He had told months before (Luke 13:6-9). In it He described a fig tree planted in a vineyard. The owner came year by year seeking fruit—but the tree remained barren. At last he gave it one more year of grace, but instructed the gardener that if the tree continued fruitless, he should cut it down.

In His earlier parable and by His actions that Monday morning, Jesus taught that time was running out for the Israelites.

But the parable and the story apply to us also. Grace is wonderful, but we must not treat it in cavalier fashion. Time runs out for individuals as well as for nations. Grace received into the life will change us—we bear fruit. Fruitless Christians are an offense to their profession.

*O Lord of the vineyard, bear fruit in me today.*

*October 6*

# THE AUTHORITY OF JESUS

*And when he was come into the temple, the chief priests and the elders of the people came unto him as he was teaching, and said, By what authority doest thou these things? and who gave thee this authority? Matt. 21:23.*

The religious leaders were still smarting from Jesus' actions the day before. They were offended by His stately procession into Jerusalem and His driving out the merchants and the money changers from the Temple. He had invaded their space and changed the rules: the sacred courts had filled with the blind and the lame and children crying hosannas.

Now, as He taught the people on that Monday morning, the chief priests and elders decided on confrontation. "By what authority do you do these things?" they challenged Jesus. "Who gave you this authority?"

The answer was implicit in their questions. *We* are the ones with authority, and *we* haven't authorized *You* to teach here.

Appealing to authority—it's a common fallback when truth hits people between the eyes. Licenses and credentials, rules and regulations, ensure that only those cast from the same mold, who will say what is safe, shall be given a chance to speak.

Most men and women still seek the word of an authority rather than testing ideas on their merits. When confronted with a new-sounding idea, they want to know who said it rather than what is said, or who accepts it rather than examining the truth claims for themselves.

Now, authority has its place both in society and in the church. Where authority fails, anarchy prevails. But authority can never substitute for truth; authority does not guarantee truth.

Truth resides in the ultimate Authority, God. And Jesus is God—which is why the Jewish leaders' question was the height of absurdity when seen in its true light.

Jesus, however, didn't rebuke them as their challenge deserved. Already they'd rejected His claims to deity, so He chose a different tack to make the same point. They wanted to raise the question of His authority. He would reply on their terms.

He answered with a question to them: "The baptism of John, whence was it? from heaven, or of men?" (verse 25).

Jesus did not evade their question. By confronting them publicly with the claims of John the Baptist, He exposed their duplicity. The answer to the question they asked Jesus was the same as the answer to His question: Jesus and John were both agents of the divine will to bring in the kingdom of heaven. God was authority for both.

Of course, the chief priests and elders had spurned John as now they were rejecting Jesus. And Jesus exposed them. They confronted Him, challenging His right to teach. He confronted them with truth.

*October 7*

# A TALE OF TWO SONS

*"Which of the two did what his father wanted?"*
*"The first," they answered.*
*Jesus said to them, "I tell you the truth, the tax collectors and the prostitutes are entering the kingdom of God ahead of you." Matt. 21:31, NIV.*

"A certain man had two sons," said Jesus, as He dialogued with the chief priests and elders. Changing the setting of Jesus' story but not its intent, it reads like this:

"Son, I want you to wash the car and sweep the driveway," Father says to First Son.

"No way! The Cowboys are playing this afternoon, and I'm not going to miss that game."

But as he sits watching football on TV, First Son begins to think about his words. He'd been downright rude as well as disobedient; he'd hurt his father. First Son begins to remember the years of loving concern—camping trips, vacations at the beach, his father's prayers.

Suddenly he jumps up and turns off the TV (it was a boring game, anyway). He puts on overalls and goes outside to hose down the car.

He finds the car still dirty, the driveway still unswept. His father, however, thinks the chores have been completed. Two hours earlier, following First Son's curt "No," he had asked Second Son to do them.

"Sure, Dad," Second Son replied.

But Second Son kept on reading the Sunday paper. After that he went out with his friends.

"Which of these two boys did his father's will?" Jesus asked at the close of the story. The answer was obvious—the son who came late to the task, regretting the foolishness of his prior behavior.

Jesus now pointed the story straight at the religious leaders. In words that stung He told them: "Tax collectors and prostitutes go into the kingdom ahead of you!" These, the most despised elements of society, the furthest from God's will, repented at the preaching of John and Jesus. Meanwhile those who scorned them, wrapping themselves in the cloak of religious privilege, failed to recognize and obey God's kingdom breaking in upon earth.

Jesus' story also cuts across lives today. It jabs our conscience with reminders of letters unwritten, promises unkept, resolutions broken, opportunities squandered, good deeds neglected. How quick we are to say, "I go, sir," but how slow to do it!

Which son did the father's will? Undoubtedly, the first. But there is a still better way: to say to God, "I will," and then to do it by His grace.

*October 8*

# THE WICKED TENANTS

*Hear another parable. There was a householder who planted a vineyard, and set a hedge around it, and dug a wine press in it, and built a tower, and let it out to tenants, and went into another country. Matt. 21:33, RSV.*

During the three and a half years of Jesus' ministry His appeals to Israel became increasingly specific and urgent. His earlier parables closed with a note of invitation, with the door of hope still open for the nation that Jesus loved so much. So the story of the loving father, commonly called the parable of the prodigal son, remains unresolved, with the father pleading with the older brother to come inside and join the party.

But on the last Monday of Jesus' ministry, as He addressed His final parable to Israel, Jesus' words were unsparing. Taking up the song of the vineyard in the book of Isaiah (Isa. 5:1-7), He predicted divine wrath to fall on the Jewish nation.

The householder, God, made full provision for Israel—He did all He could for their salvation. But they despised His messengers, beating, stoning, killing them. Finally the owner of the vineyard sent his son: "They will respect my son," he said to himself (Matt. 21:37). But instead of respect, the wicked tenants plotted to take his life. They seized him and killed him.

Jesus told this parable on Monday. Four days later He would hang on a cross outside the city gates, and the final act of madness would be complete.

Inevitably, divine retribution followed. " 'When therefore the owner of the vineyard comes, what will he do to those tenants?' They said to him, 'He will put those wretches to a miserable death, and let out the vineyard to other tenants who will give him the fruits in their seasons' " (verses 40, 41, RSV).

But the failure of Israel as a nation and her leaders in particular by no means suggests that God's displeasure rests on anyone who happens to be born a Jew. Over the centuries Christians have persecuted the Jews, calling them "Christ killers." That attitude is unjust and unbiblical. Every individual must give account to God for his own actions, not for those of his ancestors.

To each of us, more important than the failure of Israel is this question: When the Son comes to my vineyard seeking fruit, what will He find? And how will I treat Him?

*October 9*

# CORNERSTONE

*Jesus saith unto them, Did ye never read in the scriptures, The stone which the builders rejected, the same is become the head of the corner: this is the Lord's doing, and it is marvellous in our eyes? Matt. 21:42.*

Jesus is the cornerstone. We who believe, says the apostle Paul, are no longer strangers and foreigners from the household of God, but are fellow-citizens with the saints, "built upon the foundation of the apostles and prophets, Jesus Christ himself being the chief corner stone" (Eph. 2:20).

Founded on Jesus, the church stands secure. The gates of hell cannot withstand it. It casts down every stronghold of evil. The church will prevail, emerging triumphant from the reign of sin on Planet Earth.

Sometimes God's work seems so frail, so puny when measured by the successes of the enemy. Sometimes the church seems about to fall, but it does not fall. The church cannot fall, because Jesus Christ is the cornerstone.

Isaiah had prophesied of Him: "So this is what the Sovereign Lord says: 'See, I lay a stone in Zion, a tested stone, a precious cornerstone for a sure foundation; the one who trusts will never be dismayed'" (Isa. 28:16, NIV). How precious He is! More precious than the Hope Diamond or any gem that can be mined from the earth.

"Now to you who believe, this stone is precious. But to those who do not believe, 'The stone the builders rejected has become the capstone,' and, 'A stone that causes men to stumble and a rock that makes them fall.' They stumble because they disobey the message—which is also what they were destined for" (1 Peter 2:7, 8, NIV).

That is the amazing thing about Jesus. He is the cornerstone, precious beyond computation; but He is also the stone of stumbling. People may try to ignore Him, but He cannot be ignored. We either fall upon Him and let Him remake our lives into something beautiful, or one day that Stone will fall upon us in destructive power. By rejecting Him or by neglecting Him we cut ourselves off from the Source of life for the universe—we choose eternal death.

Jesus' words, spoken on that final Monday in last warning to Israel's religious leaders, fall on our ears with solemn force today: "Whosoever shall fall on this stone shall be broken: but on whomsoever it shall fall, it will grind him to powder" (Matt. 21:44).

# ROYAL WEDDING

*And Jesus answered and spake unto them again by parables, and said, The kingdom of heaven is like unto a certain king, which made a marriage for his son. Matt. 22:1, 2.*

Did you ever hear such a story? Can you imagine anyone turning down an invitation from Buckingham Palace to attend the wedding of Prince Charles and Lady Diana? or of Prince Andrew and Sarah Ferguson?

But that is what the guests do in Jesus' parable of the royal wedding (Matt. 22:1-10). They make light of the King's invitation, go merrily about their business, and even beat up the King's messengers who bear the gilt-edged invitation.

The key to understanding this perplexing story lies, as often in other parables, in Jesus' opening words: "The kingdom of heaven is like . . ." It's a story, not about earthly society, but about God's society. To illustrate spiritual truth, Jesus describes behavior that would be outrageous when measured by our customary norms.

And, spiritually speaking, the parable of the royal wedding happens every day. Men and women act just as incomprehensibly as did the crazy guests in Jesus' story.

Day by day God invites people to His heavenly banquet. He offers them a table laden with good things and best of all His own presence as Host at the wedding feast.

But what do most people do? They slight the invitation. They drown out the sweet pleading of the Holy Spirit. They go about their business and their play. Occasionally they beat up the messengers of the gospel, and yes, sometimes they even kill them.

The refusal of God's invitation in the gospel is the greatest act of madness possible to mankind. It is every bit as crazy as, and worse than, the behavior of the wedding guests in Matthew 22.

But God's banqueting hall will be filled. No, not with those who have been most privileged in the things of this life; not with the socially and spiritually advantaged.

The gospel goes out into the highways and the byways. God extends the royal invitation to life's "losers," and many of them accept it. Beaten and broken by life, they find hope, new purpose, joy, the power of the Holy Spirit to forgive and purge sins.

Praise God for His heavenly banquet—and His invitation to all of us.

*O generous Master, may I today live as a guest of Your royal wedding.*

# THE WEDDING GARMENT

*And when the king came in to see the guests, he saw there a man which had not on a wedding garment: and he saith unto him, Friend, how camest thou in hither not having a wedding garment? And he was speechless. Matt. 22:11, 12.*

Jesus not only invites us to the wedding; He supplies a tuxedo for us to wear. Without the wedding garment we will be speechless before the King.

What is the wedding garment? The book of Revelation also describes the Son's marriage supper, and it likewise refers to the dress of the saints. "Let us be glad and rejoice, and give honour to him: for the marriage of the Lamb is come, and his wife hath made herself ready. And to her was granted that she should be arrayed in fine linen, clean and white: for the fine linen is the righteousness of saints" (Rev. 19:7, 8).

We are not fit to attend the royal wedding. Even if God invites us, we will be ashamed in His presence. Even if we have the finest tailors on Seville Row or Fifth Avenue sew the most expensive suit or dress for us, we still will be embarrassed when the King mingles with the guests.

God looks on our hearts—there's the rub. He sees through the garments, beads, and baubles that we use to attract attention to ourselves. Although we try to cover up our flaws by outward adornment, He knows what we are really like.

But praise His name, He provides a tuxedo for the banquet! It is the "fine linen" of Revelation 19:8, the "white raiment" of Revelation 3:18. It is the righteousness of Jesus.

"This robe, woven in the loom of heaven, has in it not one thread of human devising" *(Christ's Object Lessons,* p. 311).

The wedding garment that Christ provides cannot be merely a cloak to cover our filthiness. Since God is interested in motives, desires, and thoughts—renewal of the inner person—the righteousness He provides extends to the complete person. When we accept Jesus, His perfect life is reckoned to us, and God accepts us as His unblemished children. But the righteousness of Jesus does not remain something altogether alien to us: the Holy Spirit makes us into new people, transforming us progressively into the image of the lovely Jesus.

Christianity does make a difference. We have new standing with God, and we also have new motivation and new power.

Praise the Lord for His wedding garment!

# GOD AND CAESAR

*Then he said to them, "Give to Caesar what is Caesar's, and to God what is God's." Matt. 22:21, NIV.*

Once again on that final Monday the enemies of Jesus tried to trap Him as He taught in the Temple. The Herodians and Pharisees, normally opposed to one another since the former favored cooperation with Rome while the latter opposed it, united in a common cause—to do away with Jesus.

They sought to disarm Him with flattery: "They sent their disciples to him along with the Herodians. 'Teacher,' they said, 'we know you are a man of integrity and that you teach the way of God in accordance with the truth. You aren't swayed by men, because you pay no attention to who they are' " (Matt. 22:16, NIV). Then they sprang the trap: "Tell us then, what is your opinion? Is it right to pay taxes to Caesar, or not?"

Jesus' enemies thought they had Him cornered. Any answer He gave, they figured, would get Him into trouble—with the people, if He said yes, with the Romans if He replied no.

But Jesus didn't give a simple answer. He called for a coin (He didn't carry money) and asked His critics whose image and subscription it bore. Obviously, the coin carried Caesar's head, and they replied accordingly.

Then Jesus said, "Give to Caesar what is Caesar's, and to God what is God's" (verse 21, NIV).

His answer is more complicated than we often realize. He distinguishes two realms of authority—God's and Caesar's—but the reaction of His hearers shows that His words involved more.

"That's why we cannot think of Jesus as calling for full support of Caesar here: His hearers didn't understand it that way. . . .

"According to Jesus, while we must render to Caesar what is his, we must render to God what is His. And God, remember, is the one before whom we can have no other gods. He is the one whose thoughts and ways are higher than ours. He is the single authority over all authorities, and we are to love Him with all our hearts and souls and minds. This is the heritage about God that Jesus upheld, and it is fundamental to the interpretation of what He said.

"That is what we must remember. God, the God who is pictured perfectly in Jesus, must be our ruler; whether we ask about working in the weapons industry or working on the Sabbath day, this truth must be our guide. It must reduce 'patriotism plus' down to healthier proportions, for if God's thoughts and ways are higher than ours, proud claims of national superiority are surely dangerous. The truth of God, after all, must shape us for *disagreement,* at least at times, with every merely human heritage. The wholesale embrace of any nation's values is idolatry, just what Jesus' saying has cast down" (Charles Scriven, "The Lady and the Lord," *Adventist Review*, Aug. 20, 1987).

*October 13*

# MARRIAGE IN HEAVEN

*Jesus answered and said unto them, Ye do err, not knowing the scriptures, nor the power of God. For in the resurrection they neither marry, nor are given in marriage, but are as the angels of God in heaven. Matt. 22:29, 30.*

What will heaven be like?

I believe the eternal home Jesus is preparing for us will surpass our fondest dreams. "But as it is written, Eye hath not seen, nor ear heard, neither have entered into the heart of man, the things which God hath prepared for them that love him" (1 Cor. 2:9).

"Let your imagination picture the home of the saved," Ellen White advises *(Steps to Christ,* p. 86). Yet, try as hard as we may, we catch but a glimpse of what will be. All that we see around us is governed by a short timespan—the "threescore years and ten" of Psalm 90:10. Indeed, in our world it isn't such an inviting prospect to live to a great age—to find oneself the last leaf on winter's bough, with family members and friends all gone.

Of this I am certain: all that is good and lovely in this life is just a taste of what God has in store for us. The powers of mind and body, the creative impulse, the conquest of ideas, the love of the beautiful—they will be not less but greater in heaven.

And all that is within me cries out for that eternal home. I was made to *live,* not to die; and so were you. God has put eternity in our hearts, the wise man tells us (Eccl. 3:11). We hunger, we thirst, for life everlasting, and through Jesus Christ one day it shall be ours.

Best of all in that heavenly home will be relationships. They are the stuff of life here, the summit of all the marvelous possibilities God has put within us. To know people—some intimately, others casually—to explore the electricity of personality meeting personality: this is life. And in heaven, I am sure, relationships will be refined and heightened in that life of all-pervasive grace, of concern for the other, of pride and joy in each others' achievement.

On this earth the closest human relationship possible to us comes through marriage. But Jesus, answering the cavilings of the Sadducees with their trick question (a woman has seven husbands in succession: whom will she have in the resurrection?), makes clear that God will change the pattern of society in heaven. We will not be dependent on marriage to explore the most exciting relationships.

How will He do it? My imagination fails, no matter how far I stretch it. But again I believe this: those dearest to us here will be no less dear to us in heaven.

And the supreme relationship? To know God. "And they shall see his face; and his name shall be in their foreheads" (Rev. 22:4).

*October 14*

# THE GREAT COMMANDMENT

***Thou shalt love the Lord thy God with all thy heart, and with all thy soul, and with all thy mind. . . . Thou shalt love thy neighbour as thyself. Matt. 22:37-39.***

Did you notice that Jesus didn't give a clear answer to the lawyer's question? The lawyer asked, "Which is the *greatest* commandment?" but Jesus gave a double-barreled answer: the greatest commandment is to love God supremely, *but* a second commandment is "like unto it"—to love our neighbor as ourselves.

Recently I met a man who to an unusual degree exhibits the twofold reply of Jesus. In Dr. Samson Kisekka, prime minister of Uganda, deep love for his Lord entwines and fills and finds expression in love for his countrymen. Religion and service have become inseparable.

Most of us cannot begin to imagine the suffering of the people of Uganda during the rule of Idi Amin and the years of anarchy that followed on his ouster. I sat one Friday evening at a dinner in Kampala and talked with my hosts about the years of terror. They told me how people simply disappeared, never to be seen again. A woman sitting opposite me had lost her husband this way. She was left with 11 children to raise. Then her brother disappeared also, and she took over his three children as well.

For several years the Seventh-day Adventist Church was banned by Idi Amin. But the church survived and even increased, largely because of the efforts of physician Samson Kisekka.

By late 1980, however, Kisekka had given up all hope for his country. A year later, facing certain arrest and death, he escaped into exile in Kenya and then England, where he coordinated the external mission of the National Resistance Movement.

When early in 1986 peace finally came to the troubled country, Kisekka was asked to serve as prime minister. He accepted the challenge of working along with President Yoweri Museveni to build a new nation. He sees politics not as a chance for self-aggrandizement, but as the management of society for happiness, justice, and prosperity.

Talking with Dr. Kisekka, head of Uganda's government, I was impressed with the spirituality, wisdom, and deep love of the people of this modern-day Daniel.

We serve God best by serving our fellowman.

*October 15*

# HOW THE PHARISEES MISSED THE MARK

*Woe to you, teachers of the law and Pharisees, you hypocrites! You give a tenth of your spices—mint, dill and cummin. But you have neglected the more important matters of the law—justice, mercy and faithfulness. You should have practiced the latter, without neglecting the former. Matt. 23:23, NIV.*

Jesus had silenced His critics. They had thrown question after question at Him, seeking to trap Him. They had sent scribes, lawyers, Pharisees, Sadducees, and Herodians in an attempt to embarrass Him publicly. But all had failed: "And no one was able to answer him a word, nor from that day did any one dare to ask him any more questions" (Matt. 22:46, RSV).

Now, either late that final Monday or on the following day, Jesus gave His last public teaching. He would impart more, and precious, instruction in the few days that remained before Calvary, but that would be reserved for the inner circle of the twelve.

Matthew 23 sets out Jesus' last teaching to the people. Strongly worded but spoken in love, it sets out a series of woes on those who of all in Israel should have recognized the Messiah—the scribes and Pharisees.

*Fault 1:* Their actions denied their profession of religion. Do what they preach, said Jesus, but don't follow their example (verses 3, 4).

*Fault 2:* They loved the praise of men more than God's commendation. They wore prominently the marks of the pious

—phylacteries. They sought the chief seats in synagogues and at feasts. They delighted in being called "teacher," "father," or "master" (verses 5-11).

*Fault 3:* They led astray honest seekers for truth. They missed the mark of God's high calling themselves, and by their example they caused others to miss it (verse 13).

*Fault 4:* Despite their pretense of piety by praying long prayers, they mistreated the unfortunate (verse 14).

*Fault 5:* They were zealous to win souls—but as followers of their misguided religion rather than as servants of God (verse 15).

*Fault 6:* They corrupted worship by theological rationalization. They had become materialistic, even in the midst of a round of religious ceremonies; so they put more value on the gold of the Temple than on the Temple itself, and on the gift on the altar than on the altar (verses 16-22).

*Fault 7:* They were scrupulous over details but were blind to the essence of the law—judgment, mercy, and faith (verses 23, 24).

*Fault 8:* They specialized in religious externals, but had not been changed from within. So while the population of Jerusalem regarded them with deference and awe, to God they were like whitewashed tombs full of decaying flesh (verses 25-28).

*O Master, whose all-searching eye reads the hearts of men and women, give me a new heart to worship You in spirit and in truth.*

*October 16*

# JERUSALEM, JERUSALEM!

*O Jerusalem, Jerusalem, thou that killest the prophets, and stonest them which are sent unto thee, how often would I have gathered thy children together, even as a hen gathereth her chickens under her wings, and ye would not! Matt. 23:37.*

Like a chicken—what a metaphor! Are we more comfortable with Jesus as the Lion of the tribe of Judah? As the King who will rule the nations with a rod of iron? As the heavenly High Priest who holds in His right hand the leaders of the church?

But here Jesus likens Himself to a hen gathering her chicks under her wings. That was what He longed to do for Jerusalem. Could she have but recognized her Lord, she might have found safety in Him.

And that is what Jesus still longs to do for you and for me. He wants to gather us in, to keep us warm and secure in the storms and struggles of life in this late twentieth century.

"Did the boy Jesus have opportunity to quietly sneak up to watch the chicks play around their mother's feet? Did He see them run beneath the hen's strong wings when frightened? And then did He think of the Messianic scriptures? When did He realize that *His* faithfulness would be the shield and rampart of salvation?

"On this day, no little roost of chickens lies before Him, but Jerusalem and indeed the whole world. He looks directly into the faces of those who will soon crucify Him. He looks around and sees Judas and Peter and John. Perhaps He sees Nicodemus, and His own mother, Mary, and the risen Lazarus. . . .

"Whatever is in His mind, suddenly He just has to say how deep is the love, how much He cares, for all of them and for us. He reaches past the condemnations, past the evil He sees in every heart, past the terrible days just ahead, and grabs on to salvation. 'It comes down to this,' He seems to be saying. 'What matters most is not that you are killers, but that there is a Saviour. A Saviour come to save you even from yourselves. Like a hen gathers her chicks, I would gather you.' . . .

"He comes to say that everything He has said and done is no more complex than this truth: God is still our refuge. He comes to remind everyone that regardless of how black the day, there is a shelter from the storm—from the storm within, from atrocities without. He comes preaching the words of Isaiah, 'Like birds hovering overhead, the Lord Almighty will shield Jerusalem; . . . he will "pass over" it and will rescue it' (Isa. 31:5). . . .

"Like a chicken, He has just one purpose for us: salvation. And like a chick, under His wings is our only safe retreat." (Ray Tetz, "Saviour Like a Chicken," *Adventist Review*, Nov. 19, 1987).

*October 17*

# THE WIDOW'S GIFT

*Calling his disciples to him, Jesus said, "I tell you the truth, this poor widow has put more into the treasury than all the others. They all gave out of their wealth; but she, out of her poverty, put in everything—all she had to live on." Mark 12:43, 44, NIV.*

With what message did the Saviour of the world ring down His public ministry?—A final call to Israel to repent? A challenge to the people to accept Him as Messiah? A prophecy of the end of all things?

No. Jesus singled someone out of the most insignificant people in society—a poor widow—and held her up for public commendation.

He sat by the Temple treasury, watching as the crowd passed by with their gifts. Many rich people threw in large amounts, causing the jaws of onlookers to drop in wonder. No one gave a second glance at the drab woman, who, shunning attention, sidled up to the treasury. No one noticed as she flung down her gift, the smallest of coins, and fled.

No one gave her a second glance—mission successful. But Jesus noticed. He called His disciples over so they could hear His praise of God's humble servant and her offering.

We commonly emphasize how small was her gift, that widow's mite. But Jesus gave it just the opposite value—how *large* it was. Jesus measured the people's offerings not by the amount they gave but by how much they had left for themselves. And by this standard the widow's mite was the greatest gift of all. Whereas the wealthy gave only a small portion of their abundance, the poor woman gave everything she had.

Today many preachers seem embarrassed to talk about giving. They're afraid that they will antagonize the flock, that the church will be dragged down to the level of a commercial enterprise. They're gun-shy because of the crass appeals for money made by high-powered televangelists.

But Jesus talked quite a bit about money—at least one-third of all His teachings deal with it. He didn't continually raise the topic in order to benefit from others' gifts—He remained poor all His life. But He knew that selfishness turns the heart from the Spirit, that giving is God's antidote to our natural tendency to greed.

Jesus stands by the treasury in church today. He watches who gives, how much, and why.

What does He see as I give?

*October 18*

# HOW THE WORLD ENDS

*And as he sat upon the mount of Olives, the disciples came unto him privately, saying, Tell us, when shall these things be? and what shall be the sign of thy coming, and of the end of the world? Matt. 24:3.*

It is Tuesday evening of Jesus' final week of life, and watching the sun set over the Temple, He sits on the Mount of Olives. Peter, James, John, and Andrew are with Him (Mark 13:3) as He begins to talk about the future.

On the way out of Jerusalem one of the disciples had pointed out the massive size of the stones of the Temple and the magnificence of the buildings. But Jesus had replied: "Not one stone here will be left on another; every one will be thrown down" (Mark 13:2, NIV).

To the disciples such unspeakable horror can mean but one thing—the end of the world. So now, as Jesus sits alone with His four closest friends, they ask when this will be. And Jesus answers their question, painting in broad strokes the course of events that will lead up to Jerusalem's capture and fall to the Roman armies in A.D. 70, but then going beyond to the end of the age.

Troubled times are ahead, He tells them—wars, famines, earthquakes, deceivers, persecution. But when the followers of Jesus see the holy city surrounded by armies, they are to flee without hesitation.

Flee when the city is surrounded? What sort of counsel is this? But the word passed down among Christians—and they waited. They saw Jerusalem besieged when the conflict between the Jews and Rome broke out in A.D. 66, and when the Romans withdrew for a little while, the Christians remembered Jesus' words and fled to Pella, where they remained safe.

But the fall of Jerusalem, terrible as it was for the Jews, would not be the end of the age. Jesus looked beyond it, spanning the centuries in a few packed sentences that reach to our day.

This is the way the world ends—not in atomic holocaust that burns up Planet Earth and leaves a few half-crazed people wandering around with their hair falling out.

This is the way the world ends—not because it is invaded by beings from outer space.

This is the way the world ends—not because eons hence the sun burns out, and all life perishes in eternal cold.

But this is the way the world ends: "And then shall appear the sign of the Son of man in heaven: and then shall all the tribes of the earth mourn, and they shall see the Son of man coming in the clouds of heaven with power and great glory" (Matt. 24:30).

And when that day comes, He who kept His people safe at Jerusalem's end will keep us at the world's end.

# HIS UNFAILING WORD

***Heaven and earth shall pass away, but my words shall
not pass away. Matt. 24:35.***

Have you ever thought what a bold statement this is?

Here is a poor Jewish carpenter, for three years an itinerant
preacher, sitting on the Mount of Olives one Tuesday evening.
Four close friends are with Him, but they, like Him, are unedu-
cated. This teacher has neither power nor influence. Although the
common people like Him, the political and religious establishment
despises Him and even now plots to murder Him.

Yet He utters a wild prophecy: His words will never pass away.
So long as heaven and earth stand, His word will endure. Let
heaven and earth pass away, His word will not.

And He was right. The word of Jesus has not failed, and it will
never fail.

During the long night of the Dark Ages that Word was taken
from mankind. It was bound, forbidden, separated by languages the
people could not understand.

But Jesus' Word did not fail. Here and there it was copied in
secret. The Waldenses in the mountain fastnesses of northern Italy
carried it secretly to those ready to receive it. Men like John
Wycliffe risked their lives to translate it so that the people could
read and understand.

At last the long night broke. The Reformation, the dawning,
sprang from the recovery of Jesus' Word. Luther translated the
Bible, working from the Greek and the Hebrew, ready to make the
plowman more knowledgeable in Scripture than the prelates who
opposed him. In God's perfect timing, movable type had been
invented about 70 years before; and soon copies of Jesus' Word
went everywhere, a tide of goodness that has not ceased to flow
since.

Two hundred years after Luther the Word faced new dangers.
Now critics and skeptics arose to deny its divine origin, pouring
energy and scholarship into dissecting, denigrating, attacking;
reducing the Lord of the Word to the status of a mere man; casting
doubt, mocking those who take the Word in simple faith, forecast-
ing the demise of Christianity.

But the word of Jesus still stands. Heaven and earth have not
passed away, nor has His word. And when they do, it will not.

*O Jesus, whose word gives life, teach me to treasure it today.
May I feast upon it, grow in it, and share it with others.*

# THE SECRET OF READINESS

*Then shall the kingdom of heaven be likened unto ten virgins, which took their lamps, and went forth to meet the bridegroom. And five of them were wise, and five were foolish. Matt. 25:1, 2.*

After Jesus had given the warning signs for the destruction of Jerusalem and the end of the age, He left three final parables with His disciples. Each, in different ways, illustrates how we are to wait for the return of Jesus: "Therefore keep watch, because you do not know the day or the hour" (Matt. 25:13, NIV).

Jesus draws the first lesson from a scene unfolding before Him. He is seated on the Mount of Olives with Peter, James, John, and Andrew. The last light has faded. Now as darkness falls they see the lights of a wedding procession. And Jesus uses the occasion to tell the story of the ten virgins—five wise, five foolish.

This isn't a parable to highlight the difference between Christians and the world. Rather, it's a parable about the church, illustrating the two classes who profess to be waiting for the Lord. "They are called virgins because they profess a pure faith. By the lamps is represented the word of God. . . . The oil is a symbol of the Holy Spirit" *(Christ's Object Lessons,* pp. 406, 407).

What is the key difference between the two groups? The wise ones had extra oil for their lamps—the Holy Spirit; the others did not.

"The Spirit works upon man's heart, according to his desire and consent implanting in him a new nature; but the class represented by the foolish virgins have been content with a superficial work. They do not know God. They have not studied His character; they have not held communion with Him; therefore they do not know how to trust, how to look and live" *(ibid.,* p. 411).

And we cannot borrow the Spirit from someone else. The foolish virgins had to seek oil for themselves, and so must we individually know our God, live by His life daily, experience His abiding presence—the Holy Spirit.

Here, then, is the first secret of readiness for the coming of the Lord: a life hid in God and nurtured by the Holy Spirit.

God alone knows our relation to Him. We can fool others, even fool ourselves; but God reads the heart.

*O Divine Master, take me to Thyself this day. May all my work be wrought in Thee, and grant me the blessed Spirit's presence and power during every moment.*

# WORKING WHILE WE WAIT

*For the kingdom of heaven is as a man travelling into a far country, who called his own servants, and delivered unto them his goods. And unto one he gave five talents, to another two, and to another one; to every man according to his several ability; and straightway took his journey. Matt. 25:14, 15.*

Jesus, in His second parable on the Mount of Olives, further showed what it means to watch for His coming.

1. *Every Christian receives at least one talent.*

The talents that Christ entrusts to His church represent the gifts and blessings imparted by the Holy Spirit, and the Spirit passes none by. No Christian can say, "I don't have any gift. Others are talented, so I will leave the work of the church to them." God has a work for every one of us; indeed, He has a *special* place of service He has ordained for each of us.

Our minds usually consider the public gifts when we speak of the talents—preaching, teaching, healing, administration. But the less spectacular gifts are equally important in God's sight. Again Paul: "On the contrary, those parts of the body that seem to be weaker are indispensable, and the parts that we think are less honorable we treat with special honor" (1 Cor. 12:22, 23, NIV).

Your talent may be in baking a loaf of bread and giving it to your neighbor. That isn't my talent, but it can convey much about the wholistic faith we profess. Your talent may be in writing letters, or in making telephone calls, or in baby-sitting—the list is endless. But whatever, you *do* have at least one talent.

2. *God expects us to develop the gifts He has entrusted to us.*

"The development of all our powers is the first duty we owe to God and to our fellow men. No one who is not growing daily in capability and usefulness is fulfilling the purpose of life. In making a profession of faith in Christ we pledge ourselves to become all that it is possible for us to be as workers for the Master," writes Ellen White *(Christ's Object Lessons,* pp. 329, 330).

A TV ad for the U.S. Army challenges: "Be all that you can be. Find your future in the Army." But God calls us to be all that He has designed us to be in His church.

3. *This life is only a doorway to eternal growth in the presence of God.*

Those who developed the talents God lent to them were given more when the Master took account. And we who work with Christ now will have the joy of working with Him in the better land.

# SURPRISED BY GRACE

*"When the Son of Man comes in his glory, and all the angels with him, he will sit on his throne in heavenly glory. All the nations will be gathered before him, and he will separate the people one from another as a shepherd separates the sheep from the goats. Matt. 25:31, 32, NIV.*

Jesus' three illustrations in Matthew 25 that instruct us in how to be ready for His second coming encompass the range of Christian experience.

The third parable, longest of all—in fact, one of the longest of all Jesus' parables—emphasizes *practical Christianity*. In the final analysis our standing before God will depend not on profession but on action, on our regard and relief for the weaker elements in society and in the church.

"Christ on the Mount of Olives pictured to His disciples the scene of the great judgment day. And He represented its decision as turning upon one point. When the nations are gathered before Him, there will be but two classes, and their eternal destiny will be determined by what they have done or have neglected to do for Him in the person of the poor and the suffering.

"In that day Christ does not present before men the great work He has done for them in giving His life for their redemption. He presents the faithful work they have done for Him" (*The Desire of Ages*, p. 637).

Those whom Christ commends aren't the famous preachers, the learned teachers, much less the rulers of government. They are the men and women who fed the hungry, gave drink to the thirsty, clothed the naked, took in the stranger, visited the sick and the prisoners.

So the "bottom line" of Christianity, after all, is works?

Yes—but not salvation by works.

Notice the *surprise* of the righteous as the Lord commends them for their good works. "Then the righteous will answer him, 'Lord, when did we see you hungry and feed you, or thirsty and give you something to drink? When did we see you a stranger and invite you in, or needing clothes and clothe you? When did we see you sick or in prison and go to visit you?' " (Matt. 25:37-39, NIV).

The righteous are rich in deeds of mercy, but they aren't conscious of the fact. All that they have done has come from an unselfish heart, a heart that does not seek to keep a score of its good deeds or to compare itself with others.

Grace has been at work on the righteous. Grace has produced a rich harvest of gentle and noble deeds. Grace has made them compassionate to the needy. Grace has made them like Jesus.

And they are surprised by grace.

*October 23*

# THE TRAITOR

*And Judas went to the chief priests and the officers of the temple guard and discussed with them how he might betray Jesus. Luke 22:4, NIV.*

How could Judas have done it—betray his Lord? Was he an irredeemably evil character, determined from birth to do this disgraceful deed?

No. Despite the abhorrence with which Judas has been held in Christian circles—his name alone among the twelve is seldom given to sons—he was not a sinister person set on a diabolical course. The startling point about him is that any one of *us* might have done what he did.

Judas started his ministry with great promise. He seemed a natural leader, brimming with talent. The other disciples urged him upon Jesus, thinking Judas would add strength to the motley band. Quickly they elevated him to responsibility: Judas became treasurer for the group.

Judas had flaws of character—as did Peter, James, John, and the others; and as do we. He was ambitious for himself and ambitious for Jesus. His eyes were set on an earthly king and kingdom, one in which he would play a leading part. He loved Jesus' proclamation of the kingdom at hand and rejoiced at the evidence of Jesus' power—His miracles of healing, raising the dead, feeding the multitudes. Gradually a scenario for Jesus—and for himself—took shape in Judas' thinking.

Judas was clever—and knew it. Eventually he was too clever by half. Jesus' words about His coming death made no sense to him. Especially Jesus' refusal to accept the crown that high day in Galilee when the crowds, their stomachs satisfied, pressed forward in acclaim, offended him. He saw Jesus as the reluctant Messiah, and at last he made a calculated move to force Jesus to act. "Judas did not, however, believe that Christ would permit Himself to be arrested. In betraying Him, it was his purpose to teach Him a lesson" (*The Desire of Ages*, p. 720).

Judas—how clever, too clever! His calculations went awry, and his life collapsed around him as he saw the impossible happen: Jesus arrested, condemned, crucified. He took his own life, a tragic individual.

Like Peter, James, John, and the others, Judas had abundant opportunity to know Jesus. But whereas they submitted to the gentle, molding influence of Christ, Judas persisted in his own ways. Priding himself in his abilities, driven by ambition, he could not grasp the true nature of Jesus' kingdom.

Judas—a story of what might have been!

*October 24*

# LOVE'S FULL MEASURE

***It was just before the Passover Feast. Jesus knew that the time had come for him to leave this world and go to the Father. Having loved his own who were in the world, he now showed them the full extent of his love. John 13:1, NIV.***

How far will love go? Love washes the feet of the disciples.

How far will love stoop? Knowing that already Judas has agreed with the religious leaders to sell Him for 30 paltry pieces of silver, Jesus washes the feet of Judas.

Behold Jesus, Creator of the Universe, Master of the world, girding Himself with a towel, pouring water in a basin, bending to wash the feet of sinful men, drying them with the towel. Around the circle He goes, one by one, taking His time, passing none by. His hands move gently, firmly; they convey love and thoughtfulness.

The disciples look on, thunderstruck. They feel a stab of conscience: *they* should be where Jesus is. When they entered the upper room for the Passover celebration that Thursday evening, they'd waited for a servant to bring in the customary basin of water to wash their dusty feet. But no servant had appeared, and each one of the twelve, jealous of rank, determined that *he* would not be the one to do the dirty work.

They waited. Nobody moved. Only Jesus.

Jesus "showed the full extent of His love." He demonstrated that love sets aside pride of place, jealous regard for self, anxiety to appear better than someone else. Love takes off its suit and puts on overalls. Love get its hands dirty.

We are complex beings, we human beings. We do very little from wholly pure motives. Always, even within the church, self intrudes into our most generous acts. We constantly are aware of what others will see, what they will think of us.

How many of us will do a good deed if we know that nobody else in the world will find out?

And even if we might do so, do we then remind ourself that God sees and takes note to reward us?

I believe that only as the love of the Lord Jesus floods our lives—only as His life becomes ours—can our good deeds approach the purity of motive that compelled Him to lay aside His robes and wash the feet of the disciples.

Only in Jesus, only in His life and love, can we act like Him. But in Him we *will* and *do* act like Him!

*O Master of the basin and the towel, may I follow Your example. Fill me with Your love and life that I may love and serve like You.*

October 25

# LORD, IS IT I?

**And they were exceeding sorrowful, and began every one of them to say unto him, Lord, is it I? Matt. 26:22.**

Lord, is it I? That is the question we must ask ourselves today.

It is a question for mature people. Have you noticed how the world of children centers in themselves? How quickly they put blame on someone else—anyone else—for a fault? How slowly their eyes open to see themselves as others see them?

We all are slow to grow up. Some people never reach maturity. They never seem able to turn the searchlight into their own heart, asking, "Lord, is it I?"

Thursday night in Jerusalem, and Jesus sits eating the Passover with the twelve. Already the bluster and bravado of Peter has been shaken. In washing the feet of the disciples, Jesus has done what he or one of the others should have done. Already John, James, Andrew, and the rest feel the chill of impending calamity.

Now Jesus adds to their apprehension. As they eat in silence Jesus says straight out: "I tell you the truth, one of you will betray me" (Matt. 26:21, NIV). They are amazed, staggered at the suggestion. They look from face to face, seeking a sign of the traitor. Peter—could it be he? Philip? Bartholomew? James?

319

Suddenly a flood of self-distrust rolls over them. Perhaps, not someone else, but *I?* "Surely not I, Lord?" (NIV).

Judas asks the same question—eventually.

"With the most painful emotion, one after another inquired, 'Lord, is it I?' But Judas sat silent. . . . The disciples had searched one another's faces closely as they asked, 'Lord, is it I?' And now the silence of Judas drew all eyes to him. Amid the confusion of questions and expressions of astonishment, Judas had not heard the words of Jesus in answer to John's question. But now, to escape the scrutiny of the disciples, he asked as they had done, 'Master, is it I?' Jesus solemnly replied, 'Thou hast said' " *(The Desire of Ages,* p. 654).

Ten centuries before, when the prophet Nathan had stood before King David and the monarch had asked him who had committed a treacherous act, the prophet replied, "Thou art the man" (2 Sam. 12:7). Now Judas gets the same message. Unlike David, however, the revelation of himself brings no repentance.

*Dear Jesus, who reads my heart, help me to see myself as You do—and as You see I may be by Your grace.*

October 26

# JESUS AND HIS FRIENDS

*And when the hour was come, he sat down, and the twelve apostles with him. And he said unto them, With desire I have desired to eat this passover with you before I suffer. Luke 22:14, 15.*

Jesus sits around the table with His friends. This is the last time they will be together. The disciples don't know it, but within a few hours Jesus will be arrested and dragged away to die on a cross.

When you are leaving on a long journey, what do you usually do? The night before, you gather your closest friends around—just the special ones—and eat together. Those final hours are precious. You remember the conversation years afterward, and so do your friends.

I remember well a family gathering in Adelaide, South Australia, in 1966. My wife and I had just flown into town, where we joined members of the Johnsson clan in celebrating Mom and Dad's fiftieth wedding anniversary. I can tell you all about that scene. I recall what Father looked like, what he said. Shortly after the celebration we left, returning to India. Dad died within four months; it was our last meeting.

And Jesus, Son of God though He was, craved the company of His closest ones that final Friday night. He savored every moment, making each word count.

The disciples never forgot that evening. Is it any surprise that the beloved John, the friend who was closest of all to Christ, recalled His words in detail? He devotes five full chapters (John 13-17) to those few hours in the upper room.

We were not present with Jesus that evening, but what the disciples remembered has passed down through the centuries and become part of our corporate memory. Just as, when children, we hear tales of our ancestors whom we have never met and appropriate their experiences to ourselves, so as Christians we enter into the Last Supper with our Lord. We recline by His side. We take the piece of bread from His hand. We drink from the cup as He passes it to us.

So those regular occasions when we gather for Communion are precious times. Jesus meets with His friends—us. He earnestly desires to spend these moments as we recall His sufferings and death.

What a pity that some Christians stay away from the Lord's Supper! Do they fear that they are unworthy? That in this solemn celebration Jesus comes with judgment on their failings? Let them see Jesus, their Friend of friends, reaching out to them, speaking gently with them, *longing* for their company.

*Lord of the upper room, draw near to me; be my friend today.*

October 27

# TELL US ABOUT HOW GOD DIED

***And as they were eating, Jesus took bread, and blessed it, and brake it, and gave it to the disciples, and said, Take, eat; this is my body. And he took the cup, and gave thanks, and gave it to them, saying, Drink ye all of it. Matt. 26:26, 27.***

The first year my wife taught kindergarten at Spicer Memorial College in India, she had many Hindu children in the class. Many of them knew little English, so imagine her surprise when one morning a bright-eyed 5-year-old boy requested, "Tell us about how God died."

Noelene decided to wait awhile until the class would be able to understand the story. The boy kept bringing up the same request, and she would whet the appetite of all by telling him to be patient—soon she would tell them about how God died.

After several months they were ready. During the next two weeks she told the story of the cross, going over and over it, adding new details. Morning by morning the little children sat transfixed in awe at what they were hearing, wanting to hear the story again. Hinduism has many gods—millions of them, a god for every hill, big tree, or rock—but none is like the God who gave His life on Calvary.

O what a story! Tell it to the little children, tell it early, tell it often. Let them wonder about how God died.

Tell it to juniors; tell it to teens. Let them weep at the betrayal, the sacrifice, the injustice, the love.

Tell it to young people; tell it to young adults. Let them fall in love with Jesus, the Man of matchless charms who went to the death for every one of us.

Tell it to adults in the prime of life; tell it to the newly married, to young parents, to families. Let it be the theme of worship, let it be the motivation for holy living.

And tell it to the aged, when cold winds blow and the leaves fall and strength ebbs and loved ones are gone. Tell it in hope; tell it in joy—the story about how God died.

"This is my body," said Jesus. "This is my blood." We take the bread and the wine—emblems of death, symbols of remembering—and make them our own. We take them in memory of that last night in the upper room, and more especially of the cross on which He died the next day. We take them in anticipation of His return, when we shall sit with Him at the heavenly banquet.

And throughout eternity we will tell that story. It will never bore us. We will hear it over and over, and want to hear it again. We will find new insights, new depths at every telling—the story about how God died.

*October 28*

# PEACE FROM JESUS

*Peace I leave with you; my peace I give to you; not as the world gives do I give to you. Let not your hearts be troubled, neither let them be afraid. John 14:27, RSV.*

"Our Lord says, Under conviction of sin, remember that I died for you. When oppressed and persecuted and afflicted for My sake and the gospel's, remember My love, so great that for you I gave My life. When your duties appear stern and severe, and your burdens too heavy to bear, remember that for your sake I endured the cross, despising the shame. When your heart shrinks from the trying ordeal, remember that your Redeemer liveth to make intercession for you" (*The Desire of Ages*, p. 659).

The One who promises us peace did not shrink when He Himself looked into the maw of death. Many men and women today are paralyzed at the threat of nonbeing. They resent the passing of the years, the ebbing away of life's forces, the prospect of the grave ahead. Sometimes prisoners of war, blindfolded and facing the firing squad but reprieved at the last moment, have been left broken, raving creatures after the blindfolds were removed. But not Jesus.

On that Thursday night in the upper room, the twelve sat around with long faces. The stench of a grim unknown was in the air. The disciples were filled with foreboding. Only Jesus—He who faced the cross but 12 hours hence—could speak of peace, and even of joy (John 15:11).

Twice that evening Jesus said to His apprehensive band of followers: "Let not your hearts be troubled."

The first time He gave them this assurance: "Believe in God, believe also in me. In my Father's house are many rooms; if it were not so, would I have told you that I go to prepare a place for you?" (John 14:1, 2, RSV).

There is the first balm for troubled hearts—the trustworthiness of Jesus. We can trust Him just as we can trust God. His word is sure; His promises fail not. He doesn't play games with us: He seeks our best good.

When the storms shake the house, we can trust Jesus. Trust Him because of *who* He is, *what* He is.

In the second passage, our text for the day, Jesus promises His peace as the cover for our fears. His peace drives out our worries, stills our nameless dread, soothes our troubled heart.

The peace of Jesus isn't like the world's. It isn't absence of trouble, removal from heartache, numbing of the senses by alcohol, drugs, or sex. Jesus gives us His peace in the midst of strife, in the heat of conflict. We have a strength beyond ourself, an inner Resource that keeps us calm, that knows that Jesus is in control of all that may befall us.

*Master who calmed the angry waves, give me Your peace throughout this day.*

*October 29*

# PETER'S FOLLY AND FALL

*But he said vehemently, "If I must die with you, I will not deny you." And they all said the same. Mark 14:31, RSV.*

Peter meant it. He could not foresee any circumstance in which he would deny his Lord. But within a few hours he would do just that. He would collapse before the inquiry of a maidservant and with cursing and swearing three times disclaim any knowledge of Jesus.

Peter wasn't an evil man—he was a good man with weaknesses. He failed miserably—but so do we. Maybe we can learn something from his fall.

We find Peter's basic problem in his words in today's text. *He was sure of himself; he could not contemplate that he might ever deny Jesus.* And so are we, all too often.

Christian life begins with realizing our own sins and weaknesses and casting ourselves on the salvation Jesus offers. And Christian life continues in just that way—and in no other way.

Within each of us lie possibilities for marvelous good or terrible ill. Enabled by God's Spirit, we can rise to sublime heights. Trusting to our own resources, we may become a Judas, a Peter in the judgment hall, a Hitler, an Idi Amin. "Wherefore let him that thinketh he standeth take heed lest he fall" (1 Cor. 10:12).

Because Peter was confident that he could never deny Jesus, he slept when he should have been praying. Three times Jesus warned him, along with the others, of the need to seek God's strength to meet the test that lay just ahead (Matt. 26:40-45).

But Peter slept. People who agonize with God in prayer know their weaknesses, feel their need of help outside themselves. But Peter slept. Sleep is good, but sometimes prayer is more important, even though we may be dog-tired.

Peter, self-confident and unfortified by prayer, was overwhelmed by what happened in the Garden that night. Against all his preconceptions, he saw Jesus arrested and led away captive. His world collapsed. It was a world built on self, not on earnest seeking of God's will, and it collapsed under the rush of events.

So at last Peter found himself in the courtyard of the high priest. He now was confused and troubled. He longed for Jesus, but followed from afar. Trying to blend in with the crowd, seeking anonymity, he failed to stand tall for his Master. It was the final step on the road to his fall.

But Peter didn't stay down. Judas failed and stayed down. He ended his life a suicide. Peter repented, and the Lord lifted him up. He became a pillar of the early church.

# THE REAL LORD'S PRAYER

*After Jesus said this, he looked toward heaven and prayed: "Father, the time has come. Glorify your Son, that your Son may glorify you." John 17:1, NIV.*

We commonly call Jesus' prayer that begins "Our Father, which art in heaven" the Lord's Prayer. But this is the disciples' prayer, because in introducing this petition Jesus said, "After this manner therefore pray *ye*" (Matt. 6:9).

John 17 gives us the real Lord's Prayer. As Jesus completed His final instruction in the upper room, He lifted His eyes toward heaven and prayed. And what a prayer it is! It breathes intercession on our behalf and communion with the Father.

Notice, Jesus hardly refers to His own wants and needs in this prayer. Although He is about to go out to the Garden of Gethsemane, where He will stand alone—betrayed, forsaken, bound—His words breathe calm assurance.

"Father, the time has come." He has waited for this hour, worked toward it. It will be the culmination of His ministry. Although to all human appearances the cross will mean the collapse of His mission in abject failure, by dying He will win the world for God. So just a few hours more and it will be over. He prays that He may glorify God now—especially now.

Most of Jesus' petition is for the disciples, however. "I pray for them," He says. "I am not praying for the world, but for those you have given me. . . . Holy Father, protect them by the power of your name—the name you gave me—so that they may be one as we are one. . . . My prayer is not that you take them out of the world but that you protect them from the evil one. . . . As you sent me into the world, I have sent them into the world" (John 17:9-18, NIV).

But Jesus' prayer reached further than Peter, James, John, Andrew, and the others. In His petition He looked down the highway of the years, saw those who would also become disciples, and He embraced them. "My prayer is not for them alone. I pray also for those who will believe in me through their message" (verse 20).

Do you believe in Jesus? Then you have a part in Jesus' prayer. He prayed for *you* that Thursday night; He prayed for me also.

Oh, what a Saviour, what a Lord! With Jesus on our side, with His intercession for us—then and now as our high priest in the heavenly courts—what have we to fear on earth or in heaven? In His name, by His grace we will go forth from strength to strength.

*Thank You, dear Lord, for including me in Your prayer in the upper room.*

# THAT THEY MAY BE ONE

*And the glory which thou gavest me I have given them; that they may be one, even as we are one: I in them, and thou in me, that they may be made perfect in one; and that the world may know that thou hast sent me, and hast loved them, as thou hast loved me. John 17:22, 23.*

What blessed harmony characterizes the Heavenly Trio! Although Father, Son, and Holy Spirit are distinct personalities, they are one in purpose, in character. They work together in love for the salvation of the world.

This is the unity for which Jesus prayed among His followers. "That they may be one, even as we are one"—think how high is His ideal for us.

Such oneness does not suggest a merging of minds that erases individuality. God loves the unique: He creates every snowflake different from the other, no two leaves exactly the same. Look at the profusion of colors with which He paints the fall landscape— gold and red and yellow and russet, with patches of lingering green. And in His church He expects to see differences—even *wants* to see differences.

As we survey the sweep of Christian history we have to conclude that this part of Jesus' intercessory prayer in John 17 has fallen far short of realization. Especially in the past, leaders of religion have sought to bend humanity's thinking to conform to their ideas. They erected the stake and the gallows to crush dissent. They fought wars to bring others to heel. They issued decrees and brooked no deviation.

In our times the opposite tendency, no less destructive of the divine plan, is more prevalent. We in the West have fallen prey to a hyperindividualism that loses sight of our corporate identity as Christians. We urgently need to recapture the meaning of the *body* of Christ.

Look out at the Christian world—so many different denominations claiming to be shepherds of the Master, even within the same church often divergent voices clamoring for the right to lead. Christians, who ought to be fighting the world and the devil, spend energy and time fighting one another, caught up in suspicion and name-calling.

One, as Jesus and the Father are one—we do not yet see it. But we catch glimpses. We *can* realize, if in part, the harmony of heaven as we fellowship together.

And we know Jesus' prayer will not go unfulfilled forever. At last, when God delivers us from the pettiness and narrowness of ourselves, we shall be together with Jesus. We will be one with Him and one with each other.

*November 1*

# EIGHTEEN HOURS THAT CHANGED THE WORLD

***And he took with him Peter and James and John, and began to be greatly distressed and troubled. And he said to them, "My soul is very sorrowful, even to death; remain here, and watch." Mark 14:33, 34, RSV.***

Jesus was arrested before midnight Thursday, perhaps around 9:00. He died the following afternoon at 3:00 p.m., 18 hours later. But those 18 hours were the most important in the history of the universe. Our salvation hung in the balance; during those 18 hours heaven watched in amazement and waited to see the outcome of Christ's struggle.

We shall follow Jesus step by step from the Garden of Gethsemane to the home of the high priest, before Herod, before Pilate, and finally as He hangs on a cross, executed between two felons. Our meditation on this 18-hour period will occupy the entire month of November.

Some of us have heard the story many times. But it bears repeating—it is *the* story of the ages. And let us pray that our hearts may be melted, that we will grasp such wondrous love, that we will sense something of the horror of sin and its penalty.

The story of the cross begins in Gethsemane. There Jesus wrestled with the awful demands of His mission; there He made the decision to take up the cross. If we would understand Calvary, we must first grasp what happened in Gethsemane.

What a change came over Jesus as He approached the garden! All evening He had been cheerful, encouraging the disciples during the supper, speaking of joy and peace. His final prayer with them made no mention of His impending struggle; it concentrated on their needs and those of believers in subsequent generations.

Furthermore, Gethsemane was His favorite place. During visits to Jerusalem in the past, He'd often spent the night there. Gethsem-

327

ane was His quiet place, where away from the crowds He relaxed and communed with His Father (John 18:1, 2).

But this night things were different. A terrible sorrow rolled over Jesus. "Every step that He now took was with labored effort. He groaned aloud, as if suffering under the pressure of a terrible burden. Twice His companions supported Him, or He would have fallen to the earth" (*The Desire of Ages*, p. 686).

Go to dark Gethsemane,
Ye that feel the tempter's power;
Your Redeemer's conflict see;
Watch with Him one bitter hour;
Turn not from His griefs away;
Learn of Jesus Christ to pray.
—James Montgomery

*November 2*

# GETHSEMANE

***And being in an agony he prayed more earnestly: and his sweat was as it were great drops of blood falling down to the ground. Luke 22:44.***

Once Satan came to Jesus in the wilderness. At the outset of the Saviour's mission, he offered Him a diabolical shortcut to the kingdom. But Jesus clung to the Word of God and bested the ancient enemy, who, says the Scriptures, "left him until an opportune time" (Luke 4:13, NIV).

Now Satan returns. The final, decisive battle in the history of our redemption has come—the moment for which the tempter had been preparing for three years. The stakes? The future of the human race.

Why was Jesus so troubled by this struggle? Because there in the Garden of Gethsemane He felt the agony of separation from His Father. He who had enjoyed eons of unbroken fellowship in the pure, unselfish love of heaven felt cut off, alone, for the first time.

Jesus became our substitute—He took our place. He felt the horror of God's displeasure with sin—He who knew no sin. "For he hath made him to be sin for us, who knew no sin; that we might be made the righteousness of God in him" (2 Cor. 5:21). He tasted death—didn't merely sip the bitter cup, but drank it to the last dregs—for every one of us (Heb. 2:9).

"Behold Him contemplating the price to be paid for the human soul. In His agony He clings to the cold ground, as if to prevent Himself from being drawn farther from God. The chilling dew of night falls upon His prostrate form, but He heeds it not. From His pale lips comes the bitter cry, 'O My Father, if it be possible, let this cup pass from Me.' Yet even now He adds, 'Nevertheless not as I will, but as Thou wilt.' "

"The humanity of the Son of God trembled in that trying hour. He prayed not now for His disciples that their faith might not fail, but for His own tempted, agonized soul. The awful moment had come—that moment which was to decide the destiny of the world. The fate of humanity trembled in the balance. Christ might even now refuse to drink the cup apportioned to guilty man. It was not yet too late. He might wipe the bloody sweat from His brow, and leave man to perish in his iniquity. He might say, Let the transgressor receive the penalty of his sin, and I will go back to My Father. Will the Son of God drink the bitter cup of humiliation and agony? Will the innocent suffer the consequences of the curse of sin, to save the guilty? The words fall tremblingly from the pale lips of Jesus, 'O My Father, if this cup may not pass away from me, except I drink it, thy will be done' " (*The Desire of Ages*, pp. 687, 690).

He suffered alone. In His moment of greatest need He sought the companionship of friends, but found none. They slept, while their salvation and ours hung in the balance. "I have trodden the winepress alone; and of the people there was none with me" (Isa. 63:3).

*O Divine Redeemer, who won my freedom by Your pain, teach me how terrible sin is and how great is the power of Your love.*

*November 3*

# THE KISS OF JUDAS

### *And forthwith he came to Jesus, and said, Hail, master; and kissed him. Matt. 26:49.*

Of all that is reprehensible in Jesus' betrayal, this is the worst. To covenant with Jesus' enemies to use the kiss, which demonstrates our closest affections, as the signal for Jesus' arrest—we loathe the thought. Ever since that night "the kiss of Judas" has stood for treachery, the stab in the back by a supposed colleague.

Think of what a kiss can mean. Do you remember your mother's kisses, her stories, songs, and prayers as you lay on your pillow, fighting to stay awake but feeling slumber roll over you, and finally the touch of her lips to your cheek and forehead as consciousness faded away? Do you remember your first kiss as an adult, perhaps stolen during academy days, maybe on a college date? And do you know the embrace of a dear one, the warm body of someone with whom your heart beats in rhythm? "Let him kiss me with the kisses of his mouth," says the Song of Solomon (1:2).

But Judas used the kiss to betray Jesus. He didn't greet Jesus simply with a quick kiss, furthermore. The Greek uses the word *katephile*, meaning that Judas kissed Jesus several times. In appearance Judas acted like one of Jesus' dearest friends, but his kisses were darts of poison.

Now, in our day kisses still are used treacherously. Kisses are used to say, "I love you," when lust rather than love motivates the action. Kisses are used as a polite greeting, a social convention that disguises the disgust or resentment that one person feels toward another. Kisses, as a part of sex, are used by spies to extract secrets of government.

Whenever we hear of such instances, we feel revulsion, sense a dehumanizing of what God intended to be beautiful.

In Psalm 2, a song of praise to Jesus, we find a verse that has puzzled many Christians: "Kiss the Son, lest he be angry, and ye perish from the way, when his wrath is kindled but a little. Blessed are all they that put their trust in him" (verse 12). I have never heard any preacher today use such language; what can it mean?

Surely it expresses the closeness we feel toward Jesus. As subjects of the few monarchs left on earth still bow before them and kiss the ring on their hand, so we bow before our Master—not in fear and cringing, but in adoration and praise.

Judas kissed the Son—but in despicable treachery. We kiss the Son as our Saviour and Lord.

*November 4*

# CAIAPHAS

***And they that had laid hold on Jesus led him away to Caiaphas the high priest, where the scribes and the elders were assembled. Matt. 26:57.***

They came by night, when the people who loved Jesus weren't around, and arrested Him, hauling Him away bound to the home of Caiaphas, the high priest of the Jews. Since Caiaphas held the highest religious office in the nation—in effect he was God's representative to the people—Jesus could be sure of getting a fair deal from him? Think again.

Caiaphas, like all the high priests of his time, belonged to the sect of the Sadducees. They were rationalists, accepting as inspired only the first five books of the Old Testament and denying the resurrection, life after death, and the existence of angels. Jesus needn't look for spiritual leadership from Caiaphas.

In fact, well before the time of Jesus the high priestly office, which commanded considerable power, had become more political than spiritual. Contenders for office schemed, plotted, bribed, and even murdered to get it. The divine ideal for the high priesthood long had been debased by holders of the office.

The few biblical passages that mention Caiaphas suggest a leader more concerned for preserving his power than for righteousness. When the Sanhedrin, flustered over the popular stir that Jesus' raising of Lazarus aroused, was called into crisis session, Caiaphas quieted them with the cynical observation: "You know nothing at all! You do not realize that it is better for you that one man die for the people than that the whole nation perish" (John 11:49, 50, NIV). Political expedience—that was Caiaphas.

"Caiaphas was a proud and cruel man," writes Ellen White, "overbearing and intolerant. Among his family connections were Sadducees, proud, bold, reckless, full of ambition and cruelty, which they hid under a cloak of pretended righteousness" (*The Desire of Ages*, p. 539).

Although Jesus was arraigned first before the leaders of His own people, His trial was a travesty of justice. So eager were the members of the Sanhedrin to be rid of Jesus that they thrust aside the provisions of Jewish law designed to safeguard the rights of the accused. They threw together a kangaroo court, called Jesus to trial in the middle of the night, and paid "witnesses" to invent testimony against Him. "He was taken from prison and from judgment: and who shall declare his generation? for he was cut off out of the land of the living: for the transgression of my people was he stricken" (Isa. 53:8).

At the close of Jesus' arraignment before Caiaphas, the high priest tore his robes in mock horror at Jesus' claim to be the Son of God. What a game in the name of God! But by doing so, Caiaphas rent more than his garment—some 12 hours later God would tear in two the veil of the Temple, and Israel's day as the chosen people would be no more.

*November 5*

# PILATE

*Very early in the morning, the chief priests, with the elders, the teachers of the law and the whole Sanhedrin, reached a decision. They bound Jesus, led him away and handed him over to Pilate. Mark 15:1, NIV.*

At its secret night trial the highest council of the Jews, the Sanhedrin, had condemned Jesus to die. But the Jews were under Roman occupation and could not carry out the death sentence without authorization of the Roman governor, Pontius Pilate. So they hauled Jesus away to the palace and summoned Pilate from his bedchamber.

They meet: the representative of Rome and the Representative of heaven. One is stern, angry at being aroused so early in the day by these Jews. The other is pale after a sleepless night in which He was bound and buffeted. Pale, but calm.

Who is this man whom history's annals will record as the one who gives the order for Jesus' execution? Because of his position we find several references to him in sources outside the Bible.

The Jewish writer Philo terms him "of nature inflexible, and, owing to stubbornness, harsh" *(Embassy to Gaius* 38). "He frequently clashed with the Jews, offending their religious feeling by many stupid acts. Once he had his soldiers march into Jerusalem carrying standards to which images of the emperor were attached. On another occasion he placed gilded shields with the name of the emperor engraved upon them in the former palace of Herod. In both cases he was forced to remove the offensive objects because of the stubborn resistance of the Jews. In the second case a direct order from Tiberius in response to a petition sent to Rome by the nobility of Judea compelled him to comply. The Jews were especially shocked when Pilate used money from the Temple treasury to pay for an aqueduct that was being built to bring water into Jerusalem. Their opposition to this misappropriation of sacred money was met with ruthless cruelty. Later Pilate massacred many Samaritans who were foolishly following an impostor who had promised to produce for them sacred gold vessels allegedly hidden by Moses on the top of Mount Gerizim" (*Seventh-day Adventist Bible Dictionary*, p. 885).

So they meet, Pilate and Jesus, and the governor's plans to dispose of this pest quickly melt away. The man is no criminal—Pilate has never seen such goodness and nobility.

Pilate doesn't know what to do with Jesus. He wants to release Him, but he doesn't want to displease the Jewish authorities. Then he sees a way out: hearing that Jesus is from Galilee, he decides to send Him to Herod, ruler of that territory. He passes the buck!

# HEROD

*And when Herod saw Jesus, he was exceeding glad: for he was desirous to see him of a long season, because he had heard many things of him; and he hoped to have seen some miracle done by him. Luke 23:8.*

Herod was glad to meet Jesus. For years he had been hearing about this remarkable rabbi from Galilee—one totally unschooled but who taught with an authority that put the lawyers to rout. He had heard that Jesus raised the dead, healed the sick, and fed the multitudes.

The opportunity that Friday morning seemed especially propitious. True, it was unusual to get a message so early in the day from the Roman governor—Herod wasn't used to doing business at 7:00 a.m. But the fact that Pilate had taken such an initiative overruled this inconvenience. For some time the two rulers hadn't been on speaking terms. Now Pilate, obviously extending the olive branch, sent his prisoner to Herod because Galilee came under Herod's jurisdiction.

So Jesus stands before Herod. The king eyes Him carefully. Yes, Jesus' clothes reflect His humble origins, but His bearing is impressive. Although He comes bound, a prisoner, He is still free in spirit—that Herod discerns.

So, miracle man, do your tricks. They say you can outdo any magician or jester at my court. Put on a good show; let's see your standup act. If it's good enough, I might even let you go—I have that power, you know. Come on, get on with it—I didn't interrupt my breakfast to be kept waiting by a rascal like you.

And Jesus did—nothing. He answered—nothing.

Herod commanded, cajoled, threatened, roared. Jesus stood silent.

Jesus gazed at Herod Antipas, murderer of His cousin John the Baptist. He thought of a scene like this a couple of years before when the king had sought an evening's entertainment that would please the guests gathered for his birthday. He brought on food and wine, and then he called for the star act—voluptuous Salome, only a girl but pretty and sensual, to dance for his guests. Salome danced—and before the evening was over one of the greatest human beings this world has ever seen lay dead, beheaded because of the foolish boast of the besotted king.

No word was fit for this contemptible creature; certainly no mighty deed to titillate his interests. Jesus did not move. He did not speak.

Puzzled, then enraged, Herod began to mock Jesus. He called his soldiers, and they put a purple robe on Him. If Jesus wouldn't play along with the king, Herod would still extract an hour of entertainment out of this obstinate fellow. The soldiers beat Jesus, blindfolded Him, slapped Him, calling on Him to prophesy.

Jesus did not move. He did not speak.

At last Herod tired of the game. The morning's fun hadn't worked out as he'd expected. What to do with this strange man? Release Him? No, since He'd refused to play ball.

Herod sent Jesus back to Pilate: he also knew how to pass the buck.

*November 7*

# PILATE AGAIN

*When Pilate saw that he could prevail nothing, but that rather a tumult was made, he took water, and washed his hands before the multitude, saying, I am innocent of the blood of this just person: see ye to it. Matt. 27:24.*

If only it were that easy—to wash away our guilt in a basin of water!

In Shakespeare's play *Macbeth,* Lady Macbeth comes down the stairs, walking in her sleep. Her conscience tortured by the murder of her husband's rival, a murder to which she has been accessory, she goes through washing motions with her hands as she cries out:

Yet here's a spot. . . .

What, will these hands ne'er be clean? . . .

Here's the smell of the blood still.

All the perfumes of Arabia

Will not sweeten this little hand.

Oh, oh, oh!

And Pilate, try to convince the rabble clamoring for the blood of Jesus that *you* are innocent as you deliver Him to them for crucifixion! Do you think they believe it? Try to convince yourself. Do you really believe that the basin of water absolves you of responsibility for His death—you who alone in this city have the authority to order this righteous man's execution?

Pilate was caught in his own game. Although the history of his rule drips with brutal acts, in his dealings with Jesus he comes across as vacillating rather than as bloodthirsty. All four Gospel writers devote space to the dialogue between Pilate and Jesus, and all four accounts indicate that Pilate wanted to release Jesus and tried to do so.

But he was caught in his own game. He did what he thought was smart: he passed the buck to Herod. But Herod turned around and passed it back.

Why was Pilate reluctant to deliver Jesus to His accusers? Surely not just because he realized Jesus was innocent; that he well knew, but questions of morality and justice hadn't troubled his conscience in the past.

Could it be that this hardened politician felt the pull of the Holy Spirit, pointing to heaven's open door? Looking on the face of Jesus, seeing His bearing and dignity, sensing the purity of this Man so utterly different from any he had ever met, did Pilate—for a moment, at least—entertain the thought that Jesus might just be what He claimed: the Son of God?

And then there was the message from his wife. "Have thou nothing to do with that just man," she said, "for I have suffered many things this day in a dream because of him" (Matt. 27:19).

Pilate's reaction to Jesus was vastly different from Herod's. The latter, a profligate playboy, saw only an object of entertainment; but Pilate's heart trembled.

Ultimately, however, Pilate's decision was every bit as terrible as Herod's. He tried once more to pass the buck, to put the guilt on the head of the Jews. But the decision to crucify Jesus was his alone.

No one can pass the buck with Jesus. Not even today.

*November 8*

# SCENES FROM THE JUDGMENT HALL

*Then came Jesus forth, wearing the crown of thorns, and the purple robe. And Pilate saith unto them, Behold the man! John 19:5.*

Let me sketch for you three dramatic scenes from that final Friday of Jesus' life, events between about 6:00-8:00 a.m. in Pilate's judgment hall.

*Scene 1:* The elders of the Jews arrive early, awakening Pilate from his bed. They drag Jesus, bound, before him.

"What do you want?" he asks.

"We have tried this fellow and find him worthy of death," they reply.

"Then you handle it," Pilate tells them.

"But we aren't permitted to execute," they remind Pilate.

Pilate goes to the judgment seat to examine Jesus formally. But the religious leaders don't go inside the court: they don't want to defile themselves and be unable to eat the Passover! (John 18:28).

Can you imagine it? Ready, anxious to put to death an innocent Man, but scrupulous about a religious ceremony! How warped can one's religion become! This scene suggests that there is no limit.

*Scene 2:* The prisoner slouches in his cell. Any day now—surely not much longer—he will hear the footsteps of the guard approaching, the key will rattle in the lock, and they will take him away. Any day now—his cross must be waiting.

The iron hand of Rome gave no quarter to revolution—and he was an insurgent. They had caught him, flogged him, thrown him into jail. Soon he would hang on a Roman cross, executed in full view of the passing crowds so everyone would get the message: Don't try to oppose Rome!

Now—the footsteps! The key in the lock—it's over!

The guard seizes him, but instead of dragging him away to execution, he unties his bonds. He leads him to the gate of the prison and turns him loose.

Barabbas, murderer and revolutionary, against all odds goes free.

Later, does someone tell Barabbas that Pilate wanted to release Jesus, but the religious leaders shouted out for Barabbas instead? Does he walk outside the city gate and see three crosses, and in the center the one that should have been his?

*Scene 3:* "And Pilate saith unto them, Behold the man!" (John 19:5).

"There stood the Son of God, wearing the robe of mockery and the crown of thorns. Stripped to the waist, His back showed the long, cruel stripes, from which the blood flowed freely. His face was stained with blood, and bore the marks of exhaustion and pain; but never had it appeared more beautiful than now" (*The Desire of Ages*, p. 735).

What a Man! What a Saviour!

*November 9*

# SIMON OF CYRENE

**And as they came out, they found a man of Cyrene, Simon by name: him they compelled to bear his cross. Matt. 27:32.**

After Pilate, acceding to the shouts of the mob, handed Jesus over to the soldiers for crucifixion, they took Him away for scourging, the customary prelude to execution. The Roman lash was no ordinary whip: its leather thongs laced with metal and bone cut deep into the bare back of the prisoner.

Now Jesus—head bloodied from the crown of thorns, face blackened by harsh blows, blood trickling from swollen lips, back lacerated—begins His last march. Rome will extract the last ounce of warning to the populace: not only will Rome's condemned die on a cross, but he must carry it through the streets of the city to the place of execution.

Jesus stumbles, falls under the weight of the cross. Not because He is a weakling—He isn't, for His muscles ripple from years of hard labor—but because the events of the past 12 hours have drained His strength. Beyond the hurt of betrayal and desertion, beyond the pain of the blows to the head and the soldiers' scourging, He carries something heavier than a Roman cross. He bears the sins of the world, and they are breaking His heart.

The prisoner is down, his cross on top of him. What to do? The soldiers certainly will not carry the despised symbol of Rome's supreme displeasure. Then they see a passerby, Simon of Cyrene, coming into the city for Passover. They order him to lift the cross and haul it behind Jesus.

Simon of Cyrene—at last we meet an encouraging character among the dismal cast of that sad Friday morning. Scripture tells that he was "the father of Alexander and Rufus" (Mark 15:21), apparently people well known among the early Christians to whom the Gospel writers first sent their inspired accounts of Jesus. That is, Simon of Cyrene in due course became a believer, and his sons as well.

"The bearing of the cross to Calvary was a blessing to Simon, and he was ever after grateful for this providence. It led him to take upon himself the cross of Christ from choice, and ever cheerfully stand beneath its burden" (*The Desire of Ages*, p. 742).

Amid the cruelty of that final Friday some people would find salvation. The cross, which brought out the radical evil of our human nature, also brought new life to people widely diverse in background—a Simon of Cyrene, a dying thief, a Roman soldier. They were the firstfruits of that harvest predicted by Jesus Himself: "And I, if I be lifted up from the earth, will draw all men unto me" (John 12:32).

Simon—he found salvation by carrying Jesus' cross. Will I take up that cross today?

# THE DAUGHTERS OF JERUSALEM

*But Jesus turning unto them said, Daughters of Jeru-salem, weep not for me, but weep for yourselves, and for your children. Luke 23:28.*

One of the features of Luke's Gospel is his interest in the socially disadvantaged—tax collectors, Samaritans, women. Luke includes in his writing incidents omitted by the other evangelists which show Jesus' interest in all classes of society and all ethnic groups.

So here, in telling the story of the cross, Luke records an incident that happened as Jesus is trudging through the streets of Jerusalem, Simon of Cyrene following and carrying Jesus' cross. A large number of people came behind, Luke says, including women who mourned and wailed for Him. They weren't disciples of Jesus. Luke a little further on mentions that the women who followed Jesus from Galilee stood at a distance from the cross, watching Jesus die (Luke 23:49).

The "daughters of Jerusalem" were city dwellers who, moved with compassion, lamented the impending execution of Jesus. Some had heard about Jesus; some, perhaps, had been healed by Him themselves or had brought their children to Him; some knew Him not but were appalled at the prospect of men going to a lingering death by crucifixion.

Jesus is weak, tired, fainting. Already He has fallen beneath the weight of the cross. All around Him men are cursing, swearing, laughing, jesting. He hears nothing. But the wailing of the women touches His heart.

And Jesus thinks of what these women soon will suffer. Not 40 years will pass before Jerusalem is surrounded by Rome's armies. In the course of a bitter four-year siege, food and water will run out and the inhabitants of the city will cannibalize their own. "For if men do these things when the tree is green, what will happen when it is dry?" He says (verse 31, NIV). That is, if the innocent One now suffers so, what must be the fate of the guilty?

Jesus of Nazareth still passes by on the road to Calvary. The crowds mock and taunt, intoxicated with laughter. Men delight to see blood flow. The condemnation of our age is that men—and even women—have become inured to scenes of violence. People are shot, stabbed, bludgeoned to death daily—and hardly anyone notices.

Who today will wail for Jesus? Who sees Him in the blood-soaked stranger lying in the gutter?

# CALVARY

*And when they were come to the place, which is called Calvary, there they crucified him, and the malefactors, one on the right hand, and the other on the left. Luke 23:33.*

The Romans did not invent the cross. That dubious honor probably belongs to the Phoenicians. But the Romans took over the cross, employed it for centuries to effectively deter opposition to the empire. They erected tens of thousands of crosses to enforce Roman rule.

The cross suited their purposes ideally. It was preeminently a means of *public* execution. The opponent of the *Pax Romana* was paraded through the streets carrying his cross or one member of it. Passersby would see—and shudder. The place of execution itself was a public one. Let the crowds see the fate of anyone who dared to rise up against Rome! And death came slowly. The victim might linger for days, nailed or tied to his cross, until exposure and loss of body fluids brought merciful release.

The Romans employed the cross extensively—but never on their own citizens. No Roman citizen was ever to be crucified. When emperors occasionally ignored this restriction, widespread indignation and rioting resulted. The cross was a symbol of shame and humiliation—too horrendous for a citizen of Rome. The apostle Paul, for example, a Roman citizen, was not crucified. He was put to death with the sword.

But Jesus of Nazareth, lacking Roman citizenship, could be crucified, and He was.

"The spotless Son of God hung upon the cross, His flesh lacerated with stripes; those hands so often reached out in blessing, nailed to the wooden bars; those feet so tireless on ministries of love, spiked to the tree; that royal head pierced by the crown of thorns; those quivering lips shaped to the cry of woe.

"And all that He endured—the blood drops that flowed from His head, His hands, His feet, the agony that racked His frame, and the unutterable anguish that filled His soul at the hiding of His Father's face—speaks to each child of humanity, declaring, It is for thee that the Son of God consents to bear this burden of guilt; for thee He spoils the domain of death, and opens the gates of Paradise. He who stilled the angry waves and walked the foam-capped billows, who made devils tremble and disease flee, who opened blind eyes and called forth the dead to life—offers Himself upon the cross as a sacrifice, and this from love to thee. He, the Sin

Bearer, endures the wrath of divine justice, and for thy sake becomes sin itself' (*The Desire of Ages*, pp. 755, 756).

# A ROMAN CROSS

### *And sitting down they watched him there. Matt. 27:36.*

The people had come out to watch Him die. Fishermen jostled for a place with merchants; priests elbowed out housewives for a better view. Some knew Him well; others hardly at all. Many had come just to see the sight—to watch Him die. Some laughed and joked as the execution proceeded. A few wept. It would take quite a while—certainly several hours—so they sat down on the grass and rocks to watch.

Soldiers were there too. Some of them stood on duty. After a while someone started a crap game. An execution was nothing new to them—they had witnessed scenes like this many times before.

Yet this public dying was different. How could these people have known that before the day's end the officer in charge would say, "Truly this man was the Son of God" (Mark 15:39)? How could they realize that the execution they were carrying out would become the symbol of a new religion?

So we take our place among the crowd. We find a clear spot on the grass and sit down. We look up at Him, watch Him as He hangs dying on the cross. We wonder, How has He come to this? "Stop this gross miscarriage of justice!" we want to shout out. "Who is responsible for this diabolical act?"

And as we watch Him, the answers come. Slowly. Four of them. Of course—the Romans were responsible! Those soldiers around the cross, that officer—all Roman. Roman authorities gave the orders for His death. They nailed Him to a Roman cross.

Legally, it is a Roman execution. The Jews did not execute by crucifixion. They stoned offenders to death. But first-century Palestine was under the subjugation of Rome, and the Jews no longer had authority to issue the death decree. "It is not lawful for us to put any man to death," they said to the Roman governor (John 18:31).

A Roman governor signed the death warrant. "Do you not know that I have power to release you, and power to crucify you?" Pontius Pilate asked Jesus (John 19:10, RSV). The presence of this strong, silent Man confused and disturbed him. He could find no fault in Him, certainly no occasion for the death decree.

And yet His own countrymen demanded His blood. Powerful men in the group—the religious hierarchy—seemed united on having Him put away. When Pilate said to them, "Shall I crucify your King?" the chief priests answered, "We have no king but Caesar." "Let him be crucified!" (John 19:15; Matt. 27:22, 23).

So legally the Romans killed Christ. He was executed at the order of a Roman governor, by Roman soldiers, on a Roman cross.

But the cross was more than this.

*November 13*

# A JEWISH CROSS

*Likewise also the chief priests mocking him, with the scribes and elders, said, He saved others; himself he cannot save. If he be the King of Israel, let him now come down from the cross, and we will believe him. Matt. 27:41, 42.*

Jesus died on a Roman cross—but it was more than this. The Romans put Jesus to death, but they did so at the instigation of His own people. The cross of Jesus is more than a legal cross; it is a cross of rejection. "He came to his own home, and his own people received him not" (John 1:11, RSV). When Pilate declared his innocence of the blood of Jesus, the crowd shouted out: "His blood be on us, and on our children" (Matt. 27:25). So the inscription on the cross, "This is Jesus the King of the Jews" (Matt. 27:37), throbs with pathos.

But were the Jews Christ-killers? While their tragic rejection of Jesus as their king is a historic fact, did God then condemn them as a people, forever to bear their guilt, forever to suffer His curse?

When we turn back to the Gospel accounts of Jesus' crucifixion, some interesting data emerge. We notice statements like these: "When the chief priests and the Pharisees heard his parables, they perceived that he was speaking about them. But when they tried to arrest him, they *feared the multitudes,* because they held him to be a prophet" (Matt. 21:45, 46, RSV).

Again, as the enemies of Jesus laid plans to take Him by stealth, they said, "Not during the feast, lest *there be a tumult among the people"* (Matt. 26:5, RSV). And at the mockery of a trial before Pilate: "Now the chief priests and the elders *persuaded the people* to ask for Barabbas and destroy Jesus" (Matt. 27:20, RSV).

The members of religious hierarchy had to persuade the population to support their demands. If we speak of Christ-killers, we should limit the term to the ecclesiastical leaders, not to the

Jews as a people. The disciples of Jesus support this view: "Our chief priests and rulers delivered him up to be condemned to death, and crucified him" (Luke 24:20, RSV).

The death of Jesus, then, does not give theological warrant for anti-Semitism. And have we forgotten His own prayer from the cross: "Father, forgive them; for they know not what they do" (Luke 23:34)? Surely His own petition is not to remain eternally unanswered!

So we sit on the grass, looking up at the dying Jesus. The cross—His cross—is legally a Roman one. Religiously, it is a Jewish one—it signifies His rejection by the leaders of His own people.

But as we continue to sit and watch, we realize that the cross represents even more. It is a divine cross.

*November 14*

# A DIVINE CROSS

***Jesus answered, Thou couldest have no power at all against me, except it were given thee from above: therefore he that delivered me unto thee hath the greater sin. John 19:11.***

When Pilate in the judgment hall boasted of his authority, Jesus gave him a surprising answer. "You would have no power over me unless it had been given you from above," He said (John 19:11, RSV). Also, in the Garden of Gethsemane at the time of His arrest—as the disciples prepared to defend Him—He said, "Do you think I cannot call on my Father, and he will at once put at my disposal more than twelve legions of angels?" (Matt. 26:53, NIV).

These ideas drastically alter our conception of the cross. It was clearly more than a miscarriage of Roman justice, more than a tragic Jewish failure. In some way God was in and behind the very death of Jesus.

Jesus, in fact, expected the cross. Months before He bore it, He had spoken of His death at Jerusalem (Matt. 16:22, 23). Throughout His ministry He spoke of "his hour," "or my time," that was "not yet" (John 7:6, 30; 8:20), looking forward to the final events of His life. As He entered upon His last week He knew what its end would be: *"The hour has come* for the Son of man to be glorified," He said (John 12:23, RSV). And then—"And I, when I am lifted up from the earth, will draw all men to myself" (verse 32, RSV).

So in a sense, neither the Romans nor the Jews killed Jesus. Neither Pilate nor the chief priests could have had power over Him unless He had permitted them.

Over the centuries the Romans erected tens of thousands of crosses. But this one stands alone in its uniqueness. It was an execution—but much more. God was working out a divine plan in the death of Jesus. "Christ died *for our sins*"—this was the affirmation of the first Christians (1 Cor. 15:3). He tasted death *for every man*—so they believed and preached (Heb. 2:9, 10). He came "to give his life a ransom for many" (Matt. 20:28).

Now we begin to understand why the cross is shrouded in mystery—divine mystery. The physical sufferings, though intense, were the least of Jesus' woes. Acute mental and spiritual anguish battered His being. His agonizing cry of desolation—"My God, my God, why hast thou forsaken me?" (Matt. 27:46)—was the cry of a soul that looks into the maw of eternal nonexistence.

So the cross is a divine cross. Through its terrible suffering Jesus dies vicariously. He is not being *punished* by God, for God has sent Him (John 3:16). Rather, through that cross God is "reconciling the world to himself" (2 Cor. 5:19, RSV).

The answers have come slowly as we have sat watching Jesus. They have surprised us. And the fourth is a shocker. Have we waited long enough to hear it?

*November 15*

# MY CROSS

*For I delivered unto you first of all that which I also received, how that Christ died for our sins according to the scriptures. 1 Cor. 15:3.*

Here is the apostle Peter speaking: "He committed no sin; no guile was found on his lips. When he was reviled, he did not revile in return; when he suffered, he did not threaten; but he trusted to him who judges justly. He himself bore *our sins* in his body on the tree, that we might die to sin and live to righteousness. By his wounds you have been healed" (1 Peter 2:22-24, RSV).

Where are the Romans? Where are the Jewish leaders? They do not come into view: only "our sins" appear.

The entire New Testament teaches that Christ died for *our* sins, not for His own. Jesus is God's Lamb "who takes away the sin of the world" (John 1:29, RSV). He is God's expiation for sins, received by faith as a free gift (Rom. 3:21-25). He is God's wisdom, whose cross is foolishness to the Greeks and a stumbling block to the Jews, but divine power to save all who believe (1 Cor. 1:18-25). And long before He came Isaiah had foretold Him as the Suffering Servant.

"Surely he has borne our griefs and carried our sorrows: yet we esteemed him stricken, smitten by God, and afflicted. But he was wounded for our transgressions, he was bruised for our iniquities; upon him was the chastisement that made us whole, and with his stripes we are healed. All we like sheep have gone astray; we have turned every one to his own way; and the Lord has laid on him the iniquity of us all" (Isa. 53:4-6, RSV).

Would we condemn the Romans? We must protest their flaunting of elemental justice in the death of Jesus. But we condemn ourselves too.

Would we call the Jews Christ-killers? We grieve at their tragic rejection of Jesus. But we condemn ourselves too. Were they not representatives of us all? We would have done no better. We would have crucified Him also. In fact, we *did* crucify Him! He died for *our* sins.

"Were you there when they crucified my Lord?" challenges the old spiritual. And now we know that we were. His cross is every person's cross—for everyone is a sinner.

And so—it is *my* cross! This is why the story of Calvary haunts mankind to this day. We see ourselves—I see *myself.*

But the good news of Christianity is that His cross *was* my cross. It no longer is mine. He took it—took it in its shame and disgrace, in its humiliation and despair. And because He took it, He transformed it from a thing of cursing into a thing of blessing; from darkness into light; from despair into hope; and from a symbol of death into a symbol of life.

Who killed Christ? The Biblical answer is almost too shocking —personally shocking—to repeat. *I* killed Christ!

But it does not leave me despairing. Because the cross is also the climax of a divine plan, it is my salvation. Through His death I find life.

*November 16*

# "FATHER, FORGIVE THEM"

***Then said Jesus, Father, forgive them; for they know not what they do. Luke 23:34.***

Putting together the four Gospel accounts of Calvary, we find seven sayings of Jesus from the cross. We will meditate on these "seven words" one by one as we spend those final six hours of Jesus' life—from about 9:00 a.m. to 3:00 p.m.—at the foot of His cross.

Jesus' first statement called down heaven's forgiveness on the very ones who were causing His agony. Some commentators suggest that He spoke these words as the soldiers were driving the nails through His hands and feet, perhaps repeating them with each blow of the hammer.

Who else could find the grace to forgive his tormentors at such a time? In the Old Testament we read about Elisha, who just after he had taken over the role of Israel's prophet from Elijah, was taunted by young men. "Go on up, you baldhead! . . . Go on up, you baldhead!" they jeered, perhaps mocking the recent translation of Elijah. Elisha turned around and called down a curse on them in the name of the Lord. "Then two bears came out of the woods" and mauled 42 of them (see 2 Kings 2:23, 24).

We understand Elisha's reaction; we would do the same. But the Son of God, hanging on the cross, did not do the same. Instead of cursing, He forgave.

Three years earlier, in Galilee, Jesus had set out for His disciples the way of the kingdom. "Love your enemies, bless them that curse you, do good to them that hate you, and pray for them which despitefully use you, and persecute you" (Matt. 5:44). Now He was putting into practice His own counsel.

And by His dying, Jesus would transform the attitude of His followers as they too faced unjust death. Erelong the eloquent Stephen, one of the first deacons of the new church, would be seized by his enemies and stoned to death. His dying words would be "Lord, do not hold this sin against them" (Acts 7:60, NIV).

During World War II, as soldiers or civilians saw the enemy committing an atrocity, they would say to each other, "Mark that man for the future!" They took a good look so that if their lives were spared, they could exact vengeance later.

But hatred cannot drive out hatred, force drive out force. Only the mind-change that comes from the One who said, "Father, forgive them; for they know not what they do" overcomes evil.

*November 17*

# "THOU SHALT BE WITH ME IN PARADISE"

***And Jesus said unto him, Verily I say unto thee, To day shalt thou be with me in paradise. Luke 23:43.***

The soldiers gambled, indifferent to what was happening nearby. The priests and religious rulers hurled taunts at Jesus, calling Him to come down from the cross and they would believe

345

in Him. The people of Jerusalem strolled by, having come out to see a hanging, gawking at the Man from the north who had claimed to be Israel's Messiah. And even from the crosses on either side of Jesus came insults: "Aren't you the Christ? Save yourself and us!" (Luke 23:39, NIV).

But after a while one of the robbers ceases to curse. His companion becomes more desperate and defiant, but he falls silent. Something is happening within him. He sees the face of Jesus contorted by pain, reads the inscription over His head, "This is Jesus, the king of the Jews." He hears the taunts from the crowd: "He saved others, . . . but he can't save himself! He's the King of Israel!" (Matt. 27:42, NIV). He watches Jesus die—racked with infinite suffering, but without cursing or reproach—and he begins to believe.

"The Holy Spirit illuminates his mind, and little by little the chain of evidence is joined together. In Jesus, bruised, mocked, and hanging upon the cross, he sees the Lamb of God, that taketh away the sin of the world. Hope is mingled with anguish in his voice as the helpless, dying soul casts himself upon a dying Saviour. 'Lord, remember me,' he cries, 'when thou comest into thy kingdom.'

"Quickly the answer came. Soft and melodious the tone, full of love, compassion, and power the words: Verily I say unto thee today, Thou shall be with Me in paradise" *(The Desire of Ages,* p. 750).

The dying thief was the only person to call Jesus Lord as He hung on the cross. While some people wept and others mocked, a felon passed from death to life.

Yes, those in power could arrest Jesus, drag Him through a kangaroo court, and at last look on as His life ebbed away at His execution, but they could not take away His power to forgive and make men whole. He *is* Israel's Messiah. He *is* the Son of God. He *is* the Lamb of God that takes away the sins of the world.

Jesus' cross, bloody and gruesome, is the place of forgiveness. Forgiveness for the entire race, as Jesus wins back a lost planet —but more. Forgiveness that is specific—forgiveness for the soldiers who drive the spikes through His hands and feet, forgiveness for the priests, for elders and scribes who taunt Him. Forgiveness for the idle watchers in the crowd. And forgiveness for a dying thief.

*Lord, remember me also when You come into Your kingdom.*

# "WOMAN, BEHOLD THY SON"

*When Jesus therefore saw his mother, and the disciple standing by, whom he loved, he saith unto his mother, Woman, behold thy son! Then saith he to the disciple, Behold thy mother! And from that hour that disciple took her unto his own home. John 19:26, 27.*

Though Jesus' agony on the cross was intense, His first three "words" concerned others instead of Himself. With the first He called down Heaven's forgiveness upon those who were crucifying Him. With the second He brought hope and assurance to a penitent robber. And with the third He provided for the future of His mother.

Mary's heart broke as she stood at the foot of the cross. We sense the tragedy of any child who dies before its parents, sense that the wheel of life has run out of its appointed course. But to have one's son executed, held up to ridicule, mocking, and cursing—how could she bear it! This man, her son, her remarkable son conceived by no human father, her son so good and kind and so different from other boys, her son over whom predictions of greatness had been uttered at birth and who seemed to promise so much during manhood—her son, Jesus, was dying on a cross!

Did the words of Simeon spoken at Jesus' circumcision come back to Mary: "A sword will pierce your own soul too" (Luke 2:35, NIV)? That sword pierced her soul now.

Jesus loved His mother with tender regard. In the Gospels we find nothing that indicates His relation to Joseph beyond statements of His obedience and work by Joseph's side as a carpenter. But Mary plays a prominent role. A girl of surprising faith, she readily accepts God's choosing her to be the mother of the Messiah. She observes Jesus closely as He grows up, pondering the mystery of His being and His mission, storing in her heart His actions and sayings. Sometimes she goes beyond the bounds, trying to tell Him how to go about His divine work, but when she does so, as at the wedding feast in Cana, He gently corrects her.

Jesus looks down from the cross at Mary. Her grief compounds His woe. Within a few hours His sufferings will be over, but she will have to face life alone. Joseph is long since dead; she will be bereft of her beloved son, also.

Jesus makes sure that Mary will have a home. He entrusts her to John, His dearest friend. From him Mary will find protection and love.

Every scene from Calvary tugs at my heart. Every word of the Saviour overwhelms me with His love. But this one of the seven, in its tender regard for Mary, touches me the most.

*November 19*

# "WHY HAST THOU FORSAKEN ME?"

***And about the ninth hour Jesus cried with a loud voice, saying, Eli, Eli, lama sabachthani? that is to say, My God, my God, why hast thou forsaken me? Matt. 27:46.***

Although on earth men mocked and taunted the Man on the center cross, leaving just a few women to weep, in heaven the songs were hushed. The Father's heart suffered with the anguish of the Son, and angels looked on in wonder at the measures to which divine love would go in order to win back a lost world.

Around noon a strange darkness fell over Jerusalem. It was as though inanimate nature, bleeding with her Creator, cast a veil over His final hours. Jesus was silent for a long while; then He uttered a terrible cry, "My God, my God, why hast thou forsaken me?"

Let those who think Christ could not have failed contemplate that moan from the cross. Let those who reason that because Jesus was God, He knew that everything would end triumphantly and so His sufferings were not real also contemplate it. It is the cry of a person forsaken by God, the cry of dereliction, the cry of despair.

And when the devil comes with his allurements, when the pleasures of sin excite our senses and the way of Jesus seems hard and dry, let us each remember that piercing cry from the darkness. Forever it tells how terrible is evil and how marvelous is the love of God.

Jesus, who had enjoyed unbroken communion with the Father, now felt forsaken. Why?

"Upon Christ as our substitute and surety was laid the iniquity of us all. He was counted a transgressor, that He might redeem us from the condemnation of the law. The guilt of every descendant of Adam was pressing upon His heart. The wrath of God against sin, the terrible manifestation of His displeasure because of iniquity, filled the soul of His Son with consternation. . . .

"Satan with his fierce temptations wrung the heart of Jesus. The Saviour could not see through the portals of the tomb. Hope did not present to Him His coming forth from the grave a conqueror, or tell Him of the Father's acceptance of the sacrifice. He feared that sin was so offensive to God that Their separation was to be eternal. Christ felt the anguish which the sinner will feel when mercy shall no longer plead for the guilty race. It was the sense of sin, bringing the Father's wrath upon Him as man's substitute, that made the cup He drank so bitter, and broke the heart of the Son of God" (*The Desire of Ages*, p. 753).

# "I THIRST"

*After this, Jesus knowing that all things were now accomplished, that the scripture might be fulfilled, saith, I thirst. John 19:28.*

When Jesus uttered that cry of dereliction, "My God, my God, why hast thou forsaken me?" He quoted from Psalm 22. This song of ancient Israel brims over with the pain of the person whose world has collapsed about him. Jesus was steeped in the Scriptures, and in His darkest, loneliest hour His mind turned to this psalm.

Christians long have recognized Psalm 22 as pointing beyond David's experience to the Messiah. Apart from the fact that Jesus quoted it, it describes God's servant scorned by mankind, mocked and insulted: "But I am a worm, and no man; a reproach of men, and despised of the people. All they that see me laugh me to scorn: they shoot out the lip, they shake the head, saying, He trusted on the Lord that he would deliver him: let him deliver him, seeing he delighted in him" (verses 6-8). It even predicts the action of the soldiers who gambled for Christ's clothing: "They part my garments among them, and cast lots upon my vesture" (verse 18).

"My strength is dried up like a potsherd; and my tongue cleaveth to my jaws; and thou hast brought me into the dust of death" (verse 15). These words originally from David's pen likewise applied to Jesus as He hung upon the cross. After His moan expressing His feelings of having been forsaken by God, He uttered the fifth word: "I thirst" (John 19:28).

One of the soldiers, touched with pity, ran and got a sponge. He filled it with wine vinegar, put it on a stick, and offered it to Jesus.

This was the second drink the soldiers had given Jesus that day. Just before the nails were driven into His flesh, they offered Him wine mingled with gall. "When one is led out to execution, he is given a goblet of wine containing a grain of frankincense, in order to benumb his senses," notes the Talmud (see *The SDA Bible Commentary*, vol. 5, p. 547). Jesus, however, merely tasted the potion, acknowledging the thought behind the offer. But then He returned the goblet: He would not let His mind be clouded in this the hour of supreme test.

Now, nearing death, He sucked the vinegar from the sponge held to His lips. Even in this He fulfilled Scripture: "They gave me also gall for my meat; and in my thirst they gave me vinegar to drink" (Ps. 69:21).

Some of those standing by, mistaking Jesus' muffled cry of dereliction, thought He called for Elijah, whom Jewish tradition had made the patron saint of pious men in the time of extremity. But the priests only mocked further: "Now leave him alone. Let's see if Elijah comes to save him" (Matt. 27:48, NIV).

Elijah didn't come. No one came. Jesus died alone—for you and me.

*November 21*

# "FATHER, INTO THY HANDS"

*And when Jesus had cried with a loud voice, he said, Father, into thy hands I commend my spirit: and having said thus, he gave up the ghost. Luke 23:46.*

Jesus died with the words of Scripture on His lips. He who had first learned the sacred Word at His mother's knee, who had defeated the tempter in the wilderness with "It is written," whose life had been shaped and ordered by the Old Testament, quoted Psalm 31:5 in His dying breath: "Into thine hand I commit my spirit: thou hast redeemed me, O Lord God of truth."

How often the people of God have turned to the psalms for comfort and courage! We still do so. Their songs of uninhibited inquiry, challenge, and supplication echo our experiences even in these times. Although 3,000 years have rolled by, our basic human condition hasn't changed—we are still weak and needy, and the psalms speak for us and to us.

They spoke to Jesus also. They identified His feelings in the cry of desolation; they likewise breathed the attitude of submission to the divine will of the sixth word of the cross.

"Into thy hands"—what a way to live! What a way to die!

The Father's hands sustained Jesus in life and in death. They will sustain us also.

The Father's hands are strong and merciful. He leads us only in paths of peace and righteousness, guiding us for our best good. Though at times we may have to walk through the dark valley, He will be with us, never forsaking us until we break out into the light.

And when we stumble and fall, those hands lift us up, set us on our feet again, and send us on our way with fresh hope.

Dying alone on Calvary, Jesus clung to the Word of God. Despite the horror of separation He felt, He trusted in the Father. "By faith He rested in Him whom it had ever been His joy to obey. And as in submission He committed Himself to God, the sense of the loss of His Father's favor was withdrawn. By faith, Christ was victor" (*The Desire of Ages*, p. 756).

The Father's hands—there is no better place to be in life or in death.

*Father of mercy, into Your hands I commit my life for this day.*

# "IT IS FINISHED!"

*When Jesus therefore had received the vinegar, he said, It is finished: and he bowed his head, and gave up the ghost. John 19:30.*

"It is finished!" What sort of utterance was this, the seventh word of the cross? Was it a groan of relief—"It's over at last"—or was it a triumphal declaration that Jesus had won the decisive battle for our salvation?

Surely the latter. "Christ did not yield up His life till He had accomplished the work which He came to do, and with His parting breath He exclaimed, 'It is finished' (John 19:30). The battle had been won. His right hand and His holy arm had gotten Him the victory. As a Conqueror He planted His banner on the eternal heights. Was there not joy among the angels? All heaven triumphed in the Saviour's victory. Satan was defeated, and knew that his kingdom was lost" (*The Desire of Ages*, p. 758).

These last words of Jesus have led evangelical Christians to speak of "the finished work of Christ." Some other Christians dislike this language because it can be used to set aside the ongoing high priestly ministry of Jesus in the heavenly courts. However, in several senses we can legitimately comfort ourselves in the fact that Christ's parting shout signaled a decisive moment in time:

1. *On the cross Jesus offered up a complete, final sacrifice for sins.*

With that cry the veil of the Jerusalem Temple was rent asunder. The system of sacrifices and offerings given anciently to Israel came to an end. All the multiplied deaths of animals in themselves could not atone for sin; they merely educated the people of God in the plan of salvation, pointing forward to the Lamb of God, who would take away the sin of the world (John 1:29).

We commemorate the dying of Jesus as we share in the Lord's Supper. But the bread and the wine are merely symbols to help us reenact Christ's last meal. They are not Christ's flesh and blood, for He died *once for all*, an all-sufficient sacrifice (Heb. 9:26, 28).

2. *The cross unmasked the character and intentions of the devil.*

The cross was the devil's final and most powerful weapon. He thought that the Majesty of heaven would never stoop to such humiliation. But He did, revealing the matchless power of love.

And thereby the devil exposed himself. He is a murderer and a liar who, despite his claims and deceptions, will stoop to any lengths to accomplish his ends.

3. *The cross sealed our salvation.*

The war goes on, but its conclusion is in no doubt. Christ won the decisive battle. Satan is a defeated foe. He wounded Christ's heel, but Calvary struck the deathblow to his head.

Praise God, "It is finished!" gives us strength in our struggles now and assurance of our eternal life in Him.


*November 23*

# HOW JESUS DIED

***But when they came to Jesus, and saw that he was dead already, they brake not his legs: But one of the soldiers with a spear pierced his side, and forthwith came there out blood and water. John 19:33, 34.***

Jesus died after only about six hours of crucifixion. That was an unusually rapid death.

One of the cruelest features of execution by crucifixion was the slowness of death. The unfortunate victim hung on the cross, unable to move a finger. Ants and other insects crawled over his body; flies settled on his wounds. The sun beat down mercilessly; the wind, rain, and frost stung the naked flesh. The body's weight drooped from the metal spikes through the "hands"—more likely the wrists, since the flesh of the hands would tear and the body drop away from the spikes.

Death took a long time. Often only after several days would exposure and loss of body fluids bring blessed relief from the hellish execution stake.

The cross was Satan's weapon, not God's. But God took it and turned it against the ancient enemy.

Jesus died early, before the robbers on either side of Him. It was Friday; Sabbath was coming. The Jewish leaders didn't want the three crosses marring the Passover celebration, so they asked Pilate to hurry death along. Soldiers broke the legs of the thieves, but when they came to Jesus, they found He was already dead. One of the soldiers pierced Jesus' side with a spear, bringing a sudden flow of blood and water.

John the Beloved emphasizes the spear thrust in the side: "And he that saw it bare record, and his record is true: and he knoweth that he saith true" (John 19:35). Why? Presumably because some people in his day questioned whether Jesus really died.

A long article in the *Journal of the American Medical Association* (March 21, 1986), "On the Physical Death of Jesus Christ," examined the Gospel accounts of Jesus' crucifixion and concluded: "Thus, it remains unsettled whether Jesus died of cardiac rupture or of cardiorespiratory failure. However, the important feature may be not *how* He died but rather *whether* He died. Clearly, the weight of historical and medical evidence indicates that Jesus was dead before the wound to His side was inflicted and supports the traditional view that the spear, thrust between His right ribs, probably perforated not only the right lung but also the pericardium and heart and thereby ensured His death."

Why is it important to know that Jesus actually died? Because the wages of sin is death (Rom. 6:23), and because of what happened Sunday morning—not a resuscitation but resurrection!

*November 24*

# THE MYSTERY OF THE CROSS

### *And almost all things are by the law purged with blood; and without shedding of blood is no remission. Heb. 9:22.*

This passage leads us into the heart of God. It tells us why Jesus had to die—and yet in the final analysis it leaves our questions unanswered.

"Without shedding of blood is no remission." So this is why Jesus must *die* if our sins are to be forgiven—because God's way of putting away sin points through death.

Adam's and Eve's first act, divinely instructed, after the Fall, showed this truth. As they took the sacrificial lamb and slew it on behalf of their transgression they learned humanity's first lesson of God's Lamb, who in God's time would give His life for the sins of the world. Every lamb offered up by the patriarchs, every one of the millions slain during the course of Israel's sacrificial services, pointed to the same event. "Without shedding of blood is no remission."

Shedding of blood shows us the terrible cost of sin. That is hard for us to grasp in these days when men and women have such a light view of sin, when psychiatrists explain it away, and television programs wallow in violence and sex. Sin isn't something that God can forgive in cavalier fashion, waving His hand in a simple, "Oh, forget it." Only the One who is infinite in holiness knows the enormity of sin and what it costs to forgive it.

And He says, "Without shedding of blood is no remission." So as God, in the counsels of eternity made provision for our salvation long before our first parents had fallen, long before they had been created, His plan of salvation meant death. God carried the cross in His heart for eons before the Romans raised it on Calvary's mountain.

And yet, in the final analysis, Hebrews 9:22 leaves unanswered our question, "Why did Jesus have to *die*?" Why could God, who is infinite in resources, not forgive us through some other means?

"Without shedding of blood is no remission." Why not? Only God knows. Hebrews 9:22 is a divine axiom, exposing a glimpse of the heart of God, but no more than a glimpse. It tells us: God has taken upon Himself our terrible problem. He Himself provides the solution, *is* the solution. And the solution comes only through the cross.

What can I give or do to take away my sin? Suppose I have killed a man in my anger—shall I now kill a lamb? How does that help? Now there is a dead man and a dead lamb also.

And look at our human courts. In no human tribunal does the law permit someone else to take my penalty, let alone to give his life to expunge my crime.

But God's way does. Transcending human law, God dies on our behalf. The cross, eternally in His heart, bears Him—and bears our sin away.

*November 25*

# FORGIVENESS AT THE CROSS

*Now when the centurion saw what was done, he glorified God, saying, Certainly this was a righteous man. Luke 23:47.*

# THE VOICE OF PROPHECY
# Reaching People for 57 Years

Radio was an infant when H. M. S. Richards began broadcasting on a single station in Los Angeles in 1930.

Today radio is a mighty giant of communication, with new stations starting every week. And people are listening. More people spend more time every week with radio than with either television or newspapers.

The Voice of Prophecy is now on the air in the United States and Canada more than 1,875 times every week.

Programs target a wide spectrum of listeners— people at home, commuters, workers on the job, university students, professional persons.

H. M. S. Richards, Jr., and Kenneth Richards catch people's ears with thought-provoking talks on many topics—from nutrition to family life, from science to current events, from coping with life in an imperfect world to hope for a better world.

But whatever the subject, the focus is always on Christ and His gospel—the good news that everyone needs to know.

Sustained by the prayers and sacrificial gifts of God's people, the Voice of Prophecy continues its work of reaching people with help for living today and hope for facing tomorrow.

*We try to present what people want—
but we never forget
to give them what they need.*

The Voice of Prophecy • Box 55 • Los Angeles, CA 90053
PRINTED IN U.S.A.

# BIBLE READING CHECK CARD

H. M. S. Richards, Jr./Director-Speaker
THE VOICE OF PROPHECY

They bound Jesus, but they could not bind His power to make men and women free. They nailed Him to a cross, but even as He hung dying He brought forgiveness to people around Him.

Consider the three men who found salvation in Him that day—Simon of Cyrene, the felon by His side, and the centurion.

Simon found Jesus by chance. He happened to be passing by when Jesus, hauling the cross on the way to Golgotha, stumbled and fell beneath its weight. As Simon paused in sympathy, the soldiers conscripted him to carry Jesus' cross.

By chance? No, not by chance. God's timing is exquisite: He put Simon at that spot at that moment. And Simon not only relieved Jesus' burden but became a believer. Jesus took Simon's burden and made him free.

The dying thief seemed the unlikeliest candidate for heaven. His life lay in ruins, with only a few grains of sand left in life's hourglass. Who could entertain hope for this hardened criminal?

But God saw differently. Never write off any individual, no matter how hopeless he or she may appear, no matter how steeped in sin. If the felon on the cross could find salvation on Good Friday, so can *any* person we may meet. The power of Jesus' love, touching a human heart in its hour of extremity, can roll back the past and bring new life.

The stranger passing by, the criminal in his death throes, and even a Roman officer—Jesus brought forgiveness as He died.

"In the bruised, broken body hanging upon the cross, the centurion recognized the form of the Son of God. He could not refrain from confessing his faith. Thus again evidence was given that our Redeemer was to see of the travail of His soul. Upon the very day of His death three men, differing widely from one another, had declared their faith—he who commanded the Roman guard, he who bore the cross of the Saviour, and he who died upon the cross at His side" (*The Desire of Ages*, p. 770).

Jesus still forgives. That cross lifted high on Calvary will never lose its power. To men and women of every race and in every circumstance it offers hope and freedom today.

Have *I* found its power? Will *I* take up the cross today?

*November 26*

# CHRIST BROKE THE CHAINS OF DEATH

*The tombs broke open and the bodies of many holy people who had died were raised to life. Matt. 27:52, NIV.*

Recently a young family visited a historic cemetery in Texas. Engrossed in looking over the old gravesites, they forgot about the time and found themselves locked in. The guard had fastened heavy chains across the gate, and the walls were too high to scale. They called and shouted, but no one came to let them out. It grew dark, and then cold. They huddled together, alone in the cemetery.

At last a guard, hearing their cries, appeared. He led them to the gate, pulled the chains aside, raised the bars, and set them free. But what amazed the family was this: the chains they thought were firmly in place had simply been thrown across the gate without any lock. They could have released them as easily as the guard had and not have spent the night in the cemetery.

Christ broke the chains of death. His parting cry, "It is finished!" not only tore asunder the veil hiding the Most Holy in the Temple; it broke open the tombs of many of God's people buried in the city.

That liberation of the dead at the death of Jesus was a sign from God for us all. It tells us that, appearances to the contrary, death no longer has power over us.

"Since by man came death, by man came also the resurrection of the dead," says Paul. "For as in Adam all die, even so in Christ shall all be made alive" (1 Cor. 15:21, 22). "Forasmuch then as the children are partakers of flesh and blood, he also himself likewise took part of the same; that through death he might destroy him that had the power of death, that is, the devil; and deliver them who through fear of death were all their lifetime subject to bondage" (Heb. 2:14, 15).

We huddle together in the graveyard of our fears. The cold winds blow; we hear the shrieks of ghosts and unearthly beings. A grim procession leads here, headed by our first parents. "Ashes to ashes, dust to dust." The tomb, never satisfied, forever yawning, is our lot.

But Christ broke the chains! By dying He entered the realm of death and destroyed it from within. "I am the Living One; I was dead, and behold I am alive for ever and ever! And I hold the keys of death and Hades," He says (Rev. 1:18, NIV).

Thine is the glory,
Risen, conquering Son;
Endless is the victory
Thou o'er death hast won.
      —Edmond Budry

# THE COSMIC CROSS

*And, having made peace through the blood of his cross,*
*by him to reconcile all things unto himself; by him, I say,*
*whether they be things in earth, or things in heaven. Col.*
*1:20.*

Jesus' cross speaks peace to the universe. It unites sinful human beings to God, and praise His name for that; but it does even more: it brings reconciliation to the entire universe.

"God was reconciling the world to himself in Christ, not counting men's sins against them," Paul tells us (2 Cor. 5:19, NIV). We need never fear that God is angry with us, that we have to curry favor with Him to somehow get Him to cast a friendly eye upon us. No, no! *Already* God has reconciled *the world*—not just good people, not just saints—to Himself. "But God commendeth his love toward us, in that, while we were yet sinners, Christ died for us. Much more then, being now justified by his blood, we shall be saved from wrath through him. For if, when we were enemies, we were reconciled to God by the death of his Son, much more, being reconciled, we shall be saved by his life" (Rom. 5:8-10).

God so loved *the world*—the whole world—that He gave His only Son for it. By the cross of Christ God bought—saved—the entire world, every man or woman, boy or girl, who has ever lived or who will live. He has reconciled us to Himself.

But reconciliation is a two-way street. God took the initiative; how shall we respond to His gesture of love? "We implore you on Christ's behalf: Be reconciled to God" (2 Cor. 5:20, NIV). God will not force Himself upon us: we can say Yes or No to His gracious invitation. But oh what peace, what joy, what sense of meaning and purpose come as we say Yes!

Paul, however, tells us that the cross effects reconciliation on a cosmic scale. "Through him to reconcile to himself all things, whether things on earth or things in heaven, by making peace through his blood, shed on the cross" (Col. 1:20, NIV). How can this be—what need can exist for unfallen intelligences to be reconciled to God?

Because Jesus died, sin will not rise up a second time. Although God did not need evil to reveal His loving character, through it He has manifested grace that takes away the breath of angels. By contrast, sin revealed itself in its enormity—lies, deception, injustice, hatred, murder.

That is why not only sinners saved from earth sing the Lamb's praises in heaven. Angelic hosts surround the throne in adoration:

"Worthy is the Lamb that was slain to receive power, and riches, and wisdom, and strength, and honour, and glory, and blessing" (Rev. 5:12).

May we one day be there to join that song!

# THE CROSS THAT HEALS

*His purpose was to create in himself one new man out of the two, thus making peace, and in this one body to reconcile both of them to God through the cross, by which he put to death their hostility. Eph. 2:15, 16, NIV.*

Of all forms of pride, that of race is most deeply rooted. We grow up unaware that we have irrational feelings of superiority toward people of a different ethnic background.

Racism seems ineradicable. Governments proclaim equality for people of all races, write equality into their constitutions, enact legislation to enforce outward conformity. But decrees and laws cannot change the heart—which is the seat of racism.

God, however, has the solution to the deep-seated human problem. The cross of Christ, which reconciles us to God, reconciles us to one another. By coming to earth and dying for every person, Jesus brought peace among us. The cross equalizes the races: no matter what our color, sex, status, or bank account, we all find salvation in exactly the same way. God made us one by creation; He made us one also by redemption.

I grew up in Australia. If you had told me as a young man that I was racist, I would have laughed at you. Why, wasn't one of my best friends an Ethiopian with skin as dark as midnight? We became pals at Avondale College, where I went to study for the gospel ministry. During one hot summer we sold books together door-to-door; he stayed as a guest in our home, ate at our table, had a bed in my room. (He also sold many more books than I did!) Racist? Never!

Yet I was. Only after I went to India and with my wife began to reflect on my roots did I realize the deep-seated pride in my heart. Totally isolated from the culture that gave me birth, I could see better where I had come from. No, I wasn't prejudiced against Black people per se; but I was racist toward the aboriginal people of Australia. I grew up thinking of them as better than animals but lower than we Whites.

Racism is like that—it's selective. Every one of us can think of people of some other race whom we like. But we probably harbor feelings of pride and superiority toward those of another race with whom life has thrown us into close proximity.

The gospel of Jesus Christ exposes the hidden pride of our hearts. It educates us, pointing to a better way. The cross is the greatest force for positive social change in the world—and that change must begin with the church.

*November 29*

# THE CROSS OF POWER

*But we preach Christ crucified, unto the Jews a stumblingblock, and unto the Greeks foolishness; but unto them which are called, both Jews and Greeks, Christ the power of God, and the wisdom of God. 1 Cor. 1:23, 24.*

When Matthew Boulton invented a better steam engine, he announced: "Here I sell what all men crave—power!"

Our message is also about power, power greater than human wisdom or invention, power to change sinful men and women into sons and daughters of God. "I decided to know nothing among you except Jesus Christ and him crucified," wrote Paul to the Corinthian Christians (1 Cor. 2:2, RSV). The crucified Jesus—there is the source of our power!

The German scholar Adolph Schlatter wrote: "And why did he die? Because I made god out of God to fill up my hunger for life and happiness. . . . Because I desired fellowship with God so that he would be my servant. . . . Because all of us, theologians, laity, church officials and politicians, proselytes and converted saints and transgressors, want to rule so that God listens to us. . . . We pray to the gods, the gods of power. Therefore Jesus bore the cross. . . . Now the religion of our claims and demands, our haughty piety and 'Christianity' by which we elevate ourselves above God comes to an end."

Jesus Christ is mighty to save. He delivers us from the threefold tyranny that would strangle our lives—the past, the present, the future.

From the past, because the guilt of our sins presses upon us, crushing us with the sense of our lostness.

From the present, because life closes in around us, the tempter lies in wait to trip us up, and we feel weak and discouraged.

From the future, because its nameless fears of nuclear annihilation, old age, or even religious persecution hang like a dead weight around our necks.

Jesus conquered the past: He erased our guilt by His cross.

Jesus conquers the present: He gives hope and strength for every need.

Jesus will conquer the future: He holds the world in His hands, and we are safe in Him.

So, counsels Ellen White, "Lift up the Man of Calvary higher and still higher; there is power in the exaltation of the cross of Christ" (*Counsels to Parents and Teachers*, p. 434).

In the cross of Christ I glory,
Towering o'er the wrecks of time;
All the light of sacred story
Gathers round its head sublime.

Bane and blessing, pain and pleasure,
By the cross are sanctified;
Peace is there that knows no measure,
Joys that through all time abide.
—John Bowring

*November 30*

# SABBATH REST FOR THE SAVIOUR

*So Joseph bought some linen cloth, took down the body, wrapped it in the linen, and placed it in a tomb cut out of rock. Then he rolled a stone against the entrance of the tomb. Mark 15:46, NIV.*

Isaiah had prophesied of Jesus: "He was assigned a grave with the wicked, and with the rich in his death" (Isa. 53:9, NIV). How strange this prediction must have seemed to those who read it during the following 700 years! If God's suffering Servant was to be numbered with transgressors, how could He be buried among the rich?

But so it came to pass with the death of Jesus. Although He died a felon, executed on a cross between two robbers, His body was placed in a wealthy man's new tomb. Joseph of Arimathaea, a ruler of the Jews, came boldly forward and requested Pilate that he be given Jesus' body. The governor, surprised to hear that Jesus was already dead, summoned the centurion to confirm the report. Then he gave Joseph permission to take Jesus' body down from the cross and to dispose of it.

Nicodemus joined Joseph in the burial. Both these men were members of the Sanhedrin, but the Council, detecting their sympathies toward Jesus, had pointedly excluded them from the deliberations of the hastily called session that had condemned

Jesus the previous night. For three years Joseph and Nicodemus had followed Jesus' teachings and ministry, attracted to Him but not quite ready to take a public stand for Him. Nicodemus had sought Jesus out at night, desiring to talk to Him but ashamed to have his colleagues know about it.

What a strange twist of events! The disciples, who had been with Jesus for three years or more, who had declared their allegiance to Him, lay desolated by His death. They fled from Him in the Garden of Gethsemane; their last hopes fled from them when He died on the cross. But the two Jewish rulers, who had kept their admiration secret, came forward to bury Jesus, knowing that by so doing they were cutting themselves off from the Sanhedrin.

So Jesus lay at rest after His hard, hard day. His body, broken and lacerated, grew cold and stiff. Wrapped in a linen sheet brought by Joseph, He slept the sleep of death in the new tomb cut from the rock. A large stone, rolled across the mouth of the cave, sealed Him in—forever, His enemies hoped.

Sleep, Saviour of the world. As once You slept in a manger with Mary by Your side, sleep now, Your work done, as angels watch over You.

*December 1*

# CONQUEROR OF DEATH

***And, behold, there was a great earthquake: for the angel of the Lord descended from heaven, and came and rolled back the stone from the door, and sat upon it. Matt. 28:2.***

How foolish to think that men could bind forever the Prince of life! How stupid to seek to imprison Him in the grave by rolling a stone across its mouth!

Before Charlemagne, blond giant of a man crowned emperor of the Holy Roman Empire on Christmas Day, A. D. 800, died, he gave orders that his tomb should be sealed so tightly that mortal hand could never break it open. So the dead monarch was buried according to his wishes—robed in purple; seated on the throne, crown on head, scepter in hand; and walled in, never again to be seen by human eye.

But dust lodged in a crack in the wall, and a seed blew in, found moisture, germinated, and began to grow. Its roots spread and developed—and eventually split asunder the dead king's resting place. The common gaze rested on what he had sought to forever hide: the crown had tumbled from his brow, the scepter lay in the dust, his robes had rotted away, and his skull grinned mockingly.

If God's tiny seed could burst a monarch's tomb, what Roman guard could forever seal the grave of Jesus? On the third day—early Sunday morning—a violent earthquake signaled the close of Jesus' sojourn in the realm of death, and His triumph over it.

Who raised Jesus from the dead? The Scriptures give three answers:

"Whom *God* hath raised up, having loosed the pains of death: because it was not possible that he should be holden of it" (Acts 2:24).

"But if *the Spirit* of him that raised up Jesus from the dead dwell in you, he that raised up Christ from the dead shall also quicken your mortal bodies by his Spirit that dwelleth in you" (Rom. 8:11).

"No man taketh it from me, but I lay it down of myself. I have power to lay it down, and *I* have power to take it again. This commandment have I received of my Father" (John 10:18).

Do these passages contradict one another? No. The members of the heavenly Trinity work together in all acts that concern our salvation, so they were united in the resurrection of Jesus.

If God planned to raise Jesus, what stone or guard could keep Him in the grave!

*Lord of life, Lord over death, give to me Your endless life today.*

*December 2*

# PHILIP'S EGG

*He is not here: for he is risen, as he said. Come, see the place where the Lord lay. Matt. 28:6.*

Harry Pritchett, Jr., tells a marvelous story about a boy named Philip, who had Down's syndrome, and his Sunday school teacher, Pritchett's friend. Despite the teacher's best efforts, Philip, with his differences, wasn't accepted by the other nine 8-year-old boys.

The teacher came up with a great idea for his class the Sunday after Easter. He collected 10 of the containers that panty hose come in—those things that look like big eggs. He gave one to each child with the assignment to go outside, find a symbol for new life, put it into the egg, and bring it back to the classroom. They would then open and share their new-life symbols and surprises one by one.

The children gathered their objects and returned to the room. As the teacher opened the eggs, the children cried out in delight as a flower, a butterfly, a rock came into view.

Then he opened another egg—and it was empty. "That's stupid," said the children.

"It's mine," Philip announced. "It's mine."

"You don't ever do things right, Philip. There's nothing there!"

"I did so do it," replied Philip. "I did do it. It's empty. The tomb is empty!"

"There was silence, a very full silence. And for you people who don't believe in miracles, I want to tell you that one happened that day last spring. From that time on, it was different. Philip suddenly became a part of that group of 8-year-old children. They took him in. He was set free from the tomb of his differences.

"Philip died last summer. His family had known since the time he was born that he wouldn't live out a full life span. Many other things had been wrong with his tiny body. And so, late last July, with an infection that most normal children could have quickly shrugged off, Philip died. The mystery simply enveloped him.

"At the funeral, nine 8-year-old children marched up to the altar, not with flowers to cover over the stark reality of death. Nine 8-year-olds, with their Sunday school teacher, marched right up to that altar and laid on it an empty egg—an empty, old, discarded panty hose egg."—Harry Pritchett, Jr. (Reprinted by permission of *The St. Luke's Journal of Theology*.)

# HE IS RISEN!

*"You are to say, 'His disciples came during the night and stole him away while we were asleep.' " Matt. 28:13, NIV.*

Early one morning my family and I set out from New Delhi, India, for the city of Agra, several hours' drive away. We arrived in Agra just after sunup. As we walked through the archway in a huge stone wall, suddenly one of the loveliest sights in this world unfolded before us—gardens, reflecting pools, and beyond a building of gleaming white, perfect in symmetry and design. I turned to my wife and asked, "Is it real?"

But the Taj Mahal is a mausoleum. The emperor Shah Jahan built it to honor his lovely wife Mumtaz—to provide a resting place for her. She lies there, together with her husband.

The Great Pyramid of Egypt, like the other pyramids, likewise was built to house the dead. According to the Greek writer Herodotus, hundreds of thousands of men labored for 20 years to build Khufu pyramid. Those numbers probably are inflated, but the sheer immensity of the structure still takes our breath away.

Jesus of Nazareth was buried in a simple rock-cut cave in a garden by Jerusalem. No one knows the site—despite tour guides' claims. No massive monument, no beautiful structure, commemorates that death. And yet Jesus' tomb is greater than Mumtaz's or Khufu's—because it is empty!

Buddha, Mahavira, Zoroaster, Muhammad—the world has produced a line of great religious teachers. One stands apart from all others: Jesus Christ, who alone rose from the dead.

Because that is the ultimate evidence that Jesus is what He claimed to be, the Son of God, enemies and critics never cease to attack the Resurrection. They began very early—on the day Jesus rose again. They bribed the soldiers to spread the story that Jesus' disciples stole the body during the night.

Plausible? Not if you consider that those same disciples became bold proclaimers that He had risen and appeared to them! If the soldiers' story were true, there would never have been a new religion based in part on Jesus' resurrection.

The soldiers' story wouldn't wash, and critics have tried to account for *the fact* of Christianity on other grounds. Why, some say, Jesus didn't really rise—His "appearances" were merely a wish fulfillment as the disciples, hoping Jesus would rise again, *imagined* they saw Him!

Two simple facts rebut this "explanation": 1. The disciples' hopes had been crushed—they didn't expect to see Jesus again. 2. And what happened to His body? For His tomb is empty. He is not dead, but alive!

*December 4*

# JESUS AND MARY

*Jesus saith unto her, Mary. She turned herself, and saith unto him, Rabboni; which is to say, Master. John 20:16.*

For centuries Christians have pondered the relationship between Jesus and Mary Magdalene. Just as John the brother of James drew close to Jesus, becoming the "disciple whom Jesus loved," so among women Mary seems to have been His dearest companion.

While all four Gospel writers mention Mary of Magdala, the fourth Gospel alone includes two significant pieces of information. John tells us that it was Mary who brought the expensive nard perfume and poured it on Jesus' feet, wiping them with her hair. And John alone records the incident by the garden tomb in which the risen Christ appeared to her before He had been seen by any others.

Early church tradition suggests that John wrote his Gospel as an old man, recalling under the guidance of the Holy Spirit stories and events from the life of Jesus that the earlier Gospels had not included. Possibly Matthew, Mark, and Luke purposely omitted the direct identification of Mary as the woman with a shady past whose anointing of Jesus' feet shocked the onlookers, since Mary was still living when they wrote. John, however, writing later brings out the full story.

In both incidents we see Jesus' tender regard for Mary. When the other disciples grumbled about waste, He rebuked them, commending Mary for her impulsive act of deep affection.

Now see Mary weeping in the garden. She had stood all day by the cross on Friday and that evening followed Joseph and Nicodemus as they laid Jesus' body in the tomb. The last picture we see of her Friday is her sitting near the tomb (Matt. 27:61). Sunday morning—and while it is still dark—Mary rises and goes to the tomb. She is first to find it empty, first to run back with the news.

And she is first to meet the risen Christ. Numb with grief, through her tears she fails to recognize Him standing near the tomb. Thinking He is the gardener, she begs, "Sir, if you have carried him away, tell me where you have put him, and I will get him" (John 20:15, NIV).

"Mary."

Just one word, but spoken in such love that she knows it can come from only One. She who loved so much and who grieved so much becomes first to see and first to believe in the Resurrection.

"They have taken my Lord away, . . . and I don't know where they have put him" (verse 13, NIV). How many people still cry out for Jesus! Jesus has been taken away—by critics' attacks on the Scriptures, by the pressures of modern living, by the doubts and fears that assail us.

But Jesus says, "Mary." One word, and we know it is He. Only He. Alive. Alive forevermore.

# JESUS AND PETER

*But go your way, tell his disciples and Peter that he goeth before you into Galilee: there shall ye see him, as he said unto you. Mark 16:7.*

"And Peter." Tell Jesus' disciples, but tell Peter in particular. Tell him that the risen Lord mentioned him apart from the others, that He plans to meet Peter in Galilee.

Oh, the thoughtfulness of Jesus! Peter in his bravado had blundered terribly, forfeiting his right to a place among the apostles, let alone to his accustomed place of leadership. There in the judgment hall as Jesus was standing before the frowning judges, He turned and looked at Peter. In sorrow, not condemnation; in love, not anger. And Peter, the words of denial and cursing still on his lips, gazed into the face of the Saviour and broke down. He rushed from the high priest's courtyard and into the night with bitter tears.

That Sabbath must have been the grayest in Peter's life. Jesus dead, his hopes in ruins, his self-confidence shattered, the other disciples now distrusting him, he wondered what lay ahead.

But now, Sunday morning, women come running. They have been to the tomb and bear an incredible message. The tomb is empty, they say, and an angel appeared to them with the astounding news that Jesus is alive! And further, that He has instructions for the disciples—and Peter.

Peter and John run to the tomb. John, being younger, gets there first. He finds the stone rolled away, stoops down, and looks within. He sees no corpse there, only the linen burial cloths lying folded, the head cloth apart from the others. Then Peter arrives and goes right inside. He also sees the linen cloths and wonders.

The message from the angel tells the disciples that Jesus will meet them in Galilee, and so back to Galilee they go. Now we look upon a fascinating scene by the lake. Peter says to Thomas, Nathanael, James, John, and two other disciples, "Let's go fishing." Why? Did he feel this was all that was left for him now? Did he wonder whether Jesus would really show up in Galilee?

So they go fishing. And it happens again: because of Jesus' instructions they haul in a huge catch. A similar miracle two years earlier had led Peter to forsake all to follow Jesus. Now the miracle repeated leads to Peter's recommitment and reintegration into the apostolic company.

After breakfast that morning Jesus asks Peter, "Do you love Me?" Three times—until Peter's heart is ready to break again. But

Jesus did it, not to bring Peter to his knees, but to give him an opportunity to confirm his loyalty in the presence of the others.

Oh, the thoughtfulness of Jesus! "And Peter." And Peter became a pillar of the early church.

# JESUS AND CLEOPAS

*And they said one to another, Did not our heart burn within us, while he talked with us by the way, and while he opened to us the scriptures? Luke 24:32.*

Sunday. Jesus has already risen from the dead hours before, but few of His disciples believe the women's report. Now two of them, Cleopas and another, are on their way to Emmaus, a village about seven miles from Jerusalem.

One subject fills their minds—the death of Jesus. As they talk and discuss, Jesus Himself draws near and joins them. And they do not recognize Him!

How could it be? First Mary in the garden and now Cleopas and his friend fail to see Jesus in the person beside them. Obviously the risen Christ wasn't bathed in light; nothing in His appearance drew their attention.

Mary, Cleopas, and the other disciple failed to recognize Jesus because they did not *expect* to meet Him. So far as they were concerned, He was dead, not alive. "Their eyes were kept from recognizing him," says Scripture (Luke 24:16, RSV)—kept by unbelief.

I wonder how often we fail to recognize Jesus because we don't expect to meet Him. How often does unbelief close our eyes?

But Jesus isn't offended. He opens to them the Old Testament prophecies showing that God's Word predicted the sufferings and death of the Messiah. (How could they have failed to know *that* voice explaining the Scriptures?)

It is getting late. The Stranger appears to be going farther, but they constrain Him: "Stay with us, for it is toward evening and the day is now far spent" (verse 29, RSV). Think—what if they hadn't bothered to invite Jesus in? What a blessing they would have lost! Have we lost similar blessings when Jesus has passed by in the form of one of His "little ones"?

So Jesus goes in to stay with them at Emmaus. They prepare for supper and invite Him to ask the blessing. He takes the bread and spreads His hands to bless it—and suddenly their eyes are opened! "The disciples start back in astonishment. Their companion spreads forth His hands in exactly the same way as their Master used to do. They look again, and lo, they see in His hands the print of nails. Both exclaim at once, It is the Lord Jesus! He has risen from the dead!" (*The Desire of Ages*, p. 800).

But He vanishes before they can worship Him. It's dark now, but Cleopas and his friend jump up from the table and head back to Jerusalem. The miles fly; their hearts leap for joy. Arriving at the city, they tell the disciples "how he was known to them in the breaking of the bread" (verse 35, RSV).

And we still recognize Jesus in the breaking of the bread—His Supper.

*December 7*

# JESUS AND THOMAS

**The other disciples therefore said unto him, We have seen the Lord. But he said unto them, Except I shall see in his hands the print of the nails, and put my finger into the print of the nails, and thrust my hand into his side, I will not believe. John 20:25.**

Who among us could believe in Jesus if those words formed the test? No wonder history has given the name "doubting Thomas" to this disciple.

Yet Scripture does not use such a designation for Thomas. James and John were dubbed boanerges—"sons of thunder"—by Jesus, but Thomas is merely called didymus, meaning "twin."

Why, then, did Thomas demand such stringent proof of the Resurrection? Because, like the other disciples, he could not grasp that Jesus really would rise again. Before we come down too hard on Thomas' unbelief, remember that the disciples in general did not accept the women's testimony that Jesus had risen—"these words seemed to them an idle tale" (Luke 24:11, RSV). Remember that Cleopas and his friend failed to recognize Jesus even though He walked and talked with them by the way. And all this despite the fact that earlier Jesus several times told all the disciples of His coming betrayal, death, and resurrection.

Thomas, however, *refused* to believe the evidence of the accumulated witnesses. He dug in his heels, setting up a test ridiculous in its extreme.

Thomas is still around. The good news about Jesus is passed on in one important way—we who know Him tell others about Him. Jesus doesn't appear in person: He has appointed the "foolishness of preaching" (1 Cor. 1:21) as the medium of salvation. That means people will always find room to question. Many still demand proof—and so never believe.

The most important matters in life cannot be "proved." I cannot prove that my wife and children love me, nor can I prove to them that I love them. But we all *know* love to be real and true.

So with Jesus: we know Him because we love Him. We learn to love Him through someone who loves Him and tells us about Him.

Interestingly, even though Thomas said he wouldn't believe in Jesus unless he could put his finger in the nail prints and his hand in Jesus' side, when he saw Jesus he forgot all about the test. He fell at Jesus' feet and confessed, "My Lord and my God" (John 20:28).

That is still true. To see Jesus is enough. He Himself rolls away our doubts. In His presence all questions dissolve; He is the only proof we need.

*Jesus, risen Lord, show me Yourself today. Take away my doubts and questions in the light of Your presence.*

*December 8*

# MISERABLE MEN

***If in this life only we have hope in Christ, we are of all men most miserable. 1 Cor. 15:19.***

I remember well a letter to the editor several years ago in *Time* magazine. The writer said he had grown up in China, the child of missionaries. As a boy he used to look forward to walking the streets of gold in the New Jerusalem and eating of the tree of life. But all those ideas had long since passed, he said. He didn't hope anymore in a life after death—this life is all there is, and that is sufficient.

Who knows what happened in the writer's heart to turn him from belief to unbelief. And what a sad note on which to end one's days!

Paul would have challenged him. If this life is all we have, Paul said, we of all people are most to be pitied. For then we would have believed a lie. We would have given our lives to proclaiming a lie.

Immediately after, however, Paul affirms: "But now is Christ risen from the dead, and become the firstfruits of them that slept. For since by man came death, by man came also the resurrection of the dead. For as in Adam all die, even so in Christ shall all be made alive" (1 Cor. 15:20-22).

"Now is Christ risen." There's the difference! The question of life after death isn't an abstract issue for debate. It can't be proved or disproved by logic. One great fact answers it for all time—*now is Christ risen!*

Occasionally you'll hear Christians say, "Even if there weren't a future life, believing in Jesus here would be worth it all." That's only a partial truth. Yes, following Christ in this life gives us a more abundant, fulfilling existence. Every bit of instruction He left us is for our good—to make us healthier, happier, more content. But we have to hear Paul again: "If in this life only we have hope in Christ, we are of all men most miserable."

Why? Because a shadow falls across our happiest experiences. Even in the midst of life we are in death.

We look before and after,
And pine for what is not:
Our sincerest laughter
With some pain is fraught;
Our sweetest songs are those that tell of saddest thought.
—Shelley, "To a Skylark"

God made us for the stars—to live forever with Him. He put eternity in our hearts; we crave immortality. Death is still the final enemy.

But we have hope in Christ not only in this life. Because He rose again, conquering death, we know that in Him we shall live forever. That makes us of all men most glad.

*December 9*

# THE LORD WHO COMMISSIONS

***Then the eleven disciples went away into Galilee, into a mountain where Jesus had appointed them. And when they saw him, they worshipped him: but some doubted. Matt. 28:16, 17.***

With this appearance of the risen Christ, Matthew closes his story of Jesus. He who once had sat on the side of a mountain in Galilee, gathering disciples about Him to announce the inauguration of the kingdom of heaven, now stood in resurrection authority to send His followers into all the world in His name.

Paul apparently refers to this final meeting in Galilee in his famous chapter of resurrection, 1 Corinthians 15. Listing the appearances of Jesus after He rose from the tomb, Paul states: "After that, he appeared to more than five hundred of the brothers at the same time, most of whom are still living, though some have fallen asleep" (verse 6, NIV). More than 500 people! That evidence alone lays to rest arguments of the critics who theorize that the appearances of Jesus were only dreams of the imagination.

And yet, Matthew tells us, some of those 500 people doubted. Even though they had been disciples of Jesus before the Crucifixion. Even though their friends believed and worshiped. Even though they saw the risen Christ. "So it will always be. There are those who find it hard to exercise faith, and they place themselves on the doubting side. They lose much because of their unbelief" (*The Desire of Ages*, p. 819).

"All authority in heaven and on earth has been given to me," proclaimed Jesus (Matt. 28:18, NIV). By virtue of that authority He gave them a threefold commission: "Go ye therefore, and teach all nations, baptizing them in the name of the Father, and of the Son, and of the Holy Ghost: teaching them to observe all things whatsoever I have commanded you: and, lo, I am with you alway, even unto the end of the world" (verses 19, 20).

The Greek original of Jesus' command makes clear that these four terms—*go, make disciples, baptize, teach* (NIV)—are not equal in force. The first, third, and fourth are subordinated to the second. In effect Jesus commands: Make disciples of all nations —this is your commission. Do this by going, baptizing, and teaching.

Notice: Jesus gave the Great Commission to *all* His followers, not just to the apostles. Every one of us to whom the good news has come becomes a channel of the good news, bringing it to others that they in turn may pass it on.

My wife and I went—we were missionaries to India for more than 15 years. But going doesn't mean only going overseas, although it includes that. We go as we *share*—with neighbor, friend, workmate, classmate. Going tells us we have been sent, commissioned, entrusted, with Heaven's choicest messages.

The risen Lord, mighty in authority, spoke from the mountain in Galilee. He still speaks. Who will go?

*December 10*

# TO KNOW HIS RESURRECTION POWER

*I want to know Christ and the power of his resurrection and the fellowship of sharing in his sufferings, becoming like him in his death, and so, somehow, to attain to the resurrection from the dead. Phil. 3:10, 11, NIV.*

"When the scholar experiences something in the spiritual realm," writes Brennan Manning, author of *Lion and Lamb: The Relentless Tenderness of Jesus* (Old Jappan, N.J.: Fleming H. Revell Co., 1986), "he discovers that he has nothing to say. He can only stutter and stammer. It would be easier to catch a hurricane in a shrimp net than to capture and adequately express the reality of the love of Jesus Christ. All else is like straw."

Jesus—He is all that matters. Not to know about Him, but to know *Him*—this is the essence of Christianity.

We serve a risen Saviour, one who walks and talks with us by the way. We know the power of His love—love that accepts us just as we are, that values us for what we are and not just for what we may become, love that will never leave us or forsake us. "Though my father and mother forsake me, the Lord will receive me," affirms the psalmist (Ps. 27:10, NIV). And in his advancing years he cries out, "O God, thou hast taught me from my youth: and hitherto have I declared thy wondrous works. Now also when I am old and greyheaded, O God, forsake me not; until I have shewed thy strength unto this generation, and thy power to every one that is to come" (Ps. 71:17, 18).

To know Christ—that is all we need. Our spiritual growth is not an end in itself: by fixating upon ourselves we fall into another form of idolatry. No, we must keep our eyes fixed on Jesus, seeking to know and love Him more every day.

Here is Paul speaking, warrior of the cross, champion of hundreds of battles for the Master. Has he attained the summit? "Not as though I had already attained," he says. But "I press toward the mark" (Phil. 3:12, 14). And that mark will ever stretch before us. Even into eternity we may grow closer to Christ, learn more about Him, love Him more fully, know Him better.

In our text for today Paul links Christ's resurrection power with fellowship in His death. That's an important link; without it, spiritual experience can run aground. The early Christians in Corinth, for instance, seemed to have so emphasized resurrection life in Christ that they had become puffed up with pride and self-exaltation. So Paul uplifted before them God's wisdom—the cross.

Forever the risen Christ wears the badge of the Crucifixion. We who would know Him, who want to walk in the power of His resurrection, must wear it too. We must share in His sufferings and day by day go to Calvary. "We always carry around in our body the death of Jesus, so that the life of Jesus may also be revealed in our body" (2 Cor. 4:10, NIV).

*Master, may I today know the power of Your resurrection.
Make me a sharer of Your sufferings as I take up the cross and
follow You.*

# TAKEN UP FROM US

*And when he had spoken these things, while they be-
held, he was taken up; and a cloud received him out of
their sight. Acts 1:9.*

For 40 days Jesus appeared to His followers after He rose from
the dead. His topic? The one with which He commenced His
ministry—the kingdom of God (Acts 1:3). During this period He
gave them instruction, and on occasion ate with them.

But those days when men and women saw the risen Christ
face-to-face and heard His sweet voice soon came to an end.
Presumably the Lord in His love gave them—and us—this period
to confirm belief that Jesus truly had broken the bands of death.

They were days of transition. The old order of animal sacrifices
had come to a close with Jesus' death on Calvary. Israel's status as
the chosen nation was also at an end; henceforth the Christian
church, made up of men and women from every ethnic background, would be the channel of God's grace.

And the time of Jesus' actual presence among us was closing
also. On that Thursday night before the cross He had told His
friends: "It is for your good that I am going away. Unless I go away,
the Counselor will not come to you; but if I go, I will send him to
you" (John 16:7, NIV). The new era was dawning—the age of the
Holy Spirit.

Jesus chose His favorite mountain for His last moments with
the disciples—the Mount of Olives. There He had often spent the
night during His visits to Jerusalem (see John 7:53; 8:1). There He
had agonized in the Garden of Gethsemane. This place, rich in
associations, would be enhanced even further as the mount of
Jesus' ascension.

"With hands outstretched in blessing, and as if in assurance of
His protecting care, He slowly ascended from among them, drawn
heavenward by a power stronger than any earthly attraction. As He
passed upward, the awestricken disciples looked with straining
eyes for the last glimpse of their ascending Lord. A cloud of glory
hid Him from their sight; and the words came back to them as the
cloudy chariot of angels received Him, 'Lo, I am with you alway,
even unto the end of the world.' At the same time there floated

373

down to them the sweetest and most joyous music from the angel choir" (*The Desire of Ages*, pp. 830, 831).

Today we walk alone. But we are not alone. Jesus has promised to be with us always, even to the end of the age. And the blessed Counselor, the Holy Spirit, brings His words to our remembrance.

But listen! The Mount of Olives one day will be honored again: "On that day his feet will stand on the Mount of Olives, east of Jerusalem" (Zech. 14:4, NIV). "This same Jesus, who has been taken from you into heaven, will come back in the same way you have seen him go into heaven" (Acts 1:11, NIV).

Even so, come, Lord Jesus!

*December 12*

# THE SECRET OF APOSTOLIC POWER

*"God has raised this Jesus to life, and we are all witnesses of the fact. Exalted to the right hand of God, he has received from the Father the promised Holy Spirit and has poured out what you now see and hear." Acts 2:32, 33, NIV.*

Why did Christianity, the religion of the crucified Jesus, spread so rapidly across the ancient world? Because of the power with which the apostles proclaimed it. And the secret of that power lay in two great affirmations: Christ is risen, and He has poured out the Holy Spirit upon us.

"God has raised this Jesus to life, and we are all witnesses of the fact." No mere theory here. No complicated message—though a startling one. Jesus is *alive*, conqueror of death; and we have seen Him.

This preaching did not invite the hearer to debate a proposition. It called to belief, to trust the testimony of these erstwhile fishermen and tax collectors. Either these fellows were crazy, lying, deceived—or what they said really happened.

"With great power the apostles continued to testify to the resurrection of the Lord Jesus, and much grace was upon them all" (Acts 4:33, NIV). Everywhere they went, from Jerusalem to Rome, their message was the same: God sent the promised Messiah, Jesus of Nazareth, and though Romans and Jewish elders crucified Him, God set His seal upon Him by raising Him from the dead.

The Resurrection was the capstone of the apostolic proclamation. Although it was a message to Jew and Greek alike, it came with the intensity of personal conviction and could not be denied: "*We* are all witnesses of the fact."

Personal witness is still the secret of power in preaching. Personal witness lies behind every successful effort to bring someone to Christ. We share what we know—rather, *whom* we know. And we *know* He is the risen one. Although we did not personally observe the Resurrection, we *know* Jesus is alive, because He is our best friend. Our message is: Let me tell you about my dear Friend, one who is so fond of me.

And the Holy Spirit testified along with the apostles' witness—this was the second secret of their power. Jesus "has received from the Father the promised Holy Spirit and has poured out what you now see and hear." No defensiveness here, no uncertainty, no skittishness about the Holy Spirit as an indwelling presence. Simply affirmation of an experience.

Why does so much preaching today lack power? Because the speakers are unsure of the two apostolic affirmations—the resurrection of Jesus and the gift of the Holy Spirit.

When we can say as did they, "Jesus is alive, because I *know* Him, and He has given me His Spirit," proclamation again will win the world for Him.

*December 13*

# LORD OF TIME

*After he had provided purification for sins, he sat down at the right hand of the Majesty in heaven. Heb. 1:3, NIV.*

I remember well an incident from my doctoral work, which was in the field of biblical studies. Every Tuesday faculty and students in this field met for lunch and discussion. Sometimes one of the students would present the gist of his dissertation thesis or some other research for feedback from the group.

On this particular day, as we sat around the table exchanging ideas, the professor who taught Jewish backgrounds—a scholar with an international reputation and a rabbi—spoke. "For you Christians, history stopped 2,000 years ago," he said. "But for us Jews, God is still active in time."

Silence. I waited for a rejoinder. Nobody seemed able to muster a convincing reply.

The rabbi was right: for most Christians divine history seems to have ended at the cross. They proclaim the life and death of Jesus and the salvation He won for the world; they also declare His resurrection—though some aren't too sure about that. But these events took place long ago; a shutter of silence has fallen over the past two millennia. If, as the New Testament claims, Jesus redeemed the world by His death on the cross, why does it look so unredeemed still? If He brought down the kingdom of God as He announced, why does our world often look more like the devil's realm?

We find answers to these troubling questions in a teaching much neglected in our day—the high priesthood of Jesus. The Bible portrays our Lord as still active for us in the heavenly courts. "Now of the things which we have spoken this is the sum: We have such an high priest, who is set on the right hand of the throne of the Majesty in the heavens; a minister of the sanctuary, and of the true tabernacle, which the Lord pitched, and not man" (Heb. 8:1, 2).

We catch only glimpses of the heavenly sanctuary and Christ's heavenly work. But we see enough to be assured that divine history didn't close 2,000 years ago. Calvary was "the consummation of the ages" (Heb. 9:26, margin), but it wasn't the end of God's activity for our salvation. Although on the cross Jesus did everything necessary to provide forgiveness for the sins of the world, the divine strategy continues from the divine headquarters, throne room of the universe.

"Like the stars in the vast circuit of their appointed path, God's purposes know no haste and no delay" (*The Desire of Ages*, p. 32). Jesus Christ is Lord of history. He who made us and all things still upholds "all things by the word of his power" (Heb. 1:3). Now exalted to highest heaven, He rules and redeems by virtue of a twofold authority: He created, and He redeemed.

We are safe in the hands of our Great High Priest.

*December 14*

# WHAT JESUS' PRIESTLY MINISTRY MEANS TO ME

*Now of the things which we have spoken this is the sum: We have such an high priest, who is set on the right hand of the throne of the Majesty in the heavens; a minister of the sanctuary, and of the true tabernacle, which the Lord pitched, and not man. Heb. 8:1, 2.*

To most Christians today the teaching of Jesus Christ as our heavenly high priest has little meaning. The language of temples, sacrifices, and blood seems to belong to an era long departed—as the biblical scholar Moffatt put it, the priest in biblical times was more like a consecrated butcher.

But the high priestly ministry of Jesus, taught in several books of Scripture, with elaboration in the book of Hebrews, still speaks powerfully. This is what it means to me:

**First, heaven is a welcome place.** I belong there. I am not a stranger. Heaven is my home, my destiny. Jesus, my Elder Brother, has blazed the trail to heaven and thrown open its gates. I come boldly into His presence—the very presence of God—through His blood (see Heb. 4:16). He who gave His life for me now stands on my behalf to plead my case. He knows all about me, understands my temptations, sympathizes in my weaknesses and struggles. "Because he himself suffered when he was tempted, he is able to help those who are being tempted" (Heb. 2:18, NIV).

**Second, my salvation rests on a Foundation outside myself.** My feelings are unreliable, changeable; I dare not place weight upon them. That I *feel* close to God does not prove it so; that I *feel* far from Him does not show it to be the case. But because Jesus is my high priest in heaven, I need no longer be overly influenced by subjective states. Nor is my salvation subject to the doubts that assail me. No—it lies outside myself. Jesus is a fixed, immovable datum. No matter what I feel or what opponents of Christianity may assert, He remains high priest in heaven for me.

**Third, because of Jesus' high priestly ministry, I need no other mediator.** Friends, yes; confidants, yes; colleagues, yes. But a human priest, a go-between to help me reach God? Never! Jesus stands apart, unique, the God-man whose person bridges the chasm between Deity and humanity. He, the eternally merciful and faithful one, is all I need, now and forever.

My studies in the book of Hebrews and meditation on Jesus as my great high priest have brought Heaven closer and made Christ more real. May you also find Jesus as your friend in the heavenly sanctuary.

> From every stormy wind that blows,
> From every swelling tide of woes,
> There is a calm, a sure retreat;
> 'Tis found beneath the mercy seat.
> —Hugh Stowell

# MIGHTY INTERCESSOR!

*Wherefore he is able also to save them to the uttermost that come unto God by him, seeing he ever liveth to make intercession for them. Heb. 7:25.*

A great preacher now gone to his rest, E. L. Minchin, used to preach on this text under the rubric "From Guttermost to the Uttermost." That's true: Jesus can save completely, forever, no matter how deep in sin's quicksand we may have sunk.

What does His intercession mean?

Let's dispose of a negative view first. Jesus' intercession does *not* signify that the Father is reluctant to accept us. Jesus doesn't placate Him, trying to get God to turn off the frown and turn on the smile. No, no! "*God* so loved the world, that he gave his only begotten Son, that whosoever believeth in him should not perish, but have everlasting life" (John 3:16). God loved us before we ever loved Him; He sent Jesus to us because He loved us. God is trying to get us into heaven, not to keep us out.

Nor should we ever set up a system of barriers within the Godhead, as though the Father is a stern God of justice, but the Son provides the balance by representing mercy. That sort of thinking has a long history—candles, Mariolatry, prayers to the saints—but it is unbiblical. When Christ accepts us—and He does—*God* accepts us, for Christ is God.

Perhaps the Old Testament sanctuary system may help us to understand Jesus' intercessory ministry, since it foreshadowed the heavenly reality. Under its services the work of the priests comprised two basic functions: sacrifice and mediation. They presided over the various animal offerings prescribed for forgiveness of transgressions, thanksgiving, or consecration. In every case the ritual required a sacrifice; but there was more—the priest or high priest would sprinkle, place, or pour out the blood in the part of the sanctuary so designated.

All these ceremonies pointed forward to Jesus. Every animal sacrifice typified His death, once for all on Calvary. Every priestly and high priestly ministration told, however feebly, the story of the work He now carries on for us in the heavenly sanctuary.

Christ does not offer actual blood to the Father. He isn't sacrificed over and over for us. But that sad, marvelous day on Calvary atoned for our sins and forms the basis of His ongoing ministry for us in heaven above. All that He does—and He is active to wind up the plan of redemption—is by virtue of His all-sufficient sacrifice.

*December 16*

# HEAVEN'S COMMAND CENTER

*Which he wrought in Christ, when he raised him from the dead, and set him at his own right hand in the heavenly places, far above all principality, and power, and might, and dominion, and every name that is named, not only in this world, but also in that which is to come. Eph. 1:20, 21.*

In this age of computer technology and space flights, heaven seems remote. Traditional images of the Father seated on a throne, angels, and books of judgment put the heavenly sanctuary in a realm and an age that no longer touches our lives.

Far from it! The heavenly sanctuary is the divine command center of the universe from which God, who in active control over His creation, directs the course of the agelong conflict between righteousness and evil, guiding all things righteous to their triumphant conclusion.

We catch only glimpses of that reality where Jesus ministers as our high priest. Prophets such as Daniel, Ezekiel, Isaiah, and John the revelator at times were privileged to see through the curtain that hides eternal verities from our eyes. They saw sights indescribable, heard words unutterable, incomprehensible—scenes of grandeur where myriads of unfallen beings sing alleluias of adoration, where messengers speed out into the farthest corners of the universe on divine missions, where, outside of time, events in time are controlled by a beneficent Hand—even the hand nailed to the cross for us.

The wilderness tabernacle that Moses made according to the divine pattern and the glorious Temple that Solomon constructed 500 years later could not adequately portray the magnificence of that structure, made not by human hands, "which the Lord pitched, and not man" (Heb. 8:2). The sanctuary where the Eternal dwells surpasses the majesty of any earthly building, and its activity supersedes that of any earthly command center.

On November 2, 1988, a 23-year-old graduate student at Cornell University, Robert Tappan Morris, introduced a computer "virus" from his office on the Cornell campus into the Internet network, which links 60,000 university and defense and corporate research computers across the United States. Despite its creator's frantic efforts, the virus spread out of control. Before long it had jammed thousands of computers across the country; only several days and millions of dollars later was it purged from the system.

Long ago a brilliant heavenly being introduced a virus into God's perfect universe. The virus multiplied and spread, causing loss and pain to millions. But God, who created Lucifer, is greater, and in His wisdom He had already prepared a program to counteract the virus—a "vaccine" that we call grace. From the center of the universe God directs that program, and one day— soon, we hope—sin's virus will be finally purged.

379

# LORD AMONG THE LAMPSTANDS

*And in the midst of the seven candlesticks one like unto the Son of man, clothed with a garment down to the foot, and girt about the paps with a golden girdle. Rev. 1:13.*

In the book of Revelation, Christ often appears in a sanctuary setting. Here in chapter 1, the first time He appears in John's vision in this book, He is clothed in priestly garments. Later, in one of the most gripping scenes of Scripture, John sees Him as a slain Lamb (Rev. 5:6). Elsewhere in Revelation we read of the altar of incense (Rev. 8:3, 4), the ark of the covenant (Rev. 11:19), and other allusions to the sanctuary, with the heavenly temple itself mentioned specifically in various places.

The book unfolds seven panoramic portrayals, and each is set in the sanctuary. That is significant: Revelation tells the story of the church from the days of John to the end-time, with focus on earth's final hours. In this comprehensive sweep of history, we see Christ in heaven's command center, directing the church and events on earth to their denouement.

I find the picture of Jesus in Revelation 1 especially striking. John sees Him standing among seven golden lampstands (verse 13), holding in His right hand seven stars (verse 16). Christ, conqueror of death and heavenly priest, explains: "The mystery of the seven stars which thou sawest in my right hand, and the seven golden candlesticks. The seven stars are the angels of the seven churches: and the seven candlesticks which thou sawest are the seven churches" (verse 20).

Then follow seven messages to the churches. They are love letters from Jesus to His people, giving instruction, warning, encouragement, and correction to His church in every place and every age. "These are the words of him who holds the seven stars in his right hand and walks among the seven golden lampstands," He says (Rev. 2:1, NIV).

Christ walks in His church, holding her leaders in His right hand—this is the message of this passage. What a message! Despite the weakness and frailty of the church, apparently so puny amid the forces of secularism and evil, Christ is with us. Although God's people individually and corporately fall short of the divine ideal, He has not cast them off and will not cast them off. Although the leaders of the church make mistakes in their human weakness, although at times they may not make the best decisions or even good decisions, Christ still holds them in His right hand.

"Enfeebled and defective as it may appear, the church is the one object upon which God bestows in a special sense His supreme regard. It is the theater of His grace, in which He delights to reveal His power to transform hearts" (*The Acts of the Apostles*, p. 12).

*Lord of the church, You who walk among us and uphold the church in Your right hand, use me today to build up Your people and to enlarge the church's borders.*

# THE JUDGE IS ON OUR SIDE

*I saw in the night visions, and, behold, one like the Son of man came with the clouds of heaven, and came to the Ancient of days, and they brought him near before him. Dan. 7:13.*

The seventh chapter of Daniel describes a dramatic court scene. Thrones are set in place, and the Ancient of days, attended by thousands of angels, takes His seat. Heaven's court sits in session, and the books of record are opened.

Who among us can endure Heaven's judgment? Most of us shrink from even appearing in a traffic court to face a speeding charge—we usually pay our fine by mail; how can we stand before God, who not only sees our offenses but reads our thoughts, motives, and desires?

The teaching of judgment, firmly rooted in both Old and New Testaments, would terrorize us except for one aspect: *the Judge is on our side!* In the same seventh chapter of Daniel we find the Son of man coming to the Ancient of days in the judgment. And to that Son, says Daniel, all authority, glory, and sovereign power are given (verse 14, NIV).

When heaven's court sits, Jesus is our judge. "For as the Father has life in himself, so he has granted the Son to have life in himself. And he has given him authority to judge because he is the Son of Man" (John 5:26, 27, NIV). What a difference that makes! He who lived among us, one with us, who gave His life for us, determines our eternal destiny.

The beloved John calls Him our advocate (1 John 2:1). When our case comes up in heaven's court, we have the best Lawyer in the universe to argue for us!

Does this arrangement—Jesus as both advocate and judge— seem impossible? In terms of the court system we know, based on an adversarial relationship between prosecutor and defendant, with the judge sitting apart objectively, it does. But not if we understand Old Testament jurisprudence. Under it the judge could become involved in a case; he could and did argue the side of the accused.

As Paul debated with the skeptical Athenians on Mars Hill, he pointed their minds to that day when God calls the world to the bar of His justice: "In the past God overlooked such ignorance, but now he commands all people everywhere to repent. For he has set a day when he will judge the world with justice by the man he has appointed. He has given proof of this to all men by raising him from the dead" (Acts 17:30, 31, NIV).

Some of the Athenians sneered when they heard about the Resurrection, and people today still sneer. Others don't want to entertain the idea of a heavenly court because it scares them. But it doesn't scare us who believe—because the Judge is on our side.

*December 19*

# WHEN JESUS JUDGES THE NATIONS

***Saying with a loud voice, Fear God, and give glory to him; for the hour of his judgment is come: and worship him that made heaven, and earth, and the sea, and the fountains of waters. Rev. 14:7.***

Heaven, according to the Scriptures, isn't a sleepy place a couple of centuries behind our technology, where they play harps instead of pipe organs and use books instead of computers. No—heaven is the command center of the universe, a hub of activity in the agelong conflict between good and evil.

Once Jesus died for us—offering up Himself a perfect unrepeatable gift for our sins. Risen from the grave, He ministers the benefits of that sacrifice—benefits never-ending and sufficient for all our needs. But time will not run on like this for countless aeons: Calvary ensures that He who *is* King of kings and Lord of lords by virtue of Creation and redemption must eventually be acknowledged as such by the entire universe. One day at the name of Jesus every knee will bow "in heaven and on earth and under the earth, and every tongue confess that Jesus Christ is Lord, to the glory of God the Father" (Phil. 2:10, 11, NIV).

The Bible calls this divine work to make things right "judgment." In both Hebrew and Greek the word for "righteousness" is the same as for "justice." Because God is righteous, He is just: His righteousness *is* justice, and His justice righteousness. When Jesus judges the nations He sets everything right.

"Judgment" in Scripture is a positive word. "How long, O Lord?" God's people cry out. How long will You let oppression reign, the poor to be trodden underfoot? How long will evil go unchecked? How long before You reveal Yourself as Lord of all and act to deliver Your people? "How long, O Lord, holy and true, dost thou not judge and avenge our blood on them that dwell on the earth?" (Rev. 6:10). God's suffering people wait in hope for God's judgment. In that judgment is their deliverance.

Now, toward the end of Scripture, they hear the glad word "The hour of his judgment is come"! Heaven's hour has struck, and God, who is always in control, who once sent the Son to earth, will act decisively to wrap up the struggle with evil.

Jesus: sacrifice, high priest, judge.

Him alone we fear—bowing in reverent respect, we will not be afraid for the terrors that signal the end of the age.

To Him alone we give glory—not to the heroes of our age or to their achievements.

Him alone we worship—Creator, Saviour, Lord of our lives.

*December 20*

# WHY I BELIEVE IN JESUS' RETURN

*And if I go and prepare a place for you, I will come again, and receive you unto myself; that where I am, there ye may be also. John 14:3.*

Every election year in the United States, it seems, some people begin to find in the Bible predictions of events about to transpire that will lead to the second coming of Jesus.

In 1984, for instance, I received a letter just before the Democratic primary convention. The writer set out a series of calculations based on Revelation 17. He concluded that Walter Mondale would be nominated for president and Edward Kennedy for vice president. The Democratic ticket would win the election, and shortly after taking office Mondale would be assassinated, with Kennedy assuming the presidency. That in turn would set in motion a chain of events that would lead to the return of Jesus.

If the writer had waited a few more days, he needn't have mailed the letter. The Democrats chose Mondale, but Kennedy wasn't his running mate (Geraldine Ferraro got the nod), and the ticket lost in November by a landslide to Reagan and Bush.

Other "prophets" don't wait till an election year! Nor are they confined to the United States, although they seem to thrive there. The news media frequently carry reports of this or that group that goes out in the sticks or charters a plane to Jerusalem to await the arrival of Jesus at a predetermined hour.

And for many levelheaded people observing the hysteria and blasted hopes, the Second Coming seems less and less likely, an illusion—a delusion.

But I still believe in Jesus' return. I do so, not because of calculations or "visions," but because of a simple but fundamental fact—He promised to come again. "I will come again," He said.

I notice many promises of Jesus in the Bible. I have tested them and find them to be true in my experience. Come to Me with your burdens, and I will give you rest, He promises (Matt. 11:28). I have tested His word; He does. If you confess your sins, I will forgive them and cleanse you, He promises (1 John 1:9). I have tried it out; He does. My peace I give to you, He promises (John 14:27). And He does.

But one promise remains: "I will come again." Jesus has kept all His other promises; He will keep this one, too.

The writers of the New Testament believed in Jesus' return. They believed His promise and wrote about it.

So do I.

*December 21*

# AS JESUS TARRIES

*Knowing this first, that there shall come in the last days scoffers, walking after their own lusts, and saying, Where is the promise of his coming? for since the fathers fell asleep, all things continue as they were from the beginning of the creation. 2 Peter 3:3, 4.*

After Jesus ascended, His followers eagerly looked to the Second Coming. Many expected to see Him come in their day; in Thessalonica excitement ran so high that some believers quit working (2 Thess. 2:1, 2; 3:6, 10).

But Jesus did not return, and some Christians began to doubt. Among those addressed in the letter to the Hebrews we hear of a falling away to the world, slackness in church attendance, and turning back from the hope of the Second Coming.

Peter in our text for the day tells us that people would openly scoff at the preaching of the Second Coming. All things continue in unbroken succession, they would assert—their thinking giving no place to the divine intervention that will bring down the present world order.

If the seeming delay in Jesus' return troubled Christians in the first century and gave grist to the mockers' mills, how much more after 1,900 years! I have observed two reactions to this promise of Jesus and plain teaching of the Scriptures:

**Eschatological burnout.** *Burnout* is a term that has become more and more familiar to people in our day. After years of hard work, a man quits his office and takes to the road. The reason? Burnout. He is tired of the routine, tired of the pressure. He may leave wife and family, change his lifestyle, or look for a totally new line of work.

Some Christians are burned out with regard to the hope of the Second Coming. Over the years they heard preachers and evangelists proclaim the signs of the times and predict Jesus would come within six months, a year, perhaps five years at most. But the years have passed; they have grown old with waiting. They have given up; they no longer come to church.

Or they may still attend church, but when they hear talk of the Second Coming they quietly turn off inside. Like the servant in Jesus' parable they say in their heart, "My lord delayeth his coming" (Matt. 24:48).

**Collapsing the Second Coming into one's death.** I heard a Christian say, "If I get wiped out on my way home from church, that's the Second Coming for me."

True—and false. True in the sense that our personal destiny will be forever fixed at the moment of our death. But false: the Second Coming is bigger than my demise. The Second Coming is universal, shattering the established order, uprooting nature, bringing in God's glorious rule.

Instead of burnout, instead of collapsing the Coming into our death, may we every day say from the heart, "Even so, come, Lord Jesus" (Rev. 22:20).

*December 22*

# WAITING FOR JESUS—1

*Therefore do not throw away your confidence, which has a great reward. For you have need of endurance, so that you may do the will of God and receive what is promised. Heb. 10:35, 36, RSV.*

How shall we wait for Jesus?

In 1914 an expedition led by Ernest Shackleton set out from England. The party hoped to make the first crossing of the continent of Antarctica. The men would sail to the Weddell Sea and traverse the continent via the South Pole, meeting the sea at McMurdo Sound.

With high hopes the party set out in the *Endurance*. But the expedition was doomed from the outset. Pack ice closed around the ship before the explorers could even reach the Antarctic continent. For nine months the *Endurance* creaked and groaned under the pressure of the ice, and then at last it split in two. What a dilemma! Shackleton and his men were at the end of the earth, trapped in a wilderness of ice.

For five months the members of Shackleton's expedition drifted around on large ice floes. Then, with the help of small boats they had salvaged from the *Endurance*, they made their way to Elephant Island. Don't be misled by the name of that island—not even a rat lives on it. It is a windswept desert of ice and snow. The nearest human habitation was 800 miles away on the island of South Georgia. But the wildest sea in the world lay between—and Shackleton had only an open whale boat to attempt the crossing.

Taking five men, Shackleton set out. As he waved goodbye to the forlorn party on Elephant Island, he wondered whether he would ever see them again. And they wondered too.

The voyage in the open whale boat was one of the epic crossings of the twentieth century. Despite the mountainous waves with which the tiny vessel had to contend, the party made landfall on the island of South Georgia.

Soon a rescue attempt was organized. The first attempt failed. The pack ice closed in, and the rescue ship could not find a way through to Elephant Island. It had to turn back. A second attempt was organized. But again the ice closed in around the island, and the ship turned back. A third attempt—and once again the ice was the victor.

Only after four rescue attempts could Shackleton find a way through to Elephant Island. As he approached that wilderness of snow and ice, he wondered what he would find. Would anyone still be alive after those months of waiting? Would there be, perhaps, a few survivors gone mad with the silence and the waiting?

Shackleton found every man alive, in good condition, and in good spirits. How had they survived? The secret lay in the leadership of the man Shackleton had left in charge. Every day he would say to his men, "Get ready, boys. The boss may come back today."

And so every day they got ready. Every day they prepared themselves. Every day they watched. Every day they waited. And despite the long silence, despite the great odds, one day Shackleton did come back.

And one day Jesus will come back for us.

# WAITING FOR JESUS—2

*Wherefore seeing we also are compassed about with so great a cloud of witnesses, let us lay aside every weight, and the sin which doth so easily beset us, and let us run with patience the race that is set before us, looking unto Jesus the author and finisher of our faith; who for the joy that was set before him endured the cross, despising the shame, and is set down at the right hand of the throne of God. Heb. 12:1, 2.*

The 1954 British Empire Games, held in Vancouver, British Columbia, provide a remarkable illustration of how to wait for Jesus. The mile race that was held there is considered to be one of the greatest races, perhaps the greatest race, of all time. It pitted the two fastest men in the world over one mile—Roger Bannister and John Landy.

Following his usual approach, Landy started fast. Unlike most runners, Landy's method was to move to the head of the pack early and by the sheer power of his physique outlast the other runners who would reserve strength for a final thrust at the tape.

The race was clearly between Bannister and Landy. Soon the other runners were dropping back, leaving Landy out in front, and Bannister well behind him.

At the end of each quarter mile the times were announced, and with each declaration the stands rocked. Landy and Bannister were setting a blazing pace, one that would surely set a new world record. But who would get to the tape first?

So the runners came to the final lap, the final quarter mile. Landy was in front, ahead of Bannister, as he had been throughout the race. Ahead of him stretched the tape, looming closer and closer. Somewhere behind him was Bannister.

And then a deafening roar arose in the stands. Landy knew what it meant: Bannister was making his last desperate effort to catch Landy.

The tape was getting closer and closer, and the roar louder and louder. Landy knew that Bannister in his last great effort was catching up. But where was he?

Just before the tape Landy turned his head so he could see just where Bannister was. And Bannister, seizing the psychological moment, threw himself past Landy on the other side and just beat him to the tape!

This famous race, the "miracle mile," is enshrined in stone in Vancouver. Go to the city and you will see the two runners—one turning his head as the other thrusts himself toward the tape.

As runners in the race of life, we are to keep our eyes fixed on Jesus. He who has begun a good thing in us will carry it forward to completion. He will present us faultless before His presence with eternal glory. He, the author of our faith, is also its finisher.

*December 24*

# WAITING FOR JESUS—3

*Let your loins be girded about, and your lights burning; and ye yourselves like unto men that wait for their lord, when he will return from the wedding; that when he cometh and knocketh, they may open unto him immediately. Luke 12:35, 36.*

In a sermon preached at Lansing, Michigan, on September 5, 1891, Ellen White gave specific instruction on how we should wait for the Lord to return.

Specifically warning us against trying to calculate the precise time of the Lord's coming, she said: "The times and the seasons God has put in His own power. And why has not God given us this knowledge? Because we would not make a right use of it if He did. A condition of things would result from this knowledge among our people that would greatly retard the work of God in preparing a people to stand in the great day that is to come. We are not to live upon time excitement. We are not to be engrossed with speculations in regard to the times and the seasons which God has not revealed. Jesus has told His disciples to 'watch,' but not for a definite time. His followers are to be in the position of those who are listening for the order of their Captain; they are to watch, wait, pray, and work, as they approach the time for the coming of the Lord; but no one will be able to predict just when that time will come; for 'of that day and hour knoweth no man.' You will not be able to say that He will come in one, two, or five years, neither are you to put off His coming by stating that it may not be for ten or twenty years" (*Selected Messages*, book 1, p. 189).

How, then, shall we wait? We will wait in hope, knowing that the One who is to come already has demonstrated the reliability of His promises a thousand times in our experience.

How, then, shall we wait? We will stand fast in the Christian way, unmoved by the currents that swirl about us. We will boldly

388

confess to the world our risen Saviour who serves in the courts above and who soon will pierce the clouds.

How, then, shall we wait? We will tell the good news near and far—to our neighbors, to our friends, to our loved ones. We will build up our fellow saints and let the world know that we are Christians.

How, then, shall we wait? We will exercise the will to believe by getting up and going to church Sabbath by Sabbath, no matter how hot or how cold it may be, no matter how inviting bed may seem.

And one day soon "he who is coming will come and will not delay" (Heb. 10:37, NIV)!

*December 25*

# MAKE-BELIEVE

*I am crucified with Christ: nevertheless I live; yet not I, but Christ liveth in me: and the life which I now live in the flesh I live by the faith of the Son of God, who loved me, and gave himself for me. Gal. 2:20.*

Sometime ago a friend sent me a clipping from the Chicago *Tribune* that related the following conversation between Robert I. Sherman and his 6-year-old son, Ricky.

"Is Cubby real or make-believe?" Sherman asked, referring to the stuffed lion that is his boy's most cherished plaything.

"Make-believe," said Ricky.

"What else is make-believe?"

"Santa Claus," Ricky said. "Jesus. The Easter bunny. Cookie Monster."

His father was deeply satisfied. "Yes," he said.

And Ricky, the little atheist, scored another chocolate baseball.

Sherman, an avowed atheist, filed suit in federal court, charging that Ricky's being required at his elementary school to say the words "under God" as his class recites the Pledge of Allegiance to the flag amounts to a school prayer—something ruled out by the United States Supreme Court. And each morning during the pledge Ricky drops his hand from his heart and closes his mouth while all the other children repeat "under God."

Santa Claus is make-believe, but not Jesus.

First, He is a man attested by history. No serious student of the past denies that Jesus of Nazareth, a carpenter who became a wandering preacher and who was executed on a Roman cross, ever existed. We don't know many facts about Him—for instance, the day of His birth, which almost certainly wasn't December 25—but we have more knowledge of His life and work than about almost any other famous person of 2,000 years ago.

If Jesus of Nazareth had never existed, there never would have been a church in His name. Jesus is not make-believe.

But there's another reason. Jesus is alive! Those of us who confess Him as Saviour and Lord know *Him*—not just about Him. We know Him as our best friend. As the gospel song "He Lives," written by Alfred H. Ackley, states, Jesus lives today within our hearts.

*December 26*

# THE CROSS AND THE CLOUD

***So Christ, having been offered once to bear the sins of many, will appear a second time, not to deal with sin but to save those who are eagerly waiting for him. Heb. 9:28, RSV.***

Some Christians dwell almost exclusively on the first coming of Jesus. They so emphasize the cross that one could think that divine history ceased 2,000 years ago.

Others, by contrast, continually focus on the future. They seem absorbed in the Second Coming and in trying to unravel the course of events that lead up to it.

How shall we live, we who believe in Jesus and look for His return?

A godly man and great preacher, the late H.M.S. Richards, founder of the *Voice of Prophecy* radio program, gave me a simple but profound answer: "The cross and the cloud—never separate them in experience or in preaching."

His words led me to restudy the teaching of the Second Coming. Although for many years I taught biblical studies, with the New Testament my specialty, I had never noticed the way in which Bible writers frequently couple together the first and second comings of Christ—the cross and the cloud. Here are some of the passages I discovered in new light:

"Behold, he cometh with *clouds*; and every eye shall see him, and they also which *pierced* him: and all kindreds of the earth shall wail because of him" (Rev. 1:7).

"For the grace of God that bringeth salvation hath appeared to all men . . . ; looking for that blessed hope, and the *glorious appearing* of the great God and our Saviour Jesus Christ; who *gave himself for us*" (Titus 2:11-14).

"For if we believe that Jesus *died* and rose again, even so them also which sleep in Jesus will God bring with him. . . . For the Lord himself shall *descend from heaven*" (1 Thess. 4:14-16).

"So Christ was once *offered* to bear the sins of many; and unto them that look for him shall he appear the *second time* without sin unto salvation" (Heb. 9:28).

The cross and the cloud: New Testament writers join them together. The cross guarantees the cloud; the cloud shows the victory Jesus won at the cross. And what God has joined let not man put asunder.

When the group I was with climbed Mount Kilimanjaro, we were surprised to find that the mountain is not one peak but two. Rising sharply out of the Tanzanian plain, visible for 100 or more miles away, the highest freestanding mountain in the world, Kilimanjaro seems from afar to stand alone, single. But it is not. As we ascended the mountain we saw that Kilimanjaro is two peaks—Mawenzi, 17,564 feet high, and Kibo, 19,340 feet. Only when we reached the heights and followed the saddle between the crests did we see the full landscape.

We who believe live between the times, traversing the saddle between the two peaks in divine history—the first and second comings of Christ. We no longer walk on the plain; we are in the highlands, and our eyes are set on the summit just ahead!

*December 27*

# A PLACE FOR US

*And if I go and prepare a place for you, I will come again, and receive you unto myself; that where I am, there ye may be also. John 14:3.*

My father worked for many years helping to build houses for other people, but he could not afford to build one for himself. One night after he died I dreamed that Jesus was showing him through a spacious new home. As Dad admired the workmanship, he asked, "Who is this for?" "It's for you," said Jesus.

"Now we know that if the earthly tent we live in is destroyed, we have a building from God, an eternal house in heaven, not built by human hands," Paul tells us (2 Cor. 5:1, NIV). God is the builder and maker of that home, and it will be glorious beyond our fondest hopes.

Jesus went to prepare a place for us. His Father's house has many rooms, and one has your name on it—and another has mine. According to His promise, He will return to earth one day to take us home.

Jesus doesn't need 2,000 years to build us a heavenly mansion. He created the world in a moment; He could prepare our place or room just as fast. When He prepares a place for us, therefore, He speaks of His work in the heavenly temple as our great high priest.

From our perspective that work seems to be taking a long time. We want quick answers to problems. We want God to wrap up the agelong struggle with evil, bring in the reign of righteousness on earth.

But our God who spoke the world into being is also maker of the giant sequoia with its slow, steady growth, and of the stalactite formed over hundreds of years one drip at a time. What He does He does perfectly.

In our experience we know that some matters are far more difficult to mend than others. We may be able to fix a flat tire in 30 minutes; a flat marriage takes longer. For thousands of years now God has been mending a universe broken by sin. When He fixes it—and He will—there'll be no question about having to go back to the repair shop, because the work will be perfectly done.

Jesus told us very little about that heavenly work in which He is now engaged. He simply said, "I go and prepare a place for you." He puts the emphasis on what means most to us—that *we* can have a place there, that He wants *us* there. And that is more important than knowing why His work seems to take so long.

*Lord Jesus, remember me—my place—in Your heavenly kingdom.*

December 28

# WHY I WANT JESUS TO COME

**Looking for that blessed hope, and the glorious appearing of the great God and our Saviour Jesus Christ. Titus 2:13.**

I want Jesus to come because I am tired of the pain, suffering, and injustice of our times. Although ours is the most learned era of history—rich in knowledge, but not in wisdom—the problems of humanity grow only worse each year. The rich get richer, the poor poorer; raw pain and misery multiply.

For centuries humanity entertained the hope of making Planet Earth a utopia. Education, science, technology, philosophy—we had the know-how to eradicate poverty, disease, and perhaps eventually even death itself. Even the church once—in the time of Augustine, who wrote *The City of God*—dreamed of extending the kingdom of God on earth until the affairs of the church would be one with the affairs of state.

Those fond hopes vanished for good with the two great wars of the twentieth century and the multiplication of human desperation in our day. Rape, murder, hunger, homelessness, corruption, treachery, deceit—our knowledgeable age is perhaps the weakest in the history of the race. "Evil men and seducers shall wax worse and worse, deceiving, and being deceived." "Ever learning, and never able to come to the knowledge of the truth" (2 Tim. 3:13, 7).

I want Jesus to come to set this world straight. "Nevertheless we, according to his promise, look for new heavens and a new earth, wherein dwelleth righteousness" (2 Peter 3:13).

I want Jesus to come because I long to see loved ones again. My godly father; my mother, rich in deeds of compassion and kindness; friends who are no longer with us, some cut off in fullness of days, some cut off at high noon—I am waiting to see them again.

One day God will restore the relationships that enriched our lives here on earth but that death severed. We shall see and know one another, retaining our individuality—what makes you yourself, and me myself—and our love and friendship will strengthen and grow in the society of life everlasting.

And I want Jesus to come so that I may be clothed with the immortal body He has for me. "Meanwhile we groan, longing to be clothed with our heavenly dwelling, because when we are clothed, we will not be found naked" (2 Cor. 5:2, 3, NIV).

There "we shall ever feel the freshness of the morning and shall ever be far from its close. . . . There the redeemed shall know, even as also they are known. The loves and sympathies which God Himself has planted in the soul shall there find truest and sweetest exercise" (*The Great Controversy*, pp. 676, 677).

For these and many other reasons I want Jesus to come. But especially because of something else, which we will discuss tomorrow.

*December 29*

# WHEN WE SEE JESUS

*And there shall be no more curse: but the throne of God and of the Lamb shall be in it; and his servants shall serve him: and they shall see his face; and his name shall be in their foreheads. Rev. 22:3, 4.*

"Blessed are the pure in heart," said Jesus, "for they shall see God" (Matt. 5:8). And God will fulfill this promise at last, for we shall see Jesus face-to-face, and His name will be on our foreheads. Of all the reasons why I want Jesus to come, the greatest is to see Him.

The Lamb will welcome me home. That name gives me hope, for it reminds me of Jesus' death on my behalf. By virtue of His shed blood I have hope, eternal life.

So we shall see Jesus. We have waited long for Him, but then we shall see Him! We see Him now only by faith, then face-to-face. "Blessed are those who have not seen and yet have believed," said Jesus in rebuke of Thomas' insistence on touching the wounds of Christ before he would believe (John 20:29, NIV).

The Lamb's name will be in our foreheads. This signifies that He is the center of our lives, the subject of our dearest thoughts, the standard of our character.

In the last days before Jesus returns, the world will divide over the issue of worship—the Lamb or the beast power (depicted in Rev. 13). Those who throw their lot in with the beast's system of counterfeit religion receive a mark on their right hand or on the forehead—they will comply because of coercion (the hand) or because they truly accept the beast's claim to worship (the forehead).

But the followers of the Lamb have His name on their foreheads only. No one who walks with Him face-to-face in heaven will be a "hand" disciple. Only those who love Him, who from a sense of His incredible love and generosity have fallen at His feet and confessed Him as Saviour and Lord, will see Him.

"The Lamb at the center of the throne will be their shepherd; he will lead them to springs of living water. And God will wipe away every tear from their eyes" (Rev. 7:17, NIV).

"And the years of eternity, as they roll, will bring richer and still more glorious revelations of God and of Christ. As knowledge is progressive, so will love, reverence, and happiness increase. The more men learn of God, the greater will be their admiration of His character. As Jesus opens before them the riches of redemption and the amazing achievements in the great controversy with Satan, the hearts of the ransomed thrill with more fervent devotion, and with more rapturous joy they sweep the harps of gold; and ten thousand times ten thousand and thousands of thousands of voices unite to swell the mighty chorus of praise" (*The Great Controversy*, p. 678).

# CHEER THE PEOPLE ON

*And let us consider how we may spur one another on toward love and good deeds. Heb. 10:24, NIV.*

In my early 40s, under the goading of two teenage children who let me know my weight was starting to increase, I took up running. Now, lest anyone think I am a great athlete, let me assure you that I ran—and still run—strictly for exercise and for fun, without concern about times.

I was able to stretch out the distances farther and still farther, until I could run 10 miles nonstop and eventually 12 or 13—at a slow pace, of course. Then we moved to Washington, D.C., and I learned of the Marine Corps Marathon. It's called "the people's marathon" because winners receive trophies rather than cash— with the result that the fastest runners don't compete. The race attracts 12,000 runners every year, with two thirds of them attempting their first marathon.

But it is still a marathon—26.2 miles. With excitement and some apprehension, I registered for the race and took my place among the 12,000 starters on the road below the Iwo Jima memorial. The Marine Corps band played, the chaplain offered up a prayer, the cannon boomed to start the race, and the mass of runners surged forward.

The first 10 miles I felt like a piece of flotsam borne along by the sea of surging humanity. Then the runners began to thin out; some slowed to a walk, others dropped out. By 15 miles I was feeling tired. We had run past the Pentagon, back across the Potomac, past the U.S. Capitol and the Washington Monument. As we approached Haynes Point near the 20-mile mark, we hit a killing head wind. By now the first runners had been finished for some time; we were straggling, wondering why we had ever got involved in such a crazy plan. We passed a man with his car parked by the road, playing over a loudspeaker the theme from *Chariots of Fire.* At the 22-mile marker we met a Scottish bagpipe band. They were playing "Amazing Grace"!

What kept me going? One thing in particular: at each mile marker along the way U.S. Marines, men and women, stood with drinks and first-aid supplies. As each runner approached they would shout out: "Keep going! You're going to make it!" When we passed the 20-mile mark and fought to keep going in face of exhaustion they encouraged: "You're almost there! Keep going— you're going to make it!"

And we did.

A great Christian leader, W. A. Spicer, used to tell his fellow-ministers: "Cheer the people on." He always spoke hope; he refused to dwell on the problems of the church.

Let us cheer one another on. We are all runners in the race of life, and in this race everyone who finishes is a winner.

By God's grace, let us make it—and encourage someone else today also to make it.

December 31

# HIS HANDS, HIS FEET

*Then said Jesus to them again, Peace be unto you: as my Father hath sent me, even so send I you. John 20:21.*

"The Word became flesh and made his dwelling among us," wrote the beloved John. "We have seen his glory, the glory of the One and Only, who came from the Father, full of grace and truth" (John 1:14, NIV).

We too have seen His glory. During this year now passing into eternity we have followed His footsteps. He whose coming was predicted by prophets and wise men in the fullness of time came to earth as a babe, born of the virgin Mary. One with us, subject to frailty and temptation, He grew up in Nazareth, obedient to parents, helping Joseph, His legal father, in the carpenter shop. But at age 30 He left carpentry and left Nazareth, heeding the Father's call to the mission for which He had left heaven. For more than three years He went about doing good, healing, preaching, teaching, making men and women whole. Then they took Him and tried Him, crucifying Him between two thieves. But the grave could not hold Him; and risen to the Father's right hand, He reigns as heavenly high priest, soon to come again to take us to the place He is preparing for us.

"Hallelujah! What a Saviour"! "Bring forth the royal diadem, and crown Him Lord of all."

But Jesus doesn't want us merely to meditate on His life and death. The "thoughtful hour" we have spent each day thinking about His life and work—and especially the closing scenes—isn't an end in itself. We have a work to do.

"As the Father has sent me, I am sending you," He says (John 20:21, NIV). On that final Thursday night before the cross, Jesus prayed to the Father, "As you sent me into the world, I have sent them into the world" (John 17:18, NIV).

Jesus was sent: He had a divine mission. So have we. We are to carry on His work.

Once Jesus' hands broke bread for the hungry, touched the lepers, patted the heads of little children. Today He has no hands but our hands.

Once Jesus' eyes looked out on the multitude with compassion, because they were harried and worn, like sheep without a shepherd. Today He has no eyes but our eyes.

Once Jesus' voice spoke hope to the broken, comfort to the sick and bereaved, forgiveness to the sinner. Today He has no voice but our voice.

Once Jesus' ears were quick to hear the cry for help. Today He has no ears but our ears.

To be Jesus' hands, feet, eyes, voice, ears—who is sufficient for these things? But to each of us He promises: "My grace is sufficient for thee: for my strength is made perfect in weakness" (2 Cor. 12:9).

# SCRIPTURE INDEX